Economic Indicators

Economic Indicators

How America Reads Its Financial Health

Joseph E. Plocek

New York Institute of Finance

New York London Toronto Sydney Tokyo Singapore

Publication Data

ts financial health / by Joseph

Includes index.
ISBN 0-13-626896-X
1. Economic indicators—United States. 2. Economic forecasting—
United States. I. Title.
HB3743.P66   1990
330.973'001'12—dc20   91-2338
                                                               CIP

This publication is designed to provide accurate and authoritative information
in regard to the subject matter covered. It is sold with the understanding
that the publisher is not engaged in rendering legal, accounting, or other
professional service. If legal advice or other expert assistance is required, the
services of a competent professional person should be sought.

*From a Declaration of Principles Jointly Adopted by
a Committee of the American Bar Association and a
Committee of Publishers and Associations*

© 1991 by Joseph E. Plocek

Printed in the United States of America

10 9 8 7 6 5 4 3 2 1

New York Institute of Finance
Simon & Schuster
A Paramount Communications Company

Contents

Preface

In the more than 12 years that I have been following economic and financial data, first as an employee of government agencies and then on Wall Street, its users (primarily participants in the financial markets, but also reporters, investors, and analysts) have become increasingly sophisticated. In large part, I believe this is due to the keen interest of the current Federal Reserve Chairman, Alan Greenspan, in the minutiae of the economic system. But it also reflects the greater dissemination of data and ready availability of high-quality analysis, such as that available on the MCM Moneywatch™ video screens. In particular, I believe Carl J. Palash, the senior real sector economist at McCarthy, Crisanti & Maffei, Inc., deserves credit for pushing forward the frontiers of understanding among market participants.

But more education is necessary to overcome the rumors and truisms that often substitute for hard data even among the individuals whose livelihoods depend on these indicators. It is my hope that this book will contribute to the market's understanding of the factors underpinning economic indicators.

A wide range of interviews and special data requests, all ably and cheerfully filled by the men and women who serve the U.S. Treasury, Labor, and Commerce departments as well as the Federal Reserve

System, have fed this book. But several individuals deserve singling out. Jill Ouseley and Roland Cook at the U.S. Treasury first sparked my interest in indicators while Paul McCarthy of MCM harbored my ambition. Special thank yous are due to Mike Strauss and Ken Gault for reading the manuscript and for encouragement; to my colleagues in economic research at MCM—Astrid Adolfson for an endless stream of fresh ideas and Carl Palash for sharing his expertise and clear thinking. Of course, any remaining errors are my own.

"The government[s] are very keen on amassing statistics—they collect them, add them, raise them to the nth power, take the cube root and prepare wonderful diagrams. But what you must never forget is that every one of those figures comes . . . from the village watchman, who just puts down what he damn pleases.

Josiah Stamp, British economist (1929)

1

Why Study Indicators?

WHAT'S THE NUMBER?

It is 8:29:20 AM Eastern Standard Time and trading screens in the stock, bond, and currencies markets have gone blank. "Market Subject" flashes before befuddled traders who seconds ago had priced hundreds of billions of dollars worth of financial instruments. Then a shout goes up across the football-sized room, "What's the number?". The answer, "20,000 nonfarm", elicits frenzied trading once again. An army of 200 salespeople frantically begin to disseminate this information over the now blinking telephone banks to the insurance companies, pension funds, money managers, and other institutional accounts who will drive bond and stock prices sharply higher for the balance of the day.

Successful traders who had correctly anticipated the event, perhaps by buying bonds the prior day, will have a steady stream of colleagues offering congratulations for the millions of dollars made. Others who did not make the grade will listen to the economics analysis staff offer explanations over their investment bank's voice box (the "hoot-and-holler" as it is called).

These traders were riveted to their video screens awaiting arguably the world's most important statistical release, the *U.S. Employment*

1

Report, which is due at 8:30 AM Eastern Standard Time on the first Friday of the month. In addition to bonds and interest rates, stock prices, currencies, and virtually every other commodity traded in the canyons of Wall Street will have been affected by the end of the day.

Financial markets react not only to the monthly *Employment Report*, but to a score of other economic data released by the federal government. *Economic Indicators* will attempt to explain the data and to give a context into which investors and financial decision makers will be able to put the numbers. Readers will be able to project the data and make independent judgments about the economy and price moves in the financial markets after completing this book. Some of the questions the reader will be able to answer might be:

Have stock prices and interest rates adequately adjusted to a weaker economy?

Will policy makers react to the data by lowering interest rates?

Are our tax laws consistent with the federal budgetary stance and the current interest rate structure?

A POLICY MAKER'S VIEW

Most policy makers at the nation's central bank, the Federal Reserve (the Fed), use a standard set of principles to analyze the effects of interest rate changes on the economy. Administration appointees at the Treasury Department, the President's Council of Economic Advisors, and the Office of Management and Budget share these constructs and use them to determine how best to sell Treasury notes and bonds and manipulate the tax code. Thus, a first step in understanding and interpreting economic indicators is to understand a typical model of the U.S. economy, a sample of which is given in Figure 1.1.

Policy makers agree that the ultimate objectives of high economic growth and stable prices (at the top of Figure 1.1) are paramount. Indeed, Congress institutionalized these objectives over 40 years ago in the *Full Employment Act of 1946*. Federal Reserve and U.S. Trea-

FIGURE 1.1 The federal policy makers model

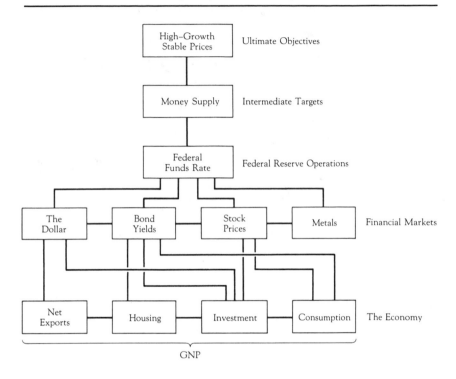

sury operations are aimed at manipulating intermediate targets such as money supply growth and the Fed funds rate (the overnight rate on reserves that commercial banks lend to each other). These are used as transmission mechanisms to the three main financial markets (stocks, the dollar, and bonds) which adjust in price.

These markets have feedback effects on particular economic indicators. For instance, bond and mortgage interest rates affect the housing market and are a factor in making investment decisions; the dollar affects the pricing of exports; and the stock market in part determines wealth and thus affects consumption. Taken together these items determine *Gross National Product* (GNP), the sum of the goods and services produced by the economy. Thus, interpreting incoming indicators becomes a focus of official Washington, as well as of Wall Street traders, economists, and individual investors.

TRADER'S EYE VIEW OF THE MARKETS

For the broker and investor, the three main markets that are the focus of federal policy makers are a vast potential source of money-making trading strategies. Bonds, stocks, and the dollar move based on economic data called *fundamentals*. But, the markets' various reactions may not be the same. For example, Figure 1.2 illustrates that weakening economic data might move interest rates down. (Since bond prices move inversely to yields, this means a rally in bonds.) But, it may also

FIGURE 1.2 The financial transmission mechanism: market reaction to economic indicators

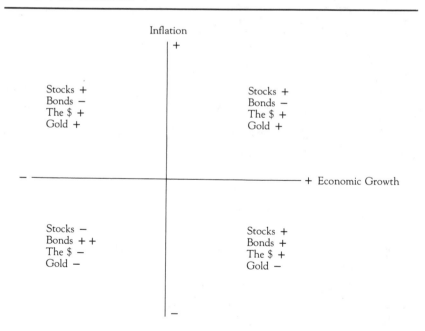

mean a lower dollar as investments overseas become more attractive. Falling stock prices may also result as lower bond yields cause portfolio adjustments (see the lower-left quadrant of Figure 1.2). Conversely, stronger economic data may mean higher stock prices and a surging dollar. But bond prices could erode since traders may anticipate a Fed policy tightening to cool the economy. Note also that high inflation is almost always good for commodities such as gold (which have relatively fixed supplies) and for stocks.

The magnitude of the price changes in the various markets depends on two factors. First, where the data fall on the continuum in Figure 1.2—the severity of any inflation problems, for instance—will be compared to Wall Street's expectations. A higher or lower number than expected will spark a relatively more severe response. Second, the anticipated Washington policy response will determine the importance assigned a particular economic release. In the traditional monetary policy view, the Fed can offset a shortfall in GNP from its long-term potential by easing short-term rates. It can also contain overheating by tightening. Thus, short-term interest rates will be watched most carefully.

A good example from the late 1980s and 1990 of economic data sparking a major financial market reaction is the broad inflation number embodied in the *Consumer Price Index* (CPI). Wall Street upgraded the CPI as a focus because Fed Chairman Greenspan was known to look at it. Greenspan was thought to believe that the economy was operating near capacity and that increases in inflation should be met with tighter money. In August 1990, a 0.4% rise in the CPI was sufficient to convince investors that the Fed would not ease short rates. Its release sparked major stock and bond selloffs.

CONSTRUCTING GNP

In a slightly simplified view, only one equation is necessary to construct quarterly GNP. The equation is generally given as:

$$C + I + G + X = GNP$$

where C = consumption spending
        I = investment spending
       G = government spending
       X = net exports (exports minus imports)

In reality, each of the four major GNP components comprises dozens of subcomponents which *econometricians* (analysts who apply statistical methods to economic indicators) attempt to specify in complicated models (see Figure 1.3). The model of the U.S. economy used at the Federal Reserve Board in Washington, for example, has 667 variables. Only some of the items that go into the four components of our simplified model will be specified here.

Consumption

Consumption is determined by wherewithal and psychology. Income (wages and salaries are the primary component) and wealth (a rising stock market and lower rates or rising home prices) give an individual his wherewithal to spend. Money earned can either be saved or spent—a conscious decision is assumed to be made. The "propensity" to consume comes from rising confidence and demographic considerations. For instance, in a growing economy most surveys show consumers intend to spend. But, the shift of the "baby boomers" into middle age is expected to raise savings rather than consumption.

Investment

To prevent double counting, *investment* is generally defined as gross private domestic. The main categories are fixed investment (residential and nonresidential) and inventories. The first is largely determined by the housing stock, business plants, and business equipment. Incremental plant and equipment spending is largely a result of an industry reaching capacity and thus needing to expand. Inventory increases, however, can be involuntary, as when consumers stop buying.

FIGURE 1.3. The GNP model for 1989*

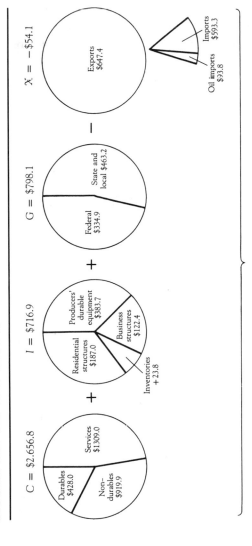

C = $2,656.8   I = $716.9   G = $798.1   X = -$54.1

C = $2,656.8

Durables $428.0

Services $1309.0

Non-durables $919.9

I = $716.9

Producers' durable equipment $383.7

Residential structures $187.0

Business structures $122.4

Inventories +23.8

G = $798.1

Federal $334.9

State and local $463.2

X = -$54.1

Exports $647.4

Oil imports $33.8

Imports $593.3

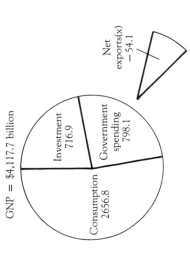

GNP = $4,117.7 billion

Investment 716.9

Consumption 2656.8

Government spending 798.1

Net exports(x) -54.1

*In billions of 1982 dollars.

7

Government

Gross federal government spending, totaling in excess of $1 trillion last year, is clearly the most important. But total state and local government spending exceeded this total. The mix of spending and tax policies can influence other variables. Increases in federal defense spending, for instance, often affect productivity and thus business fixed investment through providing technological advances.

Net Exports

Since the economy is not closed, we must measure how much output is lost to other countries. The difference between exports from the United States and imports into this country gives a net figure. In recent years, this sector has been a net drain on GNP. Oil comprises the largest dollar volume of imports, while agricultural items are among the most visible exports.

The monthly statistics released by the federal government are an attempt to gather data in each of these categories so that models of the economy can be specified. Indicators in the following chapters will be organized according to the sequence of the model. Note also that policy makers attempt to separate out price effects from "real" activity. GNP is, by definition, the product of any price changes and the quantity of goods and services produced. The individual GNP components are "deflated" using a variety of price indices, which are devoted considerable attention in Chapter 13. In most news reports and as seen in Figure 1.3, GNP is specified in real terms using 1982 dollars as a base. In this way, policy makers can tell how much of our economic growth is due to higher prices and how much to gains in output.

The Commerce Department uses two methods of GNP estimation, *product side accounting* (approximating the economy's output) and *income side accounting* (estimating the wealth produced). There are two simple approximation techniques for these methods that can be used to bring together the equations previously discussed into an estimate of current quarter real GNP. These techniques include *quar-*

TABLE 1.1
Housing Starts Data Series (SA)

January	+0.5%	April	−2.6%
February	−0.2%	May	−3.0%
March	+1.2%	June	+5.0%
Q1 Average	+0.5%	Q2 Average	−0.2%

terly averaging for a "bottom up" forecast on the product side and *summing production* for a "top down" forecast on the income side.

Quarterly Averaging

For a rough idea of how a particular sector is doing within the context of overall real GNP, it is often sufficient to use an averaging technique. First, compute the quarterly average of the monthly changes in a series for each of two quarters. Second, compare the averages to see whether the series is rising or falling. Third, plug the magnitude of the change into the appropriate segment of the GNP equation. An example is given in Table 1.1.

The averaging technique smooths out monthly fluctuations in volatile data series. In the example, it clearly shows that housing weakened in the second calendar quarter. Thus, investment will be a modest drag on GNP estimates in mid-year. Note also that the rebound in June suggests that third quarter housing growth may be significantly positive.

Hours Worked

GNP is sometimes computed as the product of hours worked (which is related to income) and productivity in the manufacturing sector. Some adjustment for lesser sectors such as agriculture and government must be included because goods-producing areas are only about 75% of

TABLE 1.2.
National Income & Product Account, 1989
GNP Reconciliation, $ billions

Personal Consumption Expenditures	$3,450.1		Compensation of Employees	$3,079.0
Durable Goods	474.6		Wages and Salaries	2,573.2
Nondurable Goods	1,130.0		Goverment	476.6
Services	1,845.5		Private	2,096.6
			Supplements to Wages and Salaries	505.8
Gross Private Domestic Investment	771.2		Employer Contributions to	
Fixed Investment	742.9		Social Insurance	263.9
Nonresidential	511.9		Other Labor Income	241.9
Structures	146.2			
Producers' Durable Equipment	365.7		Proprietors' Income*x	379.3
Residential	231.0			
Change in Business Inventories	28.3		Rental Income of Persons*	8.2
Net Exports	-46.1		Corporate Profits with Adjustments*x	311.6
Exports	626.2		Profits Before Tax	307.7
Imports	672.3		Profits Tax Liability	135.1
			Profits After Tax	172.6

Government	1,025.6
Federal	400.0
National Defense	301.1
Nondefense	98.9
State and Local	625.6

Dividends	123.5
Undistributed Profits	49.1
Inventory Valuation Adjustment	−21.7
Capital Consumption Adjustment	25.5
Net Interest	445.1
National Income	**4,223.3**
Business Transfer Payments	32.4
Indirect Business Tax and Nontax Liability	414.0
Less: Subsidies Less Current Surplus of Government Enterprises	6.3
Capital Consumption Allowances with Capital Consumption Adjustment	554.4
Statistical Discrepancy	−17.0
Gross National Product	5,200.8

Gross National Product	5,200.8

*with Capital Consumption Adjustment
×with Inventory Valuation Adjustment

the economy. All variables are computed as changes in the quarterly averages as shown in the following equation:

$$g(GNP) = g(H + (O/H) + A + G)$$

where
H	=	hours worked in the private nonfarm sector
O	=	output produced by H
A and G	=	constants for the agricultural and government sectors
g	=	growth rates

For example, a 0.5% average rise in hours plus a 0.2% productivity assumption, plus 0.4% for the agricultural and government sector suggest a quarterly GNP rate of 1.1%. This would translate to a robust 4.5% annualized rate. The overall growth rate estimated from the hours and productivity data can be used to distribute growth into the components as determined from the averaging method.

While only U.S. domestic data will be discussed in the balance of this book, the GNP accounting methods described in this chapter are in wide use internationally. The U.S. Commerce Department pioneered their use and summarized them in a system called the *National Income and Product Accounts* (NIPA) which are detailed in Table 1.2. Note that the two sides of the table must balance. Inputs to the simplified NIPA model we have specified are given by the economic indicators that comprise the balance of the remaining chapters of this book.

Appendix 1.1

Principal Source Data and Estimating Methods Used in Preparing Current-Dollar Estimates of GNP

APPENDIX 1.1

Principal Source Data and Estimating Methods Used in Preparing Current-Dollar Estimates of GNP

Component (billions of dollars)	Subcomponent (billions of dollars)	Annual estimates: Source data and methods used to determine level for benchmark and other final years or, for other years, used to prepare an extrapolator or interpolator	Preliminary quarterly estimates: Source data and methods used to prepare an extrapolator
		Income side (Charges against GNP of $4,239.9 billion in 1986)	
Compensation of employees ($2,504.9)	Wages and salaries: Private industries, State and local government, and rest of the world ($1,956.8)	For most, annual tabulations of wages and salaries of employees covered by State unemployment insurance from the Bureau of Labor Statistics; for remainder, wages from a variety of sources (such as Dept. of Agriculture for farms and Railroad Retirement Board for railroad transportation) and indirect estimation for only a few cases (such as a percentage of revenues for tips not reported as wages).	For most private, wages and salaries derived, by industry, from Bureau of Labor Statistics monthly employment times earnings times hours; for State and local government and other private, judgmental trend.
	Wages and salaries: Federal ($132.3)	Wages from the Office of Personnel Management and the Office of Management and Budget, *Budget of the United States.*	Same as annual.
	Employer contributions for social insurance ($214.7)	Contributions from the Social Security Admin., other agencies administering social insurance programs, and Census Bureau surveys of State and local government retirement funds.	For Federal programs, BEA-derived wages and salaries of employees covered by the programs; for State and local government programs, judgmental trend.
	Other labor income ($201.1)	Years except most recent—For private pension and profit-sharing funds, employer contributions from Internal Revenue Service tabulations of business tax returns when available and judgmental trend in other years; for group health and life insurance, mainly total premiums paid from trade sources and Health Care Financing Admin. and data on employer share from trade source; for workers' compensation, contributions from trade sources. Most recent year—For group health insurance, total premiums paid from Health Care Financing Admin.; for others in the category, judgmental trend.	Judgmental trend.
Proprietors' income with IVA and CCAdj ($289.8)	Nonfarm income ($217.7)	Years except most recent—Income from Internal Revenue Service tabulations of business tax returns, adjusted for understatement of income on tax returns and for several conceptual differences. Most recent year—For construction, trade, and services, indicators of activity (such as value of housing put in place); for most others, judgmental trends.	Same as annual for most recent year.
	Nonfarm IVA (−$0.2)	The IVA is described under the entry for corporate profits with IVA and CCAdj.	
	Nonfarm CCAdj ($35.1)	The CCAdj is described under the entry for capital consumption allowances with CCAdj.	
	Farm income with IVA ($45.4)	Based on Dept. of Agriculture data on net income, obtained by deriving gross earnings (cash receipts from marketing, inventory change, government payments, other cash income, and nonmoney income) and subtracting production expenses, adjusted to exclude corporate income from Internal Revenue Service tabulations of business tax returns.	Dept. of Agriculture projection adjusted for consistency with NIPA's.
	Farm CCAdj (−$8.1)	The CCAdj is described under the entry for capital consumption allowances with CCAdj.	

See footnotes at end of table.

APPENDIX 1.1 (Continued)

Component (billions of dollars)	Subcomponent (billions of dollars)	Annual estimates: Source data and methods used to determine level for benchmark and other final years or, for other years, used to prepare an extrapolator or interpolator	Preliminary quarterly estimates: Source data and methods used to prepare an extrapolator
		Income side (Charges against GNP of $4,239.9 billion in 1986)—Continued	
Rental income of persons with CCAdj ($16.7)	Rent from nonfarm nonresidential properties ($10.4)	Years except the 2 most recent—Rents paid and received by business and government, adjusted for expenses associated with property (mainly depreciation, taxes, interest, and repairs), from Internal Revenue Service tabulations of business tax returns, Census Bureau surveys, and the *Budget of the United States* prepared by the Office of Management and Budget. Two most recent years—Judgmental trend.	Same as annual for 2 most recent years.
	Rent from owner-occupied nonfarm housing ($18.5)	Derived as space rent—see the entry for nonfarm housing in personal consumption expenditures—less related expenses, including maintenance and repair from Bureau of Labor Statistics quarterly consumer expenditure survey, mortgage debt from Federal Reserve Board times an interest rate, and property taxes from Census Bureau quarterly surveys of State and local tax collections.	For owner-occupied space rent, same as annual; for depreciation, interest, and taxes, based on estimates of those components; for other expenses, based on judgmental trend.
	Rent from tenant-occupied nonfarm housing ($17.5)	Same as described under owner-occupied housing and adjusted to cover only rental income accruing to persons not primarily engaged in the real estate business.	Same as annual.
	Royalties ($10.8)	Years except most recent—Internal Revenue Service tabulations of royalties reported on individual tax returns. Most recent year—Judgmental trend.	Same as annual for most recent year.
	Rent from farms owned by nonoperator landlords ($5.1)	Prepared in conjunction with farm proprietors' income; see that entry.	Judgmental trend.
	CCAdj (−$45.5)	The CCAdj is described under the entry for capital consumption allowances with CCAdj.	
Corporate profits with IVA and CCAdj ($284.4)	Profits: Domestic, before tax ($200.7)	Years except the 2 most recent—Receipts less deductions from Internal Revenue Service tabulations of business tax returns, adjusted to include in profits the depletion allowances on domestic minerals, income of the Federal Reserve and federally sponsored credit agencies, the excess of additions to bad debt reserves over losses actually incurred, and an estimate of the amount by which income on tax returns is understated and to exclude capital gains and losses on the sale of property and dividends received from domestic corporations. Two most recent years—Separately for about 70 industries, profits from Census Bureau quarterly survey of corporate profits, regulatory agency reports, and compilations of public company reports.	For some industries in transportation, some in finance, etc., and all in services, judgmental trend; for others in this group, same as annual for 2 most recent years. (Released at time of first revision of GNP for the first, second, and third quarters and of second revision for the fourth quarter.)
	Profits: Rest of the world, before and after tax ($31.2)	Estimated as part of the balance of payments; see the entry for receipts and payments of factor income, net, under net exports of goods and services.	Judgmental trend. [1] (Released at time of first revision of GNP for the first, second, and third quarters and of second revision for the fourth quarter.)
	IVA ($6.5)	Obtained as the difference between the NIPA change in business inventories (that is, physical volume of inventories valued in prices of the current period) and the change in the book value of inventories reported by business as described in the entry for change in business inventories.	Same as annual.
	CCAdj ($46.0)	The CCAdj is described under the entry for capital consumption allowances with CCAdj.	

See footnotes at end of table.

APPENDIX 1.1 (*Continued*)

Component (billions of dollars)	Subcomponent (billions of dollars)	Annual estimates: Source data and methods used to determine level for benchmark and other final years or, for other years, used to prepare an extrapolator or interpolator	Preliminary quarterly estimates: Source data and methods used to prepare an extrapolator
		Income side (Charges against GNP of $4,239.9 billion in 1986)—Continued	
Net interest ($326.1)	Net interest: Domestic monetary ($128.9)	For farm interest paid and received, Dept. of Agriculture surveys; for residential mortgage interest, mortgage debt from Federal Reserve Board times an interest rate; for all other interest paid and received by business, Internal Revenue Service tabulations of business tax returns or, when these tabulations are not available, interest receipts and payments from regulatory agencies (such as the Federal Deposit Insurance Corporation), from trade sources, or obtained by applying an interest rate to a stock of assets/liabilities from Federal Reserve Board flow of funds accounts.	Derived by combining estimates of (1) interest received by persons, (2) government interest paid and received, and (3) interest paid by consumers to business. For (1), judgmental trend; for (2), largely from *Monthly Treasury Statement*; for (3), consumer debt from the Federal Reserve Board times BEA estimates of interest rates. [1]
	Net interest: Rest-of-the world monetary ($8.1)	Estimated as part of the balance of payments; see the entry for receipts and payments of factor income, net, under net exports of goods and services.	Judgmental trend. [1]
	Net interest: Imputed—life insurance carriers and private noninsured pension plans ($113.0)	Property income earned (and for life insurance carriers, profits) from Internal Revenue Service tabulations of business tax returns or, for the 2 most recent years, from trade sources.	Judgmental trend.
	Net interest: Imputed—banks, credit agencies, and investment companies ($76.1)	Property income earned on investment of deposits and monetary interest paid (and for mutual depositories, profits from Internal Revenue Service tabulations of business tax returns when available) from annual reports of regulatory agencies and the Federal Reserve Board. The counterentry to the interest, financial services furnished without payment, is allocated to persons, government, and rest of the world on the basis of deposit liabilities from the same sources.	Judgmental trend.
Business transfer payments ($22.3)		For corporate gifts to nonprofit institutions and bad debts incurred by consumers, Internal Revenue Service tabulations of business tax returns; for other components (such as liability payments for personal injury), information from other government and trade sources.	Judgmental trend.
Indirect business tax and nontax liability ($347.7)	Federal ($50.9)	For excise taxes and customs duties, collections from the Internal Revenue Service; for nontaxes (such as fines), receipts from the Office of Management and Budget, *Budget of the United States*.	For customs duties, the *Monthly Treasury Statement*; for other in this group, indicators of activity (such as gasoline production for gasoline tax).
	State and local ($296.8)	Receipts from Census Bureau quinquennial censuses and annual and quarterly surveys.	Judgmental trend.
Subsidies less current surplus of government enterprises ($8.7)	Federal ($23.3)	Outlays and receipts from Treasury Dept. reports; Office of Management and Budget, *Budget of the United States*; and reports of various agencies such as the Commodity Credit Corporation.	For subsidies, reports of various agencies and the *Monthly Treasury Statement*; for current surplus, agency report for the Commodity Credit Corporation and budget projections for others in this group.
	State and local (−$14.6)	For subsidies, limited to railroad, judgmental trend; for current surplus, see entry for State and local purchases other than compensation and structures.	Judgmental trend.
Capital consumption allowances with CCAdj ($456.7)	Capital consumption allowances ($477.7)	For depreciation of nonfarm sole proprietorships, partnerships, and corporations, Internal Revenue Service tabulations of business tax returns; for other depreciation (including farms, nonprofit institutions, and owner-occupied houses), perpetual-inventory calculations; for accidental damage to fixed capital, losses reported to insurance companies and government agencies.	Judgmental trend.
	CCAdj ($21.0)	Obtained in two parts: First, the part that places a historical-cost series for capital consumed on a consistent basis with regard to service lives and on a straight-line depreciation pattern is the difference between tax-return-based calculations at historical cost and the perpetual-inventory calculations; second, the part that places the historical-cost series on a current-cost basis is the difference between two perpetual-inventory calculations, one at historical cost and one at current cost.	For capital consumption allowances, judgmental trend as mentioned in preceding item; for current-cost series, perpetual-inventory calculation based on investment and on investment prices.

See footnotes at end of table.

APPENDIX 1.1 (*Continued*)

Component (billions of dollars)	Subcomponent (billions of dollars)	Annual estimates: Source data and methods used to determine level for benchmark and other final years or, for other years, used to prepare an extrapolator or interpolator	Preliminary quarterly estimates: Source data and methods used to prepare an extrapolator
		Product side (GNP of $4,235.0 billion in 1986)	
Personal consumption expenditures ($2,799.8) [2]	**Durable and nondurable goods: ($1,341.8)**		
	Most goods (goods except subcomponents listed separately) ($1,090.0)	Benchmark years—Commodity-flow method, starting with manufacturers' shipments from Census Bureau quinquennial census and including an adjustment for exports and imports from Census Bureau merchandise trade. Other years—Retail-control method, using retail trade sales from Census Bureau annual survey or, for the most recent year, monthly survey of retail trade.	Same as annual for the most recent year.
	New trucks ($27.6)	Benchmark years—Commodity-flow method, starting with manufacturers' shipments from Census Bureau quinquennial census and including an adjustment for exports and imports from Census Bureau merchandise trade. Other years except most recent—Abbreviated commodity-flow method, starting with manufacturers' shipments from Census Bureau annual survey and including an adjustment for exports and imports from Census Bureau merchandise trade. Most recent year—Physical quantity purchased times average retail price: Unit sales and information with which to allocate sales among consumers and other purchasers from trade sources and average price based on a Bureau of Labor Statistics consumer price index.	Same as annual for the most recent year.
	New and used autos ($135.3)	For new autos, physical quantity purchased times average retail price: Unit sales, information with which to allocate sales among consumers and other purchasers, and average list prices, all from trade sources. For used autos, change in the consumer stock of autos at least 1 year old plus dealers' margins based on unit sales times auction price, all from trade sources.	For new autos, same as annual; for used autos, same as annual except that change in consumer stock is based on judgmental trend.
	Gasoline and oil ($75.3)	Years except most recent—Physical quantity purchased times average retail price: Gallons consumed from the Dept. of Transportation, information with which to allocate that total among consumers and other purchasers from Federal agencies and trade sources, and monthly average retail price by grade from the Bureau of Labor Statistics. Most recent year—Physical quantity purchased times average retail price: Domestic supply from Energy Information Admin. monthly surveys and price as above.	Same as annual for most recent year.
	Food furnished employees (including military) ($8.5)	For commercial employees, number of employees of appropriate industries from Bureau of Labor Statistics tabulations times a Bureau of Labor Statistics consumer price index for food; for military personnel, outlays from the *Budget of the United States* prepared by the Office of Management and Budget.	For commercial employees, same as annual; for military personnel, number of persons in Armed Forces from the Dept. of Defense times a Bureau of Labor Statistics consumer price index for food.
	Expenditures abroad by U.S. residents ($4.0) less personal remittances in kind to foreigners ($0.5)	Estimated as part of the balance of payments; see the entry for receipts and payments for other services, net, under net exports of goods and services.	Judgmental trend.

See footnotes at end of table.

APPENDIX 1.1 (Continued)

Component (billions of dollars)	Subcomponent (billions of dollars)	Annual estimates: Source data and methods used to determine level for benchmark and other final years or, for other years, used to prepare an extrapolator or interpolator	Preliminary quarterly estimates: Source data and methods used to prepare an extrapolator
		Product side (GNP of $4,235.0 billion in 1986)—Continued	
Personal consumption expenditures— Continued	Services: ($1,450.8)		
	Nonfarm housing—space rent for owner-occupied and rent for tenant-occupied ($410.5)	Benchmark years—Based on data on housing stock and average annual rental from Census Bureau decennial census of housing and survey of residential finance. Other years—Based on data on housing stock from the Census Bureau biennial housing survey or on the number of households from Census Bureau monthly current population survey and updated average annual rental.	Same method as annual, with housing stock based on annual estimates adjusted for completions from Census Bureau survey and average rent based on annual estimates adjusted using a Bureau of Labor Statistics consumer price index for rent.
	Farm housing—rent ($9.9)	Dept. of Agriculture survey.	Judgmental trend.
	Auto and other repair, legal and funeral services, barbershops and beauty parlors, nursing homes, laundries, other recreation (except video cassette rentals, cable TV, and lotteries), hotels and motels, and commercial education ($231.0)	Benchmark years—Receipts from Census Bureau quinquennial census of service industries adjusted for receipts from business and governments. Other years—Receipts, for spectator sports from private organizations, for legitimate theaters from tabulations of wages and salaries of employees covered by State unemployment insurance from the Bureau of Labor Statistics, for others in this group from Census Bureau service annual survey.	For nursing homes, wages and salaries derived from Bureau of Labor Statistics monthly employment times earnings times hours; for legitimate theaters, receipts from trade source; for others in this group, judgmental trend.
	Physicians, dentists, and other medical professional services ($143.7)	Benchmark years—For nonprofit professional services, expenses; for others in this group, receipts, adjusted for government payments and prepayment plans, from Census Bureau quinquennial census of service industries. Other years—Receipts, adjusted for government payments and prepayment plans, from Census Bureau service annual survey.	For nonprofit professional services, wages and salaries derived from Bureau of Labor Statistics monthly employment times earnings times hours; for others in this group, judgmental trend.
	Private elementary and secondary schools, welfare activities, and other personal business ($70.1)	Benchmark years—For schools of religious organizations, enrollment from Dept. of Education times BEA estimate of average expenditures per pupil; for others in this group, receipts from Census Bureau quinquennial census of service industries. Other years—Tabulations of wages and salaries of employees covered by State unemployment insurance from the Bureau of Labor Statistics.	Wages and salaries derived from Bureau of Labor Statistics monthly employment times earnings times hours.
	Financial services furnished without payment by banks, credit agencies, and investment companies [3] ($70.9)	See entry for net interest: imputed—banks, credit agencies, and investment companies.	Judgmental trend.
	Brokerage, bank service charges, intercity transportation, and private higher education ($70.9)	For private higher education, expenses, and for others in this group, receipts, all from annual reports of government administrative agencies.	For brokerage, stock exchange transactions from trade sources; for bank service charges, judgmental trend; for intercity transportation, receipts from trade sources; for private higher education, wages and salaries for the industry derived from Bureau of Labor Statistics monthly employment times earnings times hours.
	Domestic services ($9.7)	Number of workers times weekly hours times earnings from Census Bureau monthly current population survey.	Judgmental trend.

See footnotes at end of table.

APPENDIX 1.1 (*Continued*)

Component (billions of dollars)	Subcomponent (billions of dollars)	Annual estimates: Source data and methods used to determine level for benchmark and other final years or, for other years, used to prepare an extrapolator or interpolator	Preliminary quarterly estimates: Source data and methods used to prepare an extrapolator
		Product side (GNP of $4,235.0 billion in 1986)—Continued	
Personal consumption expenditures— Continued	Services—Continued		
	Insurance, hospitals except nursing homes, religious activities, cable TV, utilities, and local transport ($373.0)	For life insurance, expenses from reports of private organizations or, for the most recent year, tabulations of wages and salaries of employees covered by State unemployment insurance from Bureau of Labor Statistics; for insurance other than life insurance, premiums and benefits from reports of private organizations; for hospitals except nursing homes, expenses from reports of private organizations; for religious activities, expenses based on contributions and membership from private organizations or, for the most recent year, judgmental trend; for cable TV and utilities, receipts from government agencies and trade sources; for local transport, receipts from reports of private organizations.	For life insurance and religious activities, wages and salaries derived from Bureau of Labor Statistics monthly employment times earnings times hours; for hospitals and electricity, reports from private organizations; for telephone and gas, reports from government agencies; for others in this group, judgmental trend. [1]
	Water and other sanitary services, and lotteries ($22.9)	Years except 2 most recent—For water and other sanitary services, expenditures from Census Bureau quinquennial censuses and annual surveys of State and local governments, adjusted to a calendar year basis from a fiscal year basis; for lotteries, net receipts from the same source. Two most recent years—Judgmental trend.	Same as 2 most recent years.
	Foreign travel by U.S. residents ($23.7) less expenditures in the United States by foreigners ($15.2)	Estimated as part of the balance of payments; see the entry for receipts and payments for other services, net, under net exports of goods and services.	Same as annual.
	Other services: Video cassette rentals and parimutuel net receipts; other housing except hotels and motels; other education and research except commercial education; bridge, etc. tolls; other household operation except repairs and insurance; and clubs and fraternal organizations ($36.9)	Various source data.	Judgmental trend.
Nonresidential structures ($137.4) [4]	Nonfarm buildings ($90.8)	Value put in place from Census Bureau monthly construction survey.	Same as annual.
	Public utilities: Telephone and telegraph ($8.2)	Value put in place from Census Bureau monthly construction survey.	Same as annual.
	Public utilities: Other ($18.0)	Expenditures from Federal regulatory agencies and trade sources.	Anticipated expenditures from BEA plant and equipment survey.
	Mining exploration, shafts, and wells ($15.8)	Benchmark years—Expenditures from Census Bureau quinquennial census of mineral industries. Other years—For petroleum and natural gas, physical quantity times average price: Footage drilled and cost per foot from trade sources; for other mining, expenditures from BEA plant and equipment survey.	Same as annual for years other than benchmark years.
	Other nonfarm structures ($2.3)	Value put in place from Census Bureau monthly construction survey.	Same as annual.
	Farm buildings ($2.0)	Expenditures for new construction from Dept. of Agriculture surveys.	Judgmental trend of value put in place from Census Bureau.

See footnotes at end of table.

APPENDIX 1.1 (Continued)

Component (billions of dollars)	Subcomponent (billions of dollars)	Annual estimates: Source data and methods used to determine level for benchmark and other final years or, for other years, used to prepare an extrapolator or interpolator	Preliminary quarterly estimates: Source data and methods used to prepare an extrapolator
		Product side (GNP of $4,235.0 billion in 1986)—Continued	
Nonresidential producers' durable equipment ($299.5)	Equipment except autos ($278.8)	Benchmark years—Commodity-flow method, starting with manufacturers' shipments from Census Bureau quinquennial census and including an adjustment for exports and imports from Census Bureau merchandise trade. Other years—Abbreviated commodity-flow method starting with manufacturers' shipments from the Census Bureau annual survey or, for the most recent year, monthly survey of manufactures and including an adjustment for exports and imports from Census Bureau merchandise trade. For trucks, for the most recent year, physical quantity purchased times average retail price: Unit sales and information with which to allocate sales among business and other purchasers from trade sources and average price based on Bureau of Labor Statistics producer price indexes.	For trucks, see entry for personal consumption expenditures; for others in this group, same as annual for years other than benchmark years except with less detail.
	New and used autos ($20.7)	For new autos, see entry in personal consumption expenditures; for used autos, change in business stock of autos at least 1 year old from trade source.	For new autos, same as annual; for used autos, judgmental trend.
Residential investment ($218.3) [5]	Permanent-site single-family housing units ($102.4)	Value put in place based on phased housing starts and average construction cost from Census Bureau monthly construction surveys.	Same as annual.
	Permanent-site multifamily housing units ($32.5)	Value put in place from Census Bureau monthly construction survey.	Same as annual.
	Mobile homes ($5.3)	Benchmark years—See entry for equipment except autos in nonresidential producers' durable equipment. Other years—Physical quantity shipped times price: Shipments from trade sources and average retail price from Census Bureau monthly survey.	Same as annual for years other than benchmark years.
	Additions and alterations, and major replacements ($54.0)	Expenditures by owner-occupants from Bureau of Labor Statistics quarterly consumer expenditure survey and by landlords from Census Bureau quarterly survey of landlords.	Judgmental trend.
	Brokers' commissions ($19.5)	Physical quantity times price times average commission rate: Number of one-family houses sold, mean sales price, and commission rates, from Census Bureau monthly construction survey and trade sources.	Same as annual.
	Producers' durable equipment ($5.4)	See entry for most goods under personal consumption expenditures.	Same as annual.
Change in business inventories ($15.7)	Manufacturing and trade ($6.3)	Benchmark years—Book values from Census Bureau quinquennial censuses converted to NIPA basis using information on the proportion of inventories reported with different accounting methods (for example, first-in-first-out), the commodity composition of goods held in inventory, and the turnover period, all from the Census Bureau censuses/surveys of manufacturing and trade, combined with cost of goods held in inventory largely from Bureau of Labor Statistics producer price indexes. Other years—Mainly book values from Census Bureau annual surveys or, for the most recent year, monthly surveys, converted to NIPA basis, as described above.	Same as annual for most recent year.
	Other nonfarm industries ($10.5)	For petroleum bulk stations in all years—physical quantities times price: Monthly quantities from the Energy Information Admin. times a Bureau of Labor Statistics producer price index. Book values converted to a NIPA basis (except when noted as physical quantity times price), as described for manufacturing and trade: For mining, Internal Revenue Service tabulations of business tax returns or, in the 2 most recent years, Census Bureau quarterly surveys of profits in those years; for services and construction, Internal Revenue Service tabulations of business tax returns or, in the 2 most recent years, judgmental trend; for transportation and electric utilities, Internal Revenue Service tabulations of business tax returns except in the two most recent years, or working capital from the Census Bureau and Federal Reserve Board in the next most recent year, or monthly quantities from the Energy Information Admin. for electric utilities and judgmental trend for transportation in the most recent year.	For electric utilities and for petroleum bulk stations—physical quantities times price: Monthly quantities from Energy Information Admin. times a Bureau of Labor Statistics producer price index; for all others, judgmental trend.
	Farm (−$1.1)	Physical quantities times current prices, from Dept. of Agriculture surveys.	Judgmental projection by BEA and Dept. of Agriculture.

See footnotes at end of table.

APPENDIX 1.1 (*Continued*)

Component (billions of dollars)	Subcomponent (billions of dollars)	Annual estimates: Source data and methods used to determine level for benchmark and other final years or, for other years, used to prepare an extrapolator or interpolator	Preliminary quarterly estimates: Source data and methods used to prepare an extrapolator
		Product side (GNP of $4,235.0 billion in 1986)—Continued	
Net exports of goods and services (−$105.5)	Merchandise exports and imports, net (−$142.6)	Estimated as part of the balance of payments: Import and export documents compiled monthly by the Census Bureau with adjustments by BEA for coverage and valuation to put them on a balance-of-payments basis and then on a NIPA basis.	Same as annual.
	Receipts and payments of factor income, net ($33.7)	Estimated as part of the balance of payments: For direct investment income, BEA surveys of U.S. companies with affiliates abroad and of U.S. affiliates of foreign companies; for other income, holdings or transactions from Treasury Dept. surveys times appropriate yields or interest rates and reports by U.S. Government agencies of interest receipts—all adjusted to NIPA basis.	Judgmental trend. [1]
	Receipts and payments for other services, net ($3.4)	Estimated as part of the balance of payments: For government transactions, reports by Federal agencies on their purchases and sales abroad; for most others in this group (including travel, passenger fares, other transportation, royalties and license fees, and private remittances), BEA quarterly or annual surveys (supplemented with data from other sources)—all adjusted to NIPA basis. Also includes financial services furnished without payment; see entry for net interest: imputed—banks, credit agencies, and investment companies.	Same as annual.
Government purchases of goods and services ($869.7)	Federal ($366.2)	Outlays from the *Budget of the United States* prepared by the Office of Management and Budget, the *United States Government Annual Report: Appendix* prepared by the Treasury Dept., and annual reports of selected agencies (such as the Commodity Credit Corporation), all adjusted to a delivery timing basis, to exclude financial transactions and transactions in land, and to exclude interest, subsidies, net expenditures of government enterprises, transfer payments, and grants-in-aid. Also includes financial services furnished without payment; see entry for net interest: imputed—banks, credit agencies, and investment companies.	Same procedures as annual but using outlays from the *Monthly Treasury Statement* and monthly reports of selected agencies.
	State and local compensation ($299.9)	Mainly tabulations of wages and salaries of employees covered by State unemployment insurance from Bureau of Labor Statistics and contributions from the Social Security Admin., other agencies administering social insurance programs, and Census Bureau surveys of State and local government retirement funds.	Judgmental trend.
	State and local structures ($61.4)	For highways, for years except the most recent, expenditures from the Dept. of Transportation or, for the most recent year, construction put in place from Census Bureau surveys; for other categories, value of construction put in place from Census Bureau monthly construction surveys.	Value put in place from Census Bureau monthly construction surveys.
	State and local other than compensation and structures ($142.2)	Years except the 2 most recent—Expenditures from Census Bureau quinquennial censuses and annual surveys of these governments, adjusted to a calendar year basis from a fiscal year basis and adjusted for exclusions and inclusions in a manner similar to that for Federal purchases. Also includes financial services furnished without payment; see entry for net interest: imputed—banks, credit agencies, and investment companies. Two most recent years—Judgmental trend.	Same as annual for 2 most recent years.

1. For insurance other than life insurance, profits and interest from the rest of the world, and parts of domestic net interest, data become available to replace the judgmental trend at the time of the second revision.

2. Includes $1.8 billion for food produced and consumed on farms, standard clothing issued to military personnel, and used trucks.

3. Also referred to as services furnished without payment by financial intermediaries except life insurance carriers and private nonprofit pension plans.

4. Includes $0.1 billion for brokers' commissions on sale of structures and net purchases of used structures.

5. Includes −$0.6 billion for other structures (dormitories, fraternity and sorority houses, nurses' homes, etc.) and net purchases of used structures.

CCAdj Capital consumption adjustment.
IVA   Inventory valuation adjustment.
NIPA National income and product account.

Source: 1986 estimates—SURVEY OF CURRENT BUSINESS, July 1987.

A Word on Seasonal Adjustment and Other Technical Items

There is an old joke on Wall Street about ground being broken for 50 new homes in Florida in the dead of winter and how the Commerce Department seasonally adjusts them into a 1.53 million unit annu- alized February pace for national housing starts (refer to Figure 2.1). This story has some basis in fact. The purpose of seasonal adjustment is to isolate regular movements and "smooth" these fluctuations over the course of a predetermined time frame such as a calendar year. For a cyclical statistical series such as housing starts, one would expect good seasonals to add back units lost during depressed periods such as the winter.

SEASONAL ADJUSTMENT

Economic series can be affected by regular intrayearly movements owing to a number of factors. The most common are:

FIGURE 2.1 Monthly housing starts from 1959

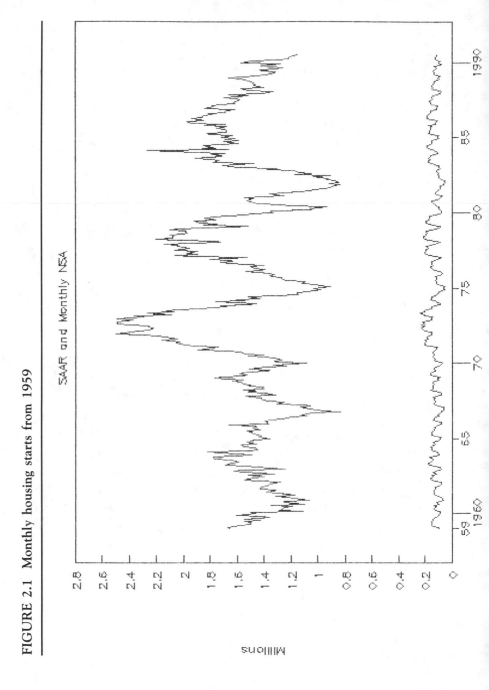

Climatic conditions

Model changeovers

Vacation practices

Holidays

Calendar quirks, such as leap year and back-to-school timing

The first attempts to isolate seasonal factors from time series data were made more than 50 years ago. The early methods depended on smoothing curves by using personal judgment. Other formal approaches involved periodogram, regression, and correlation analysis. In the mid-1950s, however, computers made more elaborate methods feasible, namely the ratio-to-moving average method. These were put into use first by the Commerce Department and then, in 1959, by the Bureau of Labor Statistics—the two agencies mainly responsible for releasing economic indicators.

The agencies now use the X-11 ARIMA Seasonal Adjustment Method developed in the 1970s by Statistics Canada. This method uses *ARIMA* (AutoRegressive Integrated Moving Average) modeling to extrapolate some extra data at the end of a time series to be seasonally adjusted. The seasonals are calculated so they move this extra data back to trend. Of course, the quantum assumption here is that a data series has an identifiable trend, so seasonals are notorious for going off track at turning points in the economy.

Seasonals are established in one of two ways—concurrently or estimated in advance. While the concurrent approach precludes the prior publication of seasonal factors and requires substantially more staff and computer resources, recent research has shown that it minimizes subsequent revisions. Also, seasonals can be estimated either for a data series as a whole or for its component parts. Recent research shows the latter is more accurate.

The Commerce Department currently uses concurrent estimation of seasonals, while the Fed estimates seasonals in advance. Since a big part of any economic analyst's job in projecting a data release is to outguess the seasonals, we will go into them in some detail.

THE MONEY SUPPLY DATA

Seasonal adjustment factors for the weekly money supply data released by the Fed are given in Table 2.1. This is a good example of advance estimating for both components and whole sections of a data series. The Fed staff creates seasonals for each of the important components of the money supply (currency, demand deposits, other checkable deposits on the first page of the table and savings deposits and thrift deposits on the second page), requiring the analyst to study each component separately. They also provide overall seasonals for catchall components (nontransaction components in M2 and in M3, on the first page of the table) for which insufficient data are available to create good seasonals.

As an example, seasonals below 1.0000 in Table 2.1 add back to the component. In the first column, the seasonal factor for currency in the December 3 week is 0.9982, indicating that currency is expected to decline. After adjustment, currency will be boosted by 0.2% (1 divided by 0.9982). Likewise, the seasonals look for demand deposits and other checkables (the checking account components) to rise. The seasonals are easily explained by a glance at the calendar and at our laws.

The Social Security Act requires retirement benefit payments to be in recipient's hands by the third day of the month. Currently, about 60% of these payments are wire transferred. Since, as shown in Table 2.1, December 3, 1990 is a Monday and the money supply computation week ends on Monday, these payments can be expected to remain on deposit for a time because not everyone will access his account right away. Thus, the Fed's seasonals for checking accounts are calculated to remove some of the bulge that would otherwise artificially bloat the money supply measures. Note that the same seasonals then boost the checking account components later in the month of December.

The money supply data, then, demonstrate the purpose of seasonal adjustment, namely, to spread out any easily explainable bulges over time and to compensate for shortfalls that can be expected to be made up later in the period (usually the calendar year). Seasonals must always sum to one, that is, add back all they have removed over the time period used. This is demonstrated in the housing starts data diagrammed in Figure 2.1. The top series is not seasonally adjusted. It is sometimes called NSA. Seasonals are demonstrated in the bottom, with the SA (seasonally adjusted) series.

Seasonals go off track on occasion. Returning to the Social Security example, in regards to the money supply data, seasonals can exacerbate the moves in checking accounts if the payments do not occur on schedule. For example, federal law requires these payments to be moved forward should the third of the month fall on a weekend or holiday. If the seasonals look for a payment on the third that is, in fact, made a few days earlier, they will inadequately depress money supply.

Recent Social Security dates and the preceding and following weeks' money supply moves are detailed in Table 2.2. The table demonstrates that even carefully specified seasonals do not prevent large weekly wiggles in money supply. These wiggles had an absolute average value of $5 billion over the four Social Security dates shown for 1990. Moreover, the seasonals inadequately depressed M1 in all instances except for July. Since the Independence Day holiday fell during mid-week in 1990, people withdrew balances from their accounts to spend. The seasonals looked for these accounts to remain full over an extra day and thus incorrectly added to the fall.

BENCHMARKING

Once a year, the statistical agencies adjust seasonal factors and produce major revisions to prior data. This is called *benchmarking*. It is intended to incorporate additional data and make a better adjustment to reality. A few times, benchmarking has changed radically the perception of the economy. A good example is in the August 1990 *Employment Report*, where nonfarm payrolls were revised down an average of 7,000 per month for the prior year but production remained

TABLE 2.1
Weekly Seasonal Factors Used to Construct M1, M2, and M3

Week ending	Currency	Nonbank travelers checks	Demand deposits	Other checkable deposits at banks	at thrifts	Nontransactions components in M2	in M3 only
	1	2	3	4	5	6	7
1990—Dec. 3	0.9982	0.9312	1.0173	0.9972	1.0014	1.0014	1.0050
10	1.0149	0.9304	1.0292	1.0228	1.0295	0.9999	1.0007
17	1.0134	0.9295	1.0392	1.0126	1.0041	0.9986	0.9975
24	1.0239	0.9287	1.0383	1.0077	0.9873	0.9962	1.0015
31	1.0082	0.9279	1.0685	1.0056	0.9846	0.9971	1.0047
1991—Jan. 7	1.0072	0.9290	1.0872	1.0486	1.0357	1.0027	0.9915
14	0.9984	0.9313	1.0423	1.0436	1.0153	1.0038	0.9986
21	0.9913	0.9337	1.0078	1.0217	0.9913	1.0007	0.9976
28	0.9814	0.9361	0.9649	0.9937	0.9560	1.0002	0.9983
Feb. 4	0.9889	0.9839	0.9839	1.0042	0.9902	0.9999	0.9984
11	0.9958	0.9448	0.9734	1.0107	0.9891	1.0003	1.0016
18	0.9942	0.9506	0.9698	0.9996	0.9729	1.0004	1.0001
25	0.9825	0.9564	0.9505	0.9908	0.9569	1.0008	0.9996
Mar. 4	0.9891	0.9613	0.9720	1.0068	0.9888	1.0012	1.0027
11	0.9998	0.9610	0.9799	1.0134	0.9998	1.0016	1.0031
18	0.9957	0.9606	0.9751	1.0049	0.9896	1.0017	1.0037
25	0.9909	0.9603	0.9562	0.9967	0.9734	1.0009	1.0091

	0.9889	0.9599	0.9835	1.0025	0.9886					
Apr. 1	0.9889	0.9599	0.9835	1.0025	0.9886					
1990—Dec. 3	0.9968	1.0104	0.9976	0.9959	0.9972	1.0052	0.9997	1.0131	1.0046	1.0187
10	0.9985	1.0130	0.9969	0.9996	0.9987	1.0083	0.9983	1.0108	1.0043	1.0067
17	0.9948	1.0112	0.9950	0.9926	0.9932	1.0066	0.9956	1.0099	1.0022	1.0042
24	0.9900	1.0063	0.9947	0.9941	0.9876	1.0030	0.9948	1.0067	0.9983	1.0021
31	0.9912	1.0108	0.9952	0.9963	0.9928	1.0050	1.0011	1.0096	0.9913	1.0057
1991—Jan. 7	0.9988	1.0183	0.9973	0.9934	0.9996	1.0093	1.0042	1.0072	0.9805	0.9901
14	0.9976	1.0156	0.9981	0.9943	0.9962	1.0072	1.0031	1.0084	0.9993	1.0361
21	0.9944	1.0095	0.9985	0.9919	0.9905	1.0013	1.0017	1.0081	1.0034	1.0416
28	0.9929	1.0051	0.9999	0.9954	0.9870	0.9992	1.0036	1.0091	1.0030	1.0425
Feb. 4	0.9909	1.0057	1.0003	0.9953	0.9900	1.0009	1.0054	1.0066	0.9977	1.0364
11	0.9943	1.0059	1.0008	0.9989	0.9916	1.0005	1.0047	1.0054	1.0028	1.0383
18	0.9939	1.0045	1.0007	0.9988	0.9892	0.9988	1.0037	1.0037	1.0058	1.0293
25	0.9932	1.0047	1.0008	1.0003	0.9873	0.9982	1.0017	0.9994	1.0071	1.0290
Mar. 4	0.9935	1.0062	1.0012	1.0036	0.9922	1.0021	1.0009	0.9953	1.0097	1.0218
11	0.9983	1.0062	1.0018	1.0053	0.9982	1.0051	0.9989	0.9938	1.0140	1.0108
18	0.9995	1.0039	1.0013	1.0062	1.0000	1.0030	0.9966	0.9919	1.0147	1.0009
25	1.0003	1.0017	1.0019	1.0101	0.9983	1.0014	0.9962	0.9939	1.0175	1.0079
Apr. 1	1.0023	1.0055	1.0042	1.0100	1.0044	1.0025	1.0006	0.9934	1.0116	1.0175

TABLE 2.2
Seasonally Adjusted M1 Changes On and After
Social Security Dates (Dollars in Billions)

Month	Prior Week	Social Security Week	Following Week
June 1990	– $3.2	+ $4.3	– $0.6
July	+ 8.8	– 7.5	– 2.6
August	+ 2.0	+ 3.8	+ 1.5
September	– 2.2	+ 4.4	+ 0.5

almost unchanged. This implied that productivity was higher and that the economy was operating at a higher rate than most analysts had assumed.

CLASSIFICATION OF DATA

It would be impossible for the government's statistical agencies to gather and disseminate data without sophisticated systems. Many of these classifications are of use to investors because they give information by industry or region and, hence, may influence stock prices or real estate values. They are also useful for designing marketing programs.

Industrial Codes

The Bureau of Labor Statistics (BLS) in the Labor Department and the other agencies closely follow a single system in order to define and classify industries in the U.S. economy. The system is called *Standard Industrial Classification* (SIC) and is based on principles set out by technical government and industry experts. These principles are:

1. Classifications must conform to the existing structure of American industry;
2. Each establishment is classified according to its primary activity; and

3. To be recognized as an industry, a group of establishments must be statistically significant in terms of payrolls or sales.

There are 11 broad divisions in the latest SIC manual. These divisions segregate the economy into sectors such as:

Agriculture;

Mining;

Construction;

Manufacturing;

Transportation, communications, electric, gas, and sanitary services;

Wholesale trade;

Retail trade;

Finance;

Services;

Public administration; and

Others.

There are 84 major groups within these 11 divisions with the classification going down to 4 digits, resulting in hundreds of subgroupings.

GEOGRAPHIC CLASSIFICATION

Statistical agencies also publish data by region, metropolitan statistical area, and labor market areas. Some of these breakdowns follow.

The *Northeast* includes the states of Connecticut, Maine, Massachusetts, New Hampshire, New Jersey, New York, Pennsylvania, Rhode Island, and Vermont. This is a heavily industrialized area which also includes many of the nation's financial concerns. Home prices and incomes are high.

The *Midwest* includes the states of Illinois, Indiana, Iowa, Kansas, Michigan, Minnesota, Missouri, Nebraska, North Dakota, Ohio,

South Dakota, and Wisconsin. Heavy manufacturing (especially auto related), minerals extraction, and farming are mainstays in this region. Home prices and incomes are high.

The *South* includes the states of Alabama, Arkansas, Delaware, Florida, Georgia, Kentucky, Louisiana, Maryland, Mississippi, North and South Carolina, Oklahoma, Tennessee, Texas, Virginia and West Virginia, as well as the District of Columbia. Tourism, textiles, farming, important ports, and some manufacturing are located here. Housing prices and incomes are among the lowest in the nation.

The *West* includes the states of Alaska, Arizona, California, Colorado, Hawaii, Idaho, Montana, Nevada, New Mexico, Oregon, Utah, Washington, and Wyoming. This is probably the most diverse group, owing in large part to the wide and varied activities in California. Major sectors include defense and aircraft manufacturing, farming and ranching, high technology, ports, and tourism. Home prices and incomes are high and vie with the Northeast for most costly.

METROPOLITAN STATISTICAL AREAS (MSA)

MSAs are large population areas (cities) together with physically adjacent communities that have a high degree of social and economic integration with that area. They are separated by rural areas. A good example is New York and Newark which, though only 40 miles apart, are separated by suburbs. MSAs are subdivided into four levels, designated A to D, based on total population. The A areas have more than 1 million people, the B areas 250,000 to 1 million, the C areas 100,000 to 250,000, and the D areas less than 100,000. In areas with over 1 million in population, primary metropolitan statistical areas may also be identified. These are large, urbanized counties that demonstrate very strong internal economic and social links.

As we will see in Chapters 4 through 9, benchmarking, seasonal adjustment, and standard classification systems are meant to make complicated economic statistics easier to understand and use. The systems described above were followed throughout the 1980s by most of the agencies that release statistics.

3

Survey Techniques
and Timing

Since the first Labor Department annual report was issued in March 1886, advanced scientific methods have been applied to most of the economic indicators released by the government. Still, most indicators are based on surveys conducted from samples rather than polling an entire industry or population (the latter is called a *census*). Thus, understanding the methodology used to choose the sample, the data collection process, and the estimating methods becomes critical to the economic analyst—if for no other reason than to understand the potential pitfalls of the data.

SAMPLING

The samples used to determine most economic indicators derived from households come from the Bureau of the Census's *Current Population Survey (CPS). The CPS sample is located in 729 areas comprising over 1,000 counties and independent cities, with coverage in every state and the District of Columbia. About 71,000 housing units are included, of which about 59,500 are occupied and about 56,600 ultimately are interviewed.*

The entire United States, consisting of 3,137 counties, is divided into 1,973 *Primary Sampling Units* (PSUs) for the CPS. Metropolitan areas within each state are used to create strata and one PSU is selected from each stratum, with the probability of selection proportionate to population size. Thus, areas such as New York City and Los Angeles are always surveyed more completely. Households within the stratum are selected based on building permit data, with sampling ranging from 1 in every 200 households to 1 in every 2,500, depending on the level of cooperation achieved in the past in various states. Part of the samples are changed each month. Therefore, the shift from one section of the country to another may impact the data. For instance, pockets of unemployment in the South could raise the unemployment rate if the South becomes overweighted after a survey change.

For wage, price, productivity, and other business data, sampling is based on *Standard Industrial Classification* (SIC) (see Chapter 2), but data gathering is conducted by the Bureau of Labor Statistics. Sales, shipments, orders, and other accounting data are garnered from yet another similar survey called the *Annual Survey of Manufacturers* (ASM) that is conducted by the Census Bureau. In both cases, businesses are chosen from publicly available data bases such as telephone books or the *Standard & Poor's Directory*, sorted according to size, and assigned probabilities in much the same procedures applied to households.

DATA COLLECTION

Statistical agencies have put in place careful review processes to determine what data to collect, to develop questionnaires that elicit the proper data, and to develop an on-going collection process. Many of the employees of these agencies are trained statisticians and economists, and even the employees conducting the day-to-day interviews are professionals who have undergone rigorous training.

Three methods are used to collect data:

1. In person interviews;
2. Telephone interviews; and
3. Mail questionnaires.

In a fairly typical example, the CPS monthly surveys are conducted during the week of the month that contains a certain date, say the nineteenth day. This helps minimize seasonal distortions. Personal visits to households are required in the first, second, and fifth month that a household remains in the sample. But in any one month, about 67% of the survey is conducted via telephone.

Completed questionnaires are forwarded to the field office the week after the survey is undertaken. Raw data are transferred to computer tapes and transmitted to the head office in Washington, D.C., where they are checked for completeness and consistency. Quality control takes two forms:

1. Re-interviews by supervisory field staff; and
2. Repeated observation during the time the household remains part of the survey.

ESTIMATING METHODS

Three adjustments are made to statistical data after it is collected. First, a noninterview adjustment is required for those segments that failed to report as a result of absence, blocked roads, refusals, or unavailability of the respondents. This adjustment is made separately for combinations of similar areas. The proportion of noninterviews is generally around 4 to 5%.

Ratio estimates are used to "blow up" the sample to the whole, weighting sample data inversely to the probability of the person being in the sample. But, the ratios are computed in two stages. The first stage is applied to 43 states, so a portion of the 729 sample areas deemed to be nonunique are chosen to represent other areas. Other areas represent only themselves. The second stage adjusts the sample proportions of age, sex, national origin, and race to match the composition in the country as a whole.

    The last adjustment to the sample data uses a composite estimating procedure. This makes use of a weighted average of the noncomposited results for the current month and the composite result for the prior month, adjusted for the net changes in the sample. The compos-

FIGURE 3.1 The survey process

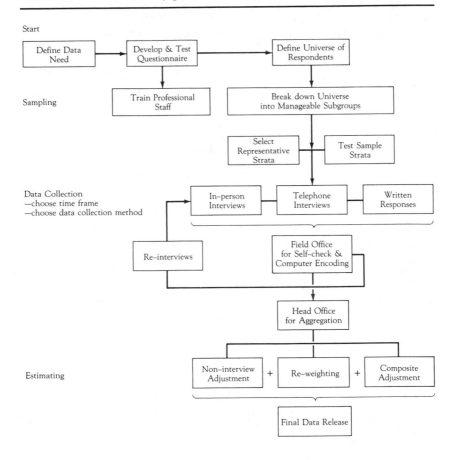

ite estimate reduces error because it does not allow for massive deviation from prior results.

Figure 3.1 demonstrates the above process from start to finish. The survey process is broken down into four stages in this chart: definition, sampling, data collection, and estimating. Of course, the addition of new data in the form of more survey responses will start part four of this process anew, producing sometimes surprising results.

Table 3.1 provides the original releases and first revisions for the Advance Retail Sales report. It illustrates that even the most advanced scientific methodology does not prevent large absolute revisions. These revisions have averaged 0.7 percentage points over the last five years—almost as much as the average initial rise! Moreover, the average revision for the first six months of 1990 was 0.34 percentage points.

RESPONSIBLE PARTIES

Most economic data in the United States are produced by one of three agencies. The Bureau of Labor Statistics in the Labor Department is responsible for wage, price, and productivity data, as well as measures

TABLE 3.1
Advance Retail Sales and Its Initial Revision (% Changes)

	Advance	Revision	Difference
January 1990	+1.6%	+1.3%	0.3 percentage point
February	−0.8%	−0.3%	0.5
March*	−0.6%	−0.3%	0.3
April	−0.6%	−0.9%	0.3
May	−0.7%	−0.6%	0.1
June	+0.5%	+1.1%	0.6
Average			0.3

*Data beyond February are as reported after benchmark revisions.

of employment and the labor force. The Census Bureau and the Bureau of Economic Analysis in the Commerce Department release numbers on the overall population and the business situation (including inventories, sales, incomes and orders), respectively. The Fed releases credit, money supply, and banking data but is also responsible for producing measures of industrial production and resource utilization.

Most of these indicators are on a regular monthly schedule, which is released at the start of each year and followed fairly carefully. This

TABLE 3.2.
Theoretical Schedule for Selected Indicators

Indicator	Time Frame
Employment Report for prior month	First Friday of the month
Consumer credit for two months prior	Fifth business day of the month
Money supply for prior week	Each Thursday evening
Advance retail sales for prior month	Second Friday of the month
Producer prices for prior month	Second or third Friday of the month
Industrial production for prior month	Fifteenth of the month
Gross National Product for prior quarter	Monday of third week of the month
Housing starts for prior month	Fifteenth business day of the month
Durable goods orders (two month lag)	Seventeenth business day of the month
Merchandise trade balance (two month lag)	Middle of third week of the month
Personal income and Consumption for prior month	Last full week of the month

schedule is given for 1991 in Appendix 3.1. There is a pattern to these releases, however, given in Table 3.2. Thus, the private analyst can plan a multi-year calendar.

Moreover, the concept of producing high-quality statistics means technical staff are always available to the private analyst to answer questions about the construction and assumptions made for each indicator. A partial contact list and their telephone numbers is given in Appendix 3.2.

SAARs

From this point forward, this book will discuss seasonally adjusted data and use rates of change calculated at an annual rate. This concept is sometimes denoted as SAAR (*seasonally adjusted annualized rate*). It is pretty much a standard within the economics profession and can be explained simply. The difference in two measurement points for a seasonally adjusted data series should be multiplied by the number of periods in a year and then divided by the base to get a SAAR. As an example for a monthly observation, total personal income rose to $4,639.5 billion in June 1990 from $4,622.9 billion in May. The difference ($4,639.5 minus $4,622.9) is $16.6 billion. This represents a 0.4% monthly gain ($16.6 billion divided by the base period, $4,622.9 billion in May, equals 0.00359 or 0.4%). In turn, this is close to a 4.3% annual pace (0.00359 times the 12 months in the year).

Appendix 3.1

Scheduled Release Dates for Economic Indicators In 1991

January 1991

Date Due	Indicator	Reference Period
Jan 2	New Construction	Nov 90
Jan 3	New One-family Home Sales	Nov 90
Jan 4	The Employment Situation	Dec 90
Jan 4	Manfacturers Shipments, Inventories & Orders	Nov 90
Jan 7	Consumer Credit	Nov 90
Jan 10	Wholesale Trade	Nov 90
Jan 11	Producer Prices	Dec 90
Jan 15	Advance Retail Sales	Dec 90
Jan 15	Industrial Production & Capacity	Dec 90
Jan 16	Consumer Prices	Dec 90
Jan 16	Manufacturing & Trade Inventories & Sales	Nov 90
Jan 17	Housing Starts & Permits	Dec 90
Jan 18	Advance Merchandise Trade	Nov 90
Jan 23	Monthly Treasury Statement	Dec 90
Jan 25	Gross National Product	90:Q4
Jan 25	Import/Export Price Indices	Dec 90
Jan 28	Personal Income & Outlays	Dec 90
Jan 29	Durable Goods Report	Dec 90
Jan 30	Leading, Lagging, & Coincident Indicators	Dec 90
Jan 31	New One-family Home Sales	Dec 90

February 1991

Date Due	Indicator	Reference Period
Feb 1	The Employment Situation	Jan 91
Feb 1	New Construction	Dec 90
Feb 5	Manufacturers Shipments, Inventories & Orders	Dec 90
Feb 7	Wholesale Trade	Dec 90
Feb 7	Consumer Credit	Dec 90
Feb 13	Advance Retail Sales	Jan 91

February 1991 (*continued*)

Date Due	Indicator	Reference Period
Feb 14	Manufacturing & Trade Inventories & Sales	Dec 90
Feb 15	Advance Merchandise Trade	Dec 90
Feb 15	Producer Prices	Jan 91
Feb 15	Industrial Production & Capacity	Jan 91
Feb 20	Consumer Prices	Jan 91
Feb 20	Housing Starts & Permits	Jan 91
Feb 22	Monthly Treasury Statement	Jan 91
Feb 26	Durable Goods Report	Jan 91
Feb 27	Gross National Product	90:Q4
Feb 28	Personal Income & Outlays	Jan 91
Feb 28	Import/Export Price Indices	Jan 91

March 1991

Date Due	Indicator	Reference Period
Mar 1	Leading, Lagging, & Coincident Indicators	Jan 91
Mar 1	New Construction	Jan 91
Mar 4	New One-family Home Sales	Jan 91
Mar 5	Manufacturers Shipments, Inventories & Orders	Jan 91
Mar 7	Consumer Credit	Jan 91
Mar 8	The Employment Situation	Feb 91
Mar 12	Wholesale Trade	Jan 91
Mar 13	Advance Retail Sales	Feb 91
Mar 14	Manufacturing & Trade Inventories & Sales	Jan 91
Mar 15	Producer Prices	Feb 91
Mar 15	Industrial Production & Capacity	Feb 91
Mar 19	Consumer Prices	Feb 91
Mar 19	Housing Starts & Permits	Feb 91
Mar 20	Advance Merchandise Trade	Jan 91
Mar 21	Monthly Treasury Statement	Feb 91

March 1991 (*continued*)

Date Due	Indicator	Reference Period
Mar 26	Durable Goods Report	Feb 91
Mar 27	Gross National Product	90:Q4
Mar 28	Personal Income & Outlays	Feb 91
Mar 28	Import/Export Price Indices	Feb 91
Mar 29	Leading, Lagging, & Coincident Indicators	Feb 91
Mar 29	New One-family Home Sales	Feb 91

April 1991

Date Due	Indicator	Reference Period
Apr 1	New Construction	Feb 91
Apr 2	Manufacturers Shipments, Inventories & Orders	Feb 91
Apr 5	The Employment Situation	Mar 91
Apr 7	Consumer Credit	Feb 91
Apr 8	Wholesale Trade	Feb 91
Apr 10	Plant & Equipment Expenditures Survey	90:Q4
Apr 11	Producer Prices	Mar 91
Apr 11	Advance Retail Sales	Mar 91
Apr 12	Consumer Prices	Mar 91
Apr 12	Manufacturing & Trade Inventories & Sales	Feb 91
Apr 15	Industrial Production & Capacity	Mar 91
Apr 16	Housing Starts & Permits	Mar 91
Apr 18	Advance Merchandise Trade	Feb 91
Apr 19	Monthly Treasury Statement	Mar 91
Apr 23	Durable Goods Report	Mar 91
Apr 25	Import/Export Price Indices	Mar 91
Apr 26	Gross National Product	91:Q1
Apr 29	Personal Income & Outlays	Mar 91
Apr 29	New One-family Home Sales	Mar 91
Apr 30	Manufacturers Shipments, Inventories & Orders	Mar 91

May 1991

Date Due	Indicator	Reference Period
May 1	Leading, Lagging, & Coincident Indicators	Mar 91
May 1	New Construction	Mar 91
May 3	The Employment Situation	Apr 91
May 7	Wholesale Trade	Mar 91
May 7	Consumer Credit	Mar 91
May 10	Producer Prices	Apr 91
May 14	Advance Retail Sales	Apr 91
May 14	Consumer Prices	Apr 91
May 15	Manufacturing & Trade Inventories & Sales	Mar 91
May 15	Industrial Production & Capacity	Apr 91
May 16	Housing Starts & Permits	Apr 91
May 17	Advance Merchandise Trade	Mar 91
May 21	Monthly Treasury Statement	Apr 91
May 23	Durable Goods Report	Apr 91
May 23	Import/Export Price Indices	Apr 91
May 29	Gross National Product	91:Q1
May 30	Personal Income & Outlays	Apr 91
May 30	New One-family Home Sales	Apr 91
May 31	Manufacturers Shipments, Inventories & Orders	Apr 91
May 31	Leading, Lagging, & Coincident Indicators	Apr 91

June 1991

Date Due	Indicator	Reference Period
Jun 3	New Construction	Apr 91
Jun 6	Plant & Equipment Spending	91:Q1
Jun 7	The Employment Situation	May 91
Jun 7	Wholesale Trade	Apr 91
Jun 7	Consumer Credit	Apr 91
Jun 13	Producer Prices	May 91

June 1991 (*continued*)

Date Due	Indicator	Reference Period
Jun 13	Advance Retail Sales	May 91
Jun 14	Consumer Prices	May 91
Jun 14	Manufacturing & Trade Inventories & Sales	Apr 91
Jun 15	Industrial Production & Capacity	May 91
Jun 18	Housing Starts & Permits	May 91
Jun 19	Advance Merchandise Trade	Apr 91
Jun 21	Monthly Treasury Statement	May 91
Jun 25	Durable Goods Report	May 91
Jun 26	Gross National Product	91:Q1
Jun 27	Import/Export Price Indices	May 91
Jun 27	Personal Income & Outlays	May 91
Jun 28	Leading, Lagging, & Coincident Indicators	May 91

July 1991

Date Due	Indicator	Reference Period
Jul 1	New Construction	May 91
Jul 2	Manufacturers Shipments, Inventories & Orders	May 91
Jul 3	New One-family Home Sales	May 91
Jul 5	The Employment Situation	Jun 91
Jul 5	Consumer Credit	May 91
Jul 10	Wholesale Trade	May 91
Jul 12	Producer Prices	Jun 91
Jul 12	Advance Retail Sales	Jun 91
Jul 15	Manufacturing & Trade Inventories & Sales	May 91
Jul 15	Industrial Production & Capacity	Jun 91
Jul 17	Consumer Prices	Jun 91
Jul 17	Housing Starts & Permits	Jun 91
Jul 18	Advance Merchandise Trade	May 91
Jul 22	Monthly Treasury Statement	Jun 91

July 1991 (*continued*)

Date Due	Indicator	Reference Period
Jul 24	Durable Goods Report	Jun 91
Jul 25	Import/Export Price Indices	Jun 91
Jul 30	Gross National Product	91:Q2
Jul 30	New One-family Home Sales	Jun 91
Jul 31	Personal Income & Outlays	Jun 91
Jul 31	Manufacturers Shipments, Inventories & Orders	Jun 91

August 1991

Date Due	Indicator	Reference Period
Aug 1	New Construction	Jun 91
Aug 2	Leading, Lagging, & Coincident Indicators	Jun 91
Aug 2	The Employment Situation	Jul 91
Aug 7	Wholesale Trade	Jun 91
Aug 7	Consumer Credit	Jun 91
Aug 9	Producer Prices	Jul 91
Aug 13	Advance Retail Sales	Jul 91
Aug 14	Consumer Prices	Jul 91
Aug 14	Manufacturing & Trade Inventories & Sales	Jun 91
Aug 15	Housing Starts & Permits	Jul 91
Aug 15	Industrial Production & Capacity	Jul 91
Aug 16	Advance Merchandise Trade	Jun 91
Aug 21	Monthly Treasury Statement	Jul 91
Aug 23	Durable Goods Report	Jul 91
Aug 25	Import/Export Price Indices	Jul 91
Aug 28	Gross National Product	91:Q2
Aug 29	Personal Income & Outlays	Jul 91
Aug 29	New One-family Home Sales	Jul 91
Aug 30	Leading, Lagging, & Coincident Indicators	Jul 91
Aug 30	Manufacturers Shipments, Inventories & Orders	Jul 91

September 1991

Date Due	Indicator	Reference Period
Sep 3	New Construction	Jul 91
Sep 5	Plant & Equipment Spending Survey	91:Q2
Sep 6	The Employment Situation	Aug 91
Sep 6	Consumer Credit	Jul 91
Sep 11	Wholesale Trade	Jul 91
Sep 12	Producer Prices	Aug 91
Sep 13	Advance Retail Sales	Aug 91
Sep 13	Consumer Prices	Aug 91
Sep 15	Industrial Production & Capacity	Aug 91
Sep 16	Manufacturing & Trade Inventories & Sales	Jul 91
Sep 18	Housing Starts & Permits	Aug 91
Sep 19	Advance Merchandise Trade	Jul 91
Sep 22	Monthly Treasury Statement	Aug 91
Sep 25	Durable Goods Report	Aug 91
Sep 26	Import/Export Price Indices	Aug 91
Sep 26	Gross National Product	91:Q2
Sep 27	Personal Income & Outlays	Aug 91

October 1991

Date Due	Indicator	Reference Period
Oct 1	Leading, Lagging, & Coincident Indicators	Aug 91
Oct 1	New Construction	Aug 91
Oct 2	New One-family Home Sales	Aug 91
Oct 3	Manufacturers Shipments, Inventories & Orders	Aug 91
Oct 4	The Employment Situation	Sep 91
Oct 7	Consumer Credit	Aug 91
Oct 8	Wholesale Trade	Aug 91
Oct 11	Producer Prices	Sep 91
Oct 11	Advance Retail Sales	Sep 91

October 1991 (*continued*)

Date Due	Indicator	Reference Period
Oct 13	Manufacturing & Trade Inventories & Sales	Aug 91
Oct 15	Industrial Production & Capacity	Sep 91
Oct 17	Consumer Prices	Sep 91
Oct 17	Advance Merchandise Trade	Aug 91
Oct 18	Housing Starts & Permits	Sep 91
Oct 22	Monthly Treasury Statement	Sep 91
Oct 24	Durable Goods Report	Sep 91
Oct 24	Import/Export Price Indices	Sep 91
Oct 29	Gross National Product	91:Q2
Oct 30	Personal Income & Outlays	Sep 91
Oct 30	New One-family Home Sales	Sep 91
Oct 31	Manufacturers Shipments, Inventories & Orders	Sep 91

November 1991

Date Due	Indicator	Reference Period
Nov 1	Leading, Lagging, & Coincident Indicators	Sep 91
Nov 1	The Employment Situation	Oct 91
Nov 1	New Construction	Sep 91
Nov 7	Wholesale Trade	Sep 91
Nov 7	Consumer Credit	Sep 91
Nov 13	Producer Prices	Oct 91
Nov 14	Consumer Prices	Oct 91
Nov 14	Advance Retail Sales	Oct 91
Nov 15	Manufacturing & Trade Inventories & Sales	Sep 91
Nov 15	Industrial Production & Capacity	Oct 91
Nov 19	Advance Merchandise Trade	Sep 91
Nov 20	Housing Starts & Permits	Oct 91
Nov 22	Monthly Treasury Statement	Oct 91
Nov 26	Gross National Product	91:Q2

November 1991 (*continued*)

Date Due	Indicator	Reference Period
Nov 27	Durable Goods Report	Oct 91
Nov 27	Personal Income & Outlays	Oct 91
Nov 27	Import/Export Price Indices	Oct 91

December 1991

Date due	Indicator	Reference Period
Dec 2	New Construction	Oct 91
Dec 3	New One-family Home Sales	Oct 91
Dec 3	Leading, Lagging, & Coincident Indicators	Oct 91
Dec 5	Manufacturers Shipments, Inventories & Orders	Oct 91
Dec 6	The Employment Situation	Nov 91
Dec 6	Consumer Credit	Oct 91
Dec 11	Wholesale Trade	Oct 91
Dec 12	Producer Prices	Nov 91
Dec 12	Advance Retail Sales	Nov 91
Dec 13	Consumer Prices	Nov 91
Dec 13	Manufacturing & Trade Inventories & Sales	Oct 91
Dec 15	Industrial Production & Capacity	Nov 91
Dec 17	Housing Starts & Permits	Nov 91
Dec 19	Advance Merchandise Trade	Oct 91
Dec 20	Monthly Treasury Statement	Nov 91
Dec 20	Gross National Product	91:Q3
Dec 23	Personal Income & Outlays	Nov 91
Dec 24	Durable Goods Report	Nov 91
Dec 27	Import/Export Price Indices	Nov 91
Dec 31	Leading, Lagging, & Coincident Indicators	Nov 91

Appendix 3.2

Schedule of Contacts

Release	Source	Telephone
Consumer Credit	Fed Board— Mr. Jim August	202-452-3741
Industrial Production	Fed Board— Mr. Dixon Traynor	202-452-2931
NAPM Survey	Purchasing Managers Assoc. Mr. Bob Bretz	203-356-6851
New One-family Houses	Commerce Dept. Mr. Barry Rappaport	301-763-7842
Housing Starts & Permits	Commerce Dept. Mr. David Fondelier	301-763-5731
Construction put in Place	Commerce Dept. Mr. Allan Meyer	301-763-5717
Advance Retail Sales	Commerce Dept. Mr. Irving True	301-763-7128
Wholesale Trade	Commerce Dept. Mr. Dombrowski	202-763-3916
Durable Goods	Commerce Dept. Ms. Ruth Runyan	202-763-2505
Inventories & Shipments	Commerce Dept. Ms. Ruth Runyan	202-763-2505
Existing Home Sales	Nat'l Assoc. of Realtors	202-383-1062
Merchandise Trade	Commerce Dept.	301-763-5140
Truck Sales	Motor Vehicle Mfgrs. Assoc. Ms. Virginia Reinfield	313-872-4311
Leading Indicators	Commerce Dept. Mr. Larry Moran	202-523-0777
Blue Chip Economic Indicators	Eggert Economics, Inc. Mr. Robert Eggert	602-282-4882
Oil Well Completions	Amer. Petroleum Inst.	202-682-8491

Release	Source	Telephone
Personal Income	Commerce Dept.	202-523-0832
	Ms. Pauline Cybert	
Dodge Capital	McGraw Hill	516-512-3794
Spending	Mr. George Christie	
Payrolls	Labor Dept.	202-523-1172
	Mr. Jerry Storch	
Producer Prices	Labor Dept.	202-272-5051
Consumer Prices	Labor Dept.	202-272-5064
	Mr. Thomas	
Unemployment	Labor Dept.	202-523-6872
Claims	Ms. Cindy Ambler	
Capacity	Fed Board	202-452-2933
Utilization		
Agricultural	Agriculture Dept.	202-447-3570
Prices		
Consumer	Conference Bd.	212-759-5224
Confidence	Ms. Newman	
Auto Production	Commerce Dept.	202-523-0807
	Mr. Paul Lally	
Income Statistics	Treasury Dept.	202-376-0083
Budget Data	Congressional Budget Office	202-226-2621
Chicago	Mr. John Pressley	312-782-7940
Purchasing		
Managers		
Association		
GNP	Commerce Dept.	202-523-0759
	Mr. Jack Triplett	

The Employment Report

The Employment Report is the most important of the monthly data releases, since it is difficult to estimate in advance and it gives the building blocks for projecting many other data series (see the GNP reconciliation in Table 1.2). *The Employment Report* consists of two sections, A and B, the first based on a survey of business firms (called *establishments*) and the second on a survey of households. Payrolls, the workweek, hourly earnings, and total hours worked for the private nonfarm sector come from the establishment survey where hours are also broken down by industry. The household survey measures the labor force, the number of people employed, and the unemployment rate. A full reproduction of the report appears in Appendix 4.1 with annotation.

ESTABLISHMENT SURVEY*

A mail survey of about 330,000 nonagricultural firms is conducted for the week of the month that contains the twelfth day. The *Bureau of Labor Statistics* (BLS) blows up the sample to get the published nonfarm payroll number. The ratio is based on an annual March survey of establishments. Payrolls are rebenchmarked each May. Seasonal factors are re-estimated then as well.

Firms in the survey fill out a questionnaire (see Figure 4.1) covering the number of workers on their payrolls, wages, and hours worked. The survey, or reference, week may not be the same as the calendar week containing the twelfth if the pay period covers another time frame such as two weeks or a month. Part- as well as full-timers are included, so payrolls can reflect individuals who worked just one day of the survey period. Strikers are excluded if they were out for the full period. The mix between full- and part-time workers affects the workweek (total hours worked divided by the number of workers) and average hourly earnings (total earnings divided by total hours worked).

The BLS does not receive all the completed questionnaires in time to include them in the preliminary report, so there are frequent revisions to nonfarm payrolls. From 130,000 to 180,000 responses are usually included in the preliminary figure. From 220,000 to 250,000 responses are included by the next month and 280,000 or higher by the third revision. As additional reports are incorporated, the total or the industry composition of payrolls can be changed (see Chapter 3 for the discussion on sampling methods). For example, the average revision to the first-reported nonfarm payroll gain was more than 100,000 in the first nine months of 1990.

HOUSEHOLD SURVEY

A sample of about 60,000 households, covering individuals aged 16 years or older is blown up by the ratio of the population to the survey size (1750:1). This survey is completed each month for the week containing the twelfth covering agriculture, the self-employed, and the armed forces in addition to payrolls. (See Figure 4.2 for a theoretical diagram of the population.) The household data are not revised, except in December when the seasonal factors are re-estimated with

FIGURE 4.1 Bureau of Labor Statistics Report on Employment, Payroll, and Hours—Manufacturing

State	Report Number	Industry

Return promptly each month in the enclosed envelope which requires no postage. Change name and mailing address if incorrect—Include Zip code.

Return to:

A. Please provide the following information in case questions arise concerning this report.

Your Name   Title   Phone Number ( )

B. Please provide the location of establishments covered by this report.

Number of establishments   City   County   State

C. Please check one: Production workers are paid ☐ each week ☐ every 2 weeks ☐ twice a month ☐ once a month ☐ other, specify:

D. Please complete columns 1-6 for the pay period checked above which includes the 12th of the month. Detailed explanations are on the reverse side.

Reference Period Please report data only for the pay period which includes the 12th of the month	(1) All Employees: Report the number of paid employees who worked during or received pay for any part of the pay period which includes the 12th of the month	(2) Women Employees: Report the number of employees from column 1 that are women	(3) Production Workers: Report the number of employees from column 1 that are production workers	(4) Production Worker Payroll: Report the total production worker payroll, including overtime, for the pay period which includes the 12th of the month (omit cents)	(5) Production Worker Hours: Report the total production worker hours, including overtime, for the pay period which includes the 12th of the month (omit fractions)	(6) Production Worker Overtime Hours: Report the total production worker overtime hours included in column 5 (omit fractions)	OFFICE USE ONLY Expl code	L/P code
DEC 1986				$				
JAN 1987								
FEB								
MAR								
APR								
MAY								
JUN								
JUL								
AUG								
SEP								
OCT								
NOV								
DEC								

E. Please report comments on significant changes in your employment, payroll, or hours on the reverse.

BLS-790 C Rev Dec 86

FIGURE 4.1 (cont'd)

For what time period should I complete this form?

Complete this form only for the single pay period checked in Part C (weekly, monthly, etc.) that includes the 12th day of the month. Payroll and hours (Part D, columns 4-6) should be reported for the entire pay period checked in Part C, regardless of its length.

If your pay period is Monday through Friday, and the 12th falls on a Saturday, please report for the week of the 6th through the 12th. When the 12th falls on a Sunday, report for the week of the 12th through the 18th.

Column 1 All Employees:
Enter the total number of persons who worked full- or part-time or received pay for any part of the pay period including the 12th of the month.

  "All Employees" includes:

  salaried officials of corporations
  executives and their staff
  persons on paid vacation
  persons on paid sick leave
  persons on other paid leave
  part-time employees
  trainees

  "All Employees" excludes:

  proprietors
  pensioners
  unpaid family workers
  partners of unincorporated firms
  persons on strike the entire pay period
  persons on leave without pay the entire pay period
  armed forces personnel on active duty the entire pay period

Column 2 Women Employees:
Enter the number of employees from column 1 that are women.

Column 3 Production Workers:
Enter the number of employees from column 1 that are production workers. "Production workers" includes all nonsupervisory workers engaged in such occupations as:

fabricating	shipping	processing
storage	trucking	assembling
receiving	packing	janitorial
warehousing	handling	repair
	maintenance	
	product development	
	recordkeeping (clerical) related to production	

"Production workers" also includes working supervisors and group leaders who may be "in charge" of a group of employees, but whose supervisory functions are only incidental to their regular work.

"Production workers" excludes:

executives	personnel	cafeterias
finance	medical	accounting
technical	professional	legal
advertising	credit	sales
collection	sales-delivery	purchasing
	recordkeeping (clerical) not related to production	
	force account construction	
	installation of products	
	servicing of products	

Column 4 Production Worker Payroll:
Enter the total amount of pay earned during the entire pay period checked in Part C (weekly, etc.) for all production workers in column 3.

  Report pay *before* employee deductions for:

  FICA (social security)
  unemployment insurance
  health insurance
  pensions
  pay deferral plans (401K plans)
  Federal, State, and local income taxes
  bonds
  union dues

Include pay for:	*Exclude:*
overtime	bonuses, unless paid regularly
holidays	lump sum payments
vacations	retroactive pay
sick leave	pay advances
other paid leave	payments-in-kind

Column 5 Production Worker Hours:
Enter the total number of hours paid for during the entire pay period checked in Part C (weekly, etc.) for all production workers in column 3. Do not convert overtime or other premium hours to straight-time equivalent hours. "Hours paid for" is the sum of:

1. Hours worked, including overtime hours.
2. Hours paid for stand-by or reporting time.
3. Hours not worked, but for which pay was received directly from the firm. Included are holidays, vacations, sick leave, or other paid leave.

Column 6 Production Worker Overtime Hours:
Enter the total number of hours from column 5 for which overtime premiums were paid because the hours were in excess of the regularly scheduled hours. Include Saturday, Sunday, 6th day, 7th day, and holiday hours only if overtime premiums were paid. Exclude hours for which only shift differential, hazard, incentive, or other similar types of premiums were paid.

If there were no overtime hours, enter "O" in column 6.

E. Comments. Check the box which best indicates the reason for significant changes in employment (Emp), payroll (PR), or hours (Hrs). Circle the item(s) (Emp, PR, or Hrs) to which the comment applies.

If none of the checkboxes apply, write your own comments here.

				seasonal increase	seasonal decrease	more business (new orders)	less business (lack of orders)	majority on paid vacation	majority on unpaid vacation	more overtime	less overtime	longer scheduled workweek	shorter scheduled workweek	higher earnings for piece work or incentive pay	lower earnings for piece work or incentive pay	general wage change—COLA	temporary or permanent shutdown	
JAN	Emp	PR	Hrs															
FEB	Emp	PR	Hrs															
MAR	Emp	PR	Hrs															
APR	Emp	PR	Hrs															
MAY	Emp	PR	Hrs															
JUN	Emp	PR	Hrs															
JUL	Emp	PR	Hrs															
AUG	Emp	PR	Hrs															
SEP	Emp	PR	Hrs															
OCT	Emp	PR	Hrs															
NOV	Emp	PR	Hrs															
DEC	Emp	PR	Hrs															

BLS-790 C Rev Dec 86

FIGURE 4.1 (cont'd)

Bureau of Labor Statistics Report on **Employment, Payroll, and Hours—Trade**

U.S. Department of Labor

This report is authorized by law 29 U.S.C. 2. Your voluntary cooperation is needed to make the results of this survey comprehensive, accurate, and timely. The information collected on this form by the Bureau of Labor Statistics and the States cooperating in its statistical programs will be held in confidence and will be used for statistical purposes only.

Form Approved
O.M.B. No. 1220-0011

State	Report Number	Industry

Return promptly each month in the enclosed envelope which requires no postage. Change name and mailing address if incorrect—Include Zip code.

Return to:

A. Please provide the following information in case questions arise concerning this report.

Your Name   Title   Phone Number
(   )

B. Please provide the location of establishments covered by this report.

Number of establishments   City   County   State

C. Please check one.
Nonsupervisory employees are paid:
☐ each week   ☐ every 2 weeks   ☐ twice a month   ☐ once a month
☐ other, specify:

D. Please check one.
Nonsupervisory employees are paid commissions:
☐ each week   ☐ every 2 weeks   ☐ twice a month   ☐ once a month
☐ no commissions are paid   ☐ other, specify:

E. Please complete columns 1-4 and 6 for the pay period checked in C above which includes the 12th of the month. Complete column 5 for the commission period checked in D above which includes the 12th of the month. Detailed explanations are on the reverse side.

Reference Period	(1) All Employees:	(2) Women Employees:	(3) Nonsupervisory Employees:	(4) Nonsupervisory Employee Payroll:	(5) Commissions of Nonsupervisory Employees:	DO NOT USE	(6) Nonsupervisory Employee Hours:	DO NOT USE	
Please report data only for the pay period which includes the 12th of the month	Report the number of paid employees who worked during or received pay for any part of the pay period which includes the 12th of the month	Report the number of employees from column 1 that are women	Report the number of employees from column 1 that are nonsupervisory employees	Report the total nonsupervisory employee payroll, excluding commissions, for the pay period including the 12th of the month (omit cents)	Report the total commissions paid for the period including the 12th of the month (omit cents)	OFFICE USE ONLY	Report the total nonsupervisory employee hours, including overtime, for the pay period including the 12th of the month (omit fractions)	OFFICE USE ONLY	
						PR		Expl code	L/P code
DEC 1986				$	$				
JAN 1987									
FEB									
MAR									
APR									
MAY									
JUN									
JUL									
AUG									
SEP									
OCT									
NOV									
DEC									

F. Please report comments on significant changes in your employment, payroll, hours, or commissions on the reverse.

BLS-790 E Rev Dec 86

FIGURE 4.1 (cont'd)

For what time period should I complete this form?

Complete Part E, columns 1-4 and 6, only for the single pay period checked in Part C (weekly, monthly, etc.) that includes the 12th day of the month. Payroll and hours (Part E, columns 4 and 6) should be reported for the entire pay period checked in Part C, regardless of its length.

Commissions (Part E, column 5) should be reported for the entire commission period checked in Part D, regardless of its length. If your commission period ends more than 2 weeks after the end of the pay period checked in Part C, do not delay this report. Instead, report commissions on a one month lag, the next time you receive this form.

If your pay period checked in Part C is Monday through Friday, and the 12th falls on a Saturday, please report for the week of the 6th through the 12th. When the 12th falls on a Sunday, report for the week of the 12th through the 18th.

Column 1 All Employees:
Enter the total number of persons who worked full- or part-time or received pay for any part of the pay period including the 12th of the month.

"All Employees" includes:

salaried officials of corporations
executives and their staff
persons on paid vacation
persons on paid sick leave
persons on other paid leave
part-time employees
trainees

"All Employees" excludes:

proprietors
pensioners
unpaid family workers
partners of unincorporated firms
persons on strike the entire pay period
persons on leave without pay the entire pay period
armed forces personnel on active duty the entire pay period

Column 2 Women Employees:
Enter the number of employees from column 1 that are women.

Column 3 Nonsupervisory Employees:
Enter the number of employees from column 1 that are nonsupervisory employees. Nonsupervisory employees are all employees in column 1 who are NOT:

officers of corporations	department heads
executives	managers

"Nonsupervisory employees" includes working supervisors and group leaders who may be "in charge" of a group of employees, but whose supervisory functions are only incidental to their regular work.

In other words, "nonsupervisory employees" includes every employee except those whose major responsibility is to supervise, plan, or direct the work of others.

Column 4 Nonsupervisory Employee Payroll:
Enter the total amount of pay earned during the entire pay period checked in Part C (weekly, etc.) for all nonsupervisory employees in column 3. Do not include commissions. Commissions are reported in column 5.

Report pay *before* employee deductions for:

FICA (social security)
unemployment insurance
health insurance
pensions
pay deferral plans (401K plans)
Federal, State, and local income taxes
bonds
union dues

Include pay for:	*Exclude:*
overtime	tips
holidays	commissions
vacations	lump sum payments
sick leave	retroactive pay
other paid leave	pay advances
	payments-in-kind (meals, etc.)
	bonuses, unless paid regularly
	travel expenses

Column 5 Commissions of Nonsupervisory Employees:
Enter commissions (not base pay, drawing accounts, or basic guarantees) paid to all nonsupervisory employees in column 3 during the entire commission period checked in Part D (weekly, etc.). If no commissions are paid, check the appropriate box in Part D and leave column 5 blank.

Column 6 Nonsupervisory Employee Hours:
Enter the total number of hours paid for during the entire pay period checked in Part C (weekly, etc.) for all nonsupervisory employees in column 3. Do not convert overtime or other premium hours to straight-time equivalent hours. "Hours paid for" is the sum of:

1. Hours worked, including overtime hours.
2. Hours paid for stand-by or reporting time.
3. Hours not worked, but for which pay was received directly from the firm. Included are holidays, vacations, sick leave, or other paid leave.

F. Comments. Check the box which best indicates the reason for significant changes in employment (Emp), payroll (PR), or hours (Hrs). Circle the item(s) (Emp, PR, or Hrs) to which the comment applies.

				seasonal increase	seasonal decrease	more business (not seasonal)	less business (not seasonal)	more overtime	less overtime	longer scheduled workweek	shorter scheduled workweek	more commissions earned	less commissions earned	general wage change—COLA	temporary or permanent shutdown	If none of the checkboxes apply, write your own comments here.
JAN	Emp	PR	Hrs													
FEB	Emp	PR	Hrs													
MAR	Emp	PR	Hrs													
APR	Emp	PR	Hrs													
MAY	Emp	PR	Hrs													
JUN	Emp	PR	Hrs													
JUL	Emp	PR	Hrs													
AUG	Emp	PR	Hrs													
SEP	Emp	PR	Hrs													
OCT	Emp	PR	Hrs													
NOV	Emp	PR	Hrs													
DEC	Emp	PR	Hrs													

BLS-790 E Rev Dec 86

FIGURE 4.2 The labor market in the United States.

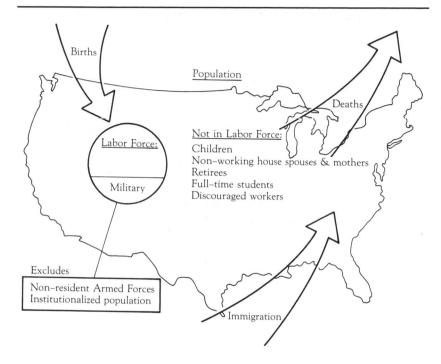

little effect on the unemployment rate. An individual is employed regardless of the number of jobs he holds. In contrast, the establishment data count jobs, not persons. Thus, payrolls tend to expand faster when the economy is strong as people moonlight. Strikers are counted as employed in the household survey so the unemployment rate is not affected by strikes though payrolls are.

The household data are less reliable than establishment data because of the smaller sample and the tendency of individuals to answer that they are employed even if this is not so. So, the unemployment rate is used to evaluate whether a monthly change in nonfarm payrolls is reliable. For example, a weak economy should show both a rising unemployment rate and slow growth in payrolls with the bulk of the growth in the latter centered in services. The household survey covers a longer time frame than the establishment survey, so it is not as sensitive as nonfarm payrolls to the weather or calendar quirks as nonfarm payrolls. An individual is defined as unemployed if he did not have a job during the survey week, but was available and looking for work during the prior four weeks.

The sampling error for the unemployment rate is 0.2 percentage points. The unemployment rate generally lags the business cycle since it excludes *discouraged workers* (people who want a job but have stopped looking). Discouraged workers increase during recessions so a sustained rise is necessary to signal a weaker economy. Note that the teenage population and unemployment are currently in a downtrend since the "baby boomers" are aging. This could result in a falling total unemployment rate over time as older people are more likely to be employed full-time while teenagers are not.

USING THE EMPLOYMENT DATA

Of particular significance to the securities markets are nonfarm payrolls, the unemployment rate, and average hourly earnings. Payrolls give an overall measure of the health of the economy. A large rise in this number implies a speed-up in growth, while a slowing indicates an economy that is not so robust. Since the report breaks out employment by industry grouping (construction, government, retail, services, mining, and manufacturing), economic analysts also use this series to project industry trends.

The unemployment rate is a confirming indicator of payrolls and a measure of labor market pressures. It is defined as the ratio of the labor force minus those who are employed, divided by the labor force. At some point, a tight labor market (low unemployment) is expected to accelerate wage gains. One current debate among policy makers in Washington is how low the unemployment rate can be permitted to drop before wage inflation gets imbedded in the price level. Supply-siders and liberal members of the Federal Reserve Board believe that a rate close to 5% is sustainable without wage pressures. The Fed's statistical model, however, suggests a sustainable non-inflationary unemployment rate is closer to 6% (a level that implied policy in 1990 should be tilted toward slowing the economy).

At the July 2–3, 1990 Federal Open Market Committee (FOMC) meeting,** for example, there was considerable debate among members about whether the Fed's staff model should be accepted at face value. The Committee felt that anecdotal evidence about the economy was considerably weighted toward a slower pace of economic growth than predicted. So, officials were divided about whether to ease interest rates immediately. Ultimately, the least common denominator which commanded a majority was a vote to leave policy unchanged with a tilt toward an easing in the not-so-distant future. The Fed did ease just 10 days after this meeting after the dissent had died down. Thus, at least one important economic analyst, Fed Chairman Alan Greenspan, bought the argument that a lower unemployment rate was acceptable.

INFLATION

Average hourly earnings (AHE) in the private nonfarm sector are used as a measure of wage inflation. Given the FOMC's pre-occupation with inflation in 1990, it is no wonder that the financial markets began to follow this early warning statistic. AHE is obtained by dividing average weekly earnings by the total hours worked in the week. Thus, it is also affected by strikes, overtime, and the mix of part- and full-time workers. So, on a monthly basis, AHE is volatile, having a pronounced tendency to surge in the first month of each calendar quarter. However, the quarterly averaging technique (see Chapter 1) smooths out AHE quite nicely. A surge in AHE would be consistent with a fall in the unemployment rate in indicating a tight labor market and an inflation problem.

ECONOMIC DATA PROJECTIONS

The computer printout from the employment report is 22 pages long and provides a wealth of information that can be plugged into other statistical series (see Appendix 4.1 for an annotated sample). Therefore, it is used to project market-moving data that are released separately later in the month. So, not only is it the first new official release each month, it is also the most important.

As mentioned in Chapter 1, income-side accounting relates the number of hours worked to real GNP growth. The percentage change in hours worked, when added to a trend estimate of productivity growth, gives an estimate of GNP growth for the current quarter. It would be statistically inconsistent to have a growing economy without increases in hours worked.

Second, the percentage change in average weekly earnings gives an estimate of the growth of nongovernment wages and salaries in the *Personal Income Report* (discussed in more depth in Chapter 6). Wages and Salaries are the largest segment of personal income (about 60% of the total). Another way to estimate wages and salaries is to multiply average hourly earnings and total hours worked and then calculate the monthly change in the product. The two methods should be consistent.

Last, insights into the *Industrial Production Report* (see Chapter 8) can be gained. The percentage change in manufacturing jobs can be used as a rough proxy for production. The percentage change in the average workweek and total hours worked are less reliable but can be used to hone this estimate.

PROJECTING THE EMPLOYMENT DATA

How do we project the components of *The Employment Report* itself? Very few analysts could afford the time and expense of duplicating the BLS's complicated survey techniques. However, *Initial Unemployment Claims* (the total of workers filing for unemployment benefits following the loss of a job) are released weekly by the BLS. Claims are compiled by the state offices which make unemployment insurance payments and are reported each week to the Bureau of Labor Statistics in Washington, which aggregates and seasonally adjusts them. Claims are a good coincident indicator of economic conditions and a good predictor of turning points in the economy since they peak two to three months prior to a cyclical trough.

However, not all workers are covered by unemployment insurance. In particular, about 50% of those in the agricultural industry in the big farm states of Texas and California are not covered. These factors lower the number of benefit recipients relative to the unemployment level. Also, the weekly and monthly changes in claims are affected by holidays and other transitory developments such as natural disasters. For instance, claims decline around holidays when the state filing offices are closed, then rebound the following week. Thus, most analysts smooth them by looking at a four-week moving average. A rise of more than 20,000 above the prior moving average in a nonholiday period probably indicates a disruption in the labor market.

Anomalies

The careful analyst of the monthly employment situation is left with only one methodology for estimating: searching out anomalies in the prior period and deciding whether they are a permanent change or reflective of a sea change in the labor market. An example is in Table B-1 of the *Employment Report* provided in Appendix 4.1.

The data demonstrate that nonfarm payrolls, the most dicey area to project, had been in a downtrend in mid-1990, reflecting both a rapidly weakening economy and the summer firing of census workers who had been brought in to take the decennial population count. We began a bottom-up estimating process with two factors in mind:

1. That any estimate should be low-balled relative to prior Septembers; and

2. that more census firings probably had taken place during the month.

The Commerce Department officials responsible for departmental payrolls subsequently indicated that about 50,000 census workers had been let go; these were subtracted from our final estimate. Table 4.1 also shows few signs of strength in manufacturing or construction in prior months. We plugged in declines of 25,000 each (close to the drops over the preceding three months).

Service-producing and retail jobs had stabilized and probably would be areas of growth ahead, especially as the Christmas season approached. Therefore, 20,000 workers were added for these categories. September is the start of the school year. Teachers, educational assistants, food workers, guards, and other support staff are rehired in that month for the nine-month season. On average, over the two prior years, the state and local government category had jumped by more than 80,000 as a result. An expanding school-age population gave every indication that this hiring would continue. But the gain could be tempered by the fact that these employees are sometimes required to report in August and may have appeared in the prior report. A five-week interval between the July and August surveys would have captured a larger payroll sample and exacerbated this

TABLE 4.1
September 1990 Estimate for Nonfarm Payrolls

Mining	− 5,000
Construction	− 25,000
Manufacturing	− 25,000
Census (Federal Government)	− 50,000
Retail	+ 20,000
Services Producing	+ 20,000
Government	+ 70,000
All Other	+ 15,000
Total	+ 20,000

possibility. Thus, only 70,000 was added for state and local government.

Last, by definition, the calling-up of armed forces reservists to serve in the Kuwait–Iraq war intervention would, by definition, lower payrolls even if they were still being paid by private firms as required by law. So, the risk was that the estimated 50,000 reservists called to active duty would also subtract from payrolls. Of course, this depended critically on firms completing the BLS survey forms correctly—an even more dicey assumption. The reservists would be captured in the categories where they had been employed.

The numbers detailed in this analysis are given in Table 4.1. The net estimate for September nonfarm payrolls was + 20,000. This slow payroll growth should have been confirmed by the *Household Survey* via a rising civilian unemployment rate which had indeed been the case since June. By definition, the unemployment rate is the ratio of unemployed persons (the labor force less those employed) to the labor force. The labor force, in turn, is defined as the civilian population (the total less the armed forces, who are employed by definition) multiplied by the participation rate. During hard economic times, the participation rate shrinks as people get discouraged from looking for work. Thus, the labor force shrinks while the population generally grows apace. As a result, the unemployment rate rise lags weakening labor market conditions.

For September, a weaker labor market was thought to be a sure thing. But, a declining labor force was also in evidence and a second technical factor was at work. Most of the prior month's 0.1 point jump in the civilian unemployment rate was attributable to a jump in teenage unemployment which surged 0.4 percentage points. As this rate is volatile, the jump could have had no economic significance. Hence, the blip could come off in the next reporting period as students returning to school also dropped out of the labor force. Thus, only a 0.1% point rise in the civilian unemployment rate was projected.

The other important data in *The Employment Report* cover inflation and hours worked and are tied to estimates for payrolls and the unemployment rate. While few analysts hazard guesses for the bulk of the data in the report, the inflation indicators are critical. *Average hourly earnings* (AHE) best reflects wage pressures. AHE is defined as average weekly earnings divided by total hours worked in the week. Weekly earnings, in turn, are influenced by the composition of the workforce. Increasing proportions of government (teachers) and service industry employees, as projected, generally indicate a moderation in AHE since they earn less than members of manufacturing unions and construction trades.

Note also that an anomaly of the report is that AHE tends to spurt at the beginning of each quarter, only to limp along subsequently. As a result, a 0.2% rise was projected, down from the 0.3% six-month average. Although it has become more controversial in recent years, some analysts still assume an inverse relationship between unemployment and the rate of inflation. So, a rising unemployment rate should also be associated with lower inflation.

The actual results for the September *Employment Report* were indicative of recession. Nonfarm payrolls fell 101,000, the civilian unemployment rate rose 0.1 percentage point to 5.7%, and AHE rose a surprising 0.5%. The latter was, indeed, a result of a shift in the composition of the workforce but reflected layoffs of lower-paid union and white collar employees. That is, the downturn evidently had steepened enough that only managers were still employed! The other data resulting from the report suggested a weakening in the other economic indicators, though not on a sustained basis, as we shall see in the analysis of income in Chapter 5.

Notes

*The following four paragraphs of this chapter are based in part on information contained in "A Guide to the Employment Report," by Carl Palash, with additions by Joseph Plocek and Astrid Adolfson, Money Market Critique of McCarthy, Crisanti, & Maffei, Inc., January 1989.

**The Federal Open Market Committee (FOMC) is a statutory body of the Federal Reserve System that is comprised of the Fed's 7 governors and 5 of the 12 regional Reserve Bank Presidents. The FOMC is charged with setting the monetary policy constructs within which the overnight interest rate is manipulated.

Appendix 4.1

Annotated Employment Report

Page 1—The first five pages of *The Employment Report* summarize the data available from both the payroll and establishment surveys. These pages parallel the briefing that the BLS Commissioner conducts for the financial press by encapsulating the outlook and indicating whether the economy is likely to grow in the month ahead, based on the latest employment situation. In August 1990, the report was fairly dismal, with the first sentence showing a continuing weak picture. Note also that the box on page 1 flags the technical adjustments made to the data—in this case, the annual benchmark revisions, the changes in the SIC codes, and the re-basing of the data to a 1982 index.

Page 6—Two pages of Explanatory Notes follow, on technical items such as the number of households and establishments surveyed. Seasonal adjustment and sampling problems are generally discussed here. The average errors for the adult male jobless rate is noted to be 0.25 percentage point, for example.

Page 8—Household data are detailed in 13 tables. The most important is the first, Table A-1, which gives the broad outlines of growth in the labor force, the participation rate, and overall unemployment rate for the entire population. Note that a growing economy with healthy demographics generally see a growing labor force—not the case in late 1990. The balance of the tables proceed to break these data down by age, sex, race, and special situation such as Hispanic origin or Vietnam-era veteran status. The seasonally adjusted data appear on the right-hand side of the tables.

Page 9—The important civilian unemployment rate is found in Table A-2 (last line for the "Total," at 5.6%).

Page 11—Table A-4 begins a breakdown of workers by industry classification, which should be compared to the nonfarm payrolls from the establishment survey. Both surveys should move in the same direction (i.e., weaken simultaneously to indicate a recession). This table also details persons at work only part time. Rising unemployment should be associated with workers being unable to find full-time jobs. This appears to have been the case since May 1990.

Page 13—Tables A-7 and A-8 give the duration of and reason for unemployment. They make an interesting commentary on the social situation but do not provide deep economic insights. Ditto for the breakdown by age, sex, occupational status, and veteran status.

Page 16—Table A-13 provides the status of the 13 most populous states—California, Florida, Illinois, Massachusetts, Michigan, New Jersey, New York, North Carolina, Ohio, Pennsylvania, and Texas. The unemployment rates in this table provide valuable clues about the regional economies. Note that the Midwest and the Northeast appeared to be experiencing high unemployment in mid-1990.

Page 18—The important payroll survey data begin here in Table B-1, with seasonally adjusted data once again on the right. The payroll total is broken down into armed forces and private, with goods-producing (mining, construction and durable and non-durable manufacturing) and services-producing (transportation, wholesale and retail trade, finance, and government) subdivisions given for the private total. Note that goods-producing employment, at 92,279 in August 1990, was below the year-earlier total. Note also the slow growth in services-producing employment. The 45,000 loss in manufacturing jobs suggests a fall in industrial production for the month.

Page 19—Table B-2 gives average weekly hours for production workers in the private sector. Note that this series was steady, implying that real GNP probably was flat.

Page 20—Table B-3 gives average hourly and weekly earnings data, expressed in dollar terms. Line 2 of the table shows that AHE rose $0.02 in August 1990 to $10.09, an increase of 0.2% ($0.02/$10.07 is 0.002 or 0.2%). Earnings in the motor vehicles and FIRE industries are the most erratic in this table, reflecting the hard times on Wall Street and the Detroit cutbacks. This suggests personal income was not strong during the month.

Page 21—Table B-5 shows an Index of weekly hours for production workers. Industry analysts use these indices to chart the progress in particular areas. Manufacturing and construction had peaked in June, while there was still strength in select areas such as tobacco products and publishing.

Page 22—Table B-6 is a little followed diffusion index, calculated as the percentage of industries with employment increasing plus one-half of the percentage with steady employment. It slipped below 50% on several occasions in 1990, showing a marked weakening beginning in April.

News

United States
Department
of Labor

Bureau of Labor Statistics   Washington, D.C. 20212

Technical information (202) 523-1371   USDL 90-461
                          523-1944
                          523-1959   TRANSMISSION OF MATERIAL IN THIS
Media contact: 523-1913   RELEASE IS EMBARGOED UNTIL
                                            8:30 A.M. (EDT), FRIDAY,
                                            SEPTEMBER 7, 1990

THE EMPLOYMENT SITUATION: AUGUST 1990

Employment continued to be weak in August and unemployment rose
slightly, the Bureau of Labor Statistics of the U.S. Department of Labor
reported today. The civilian worker unemployment rate edged up to 5.6
percent in August, after a more substantial increase in July.

Nonfarm payroll employment, as measured by the survey of business
establishments, was little changed at 110.7 million in August, the second
consecutive month it has failed to show any growth. Total civilian
employment, as measured by the survey of households, fell for the second
month in a row, to 117.7 million in August.

Unemployment (Household Survey Data)

Both the number of unemployed persons and the civilian worker
unemployment rate edged up in August, after seasonal adjustment, with the
number of unemployed reaching 7.0 million and the rate 5.6 percent. Prior
to July, the jobless rate had fluctuated around the 5.3-percent mark for
nearly 2 years. (See table A-2.)

Over-the-month movements in the jobless rates for most individual
worker groups were very small but generally upward. August rates were 5.0
percent for adult men, 4.9 percent for adult women, 16.7 percent for
teenagers, 4.8 percent for whites, 11.8 percent for blacks, and 7.8 percent
for Hispanics. (See tables A-2 and A-3.)

The number of unemployed persons who lost their last jobs rose by
280,000 in August, while there was little change in the number who
voluntarily left their last jobs or in the number who were entering the

> The establishment data shown in this news release have
> been adjusted to reflect annual benchmark revisions, the
> conversion of the industry series to 1987 Standard Industrial
> Classification (SIC) codes, and updated seasonal adjustment
> factors. In addition, all constant-dollar and indexed series
> have been rebased to 1982=100. See the note on the revisions
> beginning on page 4.

Table A. Major indicators of labor market activity, seasonally adjusted

Category	Quarterly averages 1990 I	Quarterly averages 1990 II	Monthly data 1990 June	Monthly data 1990 July	Monthly data 1990 Aug.	July-Aug. change
HOUSEHOLD DATA			Thousands of persons			
Labor force 1	126,300	126,550	126,466	126,394	126,300	-94
Total employment 1/..	119,758	119,927	120,019	119,580	119,298	-282
Civilian labor force..	124,619	124,908	124,836	124,767	124,660	-107
Civilian employment..	118,077	118,285	118,389	117,953	117,658	-295
Unemployment.........	6,541	6,623	6,447	6,814	7,003	189
Not in labor force.....	62,793	62,916	63,141	63,369	63,601	232
Discouraged workers.	747	893	N.A.	N.A.	N.A.	N.A.
			Percent of labor force			
Unemployment rates:						
All workers 1/......	5.2	5.2	5.1	5.4	5.5	0.1
All civilian workers	5.2	5.3	5.2	5.5	5.6	.1
Adult men.........	4.6	4.8	4.7	4.9	5.0	.1
Adult women.......	4.7	4.6	4.5	4.7	4.9	.2
Teenagers.........	14.5	14.8	14.1	16.3	16.7	.4
White.............	4.6	4.6	4.5	4.6	4.8	.2
Black.............	10.8	10.4	10.4	11.3	11.8	.5
Hispanic origin...	7.5	7.6	7.1	7.9	7.8	-.1
ESTABLISHMENT DATA 2/			Thousands of jobs			
Nonfarm employment....	109,911	110,541	110,829	p110,740	p110,665	p-75
Goods-producing.....	25,262	25,178	25,162	p25,100	p25,008	p-92
Service-producing...	84,649	85,363	85,667	p85,640	p85,657	p17
			Hours of work			
Average weekly hours:						
Total private.......	34.5	34.6	34.7	p34.5	p34.5	p.0
Manufacturing.......	40.8	40.9	41.0	p40.9	p41.0	p.1
Overtime..........	3.6	3.7	3.8	p3.8	p 3.9	p.1

1/ Includes the resident Armed Forces.
2/ Data have been revised to reflect March 1989 benchmarks, conversion to the 1987 Standard Industrial Classification (SIC) structure, and updated seasonal adjustment factors.

N.A.=not available.
p=preliminary.

71

labor force. The number of newly unemployed persons, those jobless for less than 5 weeks, rose by 200,000 to 3.3 million. (See tables A-7 and A-8.)

Civilian Employment and the Labor Force (Household Survey Data)

Total civilian employment fell by 300,000, seasonally adjusted, to a level of 117.7 million. Most of this decline occurred among teenagers. Total employment has declined by 730,000 in the last 2 months. As a result, the proportion of the working-age population that is employed (the employment-population ratio) declined to 62.5 percent in August, down by half a percentage point over the past 2 months. (See table A-2.)

The number of persons in the civilian labor force, 124.7 million, and the labor force participation rate, 66.2 percent, were little changed over the month, after seasonal adjustment. Over the past year, the labor force has increased by only 570,000, as growth in the working-age population has slowed and the percentage participating in the labor force has diminished. Virtually all of the reduced labor force participation has occurred among teenagers, whose participation rate was down by about 5-1/2 percentage points from a year earlier. (See table A-2.)

Industry Payroll Employment (Establishment Survey Data)

Payroll employment continued to be weak in August, as job declines occurred throughout the goods-producing sector. These losses were only partly offset by small gains in the service-producing sector. Largely because of a further decline in the number of temporary census workers, total payroll employment edged down by 75,000 over the month, following a decrease of 90,000 (as revised) in July. Employment growth in the private sector, which had been slowing since early 1989, has essentially halted during the last 2 months. (See table B-1.)

Goods-producing employment fell by 90,000 in August. The number of manufacturing jobs declined by 45,000, with virtually all of the losses occurring in durable goods industries, particularly in electronic equipment and transportation equipment. Since reaching a post-recession peak in January 1989, the number of factory jobs has declined by 455,000. The industries with the largest losses include electronic equipment (-100,000), motor vehicles (-80,000), apparel (-55,000), fabricated metals (-50,000), and instruments (-40,000).

Construction employment continued its recent downtrend with a 40,000 reduction in August and has lost nearly 100,000 jobs in the last 3 months. Employment in mining, which had grown by 60,000 since last July, decreased by 7,000 in August.

In the service-producing sector, the number of services industry jobs rose by 70,000 in August. Much of the gain came from health services, which has accounted for more than a quarter of the total job growth over the past year. In contrast, business services showed no change in August, following a small decline in July; this industry, which had seen rapid job gains during much of the expansion, has had much slower growth since early 1989.

72

State and local governments continued their employment expansion in August, adding 60,000 jobs. Overall government employment fell by 65,000 jobs, however, because of further reductions in the number of decennial census workers (which was down by an estimated 120,000 over the month). Retail trade showed little change over the month and has been unusually sluggish for most of this year. The wholesale trade, transportation and public utilities, and finance, insurance, and real estate industries all experienced small job gains in August after incurring small losses in the prior month.

Weekly Hours (Establishment Survey Data)

The average workweek of production or nonsupervisory workers on private nonfarm payrolls was unchanged in August at 34.5 hours, seasonally adjusted. In manufacturing, the workweek and overtime each edged up by 0.1 hour to 41.0 and 3.9 hours, respectively. (See table B-2.)

The index of aggregate weekly hours of private production or nonsupervisory workers--which combines the effects of employment and hours--inched downward in August to 124.6 (1982=100), after seasonal adjustment. The index for manufacturing also edged down, to 107.2. Both indexes have shown little change thus far during 1990. (See table B-5.)

Hourly and Weekly Earnings (Establishment Survey Data)

After seasonal adjustment, average hourly and weekly earnings each edged up 0.2 percent. Prior to seasonal adjustment, average hourly earnings declined 1 cent to $9.99, while average weekly earnings fell $1.35 to $347.65. Over the year, average hourly earnings rose 4.0 percent and average weekly earnings were up 3.7 percent. (See tables B-3 and B-4.)

Revisions in Establishment Survey Data

In accordance with annual practice, the establishment survey data have been revised to reflect comprehensive universe counts of payroll jobs (benchmarks). These counts were derived principally from unemployment insurance tax records for March 1989. In addition, all industry series have been converted to 1987 Standard Industrial Classification (SIC) codes. This structure replaces the 1972 SIC coding structure previously in effect for industry estimates.

The impact of SIC restructuring was negligible at the total nonfarm and major industry division levels, but more significant in some of the detailed industries presented in this release. In particular, electronic and other electrical equipment (SIC 36), instruments and related products (SIC 38), and business services (SIC 73) were affected by sizable coverage changes due to the SIC revision.

As is the usual practice with the introduction of new benchmarks, seasonal adjustment factors have been recalculated based on the experience through May 1990. As a result, seasonally adjusted series back to January 1985 are subject to revision. BLS uses the X-11 ARIMA (Auto-Regressive Integrated Moving Average) seasonal adjustment methodology to seasonally

73

adjust establishment-based employment, hours, and earnings data. In June 1989, BLS began the computation of projected factors twice a year for use in seasonally adjusting establishment-based employment, hours, and earnings data. This schedule was interrupted by the timing delays in the benchmark adjustment occasioned by the incorporation of the SIC revision (which affected some 3,600 industry series). As a result, with the release of data this month, new seasonal adjustment factors for the 9-month period, August 1990 through April 1991, are being introduced. Factors for the 6-month period May-October 1991 will be computed and incorporated with the release of May 1991 estimates, reestablishing the practice of publishing 6 months of factors in advance.

A new moving-holiday extension of X-11 ARIMA was introduced in April 1990 and was used to seasonally adjust the average weekly hours series and manufacturing overtime series. Historical seasonally adjusted series have now been recomputed from January 1980 forward to incorporate this adjustment.

All unadjusted establishment data series from April 1988 forward and all seasonally adjusted series from January 1985 forward are affected by both the benchmark and SIC revisions announced today. Industry series that are affected by revisions in the SIC have been revised back to the inception of the series, to the extent possible. Also, all published constant-dollar and indexed series have been recomputed on a 1982 base, replacing the previously published 1977-based data.

The September 1990 issue of Employment and Earnings will contain a more detailed description of the effects of the benchmark and SIC revisions, seasonal adjustment methodology, and the revised seasonal adjustment factors to be used for August 1990-April 1991. That issue will also present revised estimates for all regularly published tables containing national establishment survey data on employment, hours, and earnings. All of the revised historical series, as well as historical series unaffected by the revisions, will be published in a historical bulletin, Employment, Hours, and Earnings, United States, 1909-1990. Persons wishing further explanation of these revisions may call BLS staff members on 202-523-1172.

The Employment Situation for September 1990 will be released on Friday, October 5, at 8:30 A.M. (EDT).

Explanatory Note

This news release presents statistics from two major surveys, the Current Population Survey (household survey) and the Current Employment Statistics Survey (establishment survey). The household survey provides the information on the labor force, total employment, and unemployment that appears in the A tables, marked HOUSEHOLD DATA. It is a sample survey of about 60,000 households that is conducted by the Bureau of the Census with most of the findings analyzed and published by the Bureau of Labor Statistics (BLS).

The establishment survey provides the information on the employment, hours, and earnings of workers on nonfarm payrolls that appears in the B tables, marked ESTABLISHMENT DATA. This information is collected from payroll records by BLS in cooperation with State agencies. The sample includes over 340,000 establishments employing over 40 million people.

For both surveys, the data for a given month are actually collected for and relate to a particular week. In the household survey, unless otherwise indicated, it is the calendar week that contains the 12th day of the month, which is called the survey week. In the establishment survey, the reference week is the pay period including the 12th, which may or may not correspond directly to the calendar week.

The data in this release are affected by a number of technical factors, including definitions, survey differences, seasonal adjustments, and the inevitable variance in results between a survey of a sample and a census of the entire population. Each of these factors is explained below.

Coverage, definitions, and differences between surveys

The sample households in the household survey are selected so as to reflect the entire civilian noninstitutional population 16 years of age and older. Each person in a household is classified as employed, unemployed, or not in the labor force. Those who hold more than one job are classified according to the job at which they worked the most hours.

People are classified as *employed* if they did any work at all as paid civilians; worked in their own business or profession or on their own farm; or worked 15 hours or more in an enterprise operated by a member of their family, whether they were paid or not. People are also counted as employed if they were on unpaid leave because of illness, bad weather, disputes between labor and management, or personal reasons. Members of the Armed Forces stationed in the United States are also included in the employed total.

People are classified as *unemployed*, regardless of their eligibility for unemployment benefits or public assistance, if they meet all of the following criteria: They had no employment during the survey week; they were available for work at that time; and they made specific efforts to find employment sometime during the prior 4 weeks. Persons laid off from their former jobs and awaiting recall and those expecting to report to a job within 30 days need not be looking for work to be counted as unemployed.

The *labor force* equals the sum of the number employed and the number unemployed. The *unemployment rate* is the percentage of unemployed people in the labor force (civilian plus the resident Armed Forces). Table A-5 presents a special grouping of seven measures of unemployment based on varying definitions of unemployment and the labor force. The definitions are provided in the table. The most restrictive definition yields U-1 and the most comprehensive yields U-7. The overall unemployment rate is U-5a, while U-5b represents the same measure with a civilian labor force base.

Unlike the household survey, the establishment survey only counts wage and salary employees whose names appear on the payroll records of nonfarm firms. As a result, there are many differences between the two surveys, among which are the following:

— The household survey, although based on a smaller sample, reflects a larger segment of the population; the establishment survey excludes agriculture, the self-employed, unpaid family workers, private household workers, and members of the resident Armed Forces;

— The household survey includes people on unpaid leave among the employed; the establishment survey does not;

— The household survey is limited to those 16 years of age and older; the establishment survey is not limited by age;

— The household survey has no duplication of individuals, because each individual is counted only once; in the establishment survey, employees working at more than one job or otherwise appearing on more than one payroll would be counted separately for each appearance.

Other differences between the two surveys are described in "Comparing Employment Estimates from Household and Payroll Surveys," which may be obtained from the BLS upon request.

Seasonal adjustment

Over the course of a year, the size of the Nation's labor force and the levels of employment and unemployment undergo sharp fluctuations due to such seasonal events as changes in weather, reduced or expanded production, harvests, major holidays, and the opening and closing of schools. For example, the labor force increases by a large number each June, when schools close and many young people enter the job market. The effect of such seasonal variation can be very large; over the course of a year, for example, seasonality may account for as much as 95 percent of the month-to-month changes in unemployment.

Because these seasonal events follow a more or less regular pattern each year, their influence on statistical trends can be eliminated by adjusting the statistics from month to month. These adjustments make nonseasonal developments, such as declines in economic activity or increases in the participation of women in the labor force, easier to spot. To return to the school's-out example, the large number of people entering the labor force each June is likely to obscure any other changes that have taken place since May, making it difficult to determine if the level of economic activity has risen or declined. However, because the effect of students finishing school in previous years is known, the statistics for the current year can be adjusted to allow for a comparable change. Insofar as the seasonal adjustment is made correctly, the adjusted figure provides a more useful tool with which to analyze changes in economic activity.

Measures of labor force, employment, and unemployment contain components such as age and sex. Statistics for all employees, production workers, average weekly hours, and average hourly earnings include components based on the employer's industry. All these statistics can be seasonally adjusted either by adjusting the total or by adjusting each of the components and combining them. The second procedure usually yields more accurate information and is therefore followed by BLS. For example, the seasonally adjusted figure for the labor force is the sum of eight seasonally adjusted civilian employment components, plus the resident Armed Forces total (not adjusted for seasonality), and four seasonally adjusted unemployment components; the total for unemployment is the sum of the four unemployment components; and the overall unemployment rate is derived by dividing the resulting estimate of total unemployment by the estimate of the labor force.

The numerical factors used to make the seasonal adjustments are recalculated regularly. For the household survey, the factors are calculated for the January–June period and again for the July–December period. For the establishment survey, updated factors for seasonal adjustment are also calculated twice a year. In both surveys, revisions to historical data are made once a year.

Sampling variability

Statistics based on the household and establishment surveys are subject to sampling error, that is, the estimate of the number of people employed and the other estimates drawn from these surveys probably differ from the figures that would be obtained from a complete census, even if the same questionnaires and procedures were used. In the household survey, the amount of the differences can be expressed in terms of standard errors. The numerical value of a standard error depends upon the size of the sample, the results of the survey, and other factors. However, the numerical value is always such that the chances are approximately 68 out of 100 that an estimate based on the sample will differ by no more than the standard error from the results of a complete census. The chances are approximately 90 out of 100 that an estimate based on the sample will differ by no more than 1.6 times the standard error from the results of a complete census. At approximately the 90-percent level of confidence—the confidence limits used by BLS in its analyses—the error for the monthly change in total employment is on the order of plus or minus 358,000; for total unemployment it is 224,000; and, for the overall unemployment rate, it is 0.19 percentage point. These figures do not mean that the sample results are off by these magnitudes but, rather, that the chances are approximately 90 out of 100 that the "true" level or rate would not be expected to differ from the estimates by more than these amounts.

Sampling errors for monthly surveys are reduced when the data are cumulated for several months, such as quarterly or annually. Also, as a general rule, the smaller the estimate, the larger the sampling error. Therefore, relatively speaking, the estimate of the size of the labor force is subject to less error than is the estimate of the number unemployed. And, among the unemployed, the sampling error for the jobless rate of adult men, for example, is much smaller than is the error for the jobless rate of teenagers. Specifically, the error on monthly change in the jobless rate for men is .25 percentage point; for teenagers, it is 1.29 percentage points.

In the establishment survey, estimates for the 2 most current months are based on incomplete returns; for this reason, these estimates are labeled preliminary in the tables. When all the returns in the sample have been received, the estimates are revised. In other words, data for the month of September are published in preliminary form in October and November and in final form in December. To remove errors that build up over time, a comprehensive count of the employed is conducted each year. The results of this survey are used to establish new benchmarks—comprehensive counts of employment—against which month-to-month changes can be measured. The new benchmarks also incorporate changes in the classification of industries and allow for the formation of new establishments.

Additional statistics and other information

In order to provide a broad view of the Nation's employment situation, BLS regularly publishes a wide variety of data in this news release. More comprehensive statistics are contained in *Employment and Earnings,* published each month by BLS. It is available for $8.50 per issue or $25.00 per year from the U.S. Government Printing Office, Washington, D.C., 20204. A check or money order made out to the Superintendent of Documents must accompany all orders.

Employment and Earnings also provides approximations of the standard errors for the household survey data published in this release. For unemployment and other labor force categories, the standard errors appear in tables B through J of its "Explanatory Notes." Measures of the reliability of the data drawn from the establishment survey and the actual amounts of revision due to benchmark adjustments are provided in tables M, O, P, and Q of that publication.

76

Table A-1. **Employment status of the population, including Armed Forces in the United States, by sex**

(Numbers in thousands)

Employment status and sex	Not seasonally adjusted			Seasonally adjusted[1]					
	Aug. 1989	July 1990	Aug. 1990	Aug. 1989	Apr. 1990	May 1990	June 1990	July 1990	Aug. 1990
TOTAL									
Noninstitutional population[2]	188,286	189,763	189,901	188,286	189,326	189,467	189,607	189,763	189,901
Labor force[2]	127,132	128,527	127,652	125,758	126,543	126,643	126,466	126,394	126,300
Participation rate[3]	67.5	67.7	67.2	66.8	66.8	66.8	66.7	66.6	66.5
Total employed[2]	120,780	121,581	120,814	119,238	119,773	119,989	120,019	119,580	119,298
Employment-population ratio[4]	64.1	64.1	63.6	63.3	63.3	63.3	63.3	63.0	62.8
Resident Armed Forces	1,688	1,627	1,640	1,688	1,657	1,639	1,630	1,627	1,640
Civilian employed	119,092	119,954	119,174	117,550	118,116	118,350	118,389	117,953	117,658
Agriculture	3,633	3,573	3,473	3,275	3,133	3,305	3,348	3,085	3,137
Nonagricultural industries	115,460	116,381	115,702	114,275	114,983	115,045	115,041	114,867	114,521
Unemployed	6,352	6,945	6,837	6,520	6,770	6,653	6,447	6,814	7,003
Unemployment rate[5]	5.0	5.4	5.4	5.2	5.3	5.3	5.1	5.4	5.5
Not in labor force	61,155	61,237	62,250	62,528	62,783	62,824	63,141	63,369	63,601
Men, 16 years and over									
Noninstitutional population[2]	90,384	91,168	91,240	90,384	90,942	91,014	91,087	91,168	91,240
Labor force[2]	70,587	71,158	70,600	69,404	69,779	69,737	69,599	69,544	69,459
Participation rate[3]	78.1	78.1	77.4	76.8	76.7	76.6	76.4	76.3	76.1
Total employed[2]	67,431	67,509	67,079	65,919	66,043	66,058	66,000	65,740	65,596
Employment-population ratio[4]	74.6	74.0	73.5	72.9	72.6	72.6	72.5	72.1	71.9
Resident Armed Forces	1,519	1,462	1,475	1,519	1,499	1,472	1,465	1,462	1,475
Civilian employed	65,912	66,047	65,604	64,400	64,544	64,586	64,535	64,278	64,121
Unemployed	3,157	3,650	3,521	3,485	3,735	3,679	3,599	3,804	3,863
Unemployment rate[5]	4.5	5.1	5.0	5.0	5.4	5.3	5.2	5.5	5.6
Women, 16 years and over									
Noninstitutional population[2]	97,902	98,595	98,661	97,902	98,383	98,453	98,520	98,595	98,661
Labor force[2]	56,544	57,368	57,052	56,354	56,764	56,906	56,867	56,849	56,842
Participation rate[3]	57.8	58.2	57.8	57.6	57.7	57.8	57.7	57.7	57.6
Total employed[2]	53,349	54,072	53,735	53,319	53,729	53,931	54,019	53,839	53,702
Employment-population ratio[4]	54.5	54.8	54.5	54.5	54.6	54.8	54.8	54.6	54.4
Resident Armed Forces	169	165	165	169	158	167	165	165	165
Civilian employed	53,180	53,907	53,570	53,150	53,571	53,764	53,854	53,674	53,537
Unemployed	3,195	3,296	3,316	3,035	3,034	2,975	2,848	3,010	3,140
Unemployment rate[5]	5.7	5.7	5.8	5.4	5.3	5.2	5.0	5.3	5.5

[1] The population and Armed Forces figures are not adjusted for seasonal variation; therefore, identical numbers appear in the unadjusted and seasonally adjusted columns.
[2] Includes members of the Armed Forces stationed in the United States.

[3] Labor force as a percent of the noninstitutional population.
[4] Total employment as a percent of the noninstitutional population.
[5] Unemployment as a percent of the labor force (including the resident Armed Forces).

77

(Numbers in thousands)

Employment status, sex, and age	Not seasonally adjusted			Seasonally adjusted[1]					
	Aug. 1989	July 1990	Aug. 1990	Aug. 1989	Apr. 1990	May 1990	June 1990	July 1990	Aug. 1990
TOTAL									
Civilian noninstitutional population	186,598	188,136	188,261	186,598	187,669	187,828	187,977	188,136	188,261
Civilian labor force	125,444	126,900	126,012	124,070	124,886	125,004	124,836	124,767	124,660
Participation rate	67.2	67.5	66.9	66.5	66.5	66.6	66.4	66.3	66.2
Employed	119,092	119,954	119,174	117,550	118,116	118,350	118,389	117,953	117,658
Employment-population ratio[2]	63.8	63.8	63.3	63.0	62.9	63.0	63.0	62.7	62.5
Unemployed	6,352	6,945	6,837	6,520	6,770	6,653	6,447	6,814	7,003
Unemployment rate	5.1	5.5	5.4	5.3	5.4	5.3	5.2	5.5	5.6
Men, 20 years and over									
Civilian noninstitutional population	81,754	82,790	82,862	81,754	82,487	82,581	82,676	82,790	82,862
Civilian labor force	64,167	64,863	64,773	63,717	64,251	64,312	64,364	64,344	64,362
Participation rate	78.5	78.3	78.2	77.9	77.9	77.9	77.9	77.7	77.7
Employed	61,603	61,951	61,862	60,861	61,138	61,265	61,345	61,196	61,143
Employment-population ratio[2]	75.4	74.8	74.7	74.4	74.1	74.2	74.2	73.9	73.8
Agriculture	2,529	2,486	2,435	2,340	2,258	2,388	2,400	2,262	2,246
Nonagricultural industries	59,074	59,464	59,427	58,521	58,879	58,877	58,945	58,934	58,897
Unemployed	2,564	2,912	2,910	2,856	3,113	3,047	3,019	3,148	3,219
Unemployment rate	4.0	4.5	4.5	4.5	4.8	4.7	4.7	4.9	5.0
Women, 20 years and over									
Civilian noninstitutional population	90,684	91,581	91,688	90,684	91,330	91,414	91,495	91,581	91,688
Civilian labor force	52,000	52,853	52,974	52,352	52,954	53,146	53,174	53,211	53,315
Participation rate	57.3	57.7	57.8	57.7	58.0	58.1	58.1	58.1	58.1
Employed	49,352	50,210	50,183	49,875	50,427	50,709	50,776	50,719	50,699
Employment-population ratio[2]	54.4	54.8	54.7	55.0	55.2	55.5	55.5	55.4	55.3
Agriculture	682	676	674	642	669	680	700	585	639
Nonagricultural industries	48,670	49,533	49,509	49,233	49,758	50,029	50,077	50,135	50,060
Unemployed	2,648	2,644	2,791	2,477	2,526	2,438	2,398	2,492	2,616
Unemployment rate	5.1	5.0	5.3	4.7	4.8	4.6	4.5	4.7	4.9
Both sexes, 16 to 19 years									
Civilian noninstitutional population	14,160	13,764	13,711	14,160	13,852	13,832	13,806	13,764	13,711
Civilian labor force	9,276	9,183	8,265	8,001	7,681	7,545	7,298	7,212	6,983
Participation rate	65.5	66.7	60.3	56.5	55.4	54.6	52.9	52.4	50.9
Employed	8,137	7,794	7,129	6,814	6,551	6,376	6,268	6,038	5,815
Employment-population ratio[2]	57.5	56.6	52.0	48.1	47.3	46.1	45.4	43.9	42.4
Agriculture	422	411	364	293	206	237	249	239	251
Nonagricultural industries	7,715	7,383	6,766	6,521	6,345	6,139	6,019	5,799	5,564
Unemployed	1,140	1,389	1,136	1,187	1,130	1,169	1,030	1,174	1,168
Unemployment rate	12.3	15.1	13.7	14.8	14.7	15.5	14.1	16.3	16.7

[1] The population figures are not adjusted for seasonal variation; therefore, identical numbers appear in the unadjusted and seasonally adjusted columns.

[2] Civilian employment as a percent of the civilian noninstitutional population.

Table A-3. Employment status of the civilian population by race, sex, age, and Hispanic origin

(Numbers in thousands)

Employment status, race, sex, age, and Hispanic origin	Not seasonally adjusted			Seasonally adjusted[1]					
	Aug. 1989	July 1990	Aug. 1990	Aug. 1989	Apr. 1990	May 1990	June 1990	July 1990	Aug. 1990
WHITE									
Civilian noninstitutional population	159,470	160,468	160,550	159,470	160,170	160,271	160,365	160,468	160,550
Civilian labor force	107,597	108,930	108,238	106,485	107,133	107,353	107,273	107,230	107,135
Participation rate	67.5	67.9	67.4	66.8	66.9	67.0	66.9	66.8	66.7
Employed	102,938	103,914	103,217	101,684	102,027	102,362	102,461	102,260	101,968
Employment-population ratio[2]	64.6	64.8	64.3	63.8	63.7	63.9	63.9	63.7	63.5
Unemployed	4,659	5,016	5,022	4,801	5,106	4,991	4,812	4,970	5,167
Unemployment rate	4.3	4.6	4.6	4.5	4.8	4.6	4.5	4.6	4.8
Men, 20 years and over									
Civilian labor force	55,766	56,338	56,322	55,443	55,826	55,919	55,932	55,895	56,035
Participation rate	78.8	78.8	78.7	78.4	78.3	78.3	78.3	78.1	78.3
Employed	53,868	54,219	54,149	53,307	53,425	53,578	53,650	53,576	53,613
Employment-population ratio[2]	76.2	75.8	75.6	75.4	74.9	75.1	75.1	74.9	74.9
Unemployed	1,898	2,119	2,173	2,136	2,400	2,341	2,282	2,318	2,423
Unemployment rate	3.4	3.8	3.9	3.9	4.3	4.2	4.1	4.1	4.3
Women, 20 years and over									
Civilian labor force	43,886	44,751	44,817	44,184	44,740	44,925	45,055	45,120	45,100
Participation rate	56.8	57.5	57.5	57.2	57.6	57.8	57.9	57.9	57.9
Employed	41,948	42,844	42,795	42,391	42,895	43,165	43,292	43,321	43,227
Employment-population ratio[2]	54.3	55.0	54.9	54.9	55.2	55.5	55.6	55.6	55.5
Unemployed	1,938	1,907	2,023	1,793	1,844	1,760	1,763	1,799	1,873
Unemployment rate	4.4	4.3	4.5	4.1	4.1	3.9	3.9	4.0	4.2
Both sexes, 16 to 19 years									
Civilian labor force	7,945	7,841	7,099	6,858	6,568	6,509	6,286	6,216	5,999
Participation rate	69.1	70.8	64.3	59.6	58.8	58.4	56.6	56.1	54.3
Employed	7,122	6,852	6,273	5,986	5,707	5,619	5,519	5,363	5,128
Employment-population ratio[2]	61.9	61.9	56.8	52.0	51.1	50.4	49.7	48.4	46.4
Unemployed	823	989	826	872	861	890	767	853	871
Unemployment rate	10.4	12.6	11.6	12.7	13.1	13.7	12.2	13.7	14.5
Men	10.3	13.0	12.1	13.1	13.8	14.2	12.9	15.1	15.7
Women	10.4	12.2	11.1	12.3	12.4	13.1	11.4	12.3	13.2
BLACK									
Civilian noninstitutional population	21,060	21,318	21,337	21,060	21,228	21,261	21,289	21,318	21,337
Civilian labor force	13,694	13,799	13,584	13,476	13,570	13,587	13,472	13,379	13,366
Participation rate	65.0	64.7	63.7	64.0	63.9	63.9	63.3	62.8	62.6
Employed	12,197	12,168	12,027	11,961	12,161	12,179	12,064	11,870	11,791
Employment-population ratio[2]	57.9	57.1	56.4	56.8	57.3	57.3	56.7	55.7	55.3
Unemployed	1,497	1,631	1,557	1,515	1,409	1,408	1,407	1,510	1,575
Unemployment rate	10.9	11.8	11.5	11.2	10.4	10.4	10.4	11.3	11.8
Men, 20 years and over									
Civilian labor force	6,263	6,367	6,302	6,198	6,240	6,241	6,293	6,293	6,235
Participation rate	74.7	74.7	73.9	73.9	73.7	73.5	74.0	73.9	73.1
Employed	5,686	5,707	5,678	5,584	5,651	5,672	5,702	5,617	5,572
Employment-population ratio[2]	67.8	67.0	66.6	66.6	66.8	66.8	67.1	65.9	65.4
Unemployed	578	660	624	614	589	569	591	676	663
Unemployment rate	9.2	10.4	9.9	9.9	9.4	9.1	9.4	10.7	10.6
Women, 20 years and over									
Civilian labor force	6,338	6,342	6,331	6,362	6,451	6,516	6,377	6,328	6,358
Participation rate	60.3	59.5	59.3	60.6	60.8	61.3	59.9	59.4	59.6
Employed	5,710	5,724	5,684	5,753	5,858	5,921	5,812	5,735	5,730
Employment-population ratio[2]	54.4	53.7	53.3	54.8	55.2	55.7	54.6	53.8	53.7
Unemployed	628	619	646	609	594	595	565	592	628
Unemployment rate	9.9	9.8	10.2	9.6	9.2	9.1	8.9	9.4	9.9
Both sexes, 16 to 19 years									
Civilian labor force	1,092	1,090	951	916	879	830	802	758	773
Participation rate	50.3	50.8	44.4	42.2	40.8	38.6	37.4	35.4	36.1
Employed	801	738	664	624	652	586	550	517	489
Employment-population ratio[2]	36.9	34.4	31.0	28.7	30.3	27.3	25.6	24.1	22.8
Unemployed	291	352	287	292	227	244	252	241	284
Unemployment rate	26.6	32.3	30.2	31.9	25.8	29.4	31.4	31.8	36.7
Men	24.6	32.3	30.0	30.3	27.2	31.1	37.4	32.3	38.4
Women	28.9	32.3	30.3	33.6	24.3	27.6	25.3	31.2	35.0

See footnotes at end of table.

79

Table A-3. Employment status of the civilian population by race, sex, age, and Hispanic origin—Continued

(Numbers in thousands)

Employment status, race, sex, age, and Hispanic origin	Not seasonally adjusted			Seasonally adjusted[1]						
	Aug. 1989	July 1990	Aug. 1990	Aug. 1989	Apr. 1990	May 1990	June 1990	July 1990	Aug. 1990
HISPANIC ORIGIN									
Civilian noninstitutional population	13,853	14,317	14,356	13,853	14,198	14,238	14,277	14,317	14,356
Civilian labor force	9,494	9,830	9,841	9,361	9,618	9,669	9,651	9,665	9,707
Participation rate	68.5	68.7	68.5	67.6	67.7	67.9	67.6	67.5	67.6
Employed	8,666	9,032	9,067	8,541	8,850	8,927	8,967	8,899	8,951
Employment-population ratio[2]	62.6	63.1	63.2	61.7	62.3	62.7	62.8	62.2	62.3
Unemployed	828	798	774	820	768	742	684	767	757
Unemployment rate	8.7	8.1	7.9	8.8	8.0	7.7	7.1	7.9	7.8

[1] The population figures are not adjusted for seasonal variation; therefore, identical numbers appear in the unadjusted and seasonally adjusted columns.

[2] Civilian employment as a percent of the civilian noninstitutional population.

NOTE: Detail for the above race and Hispanic-origin groups will not sum to totals because data for the "other races" group are not presented and Hispanics are included in both the white and black population groups.

Table A-4. Selected employment indicators

(In thousands)

Category	Not seasonally adjusted			Seasonally adjusted					
	Aug. 1989	July 1990	Aug. 1990	Aug. 1989	Apr. 1990	May 1990	June 1990	July 1990	Aug. 1990
CHARACTERISTIC									
Civilian employed, 16 years and over	119,092	119,954	119,174	117,550	118,116	118,350	118,389	117,953	117,658
Married men, spouse present	40,880	40,707	40,726	40,723	40,730	40,881	40,554	40,545	40,604
Married women, spouse present	28,665	29,311	29,290	29,259	29,742	30,046	29,856	29,909	29,949
Women who maintain families	6,298	6,354	6,301	6,371	6,325	6,400	6,467	6,380	6,365
MAJOR INDUSTRY AND CLASS OF WORKER									
Agriculture:									
Wage and salary workers	1,958	1,934	1,904	1,723	1,621	1,728	1,685	1,628	1,666
Self-employed workers	1,494	1,508	1,441	1,410	1,429	1,502	1,507	1,377	1,357
Unpaid family workers	181	132	128	133	112	101	106	96	93
Nonagricultural industries:									
Wage and salary workers	106,390	107,338	106,679	105,317	105,938	106,176	105,985	105,885	105,691
Government	16,887	17,183	17,164	17,559	17,816	18,113	17,863	17,788	17,842
Private industries	89,503	90,155	89,515	87,758	88,122	88,063	88,121	88,097	87,849
Private households	1,217	1,093	1,105	1,147	957	941	1,056	989	1,033
Other industries	88,286	89,062	88,410	86,611	87,165	87,122	87,065	87,108	86,816
Self-employed workers	8,797	8,779	8,793	8,621	8,716	8,783	8,759	8,709	8,629
Unpaid family workers	273	264	229	272	258	254	226	269	229
PERSONS AT WORK PART TIME[1]									
All industries:									
Part time for economic reasons	5,125	5,610	5,368	4,802	4,871	4,831	5,013	4,870	5,036
Slack work	2,250	2,573	2,392	2,281	2,407	2,439	2,499	2,565	2,424
Could only find part-time work	2,415	2,666	2,382	2,142	2,138	2,052	2,224	2,070	2,123
Voluntary part time	12,460	12,662	12,332	15,550	15,193	15,592	15,125	15,311	15,377
Nonagricultural industries:									
Part time for economic reasons	4,849	5,355	5,072	4,567	4,630	4,666	4,734	4,710	4,780
Slack work	2,084	2,413	2,195	2,129	2,218	2,317	2,284	2,408	2,242
Could only find part-time work	2,309	2,583	2,293	2,076	2,096	2,004	2,141	2,048	2,069
Voluntary part time	11,985	12,236	11,860	15,071	14,804	15,064	14,627	14,922	14,899

[1] Excludes persons "with a job but not at work" during the survey period for such reasons as vacation, illness, or industrial dispute.

81

Table A-5. Range of unemployment measures based on varying definitions of unemployment and the labor force, seasonally adjusted

(Percent)

Measure	Quarterly averages					Monthly data		
	1989			1990		1990		
	II	III	IV	I	II	June	July	Aug.
U-1 Persons unemployed 15 weeks or longer as a percent of the civilian labor force	1.1	1.1	1.1	1.1	1.1	1.1	1.2	1.3
U-2 Job losers as a percent of the civilian labor force	2.3	2.4	2.5	2.5	2.5	2.5	2.5	2.7
U-3 Unemployed persons 25 years and over as a percent of the civilian labor force for persons 25 years and over	4.0	4.0	4.1	4.2	4.1	4.1	4.3	4.4
U-4 Unemployed full-time jobseekers as a percent of the full-time civilian labor force	4.9	5.0	5.0	4.9	5.0	4.8	5.0	5.2
U-5a Total unemployed as a percent of the labor force, including the resident Armed Forces	5.2	5.2	5.3	5.2	5.2	5.1	5.4	5.5
U-5b Total unemployed as a percent of the civilian labor force	5.3	5.3	5.3	5.2	5.3	5.2	5.5	5.6
U-6 Total full-time jobseekers plus 1/2 part-time jobseekers plus 1/2 total on part time for economic reasons as a percent of the civilian labor force less 1/2 of the part-time labor force	7.3	7.2	7.2	7.2	7.3	7.2	7.4	7.6
U-7 Total full-time jobseekers plus 1/2 part-time jobseekers plus 1/2 total on part time for economic reasons plus discouraged workers as a percent of the civilian labor force plus discouraged workers less 1/2 of the part-time labor force	8.0	7.9	7.9	7.8	8.0	N.A.	N.A.	N.A.

N.A. = not available.

82

Table A-6. Selected unemployment indicators, seasonally adjusted

Category	Number of unemployed persons (in thousands)			Unemployment rates[1]					
	Aug. 1989	July 1990	Aug. 1990	Aug. 1989	Apr. 1990	May 1990	June 1990	July 1990	Aug. 1990
CHARACTERISTIC									
Total, 16 years and over	6,520	6,814	7,003	5.3	5.4	5.3	5.2	5.5	5.6
Men, 16 years and over	3,485	3,804	3,863	5.1	5.5	5.4	5.3	5.6	5.7
Men, 20 years and over	2,856	3,148	3,219	4.5	4.8	4.7	4.7	4.9	5.0
Women, 16 years and over	3,035	3,010	3,140	5.4	5.4	5.2	5.0	5.3	5.5
Women, 20 years and over	2,477	2,492	2,616	4.7	4.8	4.6	4.5	4.7	4.9
Both sexes, 16 to 19 years	1,187	1,174	1,168	14.8	14.7	15.5	14.1	16.3	16.7
Married men, spouse present	1,308	1,393	1,463	3.1	3.3	3.3	3.2	3.3	3.5
Married women, spouse present	1,175	1,085	1,205	3.9	3.5	3.5	3.7	3.5	3.9
Women who maintain families	552	594	591	8.0	7.5	7.4	8.0	8.5	8.5
Full-time workers	5,231	5,349	5,545	4.9	5.1	4.9	4.8	5.0	5.2
Part-time workers	1,284	1,493	1,459	7.1	7.1	7.4	7.6	8.1	7.9
Labor force time lost[2]	—	—	—	6.0	6.2	6.0	5.9	6.0	6.3
INDUSTRY									
Nonagricultural private wage and salary workers	4,967	5,111	5,327	5.4	5.7	5.5	5.3	5.5	5.7
Goods-producing industries	1,831	1,918	1,989	6.3	6.9	6.7	5.9	6.6	6.9
Mining	47	30	37	6.4	4.6	3.3	3.6	4.4	4.9
Construction	634	652	680	10.2	10.6	11.5	9.7	10.2	11.1
Manufacturing	1,150	1,236	1,273	5.2	5.9	5.4	4.9	5.7	5.8
Durable goods	631	723	767	4.9	5.7	5.5	4.9	5.6	5.9
Nondurable goods	519	512	505	5.7	6.3	5.2	5.0	5.7	5.6
Service-producing industries	3,136	3,193	3,338	4.9	5.1	5.0	5.0	5.0	5.2
Transportation and public utilities	240	234	266	3.7	4.3	3.2	3.0	3.7	4.1
Wholesale and retail trade	1,415	1,425	1,468	6.0	6.2	6.3	6.2	6.0	6.2
Finance and service industries	1,481	1,534	1,604	4.4	4.5	4.4	4.5	4.5	4.7
Government workers	496	511	511	2.7	2.1	2.5	2.9	2.8	2.8
Agricultural wage and salary workers	170	192	178	9.0	11.0	7.9	10.0	10.6	9.7

[1] Unemployment as a percent of the civilian labor force.
[2] Aggregate hours lost by the unemployed and persons on part time for economic reasons as a percent of potentially available labor force hours.

Table A-7. Duration of unemployment

(Numbers in thousands)

Weeks of unemployment	Not seasonally adjusted				Seasonally adjusted						
	Aug. 1989	July 1990	Aug. 1990	Aug. 1989	Apr. 1990	May 1990	June 1990	July 1990	Aug. 1990
DURATION									
Less than 5 weeks	3,022	3,292	3,225	3,125	3,204	3,026	3,046	3,120	3,325
5 to 14 weeks	2,152	2,269	2,197	2,002	2,175	2,236	2,049	2,159	2,048
15 weeks and over	1,178	1,384	1,414	1,338	1,386	1,374	1,406	1,513	1,609
15 to 26 weeks	612	695	674	759	697	764	763	809	845
27 weeks and over	566	689	741	579	688	610	643	704	764
Average (mean) duration, in weeks	11.3	11.4	12.1	11.4	12.1	11.6	12.0	12.0	12.3
Median duration, in weeks	5.0	4.9	5.2	5.0	5.0	5.4	5.1	5.2	5.2
PERCENT DISTRIBUTION									
Total unemployed	100.0	100.0	100.0	100.0	100.0	100.0	100.0	100.0	100.0
Less than 5 weeks	47.6	47.4	47.2	48.3	47.4	45.6	46.9	45.9	47.6
5 to 14 weeks	33.9	32.7	32.1	31.0	32.2	33.7	31.5	31.8	29.3
15 weeks and over	18.5	19.9	20.7	20.7	20.5	20.7	21.6	22.3	23.0
15 to 26 weeks	9.6	10.0	9.9	11.7	10.3	11.5	11.7	11.9	12.1
27 weeks and over	8.9	9.9	10.8	9.0	10.2	9.2	9.9	10.4	10.9

84

Table A-8. Reason for unemployment

(Numbers in thousands)

Reasons	Not seasonally adjusted			Seasonally adjusted					
	Aug. 1989	July 1990	Aug. 1990	Aug. 1989	Apr. 1990	May 1990	June 1990	July 1990	Aug. 1990
NUMBER OF UNEMPLOYED									
Job losers	2,766	2,968	3,145	2,964	3,147	3,171	3,151	3,088	3,367
On layoff	736	864	824	865	999	979	918	960	973
Other job losers	2,030	2,104	2,320	2,099	2,148	2,192	2,233	2,128	2,394
Job leavers	1,122	1,071	1,078	1,031	1,179	1,014	995	1,027	984
Reentrants	1,814	2,013	1,935	1,772	1,780	1,820	1,789	1,960	1,879
New entrants	650	893	680	643	617	683	534	687	677
PERCENT DISTRIBUTION									
Total unemployed	100.0	100.0	100.0	100.0	100.0	100.0	100.0	100.0	100.0
Job losers	43.5	42.7	46.0	46.2	46.8	47.4	48.7	45.7	48.7
On layoff	11.6	12.4	12.1	13.5	14.9	14.6	14.2	14.2	14.1
Other job losers	32.0	30.3	33.9	32.7	31.9	32.8	34.5	31.5	34.7
Job leavers	17.7	15.4	15.8	16.1	17.5	15.2	15.4	15.2	14.3
Reentrants	28.6	29.0	28.3	27.6	26.5	27.2	27.7	29.0	27.2
New entrants	10.2	12.9	9.9	10.0	9.2	10.2	8.3	10.2	9.8
UNEMPLOYED AS A PERCENT OF THE CIVILIAN LABOR FORCE									
Job losers	2.2	2.3	2.5	2.4	2.5	2.5	2.5	2.5	2.7
Job leavers	.9	.8	.9	.8	.9	.8	.8	.8	.8
Reentrants	1.4	1.6	1.5	1.4	1.4	1.5	1.4	1.6	1.5
New entrants	.5	.7	.5	.5	.5	.5	.4	.6	.5

Table A-9. Unemployed persons by sex and age, seasonally adjusted

Sex and age	Number of unemployed persons (in thousands)			Unemployment rates[1]					
	Aug. 1989	July 1990	Aug. 1990	Aug. 1989	Apr. 1990	May 1990	June 1990	July 1990	Aug. 1990
Total, 16 years and over	6,520	6,814	7,003	5.3	5.4	5.3	5.2	5.5	5.6
16 to 24 years	2,437	2,316	2,387	11.0	11.2	11.0	10.3	11.0	11.5
16 to 19 years	1,187	1,174	1,168	14.8	14.7	15.5	14.1	16.3	16.7
16 to 17 years	545	457	494	17.5	17.4	20.0	16.1	17.4	19.2
18 to 19 years	623	693	653	12.8	13.0	12.8	13.4	15.2	15.0
20 to 24 years	1,250	1,142	1,219	8.8	9.3	8.5	8.2	8.3	8.8
25 years and over	4,069	4,456	4,617	4.0	4.2	4.1	4.1	4.3	4.4
25 to 54 years	3,568	3,958	4,028	4.1	4.4	4.3	4.4	4.5	4.6
55 years and over	473	494	538	3.1	3.3	3.0	2.8	3.2	3.5
Men, 16 years and over	3,485	3,804	3,863	5.1	5.5	5.4	5.3	5.6	5.7
16 to 24 years	1,330	1,279	1,253	11.5	11.8	11.2	11.1	11.6	11.6
16 to 19 years	629	656	644	15.1	15.4	16.0	15.4	17.5	17.8
16 to 17 years	295	249	287	17.7	18.1	20.6	16.4	18.4	21.5
18 to 19 years	325	387	351	13.1	13.8	13.4	14.8	16.3	15.5
20 to 24 years	701	623	609	9.4	9.8	8.6	8.9	8.5	8.5
25 years and over	2,143	2,499	2,616	3.8	4.2	4.1	4.1	4.4	4.6
25 to 54 years	1,821	2,173	2,234	3.8	4.4	4.3	4.3	4.5	4.6
55 years and over	283	321	336	3.3	3.5	3.4	3.1	3.6	3.8
Women, 16 years and over	3,035	3,010	3,140	5.4	5.4	5.2	5.0	5.3	5.5
16 to 24 years	1,107	1,037	1,134	10.4	10.5	10.7	9.3	10.4	11.4
16 to 19 years	558	518	524	14.6	13.9	14.9	12.8	14.9	15.6
16 to 17 years	250	208	207	17.2	16.7	19.4	15.9	16.4	16.6
18 to 19 years	298	306	302	12.5	12.1	12.2	11.9	13.9	14.4
20 to 24 years	549	519	610	8.1	8.7	8.4	7.5	8.0	9.3
25 years and over	1,926	1,956	2,001	4.2	4.2	4.1	4.1	4.2	4.3
25 to 54 years	1,747	1,785	1,794	4.5	4.4	4.4	4.4	4.4	4.5
55 years and over	180	173	203	2.8	2.9	2.5	2.4	2.6	3.1

[1] Unemployment as a percent of the civilian labor force.

86

Table A-10. Employment status of black and other workers

(Numbers in thousands)

Employment status	Not seasonally adjusted			Seasonally adjusted[1]					
	Aug. 1989	July 1990	Aug. 1990	Aug. 1989	Apr. 1990	May 1990	June 1990	July 1990	Aug. 1990
Civilian noninstitutional population	27,128	27,668	27,711	27,128	27,499	27,556	27,612	27,668	27,711
Civilian labor force	17,846	17,970	17,773	17,574	17,687	17,660	17,540	17,448	17,498
Participation rate	65.8	64.9	64.1	64.8	64.3	64.1	63.5	63.1	63.1
Employed	16,154	16,040	15,958	15,866	16,075	16,021	15,883	15,655	15,671
Employment-population ratio[2]	59.5	58.0	57.6	58.5	58.5	58.1	57.5	56.6	56.6
Unemployed	1,692	1,929	1,815	1,708	1,613	1,640	1,657	1,793	1,826
Unemployment rate	9.5	10.7	10.2	9.7	9.1	9.3	9.4	10.3	10.4
Not in labor force	9,282	9,698	9,938	9,554	9,812	9,896	10,072	10,220	10,213

[1] The population figures are not adjusted for seasonal variation; therefore, identical numbers appear in the unadjusted and seasonally adjusted columns.

[2] Civilian employment as a percent of the civilian noninstitutional population.

Table A-11. Occupational status of the employed and unemployed, not seasonally adjusted

(Numbers in thousands)

Occupation	Civilian employed		Unemployed		Unemployment rate	
	Aug. 1989	Aug. 1990	Aug. 1989	Aug. 1990	Aug. 1989	Aug. 1990
Total, 16 years and over[1]	119,092	119,174	6,352	6,837	5.1	5.4
Managerial and professional specialty	29,909	30,505	642	807	2.1	2.6
Executive, administrative, and managerial	15,024	15,112	317	364	2.1	2.4
Professional specialty	14,885	15,393	325	443	2.1	2.8
Technical, sales, and administrative support	36,679	36,244	1,494	1,681	3.9	4.4
Technicians and related support	3,735	3,762	83	134	2.2	3.4
Sales occupations	14,387	14,021	658	646	4.4	4.4
Administrative support, including clerical	18,557	18,461	753	901	3.9	4.7
Service occupations	16,052	16,222	1,104	1,105	6.4	6.4
Private household	925	824	67	36	6.7	4.1
Protective service	2,146	2,145	80	73	3.6	3.3
Service, except private household and protective	12,981	13,253	958	997	6.9	7.0
Precision production, craft, and repair	14,002	13,859	659	772	4.5	5.3
Mechanics and repairers	4,497	4,492	132	178	2.8	3.8
Construction trades	5,360	5,302	317	377	5.6	6.6
Other precision production, craft, and repair	4,145	4,065	211	217	4.8	5.1
Operators, fabricators, and laborers	18,350	18,351	1,490	1,467	7.5	7.4
Machine operators, assemblers, and inspectors	8,307	8,424	682	715	7.6	7.8
Transportation and material moving occupations	4,926	4,821	297	250	5.7	4.9
Handlers, equipment cleaners, helpers, and laborers	5,116	5,107	512	503	9.1	9.0
Construction laborers	845	878	147	146	14.8	14.2
Other handlers, equipment cleaners, helpers, and laborers	4,271	4,228	366	357	7.9	7.8
Farming, forestry, and fishing	4,100	3,993	218	223	5.1	5.3

[1] Persons with no previous work experience and those whose last job was in the Armed Forces are included in the unemployed total.

Table A-12. Employment status of male Vietnam-era veterans and nonveterans by age, not seasonally adjusted

(Numbers in thousands)

Veteran status and age	Civilian noninstitutional population		Civilian labor force							
			Total		Employed		Unemployed			
							Number		Percent of labor force	
	Aug. 1989	Aug. 1990	Aug. 1989	Aug. 1990	Aug. 1989	Aug. 1990	Aug. 1989	Aug. 1990	Aug. 1989	Aug. 1990
VIETNAM-ERA VETERANS										
Total, 35 years and over	7,471	7,658	6,827	6,957	6,625	6,698	202	259	3.0	3.7
35 to 49 years	6,482	6,513	6,165	6,155	5,973	5,922	192	232	3.1	3.8
35 to 39 years	1,702	1,382	1,598	1,310	1,521	1,242	77	67	4.8	5.2
40 to 44 years	3,291	3,283	3,157	3,104	3,086	2,996	72	108	2.3	3.5
45 to 49 years	1,489	1,848	1,409	1,741	1,366	1,684	43	57	3.1	3.3
50 years and over	989	1,145	662	803	652	776	10	27	1.5	3.3
NONVETERANS										
Total, 35 to 49 years	16,309	17,479	15,262	16,340	14,763	15,771	499	570	3.3	3.5
35 to 39 years	7,487	8,016	7,094	7,597	6,849	7,321	245	276	3.5	3.6
40 to 44 years	4,714	5,256	4,382	4,885	4,230	4,727	152	157	3.5	3.2
45 to 49 years	4,108	4,207	3,786	3,859	3,685	3,722	101	137	2.7	3.5

NOTE: Male Vietnam-era veterans are men who served in the Armed Forces between August 5, 1964 and May 7, 1975. Nonveterans are men who have never served in the Armed Forces; published data are limited to those 35 to 49 years of age, the group that most closely corresponds to the bulk of the Vietnam-era veteran population.

(Numbers in thousands)

State and employment status	Not seasonally adjusted[1]			Seasonally adjusted[2]					
	Aug. 1989	July 1990	Aug. 1990	Aug. 1989	Apr. 1990	May 1990	June 1990	July 1990	Aug. 1990
California									
Civilian noninstitutional population	21,518	21,961	21,999	21,518	21,834	21,877	21,918	21,961	21,999
Civilian labor force	14,678	14,965	14,940	14,574	14,677	14,801	14,801	14,751	14,816
Employed	13,994	14,115	14,126	13,899	13,881	13,998	14,073	13,995	14,010
Unemployed	684	850	813	675	796	803	728	756	806
Unemployment rate	4.7	5.7	5.4	4.6	5.4	5.4	4.9	5.1	5.4
Florida									
Civilian noninstitutional population	9,919	10,132	10,150	9,919	10,071	10,091	10,111	10,132	10,150
Civilian labor force	6,273	6,425	6,455	6,176	6,336	6,282	6,294	6,313	6,365
Employed	5,933	6,030	6,014	5,849	5,972	5,931	5,886	5,953	5,939
Unemployed	340	395	440	327	364	351	408	360	426
Unemployment rate	5.4	6.1	6.8	5.3	5.7	5.6	6.5	5.7	6.7
Illinois									
Civilian noninstitutional population	8,837	8,876	8,878	8,837	8,863	8,867	8,871	8,876	8,878
Civilian labor force	6,073	6,174	6,025	5,996	6,091	5,987	5,986	6,102	5,954
Employed	5,721	5,786	5,644	5,636	5,722	5,670	5,625	5,691	5,568
Unemployed	353	387	381	360	369	317	361	411	386
Unemployment rate	5.8	6.3	6.3	6.0	6.1	5.3	6.0	6.7	6.5
Massachusetts									
Civilian noninstitutional population	4,618	4,620	4,620	4,618	4,619	4,619	4,620	4,620	4,620
Civilian labor force	3,253	3,224	3,238	3,183	3,161	3,203	3,172	3,157	3,171
Employed	3,126	3,014	3,031	3,051	2,988	3,028	2,987	2,963	2,960
Unemployed	127	209	207	132	173	175	185	194	211
Unemployment rate	3.9	6.5	6.4	4.1	5.5	5.5	5.8	6.1	6.7
Michigan									
Civilian noninstitutional population	6,987	7,001	7,002	6,987	6,995	6,997	6,999	7,001	7,002
Civilian labor force	4,691	4,689	4,697	4,597	4,511	4,591	4,631	4,614	4,599
Employed	4,379	4,326	4,348	4,273	4,180	4,238	4,294	4,271	4,237
Unemployed	312	363	349	324	331	353	337	343	362
Unemployment rate	6.7	7.7	7.4	7.0	7.3	7.7	7.3	7.4	7.9
New Jersey									
Civilian noninstitutional population	6,032	6,028	6,028	6,032	6,028	6,028	6,028	6,028	6,028
Civilian labor force	4,012	4,134	4,104	3,974	4,002	4,012	4,037	4,073	4,066
Employed	3,842	3,922	3,915	3,798	3,805	3,820	3,845	3,879	3,872
Unemployed	170	212	189	176	197	192	192	194	194
Unemployment rate	4.2	5.1	4.6	4.4	4.9	4.8	4.8	4.8	4.8
New York									
Civilian noninstitutional population	13,804	13,802	13,801	13,804	13,799	13,800	13,801	13,802	13,801
Civilian labor force	8,727	8,874	8,731	8,588	8,709	8,775	8,732	8,686	8,586
Employed	8,306	8,415	8,311	8,152	8,286	8,328	8,287	8,222	8,155
Unemployed	421	459	420	436	423	447	445	464	431
Unemployment rate	4.8	5.2	4.8	5.1	4.9	5.1	5.1	5.3	5.0
North Carolina									
Civilian noninstitutional population	4,945	5,002	5,006	4,945	4,985	4,991	4,996	5,002	5,006
Civilian labor force	3,435	3,494	3,418	3,387	3,410	3,451	3,438	3,410	3,370
Employed	3,315	3,336	3,300	3,262	3,281	3,312	3,312	3,252	3,247
Unemployed	120	157	118	125	129	139	126	158	123
Unemployment rate	3.5	4.5	3.5	3.7	3.8	4.0	3.7	4.6	3.6
Ohio									
Civilian noninstitutional population	8,264	8,286	8,288	8,264	8,278	8,281	8,283	8,286	8,288
Civilian labor force	5,481	5,472	5,504	5,427	5,417	5,428	5,419	5,411	5,446
Employed	5,223	5,194	5,245	5,162	5,098	5,107	5,135	5,104	5,174
Unemployed	259	278	258	265	319	321	284	307	272
Unemployment rate	4.7	5.1	4.7	4.9	5.9	5.9	5.2	5.7	5.0

See footnotes at end of table.

90

Table A-13. Employment status of the civilian population for eleven large States—Continued

(Numbers in thousands)

State and employment status	Not seasonally adjusted[1]			Seasonally adjusted[2]					
	Aug. 1989	July 1990	Aug. 1990	Aug. 1989	Apr. 1990	May 1990	June 1990	July 1990	Aug. 1990
Pennsylvania									
Civilian noninstitutional population	9,369	9,390	9,392	9,369	9,382	9,385	9,387	9,390	9,392
Civilian labor force	5,879	5,974	5,877	5,762	5,945	5,941	5,894	5,869	5,777
Employed	5,648	5,664	5,624	5,508	5,604	5,648	5,623	5,574	5,496
Unemployed	231	310	253	254	341	293	271	295	281
Unemployment rate	3.9	5.2	4.3	4.4	5.7	4.9	4.6	5.0	4.9
Texas									
Civilian noninstitutional population	12,235	12,379	12,391	12,235	12,337	12,351	12,365	12,379	12,391
Civilian labor force	8,621	8,528	8,459	8,496	8,495	8,425	8,452	8,371	8,325
Employed	7,999	7,990	7,958	7,872	7,955	7,880	7,979	7,853	7,833
Unemployed	622	538	501	624	540	545	473	518	492
Unemployment rate	7.2	6.3	5.9	7.3	6.4	6.5	5.6	6.2	5.9

[1] These are the official Bureau of Labor Statistics' estimates used in the administration of Federal fund allocation programs.
[2] The population figures are not adjusted for seasonal variation; therefore, identical numbers appear in the unadjusted and the seasonally adjusted columns.

91

Table B-1. Employees on nonfarm payrolls by industry

(In thousands)

Industry	Not seasonally adjusted				Seasonally adjusted					
	Aug. 1989	June 1990	July 1990p/	Aug. 1990p/	Aug. 1989	Apr. 1990	May 1990	June 1990	July 1990p/	Aug. 1990p/
Total...........................	108,366	111,774	110,478	110,346	108,628	110,177	110,617	110,829	110,740	110,665
Total private......................	91,636	93,150	93,000	93,104	90,797	91,922	92,120	92,282	92,291	92,279
Goods-producing industries..................	25,804	25,474	25,348	25,451	25,356	25,180	25,191	25,162	25,100	25,008
Mining................................	718	748	750	749	706	734	738	744	743	736
Oil and gas extraction..................	390.8	412.1	415.2	413.5	387	405	408	413	412	409
Construction..........................	5,567	5,470	5,534	5,534	5,220	5,256	5,286	5,270	5,231	5,191
General building contractors........	1,422.6	1,375.5	1,386.3	1,378.6	1,345	1,338	1,334	1,334	1,319	1,304
Manufacturing.........................	19,519	19,256	19,064	19,168	19,430	19,190	19,167	19,148	19,126	19,081
Production workers.................	13,324	13,090	12,917	13,030	13,263	13,046	13,023	13,007	13,006	12,963
Durable goods.........................	11,412	11,267	11,122	11,121	11,416	11,229	11,217	11,201	11,175	11,126
Production workers.................	7,592	7,494	7,361	7,372	7,615	7,461	7,450	7,439	7,433	7,388
Lumber and wood products..................	771.8	758.4	756.6	755.7	753	750	748	743	740	738
Furniture and fixtures...................	522.0	514.1	501.8	510.5	525	516	516	515	512	513
Stone, clay, and glass products..........	578.9	567.7	561.8	561.5	568	560	559	556	552	551
Primary metal industries.................	771.4	760.1	750.9	755.0	772	755	755	756	758	756
Blast furnaces and basic steel products.	279.6	272.2	272.0	273.0	278	271	271	270	270	272
Fabricated metal products................	1,436.8	1,423.2	1,403.4	1,411.4	1,442	1,419	1,417	1,415	1,418	1,417
Industrial machinery and equipment.......	2,124.8	2,116.2	2,096.8	2,087.4	2,135	2,112	2,112	2,108	2,103	2,098
Electronic and other electrical equipment.	1,752.4	1,706.1	1,684.3	1,680.7	1,750	1,713	1,711	1,703	1,693	1,679
Transportation equipment.................	2,032.3	2,031.4	1,991.8	1,977.7	2,056	2,014	2,010	2,021	2,016	2,000
Motor vehicles and equipment...........	846.9	836.5	804.8	797.5	864	820	817	826	825	813
Instruments and related products........	1,029.3	1,003.2	996.9	994.8	1,027	1,005	1,002	1,000	997	992
Miscellaneous manufacturing..............	392.2	386.9	377.4	385.9	388	385	387	384	386	382
Nondurable goods..........................	8,107	7,989	7,942	8,047	8,014	7,961	7,950	7,947	7,951	7,955
Production workers.................	5,732	5,596	5,556	5,658	5,648	5,585	5,573	5,568	5,573	5,575
Food and kindred products................	1,729.6	1,644.5	1,686.1	1,731.2	1,649	1,651	1,650	1,643	1,647	1,650
Tobacco products.........................	48.4	43.6	43.6	48.0	49	46	46	47	46	48
Textile mill products....................	726.6	706.0	692.8	704.8	724	708	703	702	703	703
Apparel and other textile products.......	1,074.8	1,038.6	997.7	1,026.2	1,075	1,036	1,031	1,029	1,027	1,026
Paper and allied products................	703.9	705.7	704.7	705.8	700	699	698	699	701	702
Printing and publishing..................	1,561.1	1,584.7	1,576.3	1,578.3	1,566	1,579	1,581	1,582	1,581	1,583
Chemicals and allied products............	1,083.3	1,094.7	1,091.4	1,091.5	1,076	1,084	1,085	1,086	1,085	1,084
Petroleum and coal products..............	160.6	163.1	163.7	164.3	157	159	159	160	160	161
Rubber and misc. plastics products.......	880.8	877.8	864.6	871.0	883	869	868	871	874	874
Leather and leather products.............	137.5	129.9	121.3	126.3	135	130	129	128	127	124
Service-producing industries...............	82,562	86,300	85,130	84,895	83,272	84,997	85,426	85,667	85,640	85,657
Transportation and public utilities.........	5,566	5,881	5,842	5,854	5,561	5,809	5,833	5,846	5,840	5,849
Transportation.........................	3,453	3,649	3,607	3,615	3,467	3,588	3,613	3,627	3,625	3,630
Communications and public utilities.......	2,113	2,232	2,235	2,239	2,094	2,221	2,220	2,219	2,215	2,219
Wholesale trade............................	6,327	6,420	6,417	6,416	6,294	6,363	6,369	6,383	6,377	6,383
Durable goods..........................	3,749	3,798	3,794	3,789	3,734	3,771	3,770	3,779	3,775	3,774
Nondurable goods.......................	2,578	2,622	2,623	2,627	2,560	2,592	2,599	2,604	2,602	2,609
Retail trade..............................	19,745	19,981	19,946	19,950	19,620	19,778	19,795	19,822	19,847	19,831
General merchandise stores.............	2,481.9	2,438.3	2,435.7	2,435.7	2,537	2,493	2,487	2,496	2,496	2,490
Food stores............................	3,210.2	3,308.9	3,313.5	3,299.7	3,205	3,287	3,295	3,302	3,304	3,296
Automotive dealers and service stations.	2,131.7	2,141.7	2,154.4	2,159.1	2,106	2,118	2,121	2,120	2,129	2,133
Eating and drinking places.............	6,652.9	6,803.0	6,783.8	6,805.2	6,464	6,573	6,583	6,598	6,618	6,613
Finance, insurance, and real estate.......	6,821	6,915	6,937	6,935	6,740	6,823	6,838	6,844	6,843	6,852
Finance................................	3,334	3,364	3,367	3,365	3,312	3,336	3,338	3,344	3,337	3,342
Insurance..............................	2,116	2,152	2,159	2,161	2,109	2,135	2,139	2,143	2,148	2,155
Real estate............................	1,371	1,399	1,411	1,409	1,319	1,352	1,361	1,357	1,358	1,355
Services..................................	27,373	28,479	28,510	28,498	27,226	27,969	28,094	28,225	28,284	28,356
Business services......................	5,005.1	5,090.0	5,081.9	5,107.4	4,950	5,026	5,048	5,060	5,052	5,052
Health services........................	7,627.8	8,128.8	8,173.5	8,201.3	7,605	7,984	8,040	8,096	8,133	8,177
Government................................	16,730	18,624	17,478	17,242	17,831	18,255	18,497	18,547	18,449	18,386
Federal................................	3,011	3,365	3,197	3,053	2,996	3,151	3,346	3,338	3,161	3,038
State..................................	3,963	4,171	4,082	4,098	4,191	4,252	4,262	4,296	4,310	4,332
Local..................................	9,756	11,088	10,199	10,091	10,644	10,852	10,889	10,913	10,978	11,016

p/ = preliminary.
NOTE: Data have been revised to reflect March 1989 benchmarks, conversion to the 1987 Standard Industrial Classification (SIC) system, and updated seasonal adjustment factors.

Note on temporary census workers

The number of temporary workers associated with the 1990 census has an impact on the employment levels for the Federal government, as well as for higher aggregates. The estimate of these workers was 22,000 in January, 27,000 in February, 117,000 in March, 178,000 in April, 378,000 in May, 367,000 in June, and 194,000 in July. For August, the estimated number (preliminary) was 74,000, which may be subject to significant revision.

Table B-2. Average weekly hours of production or nonsupervisory workers[1] on private nonfarm payrolls by industry

Industry	Not seasonally adjusted				Seasonally adjusted					
	Aug. 1989	June 1990	July 1990p/	Aug. 1990p/	Aug. 1989	Apr. 1990	May 1990	June 1990	July 1990p/	Aug. 1990p/
Total private...............	34.9	34.8	34.8	34.8	34.5	34.5	34.5	34.7	34.5	34.5
Mining......................	43.5	44.4	43.6	44.0	43.4	43.4	43.6	44.4	43.7	43.9
Construction................	38.9	39.1	38.3	39.0	(2)	(2)	(2)	(2)	(2)	(2)
Manufacturing..............	40.9	41.1	40.5	40.9	41.0	40.7	40.9	41.0	40.9	41.0
Overtime hours...........	3.8	3.8	3.6	3.9	3.8	3.5	3.8	3.8	3.8	3.9
Durable goods..............	41.3	41.7	41.0	41.3	41.6	41.2	41.5	41.6	41.6	41.6
Overtime hours...........	3.9	3.9	3.7	4.0	3.5	3.5	3.9	3.9	3.9	4.0
Lumber and wood products...	40.4	40.8	40.0	40.6	40.1	40.2	40.4	40.3	40.2	40.4
Furniture and fixtures.....	39.7	39.2	38.8	39.4	39.5	39.0	39.2	39.3	39.5	39.2
Stone, clay, and glass products...	42.9	42.7	42.1	42.7	42.8	42.0	42.1	42.3	41.8	41.8
Primary metal industries...	42.4	43.2	42.8	43.5	42.8	41.8	43.5	43.3	43.1	42.9
Blast furnaces and basic steel products...	43.0	43.6	44.1	44.5	43.5	42.9	43.5	43.3	44.1	43.6
Fabricated metal products...	41.2	41.8	41.0	41.5	41.5	41.2	41.7	41.6	41.8	41.6
Industrial machinery and equipment...	41.8	42.0	41.7	41.5	41.5	41.2	42.1	42.0	42.1	42.0
Electronic and other electrical equipment...	40.8	41.0	40.2	40.6	41.0	40.9	40.9	41.0	40.8	40.8
Transportation equipment...	41.6	42.8	41.9	42.8	42.8	41.8	42.5	42.6	42.8	43.1
Motor vehicles and equipment...	44.0	44.0	42.7	40.8	42.8	41.8	42.6	43.7	43.6	41.2
Instruments and related products...	40.7	41.5	40.7	40.8	41.2	41.2	41.4	41.7	41.6	41.4
Miscellaneous manufacturing...	39.2	39.5	38.7	39.2	39.4	39.2	39.4	39.4	39.4	39.4
Nondurable goods..........	40.3	40.3	39.8	40.3	40.2	40.0	40.1	40.3	40.1	40.2
Overtime hours...........	3.6	3.6	3.6	3.9	3.6	3.4	3.6	3.6	3.6	3.7
Food and kindred products...	41.2	40.9	40.7	41.6	40.7	40.6	40.8	40.9	40.6	41.1
Tobacco products..........	37.3	39.5	38.5	38.0	(2)	(2)	(2)	(2)	(2)	(2)
Textile mill products.....	41.3	40.6	39.6	40.3	41.0	40.0	40.2	40.1	40.1	40.0
Apparel and other textile products...	37.0	36.9	36.3	36.7	36.9	36.4	36.6	36.7	36.6	36.6
Paper and allied products...	43.2	43.4	43.2	43.4	43.3	43.3	43.6	43.5	43.5	43.7
Printing and publishing....	37.9	37.6	37.6	38.2	37.8	37.8	37.9	38.0	37.9	38.1
Chemicals and allied products...	42.1	42.6	42.0	43.7	42.3	42.6	42.6	42.3	42.3	42.5
Petroleum and coal products...	43.8	46.8	44.9	43.7	(2)	(2)	(2)	(2)	(2)	(2)
Rubber and misc. plastics products...	41.7	41.7	40.9	40.9	41.2	40.9	41.4	41.6	41.5	41.1
Leather and leather products...	38.4	38.2	37.3	37.9	38.1	37.5	37.4	37.5	37.3	37.6
Transportation and public utilities...	38.9	39.4	39.4	39.4	38.6	39.0	39.1	39.2	39.0	39.1
Wholesale trade............	38.0	38.2	38.3	38.0	38.0	38.1	38.0	38.1	38.1	38.0
Retail trade...............	29.6	29.3	29.7	29.4	28.9	29.0	29.0	29.0	28.9	28.7
Finance, insurance, and real estate...	35.8	35.8	36.2	35.7	(2)	(2)	(2)	(2)	(2)	(2)
Services...................	32.8	32.7	33.0	32.9	32.5	32.6	32.5	32.6	32.6	32.6

1/ Data relate to production workers in mining and manufacturing; construction workers in construction; and nonsupervisory workers in transportation and public utilities; wholesale and retail trade; finance, insurance, and real estate; and services. These groups account for approximately four-fifths of the total employees on private nonfarm payrolls.
2/ These series are not published seasonally adjusted since the seasonal component is small relative to the trend-cycle and/or irregular components and consequently cannot be separated with sufficient precision.
p = preliminary.
NOTE: Data have been revised to reflect March 1989 benchmarks, conversion to the 1987 Standard Industrial Classification (SIC) system, and updated seasonal adjustment factors.

93

Table B-3. Average hourly and weekly earnings of production or nonsupervisory workers1/ on private nonfarm payrolls by industry

Industry	Average hourly earnings				Average weekly earnings			
	Aug. 1989	June 1990	July 1990p/	Aug. 1990p/	Aug. 1989	June 1990	July 1990p/	Aug. 1990p/
Total private...............	$9.61	$9.98	$10.00	$9.99	$335.39	$347.30	$349.00	$347.65
Seasonally adjusted.....	9.70	10.03	10.07	10.09	334.65	348.04	347.42	348.11
Mining.......................	13.22	13.66	13.65	13.59	575.07	606.50	595.14	597.96
Construction.................	13.51	13.63	13.70	13.74	525.54	532.93	524.71	535.86
Manufacturing................	10.46	10.85	10.82	10.84	427.81	445.94	440.64	443.36
Durable goods..............	10.99	11.37	11.38	11.38	453.89	474.13	466.58	469.99
Lumber and wood products...	8.90	9.09	9.17	9.16	359.56	370.87	366.80	371.90
Furniture and fixtures.....	8.30	8.52	8.51	8.58	329.51	333.98	330.58	338.05
Stone, clay, and glass products...	10.85	11.17	11.20	11.19	465.47	476.96	471.52	477.81
Primary metal industries...	12.42	12.90	13.03	12.91	526.61	557.28	557.68	548.68
Blast furnaces and basic steel products.	14.29	14.74	14.92	14.76	614.47	645.61	657.97	639.11
Fabricated metal products..	10.54	10.85	10.86	10.87	434.25	453.55	445.26	448.33
Industrial machinery and equipment.	11.37	10.75	10.78	10.82	475.27	494.68	491.23	490.53
Electronic and other electrical equipment.	10.06	10.27	10.34	10.34	410.45	421.07	415.67	419.80
Transportation equipment...	13.67	14.20	14.04	14.15	571.41	607.76	588.28	598.55
Motor vehicles and equipment.	14.16	14.85	14.56	14.68	589.06	653.40	615.89	628.30
Instruments and related products.	10.90	11.27	11.36	11.32	443.63	464.32	462.35	461.86
Miscellaneous manufacturing.	8.20	8.61	8.61	8.64	321.44	340.10	333.21	338.69
Nondurable goods..........	9.73	10.12	10.19	10.12	392.12	407.84	405.56	407.84
Food and kindred products..	9.72	9.67	9.67	9.51	383.98	395.50	393.57	395.62
Tobacco products...........	15.72	17.24	17.48	16.10	589.36	680.98	672.98	611.80
Textile mill products......	7.68	8.02	8.01	8.05	317.18	325.61	317.20	324.32
Apparel and other textile products.	6.35	6.61	6.57	6.63	234.21	243.91	238.49	243.32
Paper and allied products..	11.95	12.23	12.35	12.30	516.24	530.78	533.52	533.82
Printing and publishing....	10.91	11.16	11.26	11.30	413.49	419.62	423.38	431.66
Chemicals and allied products.	13.10	13.51	13.59	13.56	551.51	575.53	570.78	572.23
Petroleum and coal products.	15.20	16.23	16.23	15.77	665.76	759.56	717.37	689.15
Rubber and misc. plastics products.	9.47	9.77	9.87	9.84	388.27	407.41	403.68	402.46
Leather and leather products.	6.55	6.91	6.79	6.89	251.52	263.96	253.27	261.13
Transportation and public utilities..	12.61	12.86	12.96	12.95	490.53	506.68	510.62	510.23
Wholesale trade.............	10.36	10.76	10.83	10.75	393.68	411.03	414.79	408.50
Retail trade................	6.49	6.75	6.74	6.75	192.10	197.78	200.18	198.45
Finance, insurance, and real estate..	9.47	9.90	10.00	9.93	339.03	354.42	362.00	354.50
Services....................	9.30	9.75	9.78	9.76	305.04	318.83	322.74	321.10

1/ See footnote 1, table B-2.
p = preliminary.
NOTE: Data have been revised to reflect March 1989 benchmarks, conversion to the 1987 Standard Industrial Classification (SIC) system, and updated seasonal adjustment factors.

Table B-4. Average hourly earnings of production or nonsupervisory workers1/ on private nonfarm payrolls by industry, seasonally adjusted

Industry	Aug. 1989	Apr. 1990	May 1990	June 1990	July 1990p/	Aug. 1990p/	Percent change from: July 1990-Aug. 1990
Total private:							
Current dollars2/............	$9.70	$9.96	$9.98	$10.03	$10.07	$10.09	0.2
Constant (1982) dollars2/....	7.64	7.57	7.58	7.58	7.58	N.A.	(3)
Mining.......................	13.30	13.59	13.58	13.73	13.75	$13.69	-.4
Construction.................	13.55	13.62	13.71	13.73	13.76	13.78	.1
Manufacturing................	13.53	13.75	13.71	13.86	13.89	13.92	.3
Excluding overtime4/.........	10.07	10.34	10.35	10.38	10.40	10.41	.1
Transportation and public utilities	12.65	12.96	12.88	12.92	12.99	12.99	.0
Wholesale trade..............	10.42	10.74	10.74	10.80	10.85	10.81	-.4
Retail trade.................	6.56	6.74	6.76	6.78	6.79	6.82	.4
Finance, insurance, and real estate	9.56	9.88	9.87	9.98	10.08	10.03	-.5
Services.....................	9.44	9.79	9.80	9.85	9.91	9.91	.0

1/ See footnote 1, table B-2.
2/ The Consumer Price Index for Urban Wage Earners and Clerical Workers (CPI-W) is used to deflate this series.
3/ Change was 0.0 percent from June 1990 to July 1990, the latest month available.
4/ Derived by assuming that overtime hours are paid at the rate of time and one-half.

N.A. = not available.
p/ = preliminary.
NOTE: Data have been revised to reflect March 1989 benchmarks, conversion to the 1987 Standard Industrial Classification (SIC) System, and updated seasonal adjustment factors.

95

Table B-5. Indexes of aggregate weekly hours of production or nonsupervisory workers1/ on private nonfarm payrolls by industry
(1982=100)

Industry	Not seasonally adjusted				Seasonally adjusted					
	Aug. 1989	June 1990	July 1990p/	Aug. 1990p/	Aug. 1989	Apr. 1990	May 1990	June 1990	July 1990p/	Aug. 1990p/
Total private............................	125.3	127.1	127.2	127.1	122.8	124.2	124.2	125.3	124.8	124.6
Goods-producing industries..............	115.2	113.9	111.3	113.2	112.4	110.1	111.1	111.7	110.5	110.5
Mining.................................	63.8	68.3	67.2	67.5	62.4	65.2	65.9	68.0	66.7	65.9
Construction...........................	155.8	152.2	151.5	153.9	141.0	138.6	142.1	144.3	138.5	139.6
Manufacturing..........................	109.8	108.6	105.5	107.4	109.6	107.0	107.5	107.6	107.4	107.2
Durable goods..........................	108.6	108.4	104.7	105.6	109.7	106.5	107.1	107.7	107.2	106.5
Lumber and wood products.............	137.0	135.2	132.7	134.1	132.2	131.7	131.9	130.5	129.7	129.7
Furniture and fixtures...............	121.7	125.3	120.7	122.8	130.1	125.4	125.7	126.0	125.8	124.8
Stone, clay, and glass products......	117.7	114.5	111.2	112.8	113.9	110.7	110.5	110.5	108.2	109.2
Primary metal industries.............	94.6	94.7	92.4	92.2	95.5	90.9	91.5	93.5	94.3	93.2
Blast furnaces and basic steel products	83.1	82.4	82.4	81.0	83.2	80.1	81.2	80.4	81.9	81.0
Fabricated metal products............	108.7	109.1	105.1	106.9	110.1	107.2	108.3	107.8	108.6	108.0
Industrial machinery and equipment...	98.4	99.1	96.5	95.6	100.6	98.9	98.9	98.0	98.6	97.7
Electronic and other electrical equipment	111.8	109.7	105.3	106.0	112.6	109.7	109.5	109.6	108.2	107.3
Transportation equipment.............	121.4	125.0	118.7	119.0	126.2	120.2	121.6	123.3	124.3	123.8
Motor vehicles and equipment.........	130.8	136.6	125.0	125.3	138.4	126.7	131.1	133.7	133.2	134.3
Instruments and related products.....	88.7	87.5	85.3	85.8	89.2	88.4	87.7	87.2	87.0	86.5
Miscellaneous manufacturing..........	105.7	104.0	98.9	103.5	105.3	102.9	104.2	102.7	103.8	102.7
Nondurable goods.......................	111.4	108.8	106.7	110.0	109.4	107.6	107.6	108.2	107.7	108.1
Food and kindred products............	116.7	111.7	111.7	118.5	108.2	108.7	109.2	109.2	108.3	110.4
Tobacco products.....................	66.3	61.3	59.2	65.0	67.2	64.7	65.8	64.3	66.5	66.4
Textile mill products................	107.6	97.6	97.6	101.1	106.6	101.7	101.0	101.2	100.3	99.9
Apparel and other textile products...	98.4	94.4	88.7	92.4	98.2	92.9	92.9	93.0	92.6	92.5
Paper and allied products............	111.0	112.5	111.4	113.6	110.8	111.0	111.8	113.0	111.6	112.5
Printing and publishing..............	126.2	125.0	126.6	129.1	126.6	127.6	128.1	128.6	128.4	129.4
Chemicals and allied products........	105.2	105.4	103.7	103.8	104.6	104.6	104.6	104.6	103.9	103.7
Petroleum and coal products..........	88.2	95.9	90.8	90.8	86.1	88.0	88.0	93.0	87.6	87.9
Rubber and misc. plastics products...	127.1	128.4	123.5	124.9	128.3	124.6	126.0	127.3	127.6	126.2
Leather and leather products.........	67.6	61.6	57.3	60.8	65.5	62.2	61.5	61.1	59.6	59.5
Service-producing industries............	129.9	133.0	134.3	133.3	127.5	130.5	130.6	131.4	131.2	131.0
Transportation and public utilities....	110.3	117.8	117.0	117.2	109.2	115.2	116.0	116.7	115.8	116.1
Wholesale trade.........................	118.8	121.1	121.2	120.3	118.0	119.3	118.9	119.8	119.6	119.3
Retail trade............................	127.5	127.5	129.2	127.7	123.7	125.0	125.1	125.3	125.0	123.9
Finance, insurance, and real estate....	122.6	124.3	126.4	124.6	120.7	122.6	122.5	122.9	123.1	123.0
Services................................	142.6	147.4	149.0	148.3	140.4	144.4	144.6	145.8	145.9	146.2

1/ See footnote 1, table B-2.
p = preliminary.
NOTE: Data have been revised to reflect March 1989 benchmarks, conversion to the 1987 Standard Industrial Classification (SIC) system, and updated seasonal adjustment factors. In addition, the base year for the indexes has been changed to 1982=100.

Table B-6. Diffusion indexes of employment change, seasonally adjusted
(Percent)

Time span	Jan.	Feb.	Mar.	Apr.	May	June	July	Aug.	Sept	Oct.	Nov.	Dec.
Private nonfarm payrolls, 356 industries1/												
Over 1-month span:												
1989	64.5	58.7	58.0	57.0	55.6	57.3	55.8	57.7	50.0	55.2	59.6	56.6
1990	55.6	58.6	53.7	49.9	55.8	49.9	p/50.4	p/46.9				
Over 3-month span:												
1989	65.3	64.2	60.0	60.1	59.7	58.3	59.7	54.5	55.2	55.8	57.7	60.3
1990	58.4	56.7	54.8	53.1	53.7	p/54.6	p/51.3					
Over 6-month span:												
1989	67.6	65.4	65.0	61.0	61.2	58.7	57.0	58.1	56.2	58.3	57.4	58.4
1990	57.3	56.5	55.5	p/54.4	p/50.8							
Over 12-month span:												
1989	67.1	67.7	65.3	64.6	64.9	61.2	60.0	59.8	58.6	57.3	56.7	56.0
1990	p/54.1	p/54.2										
Manufacturing payrolls, 139 industries1/												
Over 1-month span:												
1989	60.4	48.6	50.4	47.1	45.3	45.7	45.0	45.7	34.2	48.6	43.5	48.2
1990	42.4	45.7	45.3	46.8	45.7	40.3	p/46.8	p/41.4				
Over 3-month span:												
1989	54.0	54.7	45.3	43.9	43.2	42.8	41.7	33.1	36.3	34.9	41.7	39.2
1990	40.3	37.1	44.2	41.4	40.6	p/42.8	p/40.6					
Over 6-month span:												
1989	56.5	49.6	49.3	43.5	42.1	37.1	36.7	34.9	34.2	35.3	33.1	36.0
1990	37.1	35.6	36.3	p/41.0	p/37.4							
Over 12-month span:												
1989	53.6	55.0	49.3	45.3	43.9	39.9	37.1	35.6	33.8	32.4	30.9	31.7
1990	p/30.2	p/32.0										

1/ Based on seasonally adjusted data for 1-, 3-, and 6-month spans and unadjusted data for the 12-month span. Data are centered within the span.

p = preliminary.

NOTE: Figures are the percent of industries with employment increasing plus one-half of the industries with unchanged employment, where 50 percent indicates an equal balance between industries with increasing and decreasing employment. Data have been revised to reflect March 1989 benchmarks, conversion to the 1987 Standard Industrial Classification (SIC) system, and updated seasonal adjustment factors.

5

Personal Income and Consumption

Since most wage earners depend on their jobs for sustenance, income is one of the most important results of the employment data discussed in Chapter 4. The Commerce Department considers personal income so important that it issues a separate monthly report showing the sources of current dollar income and its disposition.

The first section of the *Personal Income Report* is important in determining whether individuals have the wherewithal to spend (see the GNP model in Chapter 1). The second section of the report tells at what pace and specifically on what individuals are actually spending their income. Individual spending is called *consumption* or, sometimes, *personal consumption expenditures* (PCE). This is the single largest component of real GNP in the United States, accounting for about two-thirds of the total measure. Thus, the *PI Report*, as economists call it, is one of the most important determinants of an analyst's GNP forecast. It also gives industry-specific expenditures from which stock analysts can determine useful competitive indicators such as a company's market share and market potential.

SOURCES OF INCOME

Figure 5.1 shows the components of personal income in current dollars. The table is designed to encompass all the imaginable sources of income to individuals, less monies not actually received. Not surprisingly, by far the largest is wage and salary income which accounts for about 60% of the total. This differs from compensation in that it excludes taxes and other deductions from pay stubs. So, wages and salaries measure monies individuals actually have available. A separate category for "other" labor income mainly counts employers' contributions to private pension and welfare programs.

Self-employed individuals' earnings are captured in the proprietors' income category (broken down by farm and nonfarm sectors) and the rental income of persons category. Passive income is counted in the dividend and interest categories, as well as in that for transfer payments. The last is analytical jargon for programs such as Social Security benefits, direct relief, and veterans payments. Subtractions are made from PI for the employee portion of Social Security contributions. Nonfarm PI is listed separately. The latter is particularly important because government subsidy programs sometimes account for the bulk of the gain in farm income. In the GNP accounts, for instance, Commodity Credit Corporation payments used for pegging crop prices are counted as government outlays. Their impact on real economic activity is questionable.

The average rate of growth in PI over the first six months of 1990 was 6.4% or about 0.5% per month. In contrast, PCE grew at an average clip of 0.47% per month. The difference can be accounted for by taxes and the savings rate. That is, PI must be adjusted for items that prevent spending. Income taxes are the largest such item. For this reason, economic analysts sometimes prefer to look at *disposable personal income* (DPI) rather than PI. DPI grew 6.8% in the first six months of 1990, suggesting individuals paid less in taxes and thus faced a more healthy financial situation than the PI data showed on their face. This is probably why the economy took so long to slow during the year.

FIGURE 5.1 Sources of Personal Income (personal income increased $16.6 billion (annual rate) in June, following an increase of $15.2 billion in May. Wages and salaries rose $13.0 billion in June compared to a rise of $10.1 billion in May.—Series revised).

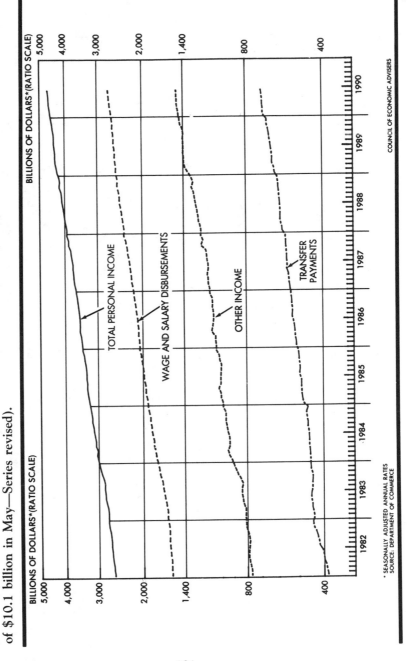

BILLIONS OF DOLLARS*(RATIO SCALE)

BILLIONS OF DOLLARS*(RATIO SCALE)

TOTAL PERSONAL INCOME

WAGE AND SALARY DISBURSEMENTS

OTHER INCOME

TRANSFER PAYMENTS

* SEASONALLY ADJUSTED ANNUAL RATES
SOURCE: DEPARTMENT OF COMMERCE

COUNCIL OF ECONOMIC ADVISERS

101

FIGURE 5.1 (continued)

[Billions of dollars; monthly data at seasonally adjusted annual rates]

Period	Total personal income	Wage and salary disbursements [1]	Other labor income [1][2]	Proprietors' income [3]		Rental income of persons [4]	Personal dividend income	Personal interest income	Transfer payments [5]	Less: Personal contributions for social insurance	Nonfarm personal income [6]
				Farm	Nonfarm						
1980	2,258.4	1,372.0	138.4	20.5	160.1	6.6	52.9	271.9	324.7	88.6	2,215.8
1981	2,520.9	1,510.3	150.3	30.7	156.1	13.3	61.3	335.4	368.1	104.5	2,465.6
1982	2,670.8	1,586.1	163.6	24.6	150.9	13.6	63.9	369.7	410.6	112.3	2,618.7
1983	2,836.6	1,676.6	173.6	12.4	178.4	13.2	68.7	393.1	442.6	120.1	2,799.0
1984	3,108.7	1,838.6	182.9	30.5	204.0	8.5	75.5	444.7	456.6	132.7	3,052.1
1985	3,325.3	1,975.4	187.6	30.2	225.6	9.2	78.7	478.0	489.8	149.3	3,271.3
1986	3,526.2	2,094.8	199.3	34.7	247.2	11.6	85.8	493.2	521.5	161.9	3,469.4
1987 r	3,766.4	2,249.7	209.4	42.8	280.6	13.7	91.8	501.3	549.9	172.9	3,702.2
1988 r	4,070.8	2,431.1	225.5	43.7	310.5	16.3	102.2	547.9	587.7	194.1	4,006.0
1989 r	4,384.3	2,573.2	241.9	48.6	330.7	8.2	114.4	643.2	636.9	212.8	4,314.6
1989: June r	4,372.5	2,566.3	241.1	41.7	328.6	9.0	113.8	649.9	634.6	212.5	4,309.8
July r	4,398.2	2,587.7	242.3	39.4	329.0	8.7	115.1	652.7	637.4	214.0	4,337.8
Aug r	4,398.7	2,578.1	243.5	38.8	329.8	8.7	115.9	655.3	642.1	213.4	4,338.9
Sept r	4,411.6	2,593.9	244.8	37.8	329.6	.0	116.3	657.6	646.1	214.5	4,352.7
Oct r	4,441.0	2,611.4	246.1	45.6	331.9	-7.4	117.4	661.2	650.8	215.9	4,374.4
Nov r	4,470.0	2,603.8	247.5	45.2	337.4	9.6	118.4	665.0	658.4	215.3	4,403.6
Dec r	4,496.7	2,623.0	248.9	46.4	338.7	10.1	118.9	668.5	658.6	216.3	4,429.2
1990: Jan r	4,532.2	2,633.3	251.6	51.1	343.3	7.7	119.7	669.5	679.8	223.9	4,459.9
Feb r	4,561.6	2,652.2	252.8	55.6	347.0	4.5	120.6	670.5	679.6	221.2	4,484.9
Mar r	4,594.7	2,669.2	254.0	65.5	349.4	4.3	121.3	671.4	683.4	223.8	4,508.1
Apr r	4,607.7	2,682.2	255.2	54.5	351.4	3.7	122.3	676.2	683.5	221.4	4,531.9
May r	4,622.9	2,692.3	256.4	51.5	352.6	4.4	123.0	681.2	685.2	223.6	4,550.1
June p	4,639.5	2,705.3	257.6	46.0	352.2	5.3	123.4	686.4	689.9	226.6	4,572.1

[1] The total of wage and salary disbursements and other labor income differs from compensation of employees (see p. 4) in that it excludes employer contributions for social insurance and the excess of wage accruals over wage disbursements.
[2] Consists primarily of employer contributions to private pension and private welfare funds.
[3] With inventory valuation and capital consumption adjustments.
[4] With capital consumption adjustment.
[5] Consists mainly of social insurance benefits, direct relief, and veterans payments.
[6] Personal income exclusive of farm proprietors' income, farm wages, farm other labor income, and agricultural net interest.

NOTE.—Series revised beginning 1987. See *Survey of Current Business*, July 1990.

Source: Department of Commerce, Bureau of Economic Analysis.

PERSONAL OUTLAYS OR CONSUMPTION

There are only two possible uses for personal income: spending or savings (see Figure 5.2). The Commerce Department collects data on outlays and treats savings as a residual, that is, the difference between PI and measured outlays. The three broadest categories for personal consumption expenditures (see Figure 5.3) follow the construction of the GNP accounts. They are durable goods, nondurable goods, and services. They are also measured in current dollars.

Durable goods are defined as having a useful life of more than three years. Examples are seen in the breakdowns in the report: motor vehicles and parts, furniture and household equipment, and other. The "other" catch-all category includes jewelry, orthodontic and opthamologic appliances, toys, recreational items (such as speed boats), books, and maps. Nondurables are items that are expected to be consumed right away but may have a slightly longer life than three years. Examples are also given in the breakdown which includes food, clothing, gasoline and oil, and other (e.g., tobacco, toiletries, cleaning supplies, and flowers and seeds). Services cover the balance of consumption and include areas as diverse as medical and dental care and hairdressing. Services are both the largest component of consumption, with over 50% of the total, and the fastest growing. The major services subcategories are housing, household operations, transportation, and medical care. Figure 5.3 gives a breakdown of PCE.

SURVEY AND DATA SOURCES

Most of the components in the PI report come from secondary sources. Labor Department wage and hour surveys undertaken as part of *The Employment Report* are used to compute wages and salaries. Other government agencies supply data on tax collections, transfer payments, and farm subsidies. But the rental and proprietors' income components must be estimated from prior trends. For consumption, the Commerce Department uses the monthly *Retail Sales Reports* (see

FIGURE 5.2 Disposition of personal income (real per capita disposable personal income fell in the second quarter of 1990—Series revised).

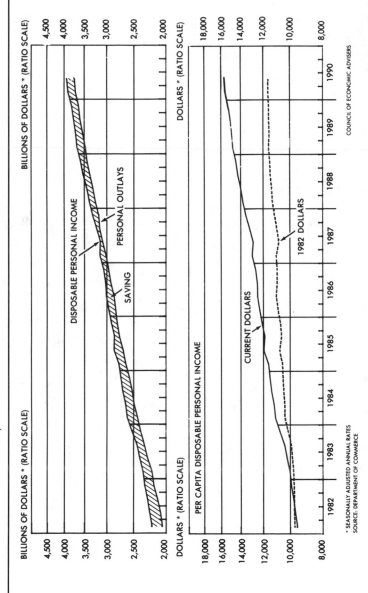

Period	Personal income	Less: Personal tax and nontax payments	Equals: Disposable personal income	Less: Personal outlays [1]	Equals: Personal saving	Disposable personal income in 1982 dollars (billions)	Per capita disposable personal income		Per capita personal consumption expenditures		Percent change in real per capita disposable personal income	Saving as percent of disposable personal income	Population, including Armed Forces abroad (thousands) [2]
							Current dollars	1982 dollars	Current dollars	1982 dollars			
	Billions of dollars					Dollars					Percent		
1980............	2,258.5	340.5	1,918.0	1,781.1	136.9	2,214.3	8,421	9,722	7,607	8,783	-1.1	7.1	227,754
1981............	2,520.9	393.3	2,127.6	1,968.1	159.4	2,248.6	9,243	9,769	8,320	8,794	.5	7.5	230,182
1982............	2,670.8	409.3	2,261.4	2,107.5	153.9	2,261.5	9,724	9,724	8,818	8,818	-.5	6.8	232,549
1983............	2,838.6	410.5	2,428.1	2,297.4	130.6	2,331.9	10,340	9,930	9,515	9,139	2.1	5.4	234,829
1984............	3,108.7	440.2	2,668.6	2,504.5	164.1	2,469.8	11,257	10,419	10,253	9,489	4.9	6.1	237,051
1985............	3,325.3	486.6	2,838.7	2,713.3	125.4	2,542.8	11,861	10,625	10,985	9,839	2.0	4.4	239,322
1986............	3,526.2	512.9	3,013.3	2,888.5	124.9	2,635.3	12,469	10,905	11,576	10,123	2.6	4.1	241,660
1987 r.........	3,766.4	571.6	3,194.7	3,102.2	92.5	2,670.7	13,094	10,946	12,335	10,311	.4	2.9	243,982
1988 r.........	4,070.8	591.6	3,479.2	3,333.6	145.6	2,800.5	14,123	11,368	13,144	10,580	3.9	4.2	246,358
1989 r.........	4,384.3	658.8	3,725.5	3,553.7	171.8	2,869.0	14,973	11,531	13,866	10,678	1.4	4.6	248,810
			Seasonally adjusted annual rates										
1982: IV.....	2,729.2	411.1	2,318.1	2,174.9	143.1	2,276.1	9,929	9,749	9,068	8,904	1.2	6.2	233,466
1983: IV.....	2,941.8	413.9	2,527.9	2,382.5	145.4	2,392.7	10,725	10,151	9,825	9,299	9.1	5.8	235,707
1984: IV.....	3,188.3	459.7	2,728.6	2,571.3	157.3	2,496.3	11,467	10,491	10,479	9,587	1.7	5.8	237,946
1985: IV.....	3,399.1	499.6	2,899.5	2,787.7	111.7	2,562.8	12,068	10,667	11,240	9,935	3.3	3.9	240,257
1986: IV.....	3,597.4	534.4	3,063.4	2,961.4	102.0	2,646.2	12,629	10,909	11,825	10,214	.3	3.3	242,579
1987: IV r...	3,890.9	588.6	3,302.3	3,172.6	129.7	2,717.9	13,483	11,097	12,572	10,347	6.4	3.9	244,925
1988: IV r...	4,186.2	607.3	3,578.9	3,430.4	148.5	2,833.9	14,470	11,458	13,474	10,669	1.2	4.1	247,329
1989: I r....	4,302.2	640.5	3,661.7	3,472.0	189.8	2,863.5	14,773	11,553	13,603	10,638	3.4	5.2	247,863
II r...	4,362.9	665.5	3,697.3	3,528.5	168.9	2,854.9	14,883	11,492	13,790	10,648	-2.1	4.6	248,431
III r..	4,402.8	659.5	3,743.4	3,588.8	154.5	2,874.3	15,026	11,538	13,986	10,739	1.6	4.1	249,127
IV r...	4,469.2	669.6	3,799.6	3,625.5	174.1	2,883.2	15,210	11,541	14,084	10,687	.1	4.6	249,818
1990: I r....	4,562.8	675.1	3,887.7	3,696.4	191.3	2,900.9	15,527	11,586	14,330	10,692	1.6	4.9	250,392
II p...	4,623.4	693.7	3,929.6	3,728.5	201.2	2,904.4	15,655	11,571	14,420	10,658	-.5	5.1	251,009

[1] Includes personal consumption expenditures, interest paid by consumers to business, and personal transfer payments to foreigners (net).
[2] Annual data are averages of quarterly data, which are averages for the period.

NOTE.—Series revised beginning 1987. See *Survey of Current Business*, July 1990.

Source: Department of Commerce (Bureau of Economic Analysis and Bureau of the Census).

FIGURE 5.3 Personal consumption expenditures (billions of dollars, except as noted; quarterly data at seasonally adjusted annual rates)

Period	Total personal consumption expenditures	Durable goods				Nondurable goods					Services	Retail sales of new passenger cars (millions of units)	
		Total durable goods	Motor vehicles and parts	Furniture and household equipment	Other	Total nondurable goods	Food	Clothing and shoes	Gasoline and oil	Other	Services	Domestics	Imports
1982	2,050.7	252.7	108.9	95.7	48.1	771.0	398.8	124.4	89.1	158.7	1,027.0	5.8	2.2
1983	2,234.5	289.1	130.4	107.1	51.6	816.7	421.9	135.1	90.2	169.5	1,128.7	6.8	2.4
1984	2,430.5	335.5	157.4	118.8	59.3	867.3	448.5	146.7	90.0	182.1	1,227.6	8.0	2.4
1985	2,629.0	372.2	179.1	129.9	63.2	911.2	471.6	156.4	90.6	192.6	1,345.6	8.2	2.8
1986	2,797.4	406.0	196.2	139.7	70.0	942.0	500.0	166.8	73.5	201.7	1,449.5	8.2	3.2
1987 ʳ	3,009.4	423.4	197.9	148.8	76.7	1,001.3	530.7	178.4	75.3	216.9	1,584.7	7.1	3.2
1988 ʳ	3,238.2	457.5	212.2	161.8	83.5	1,060.0	562.6	191.1	77.3	229.1	1,720.7	7.5	3.1
1989 ʳ	3,450.1	474.6	215.5	171.4	87.8	1,180.0	595.3	204.6	83.8	246.3	1,845.5	7.1	2.8
1982: IV	2,117.0	263.8	115.7	99.1	49.0	786.6	407.0	126.5	89.8	163.4	1,066.5	6.0	2.5
1983: IV	2,315.8	310.0	144.4	112.4	53.2	837.9	430.8	141.1	91.9	174.0	1,167.9	7.4	2.6
1984: IV	2,493.4	346.7	162.3	122.7	61.8	879.6	456.1	149.8	89.0	184.7	1,267.1	7.7	2.6
1985: IV	2,700.4	373.2	173.8	134.7	64.7	932.7	482.5	160.6	91.0	198.5	1,394.5	7.0	3.1
1986: IV ʳ	2,868.5	422.0	201.1	143.8	77.1	952.1	511.9	168.7	66.0	205.5	1,494.4	7.7	3.4
1987: IV ʳ	3,079.1	427.4	198.9	151.1	77.4	1,019.9	539.0	182.2	77.3	221.5	1,631.8	6.6	3.3
1988: IV ʳ	3,332.6	473.1	217.8	166.8	88.5	1,088.0	577.1	198.6	78.5	233.9	1,771.5	7.5	3.0
1989: I ʳ	3,371.7	466.4	211.3	170.2	84.9	1,106.7	588.8	199.3	79.0	239.7	1,798.6	7.0	2.8
II ʳ	3,425.9	473.6	216.2	170.7	86.7	1,127.1	592.5	203.4	88.2	243.0	1,825.1	7.3	3.0
III ʳ	3,484.3	487.1	226.9	171.5	88.7	1,137.3	597.6	206.9	84.5	248.3	1,859.8	7.8	2.9
IV ʳ	3,518.5	471.2	207.5	173.0	90.7	1,148.8	602.2	208.7	83.5	254.4	1,898.5	6.2	2.6
1990: I ʳ	3,588.1	492.1	221.1	178.9	92.0	1,174.7	616.4	212.9	87.1	258.2	1,921.3	7.0	2.8
II ᵖ	3,619.5	479.6	213.2	176.6	89.8	1,171.5	618.5	211.5	83.7	257.9	1,968.4	6.8	2.7

Note.—Series revised beginning 1987. See *Survey of Current Business*, July 1990.

Source: Department of Commerce, Bureau of Economic Analysis.

106

Chapter 6) to estimate non-vehicle sales. Unit sales data are available for computing car and truck sales components. Services, the largest component, are surveyed, trended, or estimated from secondary sources. Since the trending process fails to capture turning points in the economy and is subject to technical revision, it is one major source of error.

Noncurrent services are the major item in PCE that is trended, but then replaced annually in July with benchmark revisions based on additional survey information. Table 5.1 provides the major services subcategories and how they are constructed. The trending process used for a large portion of the data are based on prior growth rates inflated for the change in the cost of living. Thus, its error factor increases when the inflation rate changes sharply (individuals may switch goods or buy less, see Chapter 11) or when advances in technology rapidly change tastes.

Given the estimating procedures, major revisions to consumption are inevitable. One of the most famous examples is the aftermath of the October 1987 stock market crash. Economic theory indicates that individuals, faced with a loss of wealth, should have cut back their spending. During the winter of 1987–88, however, incoming data indicated surprising strength in consumption. Moreover, subsequent revisions to consumption numbers were generally on the higher side, indicating that Commerce Department officials had been conservative in their trend estimates. The expectation for a weakening in consumption lasted through the two subsequent years, with actual results continuing to outpace expectations. Indeed, the fall of 1988 saw another surprising upward revision to consumption that forced another realignment in market expectations.

GNP BASIS

The PCE data are measured in current dollars (i.e., not adjusted for inflation). In order to incorporate them into a real GNP forecast, it is necessary to use a deflator, the construction of which will be discussed

TABLE 5.1
PCE Services Subcomponents

Subcomponent	Source	Revision
Housing	CPS quarterly survey	Each three months
Household Operations:		
Electric & gas	Edison Elec. Inst.	Actual quarterly survey
Water & sanitation	Trended	
Domestic services	Trended	
Telephone	FCC/AT&T company data	Monthly
Transportation:		
Auto insurance	A.M. Best & Co. data	Actual quarterly data
Airlines	Air Transp. Assoc. & FAA data	Monthly
Auto repair	Trended	
Medical Care:		
Physicians & dentists	Trended	
Hospital costs	Am. Hospital Assoc. survey of 33% of hospitals	Actual quarterly data
Nursing homes & other professional services	BLS employment & earnings data	Monthly

in depth in Chapter 11. For 85 of the 115 components of PCE, the Consumer Price Index is used directly as a deflator. Thus, a quick proxy for real consumption can be obtained by subtracting the percent change in the CPI from the percent change in PCE. For example, PCE growth of 0.7% during a quarter that the CPI grew 0.5% on average indicates only modest real consumption growth of 0.2%. Since PCE accounts for about two-thirds of GNP, this would likely portend a slowing in the economy.

Appendix 5.1

Full Breakdown of PCE (millions of dollars, S.A.A.R)

TABLE 2--PERSONAL CONSUMPTION EXPENDITURES
(MILLIONS OF CURRENT DOLLARS, S.A.A.R.)

		1988	1989	IV 89	I 90	II 90	JAN 90	FEB 90	MAR 90	APR 90	MAY 90	JUN 90	JUL 90
TOTAL PCE	P.	3238192	3450085	3518542	3580051	3623944	3579135	3586520	3598493	3608089	3613811	3640930	3666524
TOTAL DURABLES	P.	457497	474614	471248	402081	472288	506605	487254	492782	481562	473771	482533	487856
MOTOR VEHICLES AND PARTS	P.												
NEW CARS (65)	P.												
NEW DOMESTIC CARS	P.												
NEW FOREIGN CARS	P.												
NEW DOMESTIC USED CARS (66)	P.												
USED TRANS MARGIN	P.												
NET PUR OF USED CARS (67)	P.												
EMPLOYEE REIMBURSEMENT	P.												
NET NEW&USED TRKS&RECR (67)	P.												
NEW AND USED TRUCKS	P.												
RECREATIONAL VEHICLES (68)	P.												
TIRES,TUBES,ACC&PARTS	P.												
ACCESSORIES AND PARTS	P.												
FURNITURE AND HOUSEHOLD EQUIP	P.												
FURN., MAT., AND BEDSP (29)	P.												
KITCH. AND HSHLD APPL (30)	P.												
CHINA,GLASSWARE,TBLWR&UTENSILS (31)	P.												
OTH FLOOR HOUSEFURN (32)	P.												
FLOOR COVERINGS	P.												
DUR HSE FURNISHINGS,NEC	P.												
WRITING EQUIPMENT	P.												
HAND TOOLS	P.												
OTHER DURABLES (18)	P.												
OPTH.&ORTH. APP (46)	P.												
BOOKS AND MAPS (83)	P.												
WHL GDS,TOYS,SP EQUIP (36)	P.												
WHEEL GOODS	P.												
BOATS	P.												
PLEASURE AIRCRAFT	P.												

NUMBERS IN ( ) REFER TO LINES IN TABLE 2.4

111

TABLE 2--PERSONAL CONSUMPTION EXPENDITURES
(MILLIONS OF CURRENT DOLLARS, S.A.A.R.)

	1988	1989	IV-89	I-90	II-90	JAN 90	FEB 90	MAR 90	APR 90	MAY 90	JUN 90	JUL 90
TOTAL NONDURABLES	1060039	1129961	1148781	1172690	1178740	1163285	1182159	1178630	1174305	1174185	1187728	1189992
TOTAL FOOD												
FOOD PUR FOR OFF PREM CONS (3)												
FOOD IN OFF PREMISE FOOD												
ALCH IN OFF PREM FOOD												
PURCH MEALS AND BEVS (4)												
FOOD IN PUR MEALS & BEVS												
ALCH IN PUR MEALS & BEVS												
FOOD FURN GOV & COMML												
FOOD SUPPLIED MIL												
FOOD PRO & CON ON FARMS (6)												
TOTAL CLOTHING & SHOES												
SHOES & OTH FOOTWEAR (11)												
WOMENS CLOTHING (14)												
MENS CLOTHING (15)												
CLOTH,ISSUSED MIL. (16)												
GASOLINE AND OIL (70)												
FUEL OIL AND COAL (40)												
OTHER NONDURABLES												
TOBACCO (7)												
EXPENDITURES ABROAD (105)												
LESS PERS REMIT IN KIND (107)												
SEMIDUR HOUSE FURN (3-5)												
DRUG PRE P& SUNDRIES (45)												
TOILETART & PREP MISC (1?)												
STATIONARY & WRITING SUP (85)												
NONDUR TOYS & SPT.EQ (89)												
FLECN.POLISH,PAPER MISC (34)												
CLIGHTING SUPPLIES												
CLEANING PREPARATIONS												
HOUSEHOLD PAPER PRODUCTS												
MAGS, NEWSPAPER, ETC (84)												

NUMBERS IN ( ) REFER TO LINES IN TABLE 2.4

TABLE 2—PERSONAL CONSUMPTION EXPENDITURES
(MILLIONS OF CURRENT DOLLARS, S.A.A.R.)

	1988	1989	IV 89	I 90	II 90	JAN 90	FEB 90	MAR 90	APR 90	MAY 90	JUN 90	JUL 90
	P. 1720656	1845510	1893513	1921280	1965916	1900246	1917107	1937486	1952222	1965855	1979669	1992676
TOTAL SERVICES												
HOUSING SVCS (23)												
OWN-OC NONFRM SPACE RENT (24)												
OWN-OC MOBILE HOMES												
OWN-OC STATIONARY UNITS												
TEN-OC NONFRM SPACE RENT (25)												
TEN-OC MOBILE HOME UNITS												
TEN-OC STATIONARY UNITS												
TENANT-LANDLORD DURABLES (26)												
RENTAL VAL OF FARM HOUSES												
OTHER HOUSING (27)												
HOTELS & MOTELS												
CLUBS & FRAT HOUSING												
HIGHER EDUCATION HSING												
ELEM & SECONDARY HOUSING												
TENANT GRP ROOM & BOARD												
TENANT GRP EMP LODGING												
HOUSEHOLD OPER SVCS (28)												
ELECTRICITY (37)												
NATURAL GAS (38)												
WATER & OTH SAN (39)												
TELEPHONE & TELEGRAPH (41)												
DOMESTIC SVCS (42)												
OTHER HSEHOLD OPER (43)												
TRANSPORTATION SVCS (63)												
AUTO REPAIR, RENTAL, ETC (69)												
BRIDGE TOLLS, ETC (71)												
NET AUTO INS PREMIUMS (72)												
PURCH LOCAL TRANS (73)												
COMMUTER RAILROAD (74)												
LOCAL TRANSIT (75)												
INTERCITY RAILROAD (76)												
INTERCITY BUSES (79)												
AIRLINES (80)												
OTHER TRANSPORTATION SVCS (81)												
MEDICAL CARE SVCS (44)												
PHYSICIANS (47)												
OTH PROFESSIONAL SVCS (49)												
PRIV HOSP & SANITORIUMS (50)												
HEALTH INSURANCE (51)												

NUMBERS IN ( ) REFER TO LINES IN TABLE 2.4

113

TABLE 2—PERSONAL CONSUMPTION EXPENDITURES
(MILLIONS OF CURRENT DOLLARS, S.A.AR.)

	1988	1989	IV 89	I 90	II 90	JAN 90	FEB 90	MAR 90	APR 90	MAY 90	JUN 90	JUL 90
PERSONAL CARE SVCS (20) P...												
SHOE CLEAN,AND REPAIR (12) P...												
CLEANING,LAUND,ETC (17,19) P...												
OTHER CLOTHING REPAIR (22) P...												
BARBERSHOPS,BEAUTY,BATHS (22) P...												
PERSONAL BUSINESS SVCS (55) P...												
BROKERAGE & INV COUNSL (56) P...												
BANK SVC CHARGE,ETC. (57) P...												
FIN SVC FURN,W/O PAY. (53) P...												
FIN SVC FURN BY OTHER P...												
COST OF HAND LIFE INS (59) P...												
LEGAL SVCS (60) P...												
FUNERAL & BURIAL EXP (61) P...												
OTHER PERSONAL BUSINESS (62) P...												
PRIV.ED., & RESEARCH (98) P.												
RECREATIONAL SERVICES (82) P...												
RADIO & TV REPAIR (88) P...												
MOTION PICTURE ADMISION (91) P...												
LEGITIMATE THEATER,ETC (92) P...												
SPECTATOR SPORTS (93) P...												
CLUBS,FRTERNL ORG (94) P...												
COMM'L PART.RECR,INSUR (95) P...												
PARI-MUTUEL RECEIPTS (96) P...												
OTHER RECREATION (97) P...												
RELIGIOUS AND WELFARE (102) P.												
NET FOREIGN TRAVEL BY US (103) P.												
US TRAVEL OUTSIDE THE US (104) P.												
LESS FOR TRAV IN US (106) P.												

NUMBERS IN ( ) REFFR TO LINES IN TABLE 2.4

114

6

Other Consumer Spending Data

The title of this chapter really ought to be "Source Data" for the other consumer spending reports. That is, many of the raw inputs to the other reports are themselves indicators that are closely watched by economic analysts. One, the monthly *Advance Retail Sales Report*, gets a lot more attention than it probably deserves (see Chapter 1 for a discussion of its revisions). Two of the other important inputs are the sales data released monthly by the automobile manufacturers and the large chain stores. These are the building blocks for the retail sales numbers and the starting point for our analysis.

AUTO SALES

The old saying "What's good for General Motors is good for the U.S.A." certainly no longer applied by the 1980s. Expenditures on motor vehicles and parts had dropped to only about 7% of consumer spending. But, the motor vehicle industry still had significant ripple effects on the economy. First, expenditures on cars are discretionary,

115

that is, they can easily be postponed until times improve so they could be a swing factor in an economic forecast. Second, even by the end of the 1980s, strikes at the major car manufacturers had the potential to plunge the economy into recession. An estimated one-third of domestic industrial production (in areas such as steel rolling, energy consumption, and glass and plastics production) depended to a great extent on demand from the auto manufacturers. Thus, changes in auto spending patterns could be the first signal that the income and production components of an economic forecast must be altered.

The convention for automobile manufacturers, begun in earnest in the 1940s when the War Control Board monitored the economy, is to release progress reports every 10 days. * These sales reports cover the number, but not the pricing, of cars sold domestically. In recent years, unit sales have ranged between six and eight million units. Sales of light trucks and vans are almost equally important, comprising about 30% of total domestic vehicle sales or three to four million units in an average year. Sales of imported vehicles affect consumption and the trade balance, and their inclusion would boost sales by another two and a half to three million units. But these data are not freely available so the financial markets focus on the domestic components.

Seasonality

The Commerce Department issues both 10-day and monthly seasonal adjustment factors that are used to compute a SAAR domestic selling rate. The seasonals adjust for time of year and holiday effects, but also take into account factors specific to the industry such as model change-over time and the number of selling days in each 10-day period (see Appendix 6.1). At the start of the year, General Motors issues a schedule of release dates for sales (see Table 6.1), and this is generally adhered to by other producers. To apply the seasonals, all the analyst need do is add up the raw sales numbers found in the news, divide by the seasonal factor, and multiply the result by 1,000. An example is given in Table 6.2.

TABLE 6.1
Sales Release Dates in 1991 for General Motors Corp. Sales
Company Contacts: Terrence Sullivan (313) 556-2019
Karen Longridge (313) 556-2035

Period Ending	Sales Release Date	No. Selling Days
Jan 10	Tues, Jan 15	8
Jan 20	Thur, Jan 24	8
Jan 31	Tues, Feb 5	10
Feb 10	Weds, Feb 13	8
Feb 20	Mon, Feb 25	9
Feb 28	Tues, Mar 5	7
Mar 10	Weds, Mar 13	8
Mar 20	Mon, Mar 25	9
Mar 31	Thur, Apr 4	9
Apr 10	Mon, Apr 15	9
Apr 20	Weds, Apr 24	9
Apr 30	Fri, May 3	8
May 10	Tues, May 14	9
May 20	Thur, May 23	8
May 31	Tues, Jun 4	9
Jun 10	Thur, Jun 13	8
Jun 20	Tues, Jun 25	9
Jun 30	Weds, Jul 3	8
Jul 10	Thur, Jun 13	8
Jul 20	Tues, Jun 25	9
Jul 30	Weds, Jul 3	8
Aug 10	Weds, Aug 14	9
Aug 20	Fri, Aug 23	8
Aug 31	Thur, Sep 5	10

TABLE 6.1
(continued)

Period Ending	Sales Release Date	No. Selling Days
Sep 10	Fri, Sep 13	7
Sep 20	Tues, Sep 24	9
Sep 30	Thur, Oct 3	8
Oct 10	Tues, Oct 15	9
Oct 20	Weds, Oct 23	8
Oct 31	Tues, Nov 5	10
Nov 10	Weds, Nov 13	8
Nov 20	Mon, Nov 25	9
Nov 30	Weds, Dec 4	8
Dec 10	Fri, Dec 13	8
Dec 20	Thur, Jan 2	9
Dec 31	Mon, Jan 6	8

Note that the "Big Three"—General Motors, Ford, and Chrysler—are still clearly the most important, but the domestically produced cars sold by foreign-based manufacturers now total more than Chrysler. Most economic analysts maintain personal contacts at the Big Three, especially GM, but cull the industry for news on the "foreign" producers. Seasonals are also produced for other auto sectors. These are used to normalize production, to compute sales of imported cars and for Canadian and Mexican imports. These are reproduced in Appendix 6.1.

In the example in Table 6.2, sales had dropped significantly to 6.5 million units from the 7.1 to 8.2 million range of September 1990. Not surprisingly, this fall came after car prices were raised at the start of the new model year and following a steep increase in the price of gasoline at the pump after Iraq invaded Kuwait. Manufacturers indicated that some of the remaining demand was due to unsustainable

TABLE 6.2
Applying 10-day Auto Seasonals, Early October 1990

	Units Reported	Seasonal
Domestic:		
General Motors	89,040	
Ford	49,190	
Chrysler	26,234	
Subtotal:	164,464	
Domestically produced by foreign companies:		
Honda	9,313	
Toyota	5,753	
Nissan	1,820	
Mazda	1,184	
Mitsubishi	1,092	
Subaru	299	
Subtotal:	19,461	
Grand Total:	183,925	28.43
Selling Pace:		

6.469 million units, rounded to a 6.5 million rate

fleet sales because businesses wanted to capture high depreciation expenses at the start of the model year. In addition, the sales pace was well below the seven million *production pace* (production that is not sold becomes unwanted inventory and may cause an economic contraction—see Chapter 7). The reduction in sales portended a slowing in the auto industry which was subsequently buffeted by severe job layoffs and production cutbacks. This was taken by many observers as the first sign of recession.

Adjustments

Car sales can be used as the raw data for other indicators, specifically the *Consumer Spending Report* detailed in Chapter 5, but caution must be used in correlating these reports. First, PCE measures dollar expenditures, not units, so pricing must be taken into account. For example, downward adjustments must be made to the average price for discounts and manufacturers' rebates, which were popular sales incentives used during the 1980s and in 1990. About half the auto manufacturers were offering incentives at any one time in early 1990. A $1,000 price reduction on just half the seven million new cars sold would reduce the PCE by $3.5 billion, or $42 billion at an annual rate. This would shave about 1.2 percentage points off consumption growth, reduce car prices by almost 7%, slice auto manufacturers' profit margins by about half, and moderate inflationary pressures.

Seasonals are generated separately for the retail sales and the PCE reports. This means they may differ slightly from the monthly unit sales seasonals. Significantly, the PCE seasonals will generally boost car sales more than the units seasonals during the cold winter months when showroom traffic is presumed to be less. So, it may take some months of weaker unit car sales before the fall-off is recognized in the GNP accounts.

CHAIN STORE SALES

The other consumer spending components for which hard data are available are the "general merchandise" area (into which department store sales fall) and "food" (some of which is marketed by large specialty stores). Collectively, these are called *chain stores* and their sales reports appear in the news monthly. The challenge for the analyst is to order the sales reports so they are of use in projecting consumption.

Same-Store Basis

Chain stores report both the dollar volume of sales and the change from a year ago (see Table 6.3). A rule of thumb in recent years is that a change of more or less than 4% on a year-over-year (y-o-y) basis represents a quick or slow pace. Some chains also have sophisticated

TABLE 6.3

Chain Store Sales (Same-store Basis, $ millions)

Department Stores	Aug 1990	Aug 1989	Y-O-Y %	% Total
Sears	$ 2,619	$ 2,516	+4.1	19.8
Walmart	2,391	2,116	+13.0	18.0
K Mart	2,133	2,099	+1.6	16.1
J.C. Penney	1,191	1,220	−2.4	9.0
Dayton Hudson	1,071	992	+8.0	8.1
F.W. Woolworth	777	758	+2.5	5.9
Melville	674	622	+8.4	5.1
May Co.	725	681	+6.5	5.5
Limited	363	359	+1.0	2.7
Carter Hawley Hale	198	198	0.0	1.5
Mercantile	173	171	+1.2	1.3
The GAP	153	134	+14.0	1.2
Neiman Marcus	118	120	−1.5	0.9
Jamesway	72	63	+15.0	0.5
Total, Department Stores	12,658	12,049	+5.1%	
Change versus comparable July 1990 data			+5.6%	
Food Stores:				
TJX Co.	217	190	+13.7	
Hills	170	185	−8.1	
Charming Shoppes	68	63	+7.0	
Gantos	13	16	−18.0	
Total, Selected Foods	468	454	+3.1%	
Change versus Comparable July 1990 data			+19.1%	

investor relations staffs (see Appendix 6.4 for a contact list) who can release details of which product areas posted the best sales or which geographical areas experienced the strongest gains. Three adjustments must be made to utilize this data in the consumption reports. Chain store sales must be put on a same-store basis to eliminate the possibility that the Commerce Department did not capture new outlets—a particular problem with a fast-growing company such as the GAP. The results should exclude finance and credit charges that may not be related to economic activity. Second, sales must be compared to volume in the prior month in order to get the appropriate (smaller) monthly change. Third, seasonal factors must be applied.

Table 6.3 details the adjustment process. Note that the y-o-y change significantly understates the monthly change in the table, especially for food stores. Also, note that, just as in the auto industry, a handful of chains dominate sales. Over five-eighths of the department store sales are attributable to four of the chains. For example, Sears and WalMart each have about 20% of all sales.

To get a sense of sales at smaller stores (the Commerce Department will attempt to include in its official report data for other stores, for instance, the corner shops which in the United States still comprise about 15% of sales in the general merchandise area), some analysts compute a change excluding the major players or equally weight the changes for the smaller and larger stores. These changes are generally much smaller on a y-o-y basis. The table also separates out specialty food store sales, which can be used as a proxy for food sales. Note also the conspicuous absence of results for privately held firms, such as Macy's.

RETAIL SALES

The Bureau of the Census issues three reports on monthly retail sales: the advance, the preliminary, and the final. The monthly change in these may differ by as much as 1 percentage point, reflecting the inclusion of additional responses and the blowing up of the survey in the manner discussed in Chapters 3 and 4. Indeed, in a typical example the *Advance Retail Sales Report* for May 1990 said retail sales fell 0.7%, *plus or minus* 1.1% (emphasis added). The financial markets and economists choose to ignore the caveat and focus instead on the reported percentage change, so we will devote this section to describing and projecting that change.

The advance retail sales estimate is based on a mail subsample of 3,200 units covering approximately 50,000 stores. Included in this are all the major department store chains called *certainty cases*. The establishment names are obtained from Internal Revenue Service records of employer identification numbers. Surveys are mailed out on the third week of the month and must be received back at the Census Bureau by the tenth of the following month. But because the reporting period is so short, officials estimate only about 30% of these written surveys are completed on time; the other 70% of the initial sample is completed by telephone follow-ups.

Classifications

The survey asks for gross dollar sales (see Figure 6.1) and inventory levels, classifying a firm according to its primary type of business. The breakdowns follow basic consumption patterns: *durables* (automobiles, building materials, and furniture and furnishings) and *nondurables* (general merchandise, food, gasoline service stations, apparel, liquor, eating and drinking, and drug stores). See Appendix 6.2 for a sample report.

Nonchain stores are divided into three reporting panels that are surveyed only quarterly for two months of data. For example, the January panel will be asked for January and December data, the February panel for January and February data, and the March panel for February and March data. Thus, only about 80% of respondents carry forward in each survey. Put another way, the survey lacks two months of data for two-thirds of the nonchains at any given time. Estimates for these missing stores are based on the results of the certainty chain stores but the inclusion of additional responses are a main source of

FIGURE 6.1 Estimated Monthly Retail Sales: December 1979–March 1990

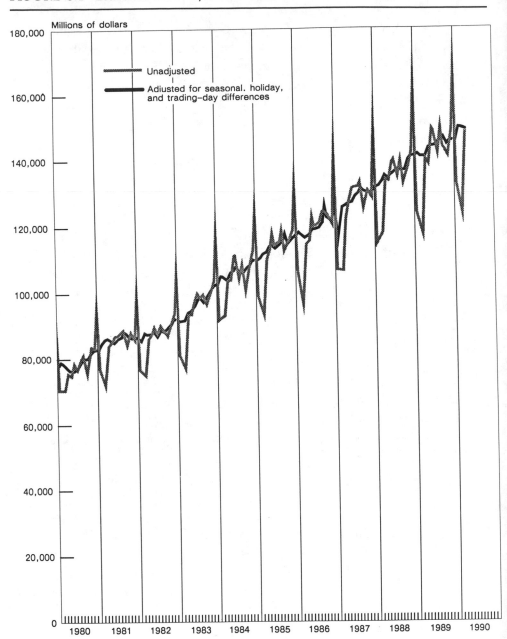

Source: U.S. Commerce Department.

revision. Eventually, the response rate builds in excess of 90% of the surveys mailed—a remarkable feat for a voluntary survey. This means the second report will cover another 12,000 establishments, while the final retail sales number covers the full 35,000 units.

Nonreporters (such as Groups 2 and 3, if this is January) are estimated, based on their classification as in other statistical reports. Suppose a significantly large retailer reports low sales one month due to an exogenous factor (say, a strike or bankruptcy) and this low number was used to estimate sales for a perfectly healthy Group 2 firm that actually benefited from the reduced competition. Then a substantial upward revision to that month would be in order as the Group 2 company's response is recorded. Suppose also that a major retailer repositioned its advertising during the period so that consumers began to perceive it as a purveyor of food rather than appliances. As a result its mix of sales shifted and the composition of retail sales overstated general merchandise sales but understated food.

Estimating Retail Sales

Given that the auto units and large chain store sales data theoretically comprise 30% of retail sales, we have a good basis for beginning an estimate. The raw data must only be seasonally adjusted and adjusted to out-guess the sampling procedure. However, the Census Bureau (which is responsible for the retail sales survey) uses concurrent seasonals, so the analyst must guess at the current year's factors using last year's factors as a guide. For example, for May 1990, the seasonal reduces auto sales by about 12%. The seasonal for department store sales boosts them by about 0.8%. These compare with the May 1989 seasonals of -12.7% and $+2.5\%$, respectively. So, this is another potential pitfall for our estimate.

In May, our chain stores proxy had a 2.6% increase y-o-y, which translated to a 27% monthly gain for department stores and a flat number for food stores. Auto unit sales had surged 7.6% to 644,300 amid discounting. Applying the appropriate seasonals suggested that autos would be down substantially (the rise in units alone did not offset the seasonal and lower prices could depress it further), food stores slightly lower (the seasonal took away), and department stores up firmly. As seen in Appendix 6.2, all three were down, contributing to the 0.7% overall fall in advance retail sales. The only anomaly was the department stores component, which was revised up in subsequent revisions to the report—in line with our raw data.

CONSUMER CREDIT

The Federal Reserve Board disseminates monthly data on the level and terms of *consumer installment credit outstanding*, which is defined as short- to intermediate-term credit extended to individuals and scheduled to be repaid in two or more installments. Strictly speaking, these data are not required to produce an economic forecast. But increasing credit usage is generally associated with an improved economic outlook, while retrenchment indicates a souring in expectations. Thus, analysts use consumer credit to measure the health of household balance sheets and the consumer's willingness to spend. As a rule of thumb, consumer credit usually trends between 20% and 23% of household liabilities. A ratio at the high end of this range suggests that the scope for more spending has been reduced.

The *Consumer Credit Report* divides credit into four categories: automobile, revolving, mobile home, and all other (see Appendix 6.3). Revolving credit is generally granted on credit cards, while the "other" category includes everything else. Some examples are:

Loans on trucks, boats, recreational vehicles;
Student loans;
Tax loans;
Home improvement loans;
Personal signature loans; and
Vacation loans.

The main swing factor is autos, where credit rises and falls along with durable goods movements. The data are also broken down by major holders—banks, finance companies, credit unions, retailers, gasoline companies, and so on.

Fed officials make their estimates using provider data. They blow up a mail survey of about 400 banks and 100 finance companies each month and then study the regulatory reports for thrifts. These data are then reconciled each quarter to the actual bank call reports submitted to regulators. But the data for retailers and gasoline companies are trended according to formulae determined from prior sales levels. These latter data are benchmarked each December to a yearly survey.

Consumer credit measures only the net change in outstanding loans, not extensions during the month. Thus, as the tax laws changed in the mid-1980s to limit the deductibility of consumer interest payments, it probably became somewhat less telling as an indicator. This is because it excluded people who use credit cards as convenience measures and pay their bills in full each period. Also, credit numbers are released with a lag of almost two months (on the fifth workday of the second month after the reference point), making them a true lagging indicator of the economy.

THE PROPENSITY TO CONSUME

Recall that in Chapter 1 we indicated that two ingredients are required for individuals to spend—rising real incomes and a desire to consume. A number of surveys have been constructed to measure consumer sentiment, the best known of which are the University of Michigan surveys begun in 1946 and the Conference Board confidence indices begun in 1967. Both are proprietary indices, so their construction cannot be discussed thoroughly here. But, both are classified as leading indicators by the Commerce Department. Indeed, the Michigan Index of Consumer Expectations is one of the components of the Commerce Department's Composite Index of Leading Indicators.

Both indices ask core questions (25 for Michigan and five for the Conference Board) designed to measure attitude changes about the overall business situation, personal finances, the job market, interest rates, and the future. Responses are scaled and weighted, then seasonally adjusted and combined into an overall index. Both indices tend to fall prior to contractions in the economy, but rise in good times. As an example, the stunning 14.4 point drop in the Michigan Index in August 1990 followed an oil shock to the economy.

But, this was not without historical precedent. The Michigan Index had contracted 5.9 points in the month after the November 1973 oil crisis and 7.2 points after the June 1979 oil problems. It also fell sharply following the imposition of credit controls in March 1980 and after the October 1987 stock market crash. All these episodes were followed by some other shocks to the economy which signaled a sea change in the outlook that manifested itself in lower consumption.

Note

*In November 1990, Chrysler indicated that it would stop disclosing its 10-day sales figures beginning in January 1991; instead it will release monthly progress reports. The last manufacturer that attempted to end 10-day reporting was American Motors in the late 1970s. Of course, this preceded the company's demise, making analysts suspicious that Chrysler was attempting to hide its deteriorating market share.

Appendix 6.1

Seasonal Factors
for Selected Components
of Auto Output

Attached are the seasonal factors for selected components of Auto Output. These seasonal factors will be used until July 1991. They were provided by the Consumption Branch, National Income and Wealth Division, Bureau of Economic Analysis, Department of Commerce, July 1990.

		Domestic Ten Day Auto Sales		
		N.S.A.	S.F.	SAAR
1987:				
	1	108.9	18.75	5.807
Jan	2	125.8	21.87	5.751
	3	193.1	32.37	5.965
	1	170.2	22.51	7.560
Feb	2	188.3	28.46	6.617
	3	199.6	27.18	7.344
	1	182.1	25.10	7.254

Domestic Ten Day Auto Sales (Continued)

	N.S.A.	S.F.	SAAR
Mar 2	217.8	30.34	7.178
3	283.5	36.65	7.736
1	193.0	27.04	7.138
Apr 2	201.5	27.27	7.390
3	299.3	38.89	7.696
1	151.1	23.37	6.466
May 2	221.1	31.93	6.924
3	250.1	35.12	7.122
1	208.7	28.96	7.207
Jun 2	223.4	30.89	7.231
3	224.6	31.98	7.023
1	165.9	23.07	7.191
Jul 2	187.6	26.11	7.186
3	257.5	34.84	7.390
1	170.4	21.09	8.080
Aug 2	234.7	25.68	9.141
3	248.9	33.13	7.513
1	177.5	23.03	7.707
Sep 2	160.2	21.56	7.429
3	275.5	34.76	7.926
1	151.0	27.93	5.406
Oct 2	154.0	24.75	6.222
3	218.9	34.18	6.405
1	139.6	22.86	6.106
Nov 2	172.6	26.86	6.425
3	173.8	25.99	6.686
1	187.1	24.00	7.796
Dec 2	154.2	20.51	7.520
3	209.4	30.63	6.837

Note: N.S.A. = Not seasonally adjusted
S.F. = Seasonal factor
SAAR = Seasonally adjusted annual rate

Domestic Ten Day Auto Sales

		N.S.A.	S.F.	SAAR
1988:				
	1	110.4	15.80	6.987
Jan	2	186.4	22.92	8.134
	3	234.4	29.89	7.841
	1	192.0	24.04	7.988
Feb	2	210.3	27.44	7.665
	3	246.8	30.45	8.104
	1	211.8	27.25	7.772
Mar	2	189.2	26.45	7.152
	3	332.7	42.19	7.886
	1	145.0	22.52	6.438
Apr	2	229.0	29.73	7.702
	3	277.6	36.69	7.566
	1	204.3	26.20	7.798
May	2	216.3	31.48	6.871
	3	281.4	35.97	7.823
	1	198.6	28.49	6.971
Jun	2	222.3	28.65	7.760
	3	301.5	34.91	8.637
	1	143.1	19.35	7.396
Jul	2	218.5	28.60	7.641
	3	243.7	32.06	7.602
	1	177.6	23.45	7.575
Aug	2	190.9	24.88	7.673
	3	234.5	35.02	6.696
	1	155.5	21.56	7.213
Sep	2	171.4	24.22	7.077
	3	251.9	34.87	7.223
	1	184.1	26.22	7.021
Oct	2	196.7	27.27	7.214
	3	210.9	31.27	6.745
	1	187.0	25.20	7.420

Domestic Ten Day Auto Sales (*Continued*)

		N.S.A.	S.F.	SAAR
Nov	2	159.6	22.51	7.089
	3	207.2	29.07	7.127
	1	167.9	22.34	7.517
Dec	2	176.1	22.47	7.837
	3	272.8	27.73	9.836

Note: N.S.A. = Not seasonally adjusted
S.F. = Seasonal factor
SAAR = Seasonally adjusted annual rate

Domestic Ten Day Auto Sales

		N.S.A.	S.F.	SAAR
1989:				
	1	107.4	17.31	6.206
Jan	2	156.7	22.41	6.993
	3	248.0	29.87	8.303
	1	158.3	24.00	6.596
Feb	2	186.1	25.68	7.246
	3	209.2	28.32	7.388
	1	172.9	26.24	6.590
Mar	2	195.0	27.33	7.136
	3	273.8	39.75	6.888
	1	188.6	25.10	7.515
Apr	2	237.3	31.29	7.584
	3	241.5	32.35	7.466
	1	207.4	28.20	7.355
May	2	224.1	30.46	7.358
	3	279.0	36.88	7.566
	1	201.2	28.13	7.152
Jun	2	198.1	29.66	6.680
	3	241.4	34.13	7.073
	1	155.3	21.34	7.279

Domestic Ten Day Auto Sales (Continued)

		N.S.A.	S.F.	SAAR
Jul	2	221.2	29.84	7.412
	3	226.9	31.69	7.160
	1	190.3	23.75	8.011
Aug	2	178.4	21.19	8.418
	3	316.7	38.65	8.193
	1	132.0	18.10	7.293
Sep	2	212.0	25.69	8.252
	3	265.7	33.68	7.890
	1	160.5	26.45	6.067
Oct	2	159.8	26.10	6.123
	3	203.9	31.99	6.374
	1	143.5	24.22	5.926
Nov	2	149.4	24.52	6.094
	3	180.7	29.96	6.031
	1	107.3	19.27	5.569
Dec	2	156.4	24.24	6.451
	3	192.1	25.73	7.466

Note: N.S.A. = Not seasonally adjusted
S.F. = Seasonal factor
SAAR = Seasonally adjusted annual rate

Domestic Ten Day Auto Sales

		N.S.A.	S.F.	SAAR			N.S.A.	S.F.	SAAR
1990:					1991:				
	1	158.8	18.61	8.533		1	____	19.15	____
Jan	2	156.4	21.97	7.119	Jan	2	____	18.86	____
	3	231.7	30.40	7.622		3	____	34.48	____
	1	173.9	23.54	7.387		1	____	20.21	____
Feb	2	164.2	26.15	6.279	Feb	2	____	28.10	____
	3	195.5	28.32	6.903		3	____	30.86	____
	1	167.1	25.73	6.494		1	____	22.09	____
Mar	2	177.6	27.84	6.379	Mar	2	____	29.92	____
	3	281.1	39.13	7.184		3	____	36.59	____
	1	164.0	25.57	6.414		1	____	27.48	____

Domestic Ten Day Auto Sales (Continued)

		N.S.A.	S.F.	SAAR			N.S.A.	S.F.	SAAR
Apr	2	192.4	30.25	6.360	Apr	2	____	29.70	____
	3	242.4	35.25	6.877		3	____	35.94	____
	1	186.4	29.01	6.425		1	____	28.02	____
May	2	161.0	26.17	6.152	May	2	____	28.53	____
	3	296.8	41.80	7.100		3	____	39.10	____
	1	151.6	24.18	6.270		1	____	26.36	____
Jun	2	213.4	31.88	6.694	Jun	2	____	32.80	____
	3	270.1	33.47	8.070		3	____	28.73	____
	1	156.7	21.73	7.211		1	____	23.35	____
Jul	2	192.2	28.85	6.662	Jul	2	____	28.32	____
	3	____	32.84	____		3	____	33.43	____
	1	____	22.96	____					
Aug	2	____	23.10	____					
	3	____	36.15	____					
	1	____	19.73	____					
Sep	2	____	26.42	____					
	3	____	28.93	____					
	1	____	28.43	____					
Oct	2	____	25.60	____					
	3	____	32.56	____					
	1	____	23.76	____					
Nov	2	____	24.98	____					
	3	____	28.96	____					
	1	____	21.00	____					
Dec	2	____	24.94	____					
	3	____	24.99	____					

Note: N.S.A. = Not seasonally adjusted
S.F. = Seasonal factor
SAAR = Seasonally adjusted annual rate

Domestic Auto Unit Sales

	NSA	S.F.	T.D.	C.F.	S.A.	SAAR
1987:						
Jan	427.8	85.68	102.6	87.91	486.7	5.840
Feb	558.1	101.49	92.0	93.37	597.8	7.174
Mar	683.4	109.84	101.0	110.94	615.8	7.390
Apr	693.8	111.20	101.1	112.42	617.3	7.408
May	622.3	111.64	97.8	109.18	569.8	6.838
Jun	656.7	110.08	100.1	110.19	596.1	7.153
Jul	611.0	97.91	103.2	101.04	604.7	7.256
Aug	654.0	94.78	100.4	95.16	687.1	8.245
Sep	613.2	96.98	98.7	95.72	640.6	7.687
Oct	523.9	101.96	102.6	104.61	500.9	6.011
Nov	486.0	93.21	97.7	91.07	533.8	6.406
Dec	550.7	85.69	104.4	89.46	615.4	7.385
1988:						
Jan	531.2	85.13	97.8	83.26	637.8	7.654
Feb	649.1	101.65	96.7	98.30	660.2	7.922
Mar	733.7	109.17	104.4	113.97	643.6	7.723
Apr	651.6	111.58	96.9	108.12	602.9	7.235
May	702.0	111.20	101.0	112.31	624.8	7.498
Jun	722.4	110.11	101.1	111.32	649.1	7.789
Jul	605.3	98.38	97.8	96.22	628.9	7.547
Aug	603.0	95.65	103.4	98.90	609.5	7.314
Sep	578.8	97.00	99.9	96.90	597.6	7.171
Oct	591.7	101.09	100.4	101.49	582.8	6.994
Nov	553.8	93.35	98.7	92.14	601.0	7.212
Dec	616.8	85.93	102.6	88.16	699.7	8.396

Note: NSA = Not seasonally adjusted
S.F. = Seasonal factor
T.D. = Trading-day factor
C.F. = Combined seasonal, trading-day factor
S.A. = Seasonally adjusted
SAAR = Seasonally adjusted annual rate

Domestic Auto Unit Sales

	NSA	S.F.	T.D.	C.F.	S.A.	SAAR
1989:						
Jan	512.1	84.86	101.0	85.71	597.3	7.168
Feb	553.6	102.04	92.0	93.88	589.8	7.078
Mar	641.7	108.58	103.2	112.05	572.6	6.871
Apr	667.4	111.28	95.7	106.49	626.8	7.522
May	710.5	111.00	103.4	114.77	618.8	7.426
Jun	640.7	110.49	99.9	110.38	580.7	6.968
Jul	603.4	99.00	100.4	99.40	607.0	7.284
Aug	685.4	95.98	104.4	100.20	683.9	8.207
Sep	609.7	96.68	96.9	93.68	651.0	7.812
Oct	524.2	100.60	101.0	101.61	515.7	6.188
Nov	473.6	93.45	101.1	94.48	501.4	6.017
Dec	455.8	86.07	97.8	84.18	541.3	6.496
1990:						
Jan	546.8	84.77	103.4	87.65	623.6	7.483
Feb	533.6	102.36	92.0	94.17	566.7	6.800
Mar	625.8	108.28	102.6	111.10	563.4	6.761
Apr	598.8	111.22	97.7	108.66	551.1	6.613
May	644.3	110.97	104.4	115.85	556.0	6.672
Jun	635.1	110.68	96.9	107.25	592.4	7.109
Jul	593.6	99.30	101.0	100.33	591.7	7.100
Aug	567.7	96.14	103.2	99.23	572.1	6.865
Sep	——	96.52	95.7	92.37	——	——
Oct	——	100.36	103.4	103.80	——	——
Nov	——	93.50	99.9	93.36	——	——
Dec	——	86.14	100.4	86.50	——	——
1991:						
Jan	——	84.73	104.4	88.48	——	——
Feb	——	102.52	92.0	94.31	——	——
Mar	——	108.14	97.8	105.79	——	——

Domestic Auto Unit Sales (*Continued*)

	NSA	S.F.	T.D.	C.F.	S.A.	SAAR
Apr	___	111.20	100.1	111.27	___	___
May	___	110.96	103.2	114.52	___	___
Jun	___	110.68	95.7	105.92	___	___
Jul	___	99.30	103.4	102.68	___	___

Note: NSA = Not seasonally adjusted
S.F. = Seasonal factor
T.D. = Trading-day factor
C.F. = Combined seasonal, trading-day factor
S.A. = Seasonally adjusted
SAAR = Seasonally adjusted annual rate

Foreign Auto Unit Sales

	NSA	C.F.	S.A.	SAAR
1987:				
Jan	197.7	92.49	213.8	2.566
Feb	223.3	86.24	258.9	3.107
Mar	251.3	99.95	251.4	3.017
Apr	244.1	97.34	250.8	3.010
May	264.3	102.57	257.7	3.092
Jun	286.1	108.47	263.8	3.166
Jul	301.9	109.60	275.5	3.306
Aug	313.5	105.43	297.4	3.569
Sep	292.0	100.08	291.8	3.502
Oct	278.5	101.74	273.7	3.284
Nov	250.8	93.77	267.5	3.210
Dec	292.7	105.59	277.2	3.326
1988:				
Jan	233.7	87.51	267.1	3.205
Feb	238.4	88.37	269.8	3.238
Mar	272.5	104.38	261.1	3.133

Foreign Auto Unit Sales (Continued)

	NSA	C.F.	S.A.	SAAR
Apr	249.6	93.89	265.8	3.190
May	272.0	105.16	258.7	3.104
Jun	287.1	109.37	262.5	3.150
Jul	257.9	103.68	248.7	2.984
Aug	282.9	111.24	254.3	3.052
Sep	251.4	100.70	249.7	2.996
Oct	246.2	97.79	251.8	3.022
Nov	242.7	97.18	249.7	2.996
Dec	265.0	103.68	255.6	3.067

Note: NSA = Not seasonally adjusted
C.F. = Combined seasonal, trading-day factor
S.A. = Seasonally adjusted
SAAR = Seasonally adjusted annual rate

Foreign Auto Unit Sales

	NSA	C.F.	S.A.	SAAR
1989:				
Jan	208.9	89.27	234.0	2.808
Feb	200.6	84.78	236.6	2.839
Mar	245.7	101.70	241.6	2.899
Apr	245.0	92.77	264.1	3.169
May	262.1	107.84	243.0	2.916
Jun	258.2	107.87	239.4	2.873
Jul	245.2	104.47	234.7	2.816
Aug	291.2	114.51	254.3	3.052
Sep	230.4	98.80	233.2	2.798
Oct	225.9	99.34	227.4	2.729
Nov	212.6	97.57	217.9	2.615
Dec	199.1	99.21	200.7	2.408
1990:				
Jan	209.1	91.43	228.7	2.744
Feb	194.2	84.55	229.7	2.756

Foreign Auto Unit Sales (*Continued*)

	NSA	C.F.	S.A.	SAAR
Mar	239.6	101.01	237.2	2.846
Apr	218.3	93.49	233.5	2.802
May	245.9	109.70	224.2	2.690
Jun	239.9	105.00	228.5	2.742
Jul	——	106.07	——	——
Aug	——	112.41	——	——
Sep	——	97.49	——	——
Oct	——	102.22	——	——
Nov	——	96.03	——	——
Dec	——	100.47	——	——
1991:				
Jan	——	93.21	——	——
Feb	——	84.44	——	——
Mar	——	96.15	——	——
Apr	——	97.54	——	——
May	——	107.05	——	——
Jun	——	103.22	——	——
Jul	——	109.20	——	——

Note: NSA = Not seasonally adjusted
      C.F. = Combined seasonal, trading-day factor
      S.A. = Seasonally adjusted
      SAAR = Seasonally adjusted annual rate

Domestic Auto Production

	NSA	S.F.	M.Y.C	C.F.	S.A.
1987:					
Jan	638.9	99.86		99.86	639.8
Feb	695.7	102.11		102.11	681.3
Mar	744.5	111.50		111.50	667.7
Apr	654.0	109.31		109.31	598.3
May	625.2	105.64		105.64	591.8
Jun	652.4	114.04		114.04	572.1

Domestic Auto Production (*Continued*)

	NSA	S.F.	M.Y.C	C.F.	S.A.
Jul	354.4	77.78	92.22	71.73	494.1
Aug	414.1	72.64	107.77	78.28	529.0
Sep	571.7	103.14		103.14	554.3
Oct	673.7	109.46		109.46	615.5
Nov	584.8	96.39		96.39	606.7
Dec	488.4	89.25		89.25	547.2
1988:					
Jan	484.8	94.74		94.74	511.7
Feb	563.7	106.22		106.22	530.7
Mar	660.9	116.62		116.62	566.7
Apr	609.1	104.67		104.67	581.9
May	692.0	111.85		111.85	618.7
Jun	731.4	113.96		113.96	641.8
Jul	367.0	72.71	84.60	61.52	596.6
Aug	500.6	78.39	115.40	90.46	553.4
Sep	626.5	100.89		100.89	621.0
Oct	670.3	108.76		108.76	616.3
Nov	652.3	104.42		104.42	624.7
Dec	572.3	85.75		85.75	667.4

Note: NSA = Not seasonally adjusted
S.F. = Seasonal factor
M.Y.C. = Model year change-over factor
C.F. = Combined seasonal factor
S.A. = Seasonally adjusted

Domestic Auto Production

	NSA	S.F.	M.Y.C.	C.F.	S.A.
1989:					
Jan	638.0	99.13		99.13	643.6
Feb	608.0	101.81		101.81	597.2
Mar	652.8	114.03		114.03	572.5
Apr	647.6	101.50		101.50	638.0

Domestic Auto Production (*Continued*)

	NSA	S.F.	M.Y.C.	C.F.	S.A.
May	679.1	118.45		118.45	573.3
Jun	612.0	111.74		114.74	547.7
Jul	276.8	74.16	67.26	49.88	554.9
Aug	546.3	77.36	132.74	102.69	532.0
Sep	573.9	99.36		99.36	577.6
Oct	620.5	113.83		113.83	545.1
Nov	538.8	102.63		102.63	525.0
Dec	429.1	83.16		83.16	516.0
1990:					
Jan	355.2	103.60		103.60	342.9
Feb	495.6	100.93		100.93	491.0
Mar	620.2	111.56		111.56	555.9
Apr	507.8	102.31		102.31	496.3
May	621.2	118.35		118.35	524.9
Jun	617.6	109.26		109.26	565.3
Jul	_____	77.46	78.12	60.51	_____
Aug	_____	74.92	121.88	91.31	_____
Sep	_____	96.48		96.48	_____
Oct	_____	119.92		119.92	_____
Nov	_____	100.25		100.25	_____
Dec	_____	84.15		84.15	_____
1991:					
Jan	_____	103.01		103.01	_____
Feb	_____	100.56		100.56	_____
Mar	_____	105.93		105.93	_____
Apr	_____	109.89		109.89	_____
May	_____	115.62		115.62	_____
Jun	_____	105.87		105.87	_____

Note: NSA = Not seasonally adjusted
S.F. = Seasonal factor
M.Y.C. = Model year change-over factor
C.F. = Combined seasonal factor
S.A. = Seasonally adjusted

Canadian Imports

	NSA	S.F.	S.A.
1987:			
Jan	66.0	102.80	64.2
Feb	67.6	100.90	67.0
Mar	62.5	109.46	57.1
Apr	54.3	113.13	48.0
May	48.9	105.62	46.3
Jun	58.3	114.99	50.7
Jul	27.9	62.00	45.0
Aug	19.5	62.10	31.4
Sep	51.0	96.23	53.0
Oct	62.7	108.85	57.6
Nov	72.6	113.79	63.8
Dec	63.3	89.79	70.5
1988:			
Jan	73.0	98.38	74.2
Feb	75.9	105.42	72.0
Mar	93.3	117.36	79.5
Apr	86.2	108.43	79.5
May	90.3	107.63	83.9
Jun	92.9	118.04	78.7
Jul	31.2	56.42	55.3
Aug	50.7	67.51	75.1
Sep	68.8	95.29	72.2
Oct	70.9	105.98	66.9
Nov	62.6	120.85	51.8
Dec	49.1	87.99	55.8

Note: NSA = Not seasonally adjusted
S.F. = Combined seasonal factor
S.A. = Seasonally adjusted

Canadian Imports

	NSA	S.F.	S.A.
1989:			
Jan	62.1	102.14	60.8
Feb	68.9	103.92	66.3
Mar	70.7	119.63	59.1
Apr	67.5	107.48	62.8
May	72.6	115.61	62.8
Jun	70.6	117.47	60.1
Jul	38.9	57.89	67.2
Aug	50.4	70.00	72
Sep	64.5	95.13	67.8
Oct	72.9	109.30	66.7
Nov	82.8	125.08	66.2
Dec	59.0	85.38	69.1
1990:			
Jan	39.8	107.70	37.0
Feb	62.6	103.60	60.4
Mar	78.7	115.90	67.9
Apr	59.2	107.41	55.1
May	78.5	115.33	68.1
Jun	_____	113.45	_____
Jul	_____	57.36	_____
Aug	_____	68.47	_____
Sep	_____	90.82	_____
Oct	_____	113.29	_____
Nov	_____	119.51	_____
Dec	_____	84.76	_____
1991:			
Jan	_____	108.94	_____
Feb	_____	103.61	_____
Mar	_____	110.37	_____
Apr	_____	111.54	_____
May	_____	114.35	_____
Jun	_____	110.26	_____
Jul	_____	60.51	_____

Note: NSA = Not seasonally adjusted
S.F. = Combined seasonal factor
S.A. = Seasonally adjusted

Mexican Imports, and U.S. Exports

	Mexican Imports			Exports		
	NSA	S.F.	S.A.	NSA	S.F.	S.A.
1987:						
Jan	4.6	100.00	4.6	32.3	73.91	43.7
Feb	0.5	100.00	0.5	56.9	106.55	53.4
Mar	1.3	100.00	1.3	66.3	130.26	50.9
Apr	7.5	100.00	7.5	58.7	117.17	50.1
May	12.6	100.00	12.6	63.6	116.48	54.6
Jun	15.2	100.00	15.2	70.0	111.64	62.7
Jul	11.8	100.00	11.8	23.5	66.95	35.1
Aug	10.4	100.00	10.4	22.2	57.07	38.9
Sep	13.1	100.00	13.1	52.9	103.93	50.9
Oct	15.1	100.00	15.1	59.9	110.11	54.4
Nov	11.6	100.00	11.6	50.0	93.81	53.3
Dec	10.1	100.00	10.1	42.5	83.66	50.8
1988:						
Jan	12.9	100.00	12.9	36.9	73.07	50.5
Feb	12.9	100.00	12.9	59.5	113.77	52.3
Mar	11.4	100.00	11.4	72.8	135.82	53.6
Apr	10.8	100.00	10.8	60.6	120.24	50.4
May	14.2	100.00	14.2	63.7	123.69	51.5
Jun	12.4	100.00	12.4	57.3	111.26	51.5
Jul	10.1	100.00	10.1	38.3	66.96	57.2
Aug	13.3	100.00	13.3	42.0	62.04	67.7
Sep	13.1	100.00	13.1	61.5	105.49	58.3
Oct	15.1	100.00	15.1	66.8	114.19	58.5
Nov	9.7	100.00	9.7	57.9	102.30	56.6
Dec	12.1	100.00	12.1	50.7	84.64	59.9

Note: NSA = Not seasonally adjusted
S.F. = Combined seasonal factor
S.A. = Seasonally adjusted

Mexican Imports, and U.S. Exports

	Mexican Imports			Exports		
	NSA	S.F.	S.A.	NSA	S.F.	S.A.
1989:						
Jan	5.1	100.00	5.1	46.3	76.53	60.5
Feb	13.7	100.00	13.7	62.0	113.55	54.6
Mar	13.3	100.00	13.3	69.0	130.68	52.8
Apr	12.7	100.00	12.7	66.8	121.68	54.9
May	18.8	100.00	18.8	54.4	125.06	43.5
Jun	17.2	100.00	17.2	53.5	110.08	48.6
Jul	18.8	100.00	18.8	27.1	66.75	40.6
Aug	9.5	100.00	9.5	40.8	63.06	64.7
Sep	5.8	100.00	5.8	53.0	106.64	49.7
Oct	5.9	100.00	5.9	49.3	118.51	41.6
Nov	7.8	100.00	7.8	52.8	98.32	53.7
Dec	4.6	100.00	4.6	51.3	83.96	61.1
1990:						
Jan	7.3	100.00	7.3	30.7	75.51	40.7
Feb	8.3	100.00	8.3	54.9	112.04	49.0
Mar	5.4	100.00	5.4	69.6	129.95	53.6
Apr	8.8	100.00	8.8	59.1	118.08	50.1
May	____	100.00	____	61.3	123.32	49.7
Jun	____	100.00	____	____	107.96	____
Jul	____	100.00	____	____	66.54	____
Aug	____	100.00	____	____	59.36	____
Sep	____	100.00	____	____	105.19	____
Oct	____	100.00	____	____	117.78	____
Nov	____	100.00	____	____	95.67	____
Dec	____	100.00	____	____	84.20	____
1991:						
Jan	____	100.00	____	____	76.20	____
Feb	____	100.00	____	____	112.07	____
Mar	____	100.00	____	____	127.39	____
Apr	____	100.00	____	____	124.50	____
May	____	100.00	____	____	117.18	____
Jun	____	100.00	____	____	107.98	____
Jul	____	100.00	____	____	67.14	____

Note NSA = Not seasonally adjusted
  S.F. = Combined seasonal factor
  S.A. = Seasonally adjusted

Domestic Auto Inventory Change Seasonally Adjusted

[Thousands of units]

	Production +	Canadian Imports +	Mexican Imports +	Sales −	Exports −	Change =	S.A. Level	I/S	NSA Level
1987:									
Jan	639.8	64.2	4.6	486.7	43.7	178.2	1693.2	3.479	1725.6
Feb	681.3	67.0	0.5	597.8	53.4	97.6	1790.8	2.996	1860.8
Mar	667.7	57.1	1.3	615.8	50.9	59.4	1850.2	3.005	1936.4
Apr	598.3	48.0	7.5	617.3	50.1	−13.6	1836.6	2.975	1903.3
May	591.8	46.3	12.6	569.8	54.6	26.3	1862.9	3.269	1903.3
Jun	572.1	50.7	15.2	596.1	62.7	−20.8	1842.1	3.090	1902.0
Jul	494.1	45.0	11.8	604.7	35.1	−88.9	1753.2	2.899	1657.1
Aug	529.0	31.4	10.4	687.1	38.9	−155.2	1598.0	2.326	1438.2
Sep	554.3	53.0	13.1	640.6	50.9	−71.1	1526.9	2.384	1396.5
Oct	615.5	57.6	15.1	500.9	54.4	132.9	1659.8	3.314	1558.9
Nov	606.7	63.8	11.6	533.8	53.3	95.0	1754.8	3.287	1691.8
Dec	547.2	70.5	10.1	615.4	50.8	−38.4	1716.4	2.789	1680.1
1988:									
Jan	511.7	74.2	12.9	637.8	50.5	−89.5	1626.9	2.551	1676.9
Feb	530.7	72.0	12.9	660.2	52.3	−96.9	1530.0	2.317	1608.5
Mar	566.7	79.5	11.4	643.6	53.6	−39.6	1490.4	2.316	1571.7
Apr	581.9	79.5	10.8	602.9	50.4	18.9	1509.3	2.503	1571.3

146

Jun	641.8	78.7	12.4	649.1	51.5	32.3	1582.1	2.437	1663.1
Jul	596.6	55.3	10.1	628.9	57.2	−24.1	1558.0	2.477	1430.9
Aug	553.4	75.1	13.3	609.5	67.7	−35.4	1522.6	2.498	1325.6
Sep	621.0	72.2	13.1	597.6	58.3	50.4	1573.0	2.632	1409.3
Oct	616.3	66.9	15.1	582.8	58.5	57.0	1630.0	2.797	1504.4
Nov	624.7	51.8	9.7	601.0	56.6	28.6	1658.6	2.760	1630.6
Dec	667.4	55.8	12.1	699.7	59.9	−24.3	1634.3	2.336	1600.8
1989:									
Jan	643.4	60.8	5.1	597.3	60.5	51.7	1686.0	2.823	1735.6
Feb	597.2	66.3	13.7	589.8	54.6	32.8	1718.8	2.914	1809.9
Mar	572.5	59.1	13.3	572.6	52.8	19.5	1738.3	3.036	1838.2
Apr	638.0	62.8	12.7	626.8	54.9	31.8	177C.1	2.824	1835.8
May	573.3	62.8	18.8	618.8	43.5	−7.4	1762.7	2.849	1844.1
Jun	547.7	60.1	17.2	580.7	48.6	−4.3	1758.4	3.028	1844.7
Jul	554.9	67.2	18.8	607.0	40.6	−6.7	1751.7	2.886	1565.3
Aug	532.0	72.0	9.5	683.9	64.7	−135.1	1616.6	2.364	1449.5
Sep	577.6	67.8	5.8	651.0	49.7	−49.5	1567.1	2.407	1439.2
Oct	545.1	66.7	5.9	515.7	41.6	60.4	1627.5	3.156	1549.0
Nov	525.0	66.2	7.8	501.4	53.7	43.9	1671.4	3.333	1658.5
Dec	516.0	69.1	4.6	541.3	61.1	−12.7	1658.7	3.064	1669.4

Domestic Auto Inventory Change Seasonally Adjusted (Continued)

	Production +	Canadian Imports +	Mexican Imports +	Sales −	Exports −	Change =	S.A. Level	I/S	NSA Level
1990:									
Jan	342.9	37.0	7.3	623.6	40.7	−277.1	1381.6	2.216	1484.0
Feb	491.0	60.4	8.3	566.7	49.0	−56.0	1325.6	2.339	1466.6
Mar	555.9	67.9	5.4	563.4	53.6	12.2	1337.8	2.375	1478.9
Apr	496.3	55.1	8.8	551.1	50.1	−40.1	1296.8	2.353	1422.1
May	524.9	68.1	8.8e	556.0	49.7	−3.9	1292.9	2.325	1470.5
Jun	565.3	—	8.8e	592.4	—	0.1	1293.0	2.183	1504.6
Jul	—	—	—	—	—	—	—	—	—
Aug	—	—	—	—	—	—	—	—	—
Sep	—	—	—	—	—	—	—	—	—
Oct	—	—	—	—	—	—	—	—	—
Nov	—	—	—	—	—	—	—	—	—
Dec	—	—	—	—	—	—	—	—	—
1991:									
Jan	—	—	—	—	—	—	—	—	—
Feb	—	—	—	—	—	—	—	—	—
Mar	—	—	—	—	—	—	—	—	—
Apr	—	—	—	—	—	—	—	—	—
May	—	—	—	—	—	—	—	—	—
Jun	—	—	—	—	—	—	—	—	—
Jul	—	—	—	—	—	—	—	—	—

148

Appendix 6.2

Advance Monthly Retail Sales, May 1990

Advance Monthly Retail Sales

U.S. Department of Commerce
BUREAU OF THE CENSUS

May 1990

CB-90-111

FOR WIRE TRANSMISSION 8:30 A.M. EDT., Wednesday, June 13, 1990

The Census Bureau of the Department of Commerce announced today that advance estimates of U.S. retail sales for May adjusted for seasonal, holiday, and trading-day differences, but not for price changes, were $146.8 billion, a decrease of 0.7 percent (± 1.1%) from the previous month, but 1.5 percent above May 1989. Total sales in the March through May period were 3.4 percent above the same period a year ago.

Durable goods decreased 1.1 percent (± 2.6%) from the previous month. Building materials decreased 4.2 percent from April and were 6.6 percent below May last year.

Nondurable goods decreased 0.5 percent (± 1.5%) from the previous month but were 3.3 percent above last year. General merchandise decreased 1.0 percent from April but was 3.3 percent above May 1989. Food stores were up 4.6 percent from the previous year.

The Advance Monthly Retail Sales Report for June is scheduled to be released July 13, 1990, at 8:30 a.m.

ESTIMATED MONTHLY RETAIL SALES
January 1988-May 1990
(Data adjusted for seasonal, holiday, and trading-day differences)

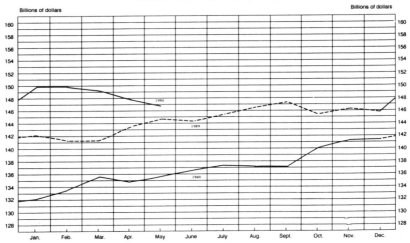

Address inquiries concerning this report to Ronald Piencykoski, Business Division, Bureau of the Census, Washington, D.C. 20233. Telephone (301) 763-5294 or 763-7561.

This report is available the day of issue through the Department of Commerce's online Economic Bulletin Board (N-8-1) (202-377-3870) and through the Census Bureau's online information service-CENDATA. CENDATA is available from Dialog Information Services, INC. (1-800-334-2464) and CompuServe (1-800-848-8199). The CENDATA staff at the Bureau of the Census (301-763-2074) can provide content information and general guidance.

Table 1. Estimated Monthly Retail Sales, by Kind of Business

(Sales in millions of dollars)

SIC code	Kind of business	Not adjusted 1990 May[2] adv.	Not adjusted 1990 Apr. prel.	Not adjusted 1990 Mar. final	Not adjusted 1989 May	Not adjusted 1989 Apr.	Adjusted[1] 1990 May[2] adv.	Adjusted[1] 1990 Apr. prel.	Adjusted[1] 1990 Mar. final	Adjusted[1] 1989 May[r]	Adjusted[1] 1989 Apr.[r]
	Retail trade, total...........	152,944	144,850	148,334	150,259	139,785	146,843	147,931	149,302	144,715	143,744
	Total (excl. auto group)..	118,604	112,459	115,008	114,902	107,196	116,060	116,965	117,818	113,156	111,933
	Durable goods, total........	57,704	53,996	54,970	58,894	53,584	53,169	53,756	54,663	54,049	53,986
52	Building mat., hardware, garden supply, and mobile home dealers..	8,790	8,020	7,456	9,446	8,150	7,319	7,639	7,890	7,834	7,786
521,3	Building mat. and supply stores.	(*)	5,747	5,446	6,512	5,695	(*)	5,679	5,806	5,692	5,684
525	Hardware stores................	(*)	1,079	1,010	1,149	1,042	(*)	1,039	1,062	1,019	984
55 ex. 554	Automotive dealers.............	34,340	32,391	33,326	35,357	32,589	30,783	30,966	31,484	31,559	31,811
551,2,5, 6,7,9	Motor vehicle and miscellaneous automotive dealers.............	31,476	29,666	30,601	32,648	30,079	28,053	28,200	28,706	28,969	29,288
551	Motor vehicle (franchised)....	(*)	25,723	26,738	28,166	26,120	(*)	(NA)	(NA)	(NA)	(NA)
553	Auto and home supply stores....	(*)	2,725	2,725	2,709	2,510	(*)	2,766	2,778	2,590	2,523
57	Furniture, home furnishings, and equipment stores................	7,584	7,189	7,541	7,331	6,908	7,755	7,841	7,804	7,510	7,494
571	Furniture and home furnishings..	(*)	3,989	4,176	4,148	3,956	(*)	4,173	4,214	4,087	4,138
5722,32	Household appliance, radio, and TV stores...............	(*)	2,560	2,676	2,608	2,381	(*)	2,932	2,847	2,780	2,706
5722	Household appliance stores....	(*)	692	698	701	632	(*)	(NA)	(NA)	(NA)	(NA)
	Nondurable goods, total.....	95,240	90,854	93,364	91,365	86,201	93,674	94,175	94,639	90,666	89,758
53	General merchandise group stores..	17,013	15,908	16,189	16,214	15,305	17,079	17,252	17,621	16,538	16,684
531	Dept. stores (ex. leased depts.)	13,741	13,000	13,248	13,056	12,482	13,852	14,024	14,322	13,377	13,538
531	Dept. stores (in. leased depts)	(*)	13,406	13,667	13,445	12,871	(*)	14,415	14,791	13,719	13,915
533	Variety stores.................	(*)	567	544	555	519	(*)	571	584	571	563
539	Misc. general mdse. stores......	(*)	2,341	2,397	2,603	2,304	(*)	2,657	2,715	2,590	2,583
54	Food stores......................	31,468	29,629	30,949	29,784	27,917	30,437	30,743	30,380	29,100	28,752
541	Grocery stores.................	29,590	27,784	29,123	28,083	26,370	28,617	28,881	28,552	27,452	27,130
554	Gasoline service stations.........	10,076	9,783	9,772	10,425	9,636	9,642	9,803	9,992	10,005	9,655
56	Apparel and accessory stores......	7,781	7,606	7,565	7,322	7,027	7,932	7,745	7,937	7,587	7,566
561	Men's and boys' clothing and furnishings stores.........	(*)	741	709	766	736	(*)	770	826	785	791
562,3,8	Women's clothing, specialty stores, furriers..............	(*)	2,721	2,686	2,655	2,545	(*)	2,782	2,824	2,718	2,696
565	Family clothing stores..........	(*)	2,037	2,099	1,917	1,811	(*)	(NA)	(NA)	(NA)	(NA)
566	Shoe stores....................	(*)	1,504	1,477	1,434	1,384	(*)	1,387	1,428	1,420	1,425
58	Eating and drinking places........	15,453	14,902	15,229	14,909	14,382	14,930	15,007	15,168	14,419	14,382
591	Drug and proprietary stores.......	5,392	5,291	5,277	5,056	4,701	5,339	5,410	5,298	5,016	4,938
592	Liquor stores....................	(*)	1,564	1,603	1,686	1,547	(*)	1,704	1,716	1,688	1,674
5961 (pt.)	Mail-order houses (department store merchandise)...............	(*)	353	370	356	339	(*)	(NA)	(NA)	(NA)	(NA)
53,56,57 594	GAF[4].............................	(*)	35,341	36,136	35,718	33,461	(*)	38,426	39,071	36,840	36,942

[4]Advance estimates are not available from the subsample panel for these kinds of business.

NA Not available.   [r] Revised

[1] Data are concurrently adjusted for seasonal variations, holiday, and trading-day differences. Concurrent seasonal adjustment uses all available unadjusted estimates as input to the X-11 program and the factors derived from the program are used in calculating all seasonally adjusted data shown in this publication. Factors and explanatory material are contained in the Monthly Retail Trade Report, BR-90-04.

[2] Advance estimates are based on early reporting by a small subsample of the full survey panel. All other estimates are based on the full sample.

[3] Includes data for leased departments operated within department stores. Data for this line not included in broader kind-of-business totals.

[4] GAF represents stores which specialize in department store types of merchandise.

Note: Totals include data for kinds of business not shown separately.

Table 2. Percent Change in Estimated Monthly Retail Sales, by Kind of Business

(Adjusted for seasonal variations, holiday, and trading-day differences)

SIC code	Kind of business	Percent change					
		May 1990 advance from--		Apr. 1990 preliminary from--		Mar. 1990 through May 1990	
		Apr. 1990 prelim.	May 1989 final	Mar. 1990 final	Apr. 1989 final	Dec. 1989 through Feb. 1990	Mar. 1989 through May 1989
	Retail trade, total....................	-0.7	+1.5	-0.9	+2.9	-0.3	+3.4
	Total (excl. automotive group).....	-0.8	+2.6	-0.7	+4.5	+0.1	+4.6
	Durable goods, total.................	-1.1	-1.6	-1.7	-0.4	-1.4	+0.6
52	Building materials, hardware, garden supply, and mobile home dealers..........	-4.2	-6.6	-3.2	-1.9	-2.6	-0.7
55 ex. 554	Automotive dealers......................	-0.6	-2.5	-1.6	-2.7	-2.0	-1.1
551,2,5, 6,7,9	Motor vehicle and miscellaneous automotive dealers........................	-0.5	-3.2	-1.8	-3.7	-2.2	-2.0
57	Furniture, home furnishings, and equipment stores................................	-1.1	+3.3	+0.5	+4.6	+2.2	+4.5
	Nondurable goods, total..............	-0.5	+3.3	-0.5	+4.9	+0.3	+5.0
53	General merchandise group stores...........	-1.0	+3.3	-2.1	+3.4	-1.6	+4.6
531	Dept. stores (ex. leased dept.).........	-1.2	+3.6	-2.1	+3.6	-1.2	+4.9
531	Dept. stores (in. leased dept.).........	(NA)	(NA)	-2.5	+3.6	(NA)	(NA)
54	Food stores.............................	-1.0	+4.6	+1.2	+6.9	+1.7	+5.9
541	Grocery stores..........................	-0.9	+4.2	+1.2	+6.5	+1.6	+5.6
554	Gasoline service stations...................	-1.6	-3.6	-1.9	+1.5	-2.0	+1.4
56	Apparel and accessory stores..............	+2.4	+4.5	-2.4	+2.4	+2.0	+5.7
58	Eating and drinking places.................	-0.5	+3.5	-1.1	+4.3	+1.4	+4.5
591	Drug and proprietary stores................	-1.3	+6.4	+2.1	+9.6	+0.4	+7.2

Table 3. Estimated Monthly Retail Sales of Group II Companies, by Kind of Business

(Sales in millions of dollars)

SIC code	Kind of business	Not adjusted			Adjusted[1]		
		Apr. 1990 prelim.	Mar. 1990 final	Apr. 1989	Apr. 1990 prelim.	Mar. 1990 final	Apr.ʳ 1989
	Retail trade, total....................	53,769	55,359	50,659	56,370	56,837	53,374
53	General merchandise group stores..........	14,612	14,902	14,036	15,907	16,288	15,354
531	Dept. stores (ex. leased dept.)..........	12,596	12,826	12,044	13,588	13,926	13,049
531	Dept. stores (in. leased dept.)..........	12,987	13,232	12,421	13,980	14,320	13,414
533	Variety stores...........................	445	427	413	455	460	452
539	Miscellaneous general merchandise stores.	1,571	1,649	1,579	(NA)	(NA)	(NA)
54	Food stores..............................	16,559	17,574	15,647	(NA)	(NA)	(NA)
541	Grocery stores...........................	16,313	17,343	15,468	16,975	16,805	15,914
56	Apparel and accessory stores..............	4,187	4,232	3,783	4,232	4,415	4,121
562,3,8	Women's clothing, specialty stores, furriers...............................	1,449	1,460	1,375	1,485	1,526	1,485
566	Shoe stores..............................	989	955	858	903	917	913
591	Drug stores and proprietary stores.........	3,262	3,181	2,763	3,346	3,213	2,952

NA Not available.   ʳ Revised

[1] Data are concurrently adjusted for seasonal variations, holiday, and trading-day differences. Concurrent seasonal adjustment uses all available unadjusted estimates as input to the X-11 program and the factors derived from the program are used in calculating all seasonally adjusted data shown in this publication. Factors and explanatory material are contained in the Monthly Retail Trade Report, BR-90-04.

[2] Includes data for leased departments operated within department stores. Data for this line not included in broader kind-of-business totals.

Note: The Group II component of the sample consists of companies which had 11 or more retail establishments according to the most recent update of multi-establishment files and which were selected with certainty (i.e., their sales size exceeded specified dollar volume cutoffs which vary by kind of business).

U.S. Department of Commerce
BUREAU OF THE CENSUS
Washington, D.C. 20233

Official Business

Penalty for Private Use, $300

POSTAGE AND FEES PAID
U S DEPARTMENT OF COMMERCE

COM 202

_____ First Class Mail

Sample Design and Reliability of Data

The advance sales estimates are based on early reporting of sales by a small subsample of the Bureau's retail survey panel. Because of the early reporting, the advance estimates can differ from the subsequent estimates which are based on monthly reports obtained from the full sample of retail stores. In addition, sampling variability between the sub-sample used for the advance estimates and the full sample can cause a difference.

Percentage differences between advance and full sample preliminary estimates of month-to-month percentage change in seasonally adjusted total retail store sales have ranged from approximately - 0.4 percent to + 1.2 percent with the average of the absolute differences about 0.4 percent for the past 12 months. For individual kind-of-business groups, these differences tend to be higher. Sampling variablility of and revisions to advance-to-preliminary estimates are shown in table 4 below.

Preliminary estimates for April 1990 and final estimates for March 1990 based on the full sample are published later this month in the Monthly Retail Trade Report for April (BR-90-04). The complete report will provide sales estimates in greater detail and will present a description of revisions and the techniques used in developing the estimates.

The margin of sampling error, as used on page 1, indicates a range about the estimate which corresponds to a 90 percent confidence interval. If, for example, the estimate is up .8 percent and the margin of sampling error is 1.2 percentage points above or below the estimate, then the indicated range is - .4 percent to + 2.0 percent. If the range contains 0, it is uncertain whether there was an increase or decrease. The Monthly Retail Trade Report includes explanations of confidence intervals and sampling variability along with additional measures of sampling variability.

Table 4. **Sampling Variability of and Revision to Advance-to-Preliminary Estimate**

| SIC code | Kind of Business | Estimated coefficient of Variation in percent of the | | | | | | Preliminary-to-final percent change minus the Advance-to-preliminary percent change | | | |
| | | Advance-to-preliminary ratio | | Ratio to same month a year ago | Dollar volume sales est. | Ratio of current quarter to prev. quarter | | | | |
		Range[1] From	To	Median	Median	Median	Median	Range[2] From	To	Mean	Aver. of absolute diff.
	Retail trade, total........	0.5	0.6	0.6	0.9	0.8	1.0	-0.4	+1.2	+0.1	0.4
	Total (excl. auto).	0.5	0.7	0.6	0.8	0.7	0.9	-0.3	+0.5	+0.1	0.2
	Durable goods, total..	1.4	2.0	1.6	2.3	1.8	2.2	-0.9	+1.7	-0.1	0.7
52	Building materials, group stores...............	1.1	3.0	1.7	3.8	3.2	3.1	-1.9	+3.1	0.0	0.7
55 ex. 554	Automotive dealers..........	1.6	2.4	2.0	3.2	2.6	3.0	-2.1	+2.9	-0.1	0.9
551,2,5, 6,7,9	Motor vehicle and misc. automotive dealers.......	1.3	2.0	1.6	4.0	2.8	3.3	-2.5	+3.3	-0.1	1.0
57	Furniture, home furn, and equipment stores...........	1.3	3.8	2.1	4.2	3.9	3.1	-1.9	+5.0	+0.5	1.5
	Nondur. stores, total...	0.5	0.7	0.6	1.0	0.7	0.9	-0.2	+0.7	+0.1	0.2
53	General merch. group, total.	0.2	0.9	0.4	0.4	0.4	0.5	-0.9	+1.3	0.0	0.4
531	Dept. stores (ex. leased depts.)..................	0.1	0.3	0.2	0.2	0.2	0.1	-0.5	+1.2	+0.1	0.4
54	Food stores.................	0.8	1.3	1.0	1.7	1.3	1.6	-0.4	+1.5	+0.2	0.4
541	Grocery stores.............	0.2	0.5	0.3	1.8	1.3	1.6	-0.5	+1.3	+0.2	0.4
554	Gasoline service stations...	0.6	1.0	0.9	2.9	2.1	2.7	-1.8	+1.9	0.0	0.7
56	Apparel and acc. stores......	1.1	3.6	1.7	2.5	2.0	1.9	-3.9	+3.8	+0.2	1.4
58	Eating and drinking	0.4	1.9	0.8	2.7	2.3	2.6	-1.3	+1.6	+0.2	0.8
591	Drug and proprietary	0.6	1.8	0.7	2.5	1.9	2.1	-1.7	+2.1	+0.3	0.7

[1] The ranges of sampling variability shown are based on sales estimates unadjusted for seasonal variation, holiday, and trading-day differences for the data months of November 1988 - October 1989.

[2] The ranges shown for the retail trade total are based on sales estimates adjusted for seasonal variations, holiday, and trading-day differences for the 12-month period, May 1989 - April 1990. The ranges for all other totals and kinds of business are based on the 12-month period October 1988 - September 1989.

Note: Coefficients of variation for the ratio of current quarter to current quarter a-year-ago estimates are approximately the same as those for the ratio of current quarter to previous quarter. See appendix B, Reliability of Data, in the Monthly Retail Trade Report for a discussion on the measures of sampling variability.

153

Appendix 6.3

Consumer Credit
Statistical Release

FEDERAL RESERVE statistical release

For immediate release
August 7, 1990

G.19

CONSUMER INSTALLMENT CREDIT

Consumer installment credit outstanding grew $0.5 billion in June, following a $3.7 billion rise in May. The rate of advance, at 0.8 percent, was slightly above that in April but well below the May increase. Outstanding auto loans declined while growth in revolving credit slowed. "Other" credit outstanding rose and mobile home loans fell.

	Net change in amount outstanding (millions of dollars) 1990			Annual rate of growth (percent) 1990		
	Jun p	May r	Apr	Jun p	May r	Apr
CHANGE IN CREDIT, BY TYPE 1/ (seasonally adjusted)						
Total	463	3,650	390	0.8	6.1	0.6
Automobile	-1,584	-5	-1,996	-6.6	0.0	-8.2
Revolving	1,304	3,188	1,702	7.6	18.8	10.1
Mobile home	-85	113	-6	-4.5	6.0	-0.3
Other	827	353	689	4.8	2.1	4.0

	1990				1989-
	Jun	May	Apr	Mar	Jun
TERMS OF CREDIT 2/ (not seasonally adjusted)					
Interest rates					
Commercial banks					
48-mo. new car loan	n.a.	11.82	n.a.	n.a.	n.a.
24-mo. personal loan	n.a.	15.41	n.a.	n.a.	n.a.
120-mo. mobile home loan	n.a.	14.09	n.a.	n.a.	n.a.
Credit card plan	n.a.	18.14	n.a.	n.a.	n.a.
Auto finance companies					
New car loan	12.58	12.23	12.21	12.31	11.96
Used car loan	16.00	16.03	16.02	15.97	16.45
Other terms at auto finance companies					
Maturity (months)					
New car loan	54.8	54.5	54.2	54.3	53.0
Used car loan	46.2	46.1	46.5	46.4	46.5
Loan-to-value ratio (percent)					
New car loan	87	87	87	88	91
Used car loan	95	96	96	95	97
Amount financed (dollars)					
New car loan	12,108	12,064	12,089	12,216	12,065
Used car loan	8,296	8,169	8,105	8,132	7,921

CONSUMER INSTALLMENT CREDIT, BY HOLDER AND TYPE 1/
Millions of dollars

	Jun p 1990	May r 1990	Apr 1990	Mar 1990	Feb 1990	Jun 1989	May 1989
			seasonally adjusted				
Total	724,948	724,485	720,835	720,445	717,869	697,262	695,627
Automobile	287,348	288,931	288,936	290,932	289,629	290,583	290,954
Revolving	208,458	207,153	203,965	202,263	199,927	184,239	182,847
Mobile home	22,731	22,815	22,702	22,708	22,633	23,309	23,505
Other	206,412	205,585	205,232	204,543	205,680	199,130	198,320
			not seasonally adjusted				
Total	723,300	720,045	715,801	713,138	717,062	695,602	691,223
Major holder							
Commercial banks	335,951	339,328	337,576	334,645	339,418	324,967	323,055
Finance companies	138,642	138,384	138,174	137,857	139,115	143,858	142,207
Credit unions	90,482	89,913	89,689	89,556	90,127	89,694	89,235
Savings institutions	52,902	53,301	53,606	54,095	54,771	60,208	61,471
Retailers	37,382	37,347	37,207	37,302	37,904	37,899	38,269
Gasoline companies	4,192	4,024	3,928	3,792	3,803	3,957	3,768
Pools of securitized assets 3/	63,749	57,748	55,621	55,891	51,924	35,019	33,218
Major credit type 4/							
Automobile	287,434	287,140	286,220	286,539	288,036	290,554	289,034
Commercial banks	126,992	127,056	126,483	126,289	127,149	124,596	123,447
Finance companies	78,273	78,927	79,295	79,523	80,227	89,312	88,204
Pools of securitized assets 3/	21,043	20,151	19,406	19,563	18,931	12,699	13,397
Revolving	206,915	204,854	201,783	199,937	200,147	182,839	180,744
Commercial banks	122,142	125,433	124,039	122,024	124,821	115,580	115,018
Retailers	32,884	32,857	32,721	32,794	33,378	33,486	33,868
Gasoline companies	4,192	4,024	3,928	3,792	3,803	3,957	3,768
Pools of securitized assets 3/	36,125	30,913	29,403	29,542	26,204	17,172	14,623
Mobile homes	22,642	22,610	22,484	22,426	22,726	23,218	23,303
Commercial banks	9,294	9,295	9,231	9,142	9,162	9,004	8,974
Finance companies	5,266	5,224	5,168	5,178	5,410	5,659	5,638
Other	206,309	205,441	205,314	204,236	206,153	198,991	198,142
Commercial banks	77,523	77,544	77,823	77,190	78,286	75,787	75,616
Finance companies	55,103	54,233	53,711	53,156	53,478	48,887	48,365
Retailers	4,498	4,490	4,486	4,508	4,526	4,413	4,401
Pools of securitized assets (incl. mobile homes) 3/	6,581	6,684	6,812	6,786	6,789	5,148	5,198

1. The Board's series on amounts of credit covers most short- and intermediate-term credit
extended to individuals that is scheduled to be repaid (or has the option of repayment) in two
or more installments, excluding loans secured by real estate.
2. Interest rates are annual percentage rates as specified by Regulation Z. Commercial
bank data are simple unweighted averages of each bank's "most common" rate charged during
the first calendar week of the month. Finance company data from the subsidiaries of the
three major U.S. automobile manufacturers are volume-weighted averages covering all loans
of each type purchased during the month.
3. Outstanding balances of pools upon which securities have been issued; these balances
are no longer carried on the balance sheets of the loan originator.
4. Type-of-credit totals include estimates for certain holders for which only consumer
credit totals are available.

r = revised.   p = preliminary.

The G.19 Statistical Release is issued around the fifth working day of each month. The exact
date and time may be obtained by calling (202) 452-3206.

Appendix 6.4

Retail Industry Contact List

Company	Contact	Telephone
Allied Stores	Orren Knauer, Dir. of Investor Relations	212-764-2541
Carter Hawley Hale	Harlin Smith, VP of Investor Relations	213-239-6626
Dayton Hudson	Douglas Ewing, Director, Financial Relations	612-370-5500
Federated Stores	Jack Kuresman, Director, Investor Relations	513-579-7780
K-Mart	Mike Gerych	313-643-1040
The May Cos.	Mr. Jan Kniffen, VP & Treasurer	314-342-6403
Montgomery Ward	Joseph Sarnowski or Carol Harms, Treasurer	312-467-3242
J.C. Penney	Ely Akresh, Manager, Investor Relations	212-957-5953
Sears, Roebuck & Co.	John McGrail Mark Kennedy	312-875-0815
F.W. Woolworth & Co.	Roy Garafalo, VP, Investor Relations	212-553-2532

7

Industrial Sector Data

Factory production affects incomes and output (especially in the form of inventories) and may fuel inflation at too full resource utilization (see Chapter 4). So, Washington's statistics mills spend considerable time grinding out data on the status of the business sector of the economy, even though about 54% of its output is used by other businesses and thus is not counted in our final product definition of GNP.

INDUSTRIAL PRODUCTION

Aggregating data on the output of U.S. industries is the responsibility of the Federal Reserve Board. The Fed produces measures of *Industrial Production* (IP) and *Capacity Utilization* each month from 250 other individual data series obtained primarily from private trade associations and internal estimates. The IP data takes two forms—output measures in physical units and data on inputs to the production process from which output is measured. The latter sometimes allows surprising judgmental adjustments to the monthly IP number. The estimation process covers 40 to 45% of the IP index and is based on the historical relationships between production worker hours, kilowatt hours (or a combination of the two), and real output.

Technological advances that allow workers to operate more efficiently and slippages, such as inventory building and increased overseas trade, may cause these historical estimates to go off track. One such example occurred in the summer of 1990 when the IP data failed to correlate closely with the weakening GNP accounts. Layoffs raised productivity at that time as inventories rose. The physical input data that Fed statisticians used to construct IP suggested growth was more robust than the Commerce Department found convincing. Higher productivity was one reason.

IP is subdivided in two ways: by major markets and by industry groups (see Table 7.1). Major markets are comprised of final products (consumer goods, business equipment, and construction supplies), intermediate products, and materials. The industry groups are manufacturing (durable and nondurable goods), mining, and electric and gas utilities. Each is expressed as an index with a base period (currently 1987).

Weights are assigned to the individual industries that comprise IP based on each industry's proportion in the total value-added output of all industries. The overall IP index is built in five-year segments that extend back to 1919 and have been linked together. Each segment has a base period (e.g., 1987 for the period from 1987 to the present, 1982 for the 1982–86 period, and 1977 for the 1977–81 period) and is a Laspeyres quality index (see Chapter 13) which shows both changes in quantities and prices. This construction allows for dynamic adjustments, to the extent that an individual industry grows faster than the total index after the fixed base period, its current proportion will rise.

Changes in IP are expressed as percent changes. See Figure 7.1. The average revision to the percent change in the IP index between its first publication and third publication over the 1972–88 period was 0.27 percentage points (almost the entire gain during periods of slow growth). Nonetheless, the financial markets pay vast attention to IP, in part because it is produced by the Federal Reserve Board (the same

TABLE 7.1
Industrial Production and Capacity Utilization: Summary

Seasonally adjusted

Industrial Production	Index 1987 = 100				Percent change				
	1990 Mar^r	Apr^r	May^r	Jun^p	1990 Mar^r	Apr^r	May^r	Jun^p	Jun 89 to Jun 90
Total Index	108.9	108.7	109.3	109.8	0.4	-0.2	0.6	0.4	1.2
Previous estimates	109.0	109.0	109.7		0.5	0.0	0.6	0.6	
Major market groups:									
Products, total	110.7	110.2	111.2	112.0	0.9	-0.4	0.9	0.7	2.0
Consumer goods	107.5	106.9	107.5	108.2	0.5	-0.5	0.5	0.7	1.8
Business equipment	122.2	121.4	123.4	124.6	1.8	-0.6	1.6	0.9	2.6
Construction supplies	107.3	106.5	106.0	105.5	-0.8	-0.8	-0.5	-0.5	-0.6
Materials	107.1	107.2	107.6	107.8	0.0	0.1	0.3	0.2	0.2
Major industry groups:									
Manufacturing	109.8	109.3	110.2	110.7	0.2	-0.4	0.8	0.5	1.3
Durable	111.9	110.9	112.4	113.0	1.1	-0.9	1.3	0.5	1.1
Nondurable	107.2	107.3	107.4	107.8	-1.0	0.1	0.1	0.4	1.6
Mining	101.1	103.3	102.6	101.0	0.2	2.2	-0.7	-1.5	0.6
Utilities	106.2	106.2	106.9	109.2	2.2	-0.0	0.7	2.1	2.7

Capacity Utilization	Percent of Capacity								Capacity growth
	Average 1967–89	1982 Low	1988–89 High	1980 Jun	1990 Mar^r	Apr^r	May^r	Jun^p	Jun 89 to Jun 90
Total Industry	82.2	71.8	85.0	84.6	83.4	83.0	83.3	83.5	2.6
Manufacturing	81.5	70.0	85.1	84.4	82.9	82.3	82.7	82.9	3.1
Advanced processing	81.1	71.4	83.6	83.2	82.0	81.3	81.9	82.0	3.3
Primary processing	82.3	66.8	89.0	87.0	85.2	84.9	84.9	85.2	2.4
Mining	87.3	80.6	87.2	85.8	87.5	89.6	89.1	87.8	-1.6
Utilities	86.8	76.2	92.3	84.8	84.2	84.1	84.6	86.3	0.9

FIGURE 7.1

Converting an Index into a Monthly Change

Changes in indices from one month to the next are usually expressed as percent changes rather than as movements in index points because the latter are affected by the level of the index in relation to its base period. To compute a percent change from an index, take the point change and divide by the prior index. Multiply the result by 100 to normalize it. As an example, the June IP index was 109.8 and the May index was 109.3. The 0.5 point difference must be divided by 109.3 (0.5 points over 109.3 is 0.004) and then multiplied by 100 (0.004 times 100 is 0.4%) to get the 0.4% rise in IP for June.

---

body that makes monetary policy). Thus, economic analysts are often called on to make specific projections for monthly IP.

The two best estimators of IP are data in the employment report and the Business Week Index. As mentioned in Chapter 4, the percentage change in manufacturing jobs gives an approximation of the change in IP. Jobs must be adjusted, however, for productivity (high at the start of an economic cycle, modest in the middle, and low at the end) and for timing (recall that *The Employment Report*'s survey encompasses the week of the month containing the twelfth, while IP covers the entire month). Thus, this predictor goes awry on occasion. June 1990 serves as an example. During that month, manufacturing jobs fell by 19,000 in the *Employment Report* but IP rose 0.4%. IP was pushed up by increased motor vehicle output late in the month (jobs in this category increased 9,000 and productivity increased). Extremely hot weather pumped up utility output (where productivity gains are large when the industry is operating close to capacity).

THE BUSINESS WEEK INDEX (BW INDEX)

In contrast to the employment report, the BW Index had projected a
larger June IP gain since it rose 1.1% over the same month. This index
is produced by the magazine of the same name and is constructed to
give concurrent evidence on the status of manufacturing. The BW
Index contains 13 components listed in Table 7.2. The components
represent industry either by direct measure (steel, crude oil, and auto
assemblies) or by proxy (electricity output, paperboard, and trucking
and rail shipments). The production series comprise 46% of the index,
while the proxies are another 40% and electricity is 14%.

The differing composition and separate seasonal factors sometimes

TABLE 7.2
Structure of the Business Week Index

Component	Weight	Source
Rail freight traffic	22	Assoc. of American Railroads
Intercity trucking	18	American Trucking Assns.
Machinery production	17	Federal Reserve
Electric power output	14	Edison Electric Institute
Defense & space equipment	8	Federal Reserve
Crude oil refinery runs	6	Am. Petroleum Institute
Raw steel production	4	Am. Iron & Steel Institute
Automobile assemblies	4	Ward's Automotive Reports
Lumber production	3	Western Wood Products Assoc. & Southern Forest Products Assoc.
Paper production	2	American Paper Institute
Paperboard production	1	American Paper Institute
Coal production	1	U.S. Bureau of Mines
Truck assemblies	1	Ward's Automotive Reports

cause divergences between the BW Index and IP. The BW Index's trucking and rail measures are indirect indicators of production that do not appear in the Fed's IP numbers. They sometimes go off track in indicating that an idle economy is still expanding when inventories are being shipped but not sold.

Modeling

Another methodology for estimating IP is in Table 7.3, which demonstrates how raw data are collected and organized in a method that parallels the IP series. It uses a weighted average percent change in the component series to estimate the change in IP. The weights are the

TABLE 7.3
Industrial Production Alternative Proxy: October 1989

			Levels		
Data Series	Number of Days	Weight	Prior Month	This Month	% Change
Raw Steel (thousands of net tons)	21	0.51	264.9	269.0	+1.55
Auto Production (SAAR)	28	1.82	6800	6739	−0.90
Truck Production (SAAR)	28	1.03	3600	3500	−2.78
Paper Production (thousands of tons)	14	0.44	103.9	106.2	+2.21
Paperboard (thousands of tons)	14	0.44	131.3	132.0	+0.53

TABLE 7.3 (Continued)

Data Series	Number of Days	Weight	Levels Prior Month	Levels This Month	% Change
Lumber (millions of feet)	14	1.25	93.8	100.9	+7.57
Bituminous Coal (thousands of net tons)	21	1.58	3954	3843	+6.93
Electric Power (millions of KiloWatt hours)	21	4.17	7792	7750	−0.54
Petroleum Refining (refinery runs per day)	21	2.21	1920	1941	+1.09
Crude Refining (domestic daily output, including condensation)	13	3.46	1079	1058	−1.95
Oil & Gas Extraction (weekly rigs in operation)	23	0.99	145.6	141.2	−3.02
Weighted % Change		**17.9**			**0.47**

proportions in the IP index; on some occasions the data must be judgmentally adjusted for calendar quirks such as a truncated work-week. In this case, the model projected a 0.4% rise for October 1989. This estimate overstated the actual 0.5% decline in IP because the strength came from raw materials that did not translate into produc-tion.

IP is a coincident indicator of economic conditions. That is, it rises when the economy is expanding and flattens at the peak in activity. IP dips only during recessions as shown in Figure 7.2. IP has fallen as little as 5.8% in the eight recessions (peak to trough) in the post-WW II period and as much as 14.8%, with the average decline at 9.8%. As seen in Figure 7.2, IP flattens for a period of mere months prior to recessions.

CAPACITY UTILIZATION

After measuring the change in output, it is necessary to put the data to some use, namely as an indicator of whether the business sector is operating at a pace that is likely to cause the economy to overheat. The Fed's index of *capacity utilization*, defined as output (as measured by IP) divided by overall production capability, is how this is accom-plished (see Figure 7.3). The business sector's sustainable practical capacity is computed first as a cap on total output. *Capacity* is defined as the greatest level of output that a plant can sustain within the framework of a realistic work schedule, taking account of downtime and assuming adequate supplies of raw materials.

There are 74 individual capacity indices that are based on trade association data, surveys, and estimates of the growth of the capital stock. The last allows the Fed's analysts some leeway in the estimates and is a potential error source either when business spending picks up sharply and expands capacity or when capacity constraints make refurbishing of old plants more likely. This is usually the case at business cycle peaks.

FIGURE 7.2 Industrial Production and Capacity Utilization

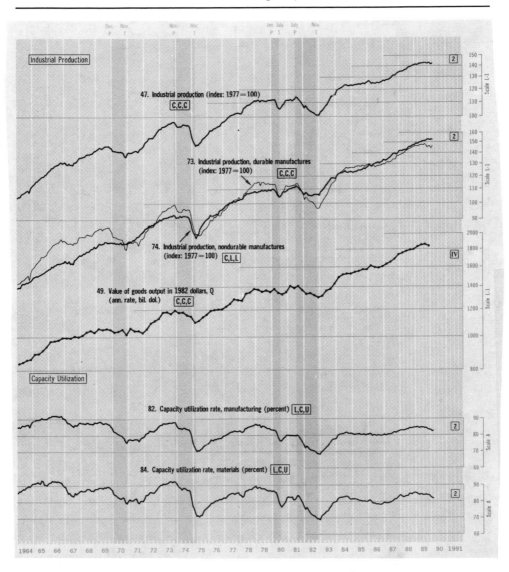

167

FIGURE 7.3 Capacity Utilization

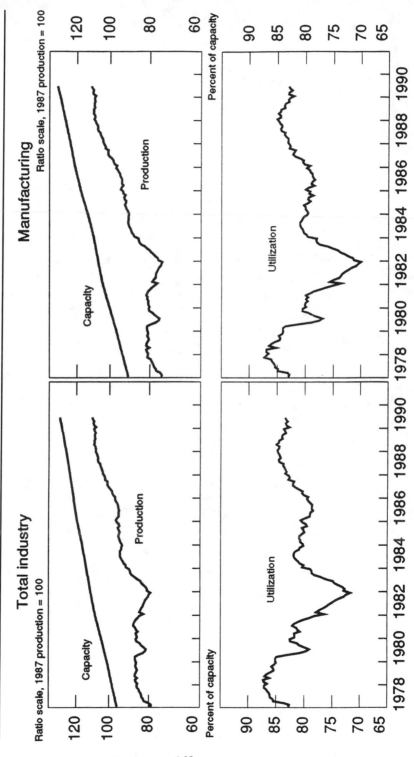

The individual indices are weighted and aggregated in much the same manner as the IP index using value-added proportions. *Capacity Utilization* is published as an overall index for total industry and is also broken down into subcategories for manufacturing (advanced and primary processing), mining, and utilities. Overall rates of capacity utilization in the 84 to 85% range indicate that the economy is close to full resource utilization and often precede inflationary episodes (see Figure 7.4). These levels have been achieved in the mid-1970s and again in 1988–89, just prior to economic peaks. Recent research has indicated that capacity utilization at 81.5% is the "steady state" level that allows inflation to be contained.

Why does inflation erupt at such low capacity utilization levels? Individual industries operate at startlingly varying levels. At an 84%

FIGURE 7.4. Change in Inflation and Capacity Utilization Rates, 1950–88

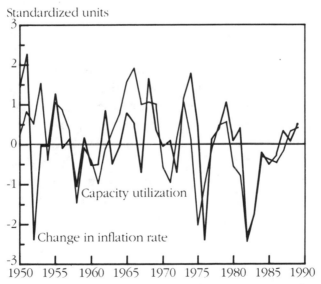

NOTE: Series were standardized to have a mean of zero and a variance of one.
SOURCES: U.S. Department of Labor, Bureau of Labor Statistics, and Board of Governors of the Federal Reserve System.

overall rate, the raw input industries are generally overtaxed. This is seen in the capacity utilization measures for primary metals which were operating at over 100%. These levels sparked overtime wages and additional spending for new factories but could not be sustained.

The *capacity utilization index* also gives proportions of each industry to the total. So, the economic analyst can tell, for instance, that transportation accounts for about 10% of production, equally divided between autos and aircraft. Within the breakdowns, the machinery industry is another important component, accounting for almost 19% of capacity. This industry is also the source of many of the exports from the United States and the source of equipment used in the production process. Thus, a step-up in capacity utilization in machinery may portend more economic growth. A complete listing of source data for IP and capacity utilization is given in Appendix 7.1.

THE NATIONAL ASSOCIATION OF PURCHASING MANAGERS INDEX

The *National Association of Purchasing Managers* (NAPM) surveys 250 industrial purchasing managers who indicate better, the same, or worsening conditions in new orders, production, employment, inventories, and vendor delivery speed; it also asks about prices but these are not part of the index. The survey starts from even each month—that is, the basis of comparison is the prior period so that 50% is used as a base. The NAPM Index is a weighted average of the components (strictly speaking, a *diffusion index*), seasonally adjusted using factors computed by the Commerce Department (see Table 7.4). The financial markets pay close attention to the NAPM Index because it is generally the first indicator released each month. The NAPM Index also has sometimes turned prior to the government's economic reports and thus may provide an early warning signal for moves in the industrial sector.

A well-known rule is that a NAPM Index below 50% signals a

TABLE 7.4
Seasonal Adjustment Factors for NAPM Indexes in 1990

(Prepared by Theodore Torda, Sr. Economist, U.S. Dept. of Commerce, 202/377-2894)

	New Orders	Production	Employment	Supplier Deliveries	Inventories	Prices
January	1.047	1.013	.987	1.017	1.005	1.047
February	1.023	1.039	.975	.994	1.054	1.008
March	1.072	1.020	1.039	1.027	1.033	1.017
April	1.063	1.075	1.064	.998	1.022	1.043
May	.994	.995	1.023	.998	1.059	.999
June	.957	1.002	1.025	.967	1.002	1.021
July	.985	.922	1.016	1.005	.955	.993
August	.980	.969	.974	.988	1.009	.962
September	1.045	1.043	.976	1.003	1.018	.981
October	.970	.999	.994	1.014	.965	.982
November	.952	.970	.981	.988	.923	.975
December	.913	.953	.950	1.012	.956	.972
WEIGHT	.30	.25	.20	.15	.10	(Not part of Purchasing Managers' Index)

Source: NAPM.

171

slowing in economic activity. However, recent research indicates that a better cut-off point is 45% and that the magnitude of the change in the NAPM Index tells little about the magnitude of the move in the economy. This is because the NAPM Index measures only a "feeling," not hard data; because the regions exclude some economically important areas such as California; and because production does not always translate into demand.

Regional Reports

The NAPM is divided into 10 regions, some of which issue their own reports (see Table 7.5). There are also cities within the regions which issue separate reports. As the level of disaggregation grows, however, these reports may be a more useful indicator of local conditions (which are reflective of particular industries or the weather) than of the national economy. Some of the recent reports include indices for Chicago, Milwaukee, Detroit, and Denver.

Financial markets do give attention to the Chicago area's *Purchasing Managers Index* (Chicago PMI). Chicago is considered the industrial heartland and its PMI release also precedes the NAPM index.

TABLE 7.5
Purchasing Managers' Regions

Arizona	Hal Fearon	(602) 752-6276
Austin, TX	Gary Euscher	(512) 250-7580
Buffalo, NY	Rosemary Rusch	(716) 695-3960
Chicago, IL	John Pressley	(312) 390-5119
Cleveland, OH	G. Alan Thayer	(216) 641-8580
Detroit, MI	David Littman	(313) 336-1570
Grand Rapids, MI	Clyde Eckman	(616) 949-6600
Toledo, OH	Alan Flashner	(419) 470-2212
Oregon	Alan Raedels	(503) 645-1118
Rochester, NY	Barry Swanson	(716) 546-8464

FIGURE 7.5   Philadelphia Fed Index (January 1969–September 1990)*

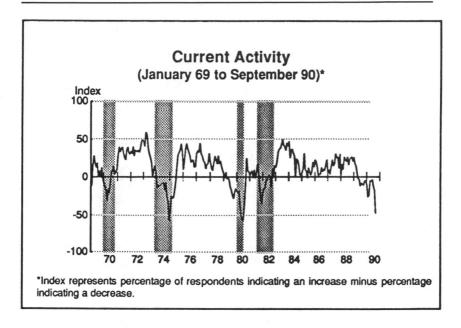

Current Activity
(January 69 to September 90)*

*Index represents percentage of respondents indicating an increase minus percentage indicating a decrease.

The index released to the press is NSA and so must be translated using seasonals provided by the association. In general, the seasonals adjust up the index in the winter and during the summer vacation season. While an argument can be made that the Chicago PMI can be used to adjust one's expectation for the NAPM Index, in recent years, the Chicago PMI has not correlated perfectly with the rest of the country. This is because the Chicago Index includes order backlog (with about a 15% weight), while the NAPM asks about import orders.

THE PHILADELPHIA FED SURVEY

Manufacturing activity is also tested monthly by the Federal Reserve Bank of Philadelphia's Economic Research Department in its *Business Outlook Survey*. This survey also produces a seasonally adjusted diffusion index which represents the percentage of respondents indicating an increase in general business activity minus the percentage indicating a decrease (see Figure 7.5). The survey also compiles data on a broad spectrum of questions meant to parallel the items in the NAPM including orders, shipments, delivery time, inventories, employment, and prices. Since the Philadelphia Survey includes questions about the workweek and capital expenditures but not production, it cannot be used to duplicate the NAPM precisely. But, forecasters also use it to refine their NAPM estimates.

Appendix 7.1

Source and Description Information: Industrial Production and Capacity Utilization

Source: Federal Reserve Board.

Industry structure and series composition of industrial production: classifications, value-added weights, and description of series
(Footnotes follow the table.)

Names of groups and series in them[1]	Classification[2] SIC code (1977)	Classification[2] Market	Value Added[3] 1977 Millions of dollars	Value Added[3] 1977 Proportion	Value Added[3] 1982 Millions of dollars	Value Added[3] 1982 Proportion	Value Added[3] 1987 Millions of dollars	Value Added[3] 1987 Proportion	Type of series[4]	Series sources, units, and beginning date
TOTAL INDEX			704,532	100.00	1,111,204	100.00	1,397,209	100.00		1919
Manufacturing, total			593,321	84.21	830,223	74.71	1,179,848	84.44		1919
Durable			345,942	49.10	470,655	42.36	660,477	47.27		1919
Nondurable			247,379	35.11	359,568	32.36	519,371	37.17		1919
Mining			69,250	9.83	188,056	16.92	110,769	7.93		1919
Utilities			41,961	5.96	92,925	8.36	106,592	7.63		1919
MINING			69,250	9.83	188,056	16.92	110,769	7.93		1919
Metal mining	10		3,504	.50	3,215	.29	4,427	.32		1947
Iron ores	101	Mdn	1,046	.15	770	.07	768	.05	Prod.	Tons, usable iron ore excluding ore containing 5 percent or more manganese, Bureau of Mines, 1954
Nonferrous ores	102-6,8,9		2,458	.35	2,445	.22	3,659	.26		1954
Copper ore	102	Mdn	1,067	.15	672	.06	1,298	.09	Prod.	Tons, recoverable copper, Bur. of Mines. 1954
Lead and zinc ores	103	Mdn	329	.05	201	.02	191	.01	Prod.	Tons, recoverable lead and zinc, Bur. of Mines. 1954
Gold and silver ores	104	Mdn	161	.02	650	.06	1,635	.12	Prod.	Troy ounces, gold and silver ores, Bur. of Mines. 1972
Ferroalloy ores	106	Mdn	256	.04	146	.01	110	.01	Prod.	Lbs., molybdenum ores, Burr. of Mines. 1972
Misc. metal ores[a]	105,8,9	Mdn	645	.09	776	.07	425	.03	Kwh	1967
Anthracite	11	Me	123	.02	176	.02	109	.01	Prod.	Tons, Dept. of Energy. 1954
Bituminous coal	12	Me	11,143	1.58	18,455	1.66	16,904	1.21	Prod.	Tons, includes lignite, Dept. of Energy. 1954
Oil and gas extraction	13		49,825	7.07	159,937	14.39	79,994	5.73		1947
Crude oil and natural gas	131		39,565	5.62	126,035	11.34	67,897	4.86		1954
Crude oil, total			24,349	3.46	83,057	7.47	43,115	3.09	Prod.	Includes condensate. 1954
Texas		Me	9,453	1.34	26,248	2.36	10,636	.76	Prod.	Barrels, Dept. of Energy. 1954
Alaska and California		Me	4,039	.57	23,570	2.12	15,841	1.13	Prod.	Barrels, Dept. of Energy. 1954
Louisiana and other		Me	10,857	1.54	33,239	2.99	16,638	1.19	Prod.	Barrels, Dept. of Energy. 1954
Natural gas		Me	15,216	2.16	42,978	3.87	24,782	1.77	Prod.	Cubic feet, marketed production, Dept. of Energy. 1954
Natural gas liquids	132	Cs	3,286	.47	8,865	.80	4,050	.29		1954
Propane			332	.05	669	.06	279	.02	Prod.	Barrels, at gas processing plant, Dept. of Energy. 1967

Names of groups and series in them	SIC code (1977)	Market	1977 Millions of dollars	1977 Pro-por-tion	1982 Millions of dollars	1982 Pro-por-tion	1987 Millions of dollars	1987 Pro-por-tion	Type of series[4]	Series sources, units, and beginning date
Liquified petroleum..........		Me	2,954	.42	8,196	.74	3,771	.27	Prod.	Barrels, natural gas liquids minus propane at gas processing plants, Dept. of Energy. 1967
Oil and gas well drilling.........	138	Es	6,974	.99	25,037	2.25	8,047	.58	Prod.	Number of rotary rigs running, Hughes Tool Co. 1954
Stone and earth minerals.....	14		4,655	.66	6,273	.56	9,335	.67		1947
Stone, sand, and gravel*.....	141,2,4	Ic	2,556	.36	3,173	.29	5,969	.43	Kwh	Production worker hours for 1954-62. 1954
Chemical & fert. materials*.....	147	Mnt	1,433	.20	2,237	.20	2,014	.14	Prod.	Tons, soda ash, sodium phosphate rock and sulfur, Bureau of Mines. 1972
Misc. stone & earth minerals*.....	145,8,9	Mnn	666	.09	863	.08	1,352	.10	Kwh	Production worker hours for 1954-62. 1972
MANUFACTURING..........			593,321	84.21	830,223	74.71	1,179,848	84.44		1919
Foods...........	20		56,062	7.96	88,415	7.96	122,424	8.76		1947
Meat products.......	201		7,478	1.06	11,002	.99	13,730	.98		1954
Beef..........		Cs	3,043	.43	4,786	.43	4,659	.33	Prod.	lbs., Dept. of Agriculture. 1954
Pork..........		Cs	1,766	.25	3,363	.30	4,298	.31	Prod.	lbs., Dept. of Agriculture. 1954
Poultry..........		Cs	1,429	.20	2,328	.21	4,184	.30	Prod.	lbs., Dept. of Agriculture. 1972
Misc. meats.......		Cs	1,240	.18	525	.05	589	.04	Prod.	lbs., weighted combination of veal, lamb, and lard; Dept. of Agriculture. 1972
Dairy products.........	202	Cs	5,648	.80	8,359	.75	11,891	.85		1954
Butter..........	2021	Cs	75	.01	135	.01	155	.01	Prod.	lbs., Dept. of Agriculture. 1954
Cheese..........	2022	Cs	949	.13	1,777	.16	2,612	.19	Prod.	lbs., Dept. of Agriculture. 1954
Concentrated milk......	2023	Cs	805	.11	1,448	.13	2,382	.17	Prod.	lbs., evaporated, condensed, dry milk, whey, and lactose; Dept. of Agriculture. 1954
Frozen desserts......	2024	Cs	643	.09	910	.09	1,262	.09	Prod.	Gallons, ice cream, ice milk, sherbet, and mellorine type; Dept. of Agriculture. 1954
Milk & misc. dairy products*.....	2026	Cs	3,176	.45	4,089	.37	5,479	.39	Prod.	Gallons, fluid milk, Dept. of Agriculture; estimated 1959-66 with Federal Reserve interpolation. 1954
Canned and frozen food......	203	Cs	7,684	1.09	12,353	1.11	17,850	1.28	Kwh	Production worker hours for 1954-62. 1954
Grain mill products.........	204	Mnn	6,626	.94	10,332	.93	15,229	1.09		1954
Flour..........	2041	Cs	824	.12	1,094	.10	1,326	.09	Prod.	lbs., wheat flour, Bureau of the Census. 1977
Cereal products*.....	2043-5	Cs	2,197	.31	3,612	.32	6,631	.47	Pwh	1954
Corn oil*..........	2046pt	Cs	110	.02	109	.01	341	.02	Prod.	lbs., Census. 1977
Corn syrup and starch*.....	2046pt	Mnn	557	.08	1,048	.09	1,689	.12	Prod.	1954
Pet foods*.........	2047	Cs	1,393	.20	2,281	.20	2,738	.20	Pwh	lbs., shipments, Corn Refiners Assn. 1977
Feeds*..........	2048	Ib	1,545	.22	2,188	.20	2,504	.18	Kwh	1972 / Production worker hours for 1954-62. 1954

| Names of groups and series in them | Classification[2] | | Value Added[3] | | | | | | Type of series[4] | Series sources, units, and beginning date |
	SIC code (1977)	Market	1977 Millions of dollars	1977 Proportion	1982 Millions of dollars	1982 Proportion	1987 Millions of dollars	1987 Proportion		
Bakery products...........	205	Cs	7,073	1.00	10,650	.96	14,630	1.05	Kwh	Production worker hours for 1954-62. 1954
Sugar*..........	2061-3	Mnn	1,147	.16	1,352	.12	1,567	.11	Prod.	Tons, refined, quarterly, Dept. of Agriculture. 1954.
Confectionery*...........	2065-7	Cs	3,004	.43	4,882	.44	4,855	.35	Pwh	Lbs., factory sales of confectionery including chocolate, Census, 1954-76. 1954
Fats and oils..........	207		1,905	.27	2,785	.25	3,252	.23	Prod.	Lbs., crude cottonseed, and soybean oils, cakes and meals; Census. 1972
Vegetable oils*..........	2074-6	Mnn	630	.09	961	.09	1,214	.09	Prod.	1954
Grease and tallow*..........	2077	Mnn	584	.08	562	.05	743	.05	Prod.	Lbs., inedible tallow and grease, Census. 1954
Edible oil products*..........	2079	Cs	691	.10	1,262	.11	1,295	.09	Prod.	Lbs., margarine and baking/frying fats, soybean, salad and cooking oils; Census. 1954
Beverages...........	208	Cs	9,901	1.41	16,683	1.50	22,807	1.63		1954
Beer and ale..........	2082,3	Cs	2,704	.38	4,701	.42	7,419	.53	Prod.	Barrels (31 gals.), Internal Revenue Service. 1954
Wines and brandy..........	2084	Cs	510	.07	997	.09	1,312	.09	Prod.	Wine gallons, taxable withdrawals of still wines effervescent wines, and brandy; IRS. 1954
Liquors...........	2085		1,150	.16	1,459	.13	2,145	.15		1954
Liquor distilling*..........		Mnn	132	.02	182	.02	465	.03	Prod.	Tax gallons, IRS. 1954
Liquor bottling*..........		Cs	1,018	.14	1,277	.11	1,680	.12	Prod.	Wine gallons, bottled-in-bond, IRS. 1954
Soft drinks..........	2086,7	Cs	5,537	.79	9,526	.86	11,931	.85	Kwh	Number of cases for 1954-62, National Soft Drink Assn. 1954
Coffee and misc. foods..........	209	Cs	5,596	.79	10,017	.90	16,613	1.19		1954
Roasted coffee*..........	2095	Cs	988	.14	2,070	.19	2,603	.19	Prod.	Bags (60 kilos) green coffee roasted, George Gordon Patton and Co. 1972
Misc. foods, n.e.c.*..........	2091,2, 7-9	Cs	4,608	.65	7,947	.72	14,010	1.00	Pwh	1972
Tobacco products..........	21		4,334	.62	8,964	.81	14,260	1.02		1947
Cigarettes..........	211	Cs	3,803	.54	8,098	.73	12,967	.93	Prod.	Units, IRS. 1954
Cigars*..........	212	Cs	126	.02	133	.01	106	.01	Prod.	Units, IRS. 1954
Misc. tobacco*..........	213,4	Cs	405	.06	733	.07	1,186	.08	Kwh	Lbs., IRS., 1954-62. 1954
Textile mill products..........	22		16,105	2.29	18,549	1.67	25,705	1.84		Index, production of broadwoven goods, American Textile Manufactures Institute (ATMI). 1954
Fabrics..........	221-4		5,399	.77	5,940	.53	7,371	.53	Prod.	Shipments, lbs., filament fibers from Fiber Economics Bureau. 1954
Cotton and synthetic fabrics..........	221,2	Mnt	4,735	.67	5,126	.46	6,254	.45		
Wool fabrics*..........	223	Mnt	313	.04	349	.03	507	.04	Kwh	Linear yds., wool apparel fabrics (gray), Census, 1954-76. 1954
Narrow fabrics*..........	224	Mnt	351	.05	465	.04	610	.04	Pwh	1972

Names of groups and series in them [1]	Classification [2] SIC code (1977)	Market	Value Added [3] 1977 Millions of dollars	Proportion	1982 Millions of dollars	Proportion	1987 Millions of dollars	Proportion	Type of series [4]	Series sources, units, and beginning date
Knit goods.................	225		3,863	.55	4,985	.45	6,103	.44	Prod.	1954
Hosiery..................	2251,2	Cs	859	.12	1,395	.13	1,729	.12	Prod.	Pairs, weighted combination of total hosiery and pantyhose, National Assn. of Hosiery Manufacturers. 1954
Knit garments.............	2253,4, 7-9	Cs	3,004	.43	3,590	.32	4,374	.31	Kwh	Production-worker hours for 1954-62. 1954
Fabric finishing*..........	226	Mnt	1,417	.20	1,590	.14	2,308	.16	Prod.	Index, production of broadwoven goods by weaving mills, ATMI. 1954
Carpeting.................	227		1,530	.22	1,712	.15	3,181	.23	Prod.	1954
Woven carpets*...........	2271,9	Ch	92	.01	127	.01	248	.02	Prod.	Sq. yds., Carpet and Rug Inst. 1954
Tufted carpeting*........	2272	Ch	1,438	.20	1,585	.14	2,933	.21	Prod.	Sq. yds., Carpet and Rug Inst. Production worker hours for 1954-62. Kilowatt hours for 1963-66. 1954
Yarn and misc. textiles....	228,9		3,896	.55	4,322	.39	6,742	.48	Prod.	1954
Yarn and thread*.........	228		2,255	.32	2,318	.21	3,822	.27	Prod.	Tons, consumption of cotton and synthetic fibers 1954
Misc. textiles*...........	229	Mnt	1,641	.23	2,004	.18	2,920	.21	Kwh	Production worker hours for 1954-62. 1954
Apparel products...........	23		19,671	2.79	26,060	2.34	32,911	2.36		1947
Men's outerwear*..........	231,2		6,509	.92	8,304	.75	10,411	.75		1954
Men's suits and coats*...	231	Cs	1,574	.22	1,683	.15	1,945	.14	Pwh	Units cut, Census, 1954-76. 1954
Men's furnishings*.........	232	Cs	4,935	.70	6,621	.60	8,466	.61	Pwh	Units cut; work pants, dungarees, waistband overalls, jeans, separate trousers, & shirts; Census, 1954-76. 1954
Women's outerwear*.........	233		6,430	.91	8,576	.77	9,918	.71		1954
Women's suits and coats*..	2331,7,9	Cs	4,196	.60	6,163	.55	6,752	.48	Pwh	Units cut; blouses, skirts, coats, and suits; Census, 1954-76. 1954
Women's dresses*..........	2335	Cs	2,234	.32	2,413	.22	3,166	.23	Pwh	Units cut; women's and misses' dresses; Census, 1954-76. 1954
Misc. apparel and allied goods*....	234-9		6,732	.96	9,180	.83	12,581	.90		1954
Children's & misc. garments*.....	234-8	Cs	3,273	.46	4,682	.42	5,691	.41	Kwh	Kilowatt-production-worker hours 1963-66; production worker hours for 1954-62. 1954
Misc. fabricated textile products*	239	Ch	3,459	.49	4,498	.49	6,890	.49	Pwh	Kilowatt-production worker hours for 1963-66; production worker hours for 1954-62. 1954

Names of groups and series in them[1]	Classification[2] SIC code (1977)	Classification[2] Market	Value Added[3] 1977 Millions of dollars	1977 Proportion	1982 Millions of dollars	1982 Proportion	1987 Millions of dollars	1987 Proportion	Type of series[4]	Series sources, units, and beginning date
Lumber and products...........	24		16,223	2.30	15,617	1.41	27,941	2.00		1947
Logging and lumber*..........	241,2	Mdn	7,394	1.05	6,250	.56	11,772	.84		1954
Logging*..................	241	Ic	2,419	.34	2,502	.23	4,149	.30	Pwh	Board feet, National Forest Products Assn. 1972
Lumber*...................	2421,9	Ic	4,562	.65	3,303	.30	6,770	.48	Prod.	Board feet, National Forest Products Assn. 1972
Flooring*.................	2426	Ic	413	.06	445	.04	852	.06	Prod.	1954
Lumber products...............	243-5,9		8,829	1.25	9,367	.84	16,169	1.16		1954
Millwork and plywood.........	243		4,700	.67	4,460	.40	9,495	.68		1954
Millwork and prefab.products*.	2431,4,9	Ic	2,696	.38	3,187	.29	6,834	.49	Pwh	Units of exterior frames, doors and window sash; National Woodwork Manufacturers Assn., Inc., 1954-1966. 1954
Plywood*..................	2435,6	Ic	2,004	.28	1,273	.11	2,661	.19	Prod.	Sq. Ft., structural panels, American Plywood Assn. 1954
Wood containers*.............	244	Mnc	540	.08	703	.06	871	.06	Kwh	Production worker hours for 1954-62. 1954
Manufactured homes...........	245	Es	1,789	.25	1,981	.18	2,444	.17	Prod.	Units, Manufactured Housing Inst. 1954
Misc. wood products*.........	249	Mdn	1,800	.26	2,223	.20	3,358	.24	K-Pwh	Production worker hours for 1954-62. 1954
Furniture and fixtures........	25		8,922	1.27	12,829	1.15	20,207	1.45		1947
Household furniture*.........	251	Ch	5,213	.74	6,455	.58	9,473	.68	Kwh	Production worker hours for 1954-62. 1954
Off. furniture, fixtures,and misc.	252,4,9	Ebo	3,294	.47	5,795	.52	9,888	.71	Kwh	Production worker hours for 1954-62. 1954
Public building furniture*...	253	Ic	415	.06	579	.05	847	.06	Pwh	1954
Paper and products............	26		22,171	3.15	33,376	3.00	50,022	3.58		1947
Pulp and paper*..............	261-3		9,394	1.33	13,808	1.24	22,874	1.64		1954
Wood pulp*................	261	Mnt	3,131	.44	1,114	.10	2,246	.16	Prod.	Tons, American Paper Institute (API); Census for 1954-81. 1954
Paper*...................	262	Mnt	3,132	.44	8,954	.81	13,626	.98	Prod.	Tons, API; Census for 1954-81. 1954
Paperboard................	263	Mnt	3,131	.44	3,740	.34	7,002	.50	Prod.	Tons, API; Census for 1954-81. 1954
Converted paper products.....	264		7,263	1.03	12,014	1.08	16,951	1.21		1954
Paper coating*.............	2641	Mnt	1,507	.21	2,331	.21	3,317	.24	Prod.	Tons, shipments, coated printing and converting, paper, API; Census for 1954-81. 1954
Paper business supplies*.....	2642-6,8,9	Ib	3,562	.51	5,342	.48	7,366	.53	Prod.	Tons; free sheet, cotton, and thin paper, API; Census 1954-81. 1954
Sanitary paper products*.....	2647	Cs	2,194	.31	4,341	.39	6,268	.45	Prod.	Tons, tissue paper, API; Census 1954-81. 1954
Paperboard containers........	265	Mnc	5,296	.75	7,396	.67	9,867	.71	Prod.	Sq. ft., shipments of corrugated and solid fiber shipping containers, Fiber Box Assn. 1954
Building paper and board*....	266	Ic	218	.03	158	.01	330	.02	Pwh	Tons, construction paper and board, Census, 1954-76. 1954

Names of groups and series in them[1]	Classification[2] SIC code (1977)	Classification[2] Mar-ket[4]	Value Added[3] 1977 Millions of dollars	Value Added[3] 1977 Pro-por-tion	Value Added[3] 1982 Millions of dollars	Value Added[3] 1982 Pro-por-tion	Value Added[3] 1987 Millions of dollars	Value Added[3] 1987 Pro-por-tion	Type of series[4]	Series sources, units, and beginning date
Printing and publishing............	27		31,979	4.54	54,423	4.90	88,969	6.37		1947
Newspapers.......................	271		9,519	1.35	15,275	1.37	24,268	1.74		Tons; newsprint consumption series separated by Federal Reserve into circulation and advertising, American Newspaper Publishers Assn. 1954
Newspaper circulation*............		Cs	2,332	.33	3,559	.32	5,072	.36	Prod.	Federal Reserve estimates based on Newspaper Advertising Bureau annual circulation data. 1954
Newspaper advertising*............		Ib	7,187	1.02	11,716	1.05	19,196	1.37	Prod.	Index derived by deducting circulation series from newsprint consumption series. 1954
Periodicals, books, and cards.....	272,3,7	Cs	8,710	1.24	14,981	1.35	24,233	1.73	Kwh	Production worker hours for 1954-62. 1954
Job printing.....................	274-6,8,9	Ib	13,750	1.95	24,167	2.17	40,468	2.90	Kwh	Production worker hours for 1954-62. 1954
Chemicals and products............	28		56,721	8.05	75,722	6.81	120,191	8.60		1947
Indus.chemicals & synthetic mat...	281,2,6		27,205	3.86	30,571	2.75	50,468	3.61		1954
Basic chemicals..................	281		6,487	.92	8,828	.79	11,087	.79		1954
Alkalies and chlorine............	2812	Mnt	823	.12	729	.07	720	.05	Prod.	Tons; sodium hydroxide and chlorine gas (liquid), Census. 1972
Industrial gases.................	2813	Mnt	733	.10	1,055	.09	1,601	.11	Prod.	Cu. ft., hydrogen, oxygen, acetylene, argon, nitrogen, and carbon dioxide; Census. 1972
Inorganic pigments...............	2816	Mnt	568	.08	723	.06	1,410	.10	Prod.	Tons, chrome colors and titanium dioxide, Census. 1972
Inorganic chemicals n.e.c........	2819		4,363	.62	6,321	.57	7,356	.53		1954
Acids and other chemicals.......			2,808	.40	3,778	.34	4,400	.31		1954
Acids, phosphates, & sulf.*		Mnt	702	.10	1,027	.09	1,200	.09	Prod.	Tons, sulfuric acid, hydrochloric acid, aluminum sulfate, sodium phosphate tripoly, phosphorus, hydrofluoric acid, and calcium phosphate; Census. 1972
Other inorganic chemicals*.		Mnt	2,106	.30	2,751	.25	3,200	.23	Prod.	Tons, calcium carbide, hydrogen peroxide, sodium chlorate, sodium metal, sodium silicate, and potassium pyrophosphate; Census. 1972
Nuclear manufacturing*...........			1,555	.22	2,543	.23	2,956	.21		1954
Nuclear manuf., defense*.		Ed	855	.12	1,526	.14	1,772	.13	Prod.	Production contractor employees, Dept. of Energy. 1954
Nuclear materials*...............		Me	700	.10	1,017	.10	1,184	.08	Prod.	Use of electricity mainly for nuclear materials and reactors, Dept. of Energy. 1967

Names of groups and series in them[1]	Classification[2] SIC code (1977)	Classification[2] Market	Value Added[3] 1977 Millions of dollars	Value Added[3] 1977 Proportion	Value Added[3] 1982 Millions of dollars	Value Added[3] 1982 Proportion	Value Added[3] 1987 Millions of dollars	Value Added[3] 1987 Proportion	Type of series[4]	Series sources, units, and beginning date
Synthetic materials..........	282		7,843	1.11	9,402	.85	17,840	1.28	Prod.	1954
Plastics materials..........	2821	Mnt	4,143	.59	4,746	.43	10,876	.78	Prod.	Lbs., thermosetting and thermoplastic resins, Society of the Plastics Industry, Inc.; U.S. Tariff Comm. 1954-70. 1954
Synthetic rubber..........	2822	Mnt	569	.08	909	.08	1,261	.09	Prod.	Tons, Rubber Manufacturers Assn. 1954
Synthetic fibers..........	2823,4	Mnt	3,131	.44	3,747	.34	5,704	.41	Prod.	Lbs.; noncellulosic, rayon, and acetate fibers, Textile Economics Bureau, Textile Organon. 1954
Industrial organic chemicals......	286	Mnt	12,875	1.83	12,341	1.11	21,540	1.54	Pwh	1972
Chemical products..........	283-5,9		25,708	3.65	40,054	3.60	63,407	4.54		1954
Drugs and medicines..........	283	Cs	9,940	1.41	16,981	1.53	28,062	2.01	Kwh	Production worker hours for 1954-62. 1954
Soap and toiletries..........	284	Cs	9,407	1.34	14,245	1.28	21,394	1.53	Kwh	Two series before 1967. 1954
Paints..........	285		2,822	.40	3,953	.36	5,747	.41		1954
Construction paints*		Ic	1,520	.22	2,182	.20	3,254	.23	Prod.	Gallons, trade sales products, Census. 1954
Industrial paints*..........		Mdn	1,302	.18	1,771	.16	2,493	.18	Prod.	Gallons, industrial product finishes and special coatings, Census. 1954
Misc. chemical products*..........	289	Ib	3,539	.50	4,875	.44	8,204	.59	K-Pwh	1972
Agricultural chemicals..........	287		3,808	.54	5,097	.46	6,314	.45		1954
Fertilizer materials*	2873,4,5	Mnt	2,509	.36	2,148	.19	2,461	.18	Prod.	Tons, synthetic anhydrous ammonia, ammonia nitrate, ammonium sulfate, nitrogen solutions, nitric acid, phosphoric acid, and phosphatic fertilizer materials; Census. 1967
Agricultural chemicals, n.e.c.*....	2879	Ib	1,299	.18	2,949	.26	3,852	.28	Kwh	Production worker hours for 1954-62. 1954
Petroleum products..........	29		16,877	2.40	22,068	1.99	18,434	1.32		1947
Petroleum refining & misc. prods..	291,9		15,605	2.21	20,325	1.83	15,568	1.11		Barrels for products listed at refineries, Dept. of Energy. 1954
Automotive gasoline..........		Cs	6,792	.96	9,453	.85	7,230	.52	Prod.	1954
Distillate fuel oil..........		Cs	3,053	.43	3,764	.34	2,641	.19	Prod.	1954
Residual fuel oil..........		Me	1,087	.15	1,190	.11	668	.05	Prod.	1954
Aviation fuel & kerosene..........		Ib	1,265	.18	1,748	.16	1,406	.10	Prod.	1954
Misc. petroleum products..........		Ib	3,408	.48	4,170	.38	3,623	.26	Prod.	1954
Refinery fuel, n.e.c.*		Me	627	.09	864	.08	654	.05	Prod.	Liquefied refinery gases (including LRG propane) for fuel use, still gas for fuel, and petroleum coke. 1967

Names of groups and series in them[1]	SIC code (1977)[2]	Market[2]	Value Added[3] 1977 Millions of dollars	1977 Proportion	1982 Millions of dollars	1982 Proportion	1987 Millions of dollars	1987 Proportion	Type of series[4]	Series sources, units, and beginning date
Refinery nonfuel materials*		Mnt	1,837	.26	1,862	.17	1,278	.09	Prod.	Ethane, liquified refinery gases (including LRG propane) for chemical use, special naphthas, petrochemical feedstocks, wax, misc. products at refineries. 1967
Refinery products, n.e.c.*		Ib	944	.13	1,444	.13	1,691	.12	Prod.	Asphalt, road oil, and lubricants. 1967
Paving & roofing materials*	295	Ic	1,272	.18	1,743	.16	2,866	.21	Kwh	Sq. ft., Census, 1954-71. 1954
Rubber and plastics products	30		19,740	2.80	27,218	2.45	42,223	3.02		1947
Tires*	301	Ca	4,348	.62	4,660	.42	5,559	.40	Prod.	1954
Replace. tires, consumer*			1,806	.26	2,280	.21	2,475	.18	Prod.	Units, passenger car tires (radial and other); Manufacturers Assn. (RMA). 1954
Replace. tires, business*	301	Ib	1,160	.16	1,505	.14	1,813	.13	Prod.	Units, truck and bus tires (radial and other), tractor implement, industrial and utility; RMA. 1967
Original equipment tires, consumer*		Mdc	885	.13	595	.05	860	.06	Prod.	Units, passenger car tires RMA. 1954
Original equipment tires, business*		Mde	497	.07	280	.03	411	.03	Prod.	Units, truck and bus tires (radial and other); tractor implement, industrial, and utility RMA. 1967
Other rubber products	302-4,6	Cs	3,622	.51	4,623	.42	6,197	.44	Prod.	1954; Pairs, Census; Production worker hours for 1954-77. 1954
Rubber footwear*	302	Cs	272	.04	360	.03	325	.02	Prod.	
Misc. rubber products*	303,4,6	Mdn	3,350	.48	4,263	.38	5,872	.42	Kwh	Production worker hours 1954-62. 1954
Plastics products, n.e.c.*	307		11,770	1.67	17,935	1.61	30,467	2.18		1954
Plastics shapes and parts*			10,381	1.47	15,862	1.43	26,991	1.93		1954
Construction plastics*		Ic	1,459	.21	1,625	.15	3,118	.22	Kwh	1967
Misc. plastics mat*		Mdn	8,922	1.27	14,237	1.28	23,873	1.71	Kwh	1967.
Plastics containers*		Mnc	1,389	.20	2,073	.19	3,476	.25	Est.	Federal Reserve estimates; Census 1954-83. 1954
Leather and products*	31	Mnn	3,719	.53	4,773	.43	4,232	.30	Kwh	1947
Leather and belting*	311		535	.08	580	.05	743	.05	Kwh	Number of hides, Tanners Council of America, 1954-66. 1954
Personal leather goods	313,5-7,9	Cs	1,114	.16	1,384	.12	1,384	.10	Pwh	1954
Shoes*	314	Cs	2,070	.29	2,809	.25	2,105	.15	Prod.	Pairs, shoes and slippers, Census. 1954

183

| Names of groups and series in them | Classification[2] | | Value Added[3] | | | | | | Type of series[4] | Series sources, units, and beginning date |
	SIC code (1977)	Market	1977 Millions of dollars	Proportion	1982 Millions of dollars	Proportion	1987 Millions of dollars	Proportion		
Stone, clay, and glass products..	32		19,130	2.72	23,533	2.12	34,434	2.46		1947
Flat glass and products*	321,3	Ic	1,891	.27	2,330	.21	4,456	.32	Pwh	1954
Pressed and blown glass*	322		3,592	.51	4,724	.43	4,958	.35		1954
Glass containers	3221	Mnc	2,139	.30	2,739	.25	2,610	.19	Prod.	Gross, Census. 1954
Pressed and blown glass, n.e.c.*	3229		1,453	.21	1,985	.18	2,348	.17		1954
Consumer glassware		Ch	479	.07	293	.03	791	.06	Kwh	Doz. tumblers pressed and blown, American Glassware Assn., 1954-76. 1954
Misc. glassware*		Mdn	974	.14	1,692	.15	1,557	.11	Kwh	Production worker hours for 1954-62. 1954
Cement	324	Mdn	1,672	.24	1,816	.16	2,283	.16	Prod.	Barrels (376 lbs.), Bureau of Mines. 1954
Structural clay products	325		1,058	.15	995	.09	1,727	.12		1954
Brick	3251	Ic	468	.07	339	.03	766	.05	Prod.	Units, building or common and face brick, Census. 1954
Clay, firebrick, pipe, and tile*	3253,5,9		590	.08	656	.06	961	.07		1954
Clay sewer pipe*	3259	Ic	126	.02	78	.01	98	.01	Prod.	Vitrified clay sewer pipe, Census. 1972
Clay tile*	3253,5	Ic	464	.07	578	.05	863	.06	Prod.	Clay floor and wall tile, including quarry tile; glazed wall tile; Census. 1972
Concrete and misc. earth mfrs.	326-9		10,917	1.55	13,668	1.23	21,010	1.50		1954
Pottery products*	326		894	.13	1,174	.11	1,621	.12	Kwh	1954
Construction pottery*	3261,4	Ic	531	.08	664	.06	968	.07	Pwh	Production worker hours for 1954-62. 1954
Consumer pottery*	3262,3,9	Ch	363	.05	510	.05	653	.05	Kwh	Production worker hours for 1954-62. 1954
Concrete & plaster products*	327	Ic	5,391	.77	6,903	.62	11,660	.83	Prod.	Production worker hours for 1954-62. 1954
Misc.stone and earth mfrs*	328,9	Mdn	4,632	.66	5,591	.50	7,729	.55	Kwh	Production worker hours for 1954-62. 1954
Primary metals	33		37,568	5.33	30,333	2.73	46,422	3.32		1947
Iron and steel	331,2		24,555	3.49	17,124	1.54	27,193	1.95		1947
Basic steel and mill products	331		18,318	2.60	11,763	1.06	20,987	1.50		1954
Pig iron and steel			7,801	1.11	5,582	.50	5,115	.37		1954
Raw steel		Mdn	2,967	.42	2,962	.27	2,811	.20	Prod.	Tons, American Iron and Steel Inst. (AISI) 1954
		Mdn	3,619	.51	1,343	.12	1,494	.11	Prod.	Tons, weighted combination of carbon, alloy, and stainless; AISI. 1954
Coke and products*		Me	1,215	.17	1,277	.11	810	.06	Prod.	Tons, coke, quarterly, Dept. of Energy. 1954
Steel mill products			10,517	1.49	6,181	.56	15,872	1.14		AISI shipments data in tons, inventory data from Census Bureau. 1954
Consumer durable steel		Mdc	2,682	.38	1,576	.14	4,047	.29	Prod.	Tons, automotive, appliances, utensils, and cutlery; AISI. 1954
Equipment steel		Mds	2,556	.36	1,502	.14	3,857	.28	Prod.	Tons, AISI. 1954[5]
Construction steel		Ic	1,314	.19	772	.07	1,982	.14	Prod.	Tons, construction including maintenance and contractors' products, AISI. 1954

| Names of groups and series in them | Classification[2] | | Value Added[3] | | | | | | Type of series[4] | Series sources, units, and beginning date |
	SIC code (1977)	Market	1977 Millions of dollars	1977 Proportion	1982 Millions of dollars	1982 Proportion	1987 Millions of dollars	1987 Proportion		
Can and closure steel.........		Mdn	694	.10	408	.04	1,048	.08	Prod.	Tons, AISI. 1954
Misc. steel..............		Mdn	3,271	.46	1,923	.17	4,938	.35	Prod.	Tons, all other AISI classifications, incl. warehouses and exports, AISI. 1954
Iron and steel foundries........	332	Mdn	6,237	.89	5,361	.48	6,205	.44	Prod.	Tons; castings of gray ductile iron, and malleable iron, steel; Census. 1954
Nonferrous metals.............	333-6,9		13,013	1.85	13,209	1.19	19,229	1.38		1947
Primary nonferrous metals.....	333		3,619	.51	2,311	.21	3,128	.22		1954
Copper...................	3331	Mdn	904	.13	440	.04	443	.03	Prod.	1954
Copper smelting*..........		Mdn	372	.05	204	.02	205	.02	Prod.	Tons, American Bureau of Metal Statistics. 1954
Copper refining*..........		Mdn	532	.08	236	.02	238	.02	Prod.	Tons, American Bureau of Metal Statistics. 1954
Aluminum.................	3334	Mdn	1,981	.28	1,134	.10	1,903	.14	Prod.	Tons, primary aluminum ingots, Aluminum Assn. 1954
Misc. nonferrous metals*.....	3332,3,9	Mdn	734	.10	737	.07	782	.06	Prod.	Lead and primary slab zinc refining, Amer. Bur. of Metals Statistics. 1954
Secondary nonferrous metals.....	334	Mdn	769	.11	620	.06	945	.07	Prod.	Tons; aluminum alloys and brass ingot at secondary smelters and secondary lead, Bur. of Mines. 1954
Nonferrous products.........	335,6		7,862	1.12	9,280	.84	13,366	.96		1954
Nonferrous mill products......	335		5,902	.84	6,822	.61	10,151	.73		1954
Copper mill products.........	3351	Mdn	974	.14	958	.09	1,556	.11	Prod.	Tons, refined copper consumption by U.S. fabricators, Amer. Bur.of Metal Statistics,1954
Aluminum mill products......	3353-5	Ic	2,242	.32	2,044	.18	3,261	.23	Prod.	lbs.; net shipments, Census. 1954
Construction aluminum........			630	.09	859	.08	1,345	.10	Prod.	Extruded shapes. 1967
Misc. aluminum materials*.....		Mdn	1,612	.23	1,185	.11	1,916	.14	Prod.	Aluminum mill products other than extruded shapes. 1967
Misc. nonferrous mill prods.*	3356,7	Mdn	2,686	.38	3,820	.34	5,334	.38	Pwh	1972
Nonferrous foundries...........	336	Mdn	1,960	.28	2,458	.22	3,215	.23	Prod.	Lbs., shipments for sale and own use, Census. 1954
Misc. primary metals*.........	339	Mdn	763	.11	998	.09	1,790	.13	Kwh	Tons, ferrous and nonferrous forgings, Forgings Industry Assn. 1954-66. 1954
Fabricated metal products.........	34	Mdn	45,511	6.46	58,930	5.30	75,137	5.38		1947
Metal containers...............	341	Mdn	3,644	.52	4,444	.40	4,034	.29		1954
Metal cans*................	3411	Mnc	3,254	.46	4,072	.37	3,628	.26	Kwh	Tons, shipments of metal cans for 1954-62, Census. 1954
Metal barrels*...............	3412	Mnc	390	.06	372	.03	406	.03	Pwh	1954

Names of groups and series in them	Classification[2] SIC code (1977)	Classification[2] Mar-ket	Value Added[3] 1977 Millions of dollars	Value Added[3] 1977 Pro-por-tion	Value Added[3] 1982 Millions of dollars	Value Added[3] 1982 Pro-por-tion	Value Added[3] 1987 Millions of dollars	Value Added[3] 1987 Pro-por-tion	Type of series[4]	Series sources, units, and beginning date
Hardware, tools, and cutlery......	342		5,177	.73	6,041	.54	8,040	.58		1954
Cutlery*..................	3421	Ch	492	.07	684	.06	803	.06	Pwh	1954
Hardware and tools*.........	3423,5,9	Mdc	4,685	.66	5,357	.48	7,237	.52	Kwh	Production worker hours for 1954-62. 1954
Plumbing and heating products*...	343	Ic	1,573	.22	2,023	.18	2,769	.20	Kwh	Units; shipments of oil burners, warm air furnaces, and heating stoves; Census, 1954-71. 1954
Structural metal products........	344		11,785	1.67	15,467	1.39	18,780	1.34		1954
Structural metal, n.e.c.*.......	3441,2,4,6,8,9	Ic	7,710	1.09	11,331	1.02	15,385	1.10	Pwh	Kilowatt hours for 1963-66. Production worker hours for 1954-62. 1954
Boiler shop products*..........	3443	Ebn	4,075	.58	4,136	.37	3,395	.24	Pwh	1954
Other fabricated metal products*..	345-9		23,332	3.31	30,955	2.79	41,514	2.97		1954
Fasteners, stampings, etc........	345-7		13,740	1.95	15,915	1.43	22,800	1.63		1967
Bolts and fasteners*..........	345	Mdn	2,864	.41	3,309	.30	4,749	.34	Kwh	Production worker hours for 1954-62. 1954
Metal stampings*..........	346	Mdc	8,913	1.27	9,710	.87	13,332	.95	Kwh	Kilowatt production-worker hours 1963-66; production worker hours, 1954-62. 1954
Metal services, wire prod*.......	347	Mdn	1,963	.28	2,896	.26	4,719	.34	Kwh	Production worker hours, 1954-62. 1972
Ordnance*..................	348	Ed	1,737	.25	3,442	.31	5,340	.38	Pwh	1972
Fabricated metal prods., n.e.c.*	349		7,855	1.11	11,598	1.04	13,374	.96	Pwh	1954
Valves, pipes, & fittings*.......	3494,8	Mde	4,273	.61	6,662	.60	6,351	.45	Pwh	Kilowatt hours for 1963-66. Production worker hours from 1954-62. 1954
Misc. metal products*..........	3493,5-7,9	Ib	3,582	.51	4,936	.44	7,023	.50	Pwh	1954
Nonelectrical machinery........	35		67,222	9.54	102,270	9.20	119,499	8.55	Pwh	1947
Engines and turbines..........	351		4,960	.70	6,070	.55	7,011	.50		1954
Turbines*..................	3511	Ebn	1,553	.22	2,153	.19	1,967	.14	Pwh	1954
Internal combustion engines*.....	3519	Mde	3,407	.48	3,917	.35	5,044	.36	Pwh	1954
Farm and garden equipment......	352	Ebn	5,490	.78	6,146	.55	5,624	.40	K-Pwh	1977

186

Names of groups and series in them[1]	Classification[2] SIC code (1977)	Classification[2] Mar-ket	Value Added[3] 1977 Millions of dollars	Value Added[3] 1977 Pro-por-tion	Value Added[3] 1982 Millions of dollars	Value Added[3] 1982 Pro-por-tion	Value Added[3] 1987 Millions of dollars	Value Added[3] 1987 Pro-por-tion	Type of series[4]	Series sources, units, and beginning date
Construction and allied equipment	353		11,835	1.68	16,454	1.48	15,512	1.11		1954
Construction & mining equip*	3531-3	Ebn	9,200	1.31	13,137	1.18	11,675	.84	Kwh	1977
Materials handling mach.*	3534-7	Ebn	2,635	.37	3,317	.30	3,837	.27	Pwh	1954
Metalworking machinery	354	Ebn	8,747	1.24	11,284	1.02	13,006	.93	Kwh	Production worker hours for 1954-62. 1954
Special industry machinery	355	Ebn	5,271	.75	7,416	.67	9,590	.69	Pwh	Kilowatt hours for 1963-66. Production worker hours for 1954-62. 1954
General industrial machinery	356		9,673	1.37	13,587	1.22	12,173	.87		1954
Gen. industrial equip.*	3561,3-5, 7,9	Ebn	6,388	.91	9,573	.86	7,225	.52	Kwh	Production worker hours for 1954-62. 1954
Bearings and gears*	3562,6,8	Mde	3,285	.47	4,014	.36	4,948	.35	Pwh	1954
Office & computing machines	357		9,921	1.41	23,386	2.10	34,305	2.46		1954
Office & computing equipment	357pt	Ebi	8,213	1.17	18,148	1.63	27,074	1.94	Kwh	1977
Computer parts*	357pt	Mde	1,708	.24	5,238	.47	7,231	.52	Kwh	1977
Service industry machines	358		5,963	.85	8,121	.73	10,984	.79		1954
Service industry equip*		Ebo	5,582	.79	7,698	.69	10,472	.75	Kwh	Production worker hours for 1954-62. 1954
Air conditioners, room*		Ch	381	.05	423	.04	512	.04	Prod.	Units, room air conditioners and dehumidifiers, Assn of Home Appliance Mfrs. (AHAM) 1954
Misc. machinery*	359	Mdn	5,362	.76	9,806	.88	11,294	.81	Kwh	Production worker hours for 1954-62. 1954
Electrical machinery	36		50,366	7.15	84,605	7.61	120,481	8.62		1947
Major electrical eq. and part	361,2		8,950	1.27	12,503	1.12	12,968	.93		1954
Elect. distribution equip*	361	Ebn	3,336	.47	4,584	.41	5,694	.41	Kwh	Production worker hours for 1954-62. 1954
Elect. industrial apparatus*	362	Mde	5,614	.80	7,919	.71	7,274	.52	Kwh	Production worker hours for 1954-62. 1954
Household appliances	363		5,276	.75	5,776	.52	7,580	.54		1954
Cooking equipment	3631	Ch	784	.11	941	.08	1,290	.09	Prod.	Units, freestanding, built-in electric ranges, and microwaves, AHAM; gas ranges and ovens, Gas Appliance Mfrs. Assn., Inc. (GAMA). 1954
Refrigeration and freezers	3632		1,166	.17	1,032	.09	1,450	.10		1954
Refrigerators*		Ch	989	.14	879	.08	1,346	.10	Prod.	Units, AHAM. 1954
Home freezers*		Ch	177	.03	153	.01	104	.01	Prod.	Units, upright and chest freezers, AHAM. 1954
Laundry appliances	3633		845	.12	984	.09	1,405	.10		1954
Washing machines*		Ch	596	.08	734	.07	1,054	.08	Prod.	Units, automatic and wringer washers, AHAM. 1954
Clothes dryers*		Ch	249	.04	250	.02	351	.03	Prod.	Units, electric and gas dryers, AHAM, 1954

Names of groups and series in them	SIC code (1977)	Market	1977 Millions of dollars	1977 Proportion	1982 Millions of dollars	1982 Proportion	1987 Millions of dollars	1987 Proportion	Type of series[4]	Series sources, units, and beginning date
Miscellaneous appliances	3634-6,9		2,481	.35	2,819	.25	3,435	.25		1954
Electrical housewares*	3634	Ch	1,366	.19	1,512	.14	1,364	.10	Pwh	1954
Vacuum cleaners*	3635	Ch	379	.05	464	.04	852	.06	Est.	Federal Reserve estimates; units, Vacuum Cleaner Mfrs. Assn. 1954-84. 1954
Appliances n.e.c.*	3636,9		736	.10	843	.06	1,219	.09		1954
Electric water heaters*		Ch	147	.02	188	.02	212	.02	Prod.	Units; shipments of residential electric storage water heaters, GAMA. 1954
Gas water heaters*		Ch	174	.02	226	.02	295	.02	Prod.	Units; shipments of residential gas-fired automatic storage water types, GAMA. 1954
Dishwashers & disposals*		Ch	415	.06	429	.04	712	.05	Prod.	Units; built-in and portable types, AHAM. 1954
Lighting and wiring products*	364	Ic	4,741	.67	6,619	.60	10,700	.77	Kwh	Production worker hours for 1954-62. 1954
Television and radio sets	365		3,078	.44	3,200	.29	2,960	.21		1954
Television sets*	3651pt		1,390	.20	1,257	.11	1,053	.08	Prod.	Units; monochrome and color sets, Electronic Industries Assn. (EIA). 1954
Home audio*	3651pt,2	Ch	1,688	.24	1,943	.17	1,907	.14	Est.	Federal Reserve estimates; units; home radio, audio components; EIA, 1954-84. 1954
Communication equipment	366		14,130	2.01	28,299	2.55	42,113	3.01		1954
Telephone apparatus*	3661	Ebi	4,192	.60	7,121	.64	6,809	.49	Pwh	1954
Electronic communications*	3662		9,938	1.41	21,178	1.91	35,304	2.53		1954
Defense*		Ed	3,313	.47	7,060	.64	11,768	.84	Pwh	1967
Nondefense*		Ebi	3,313	.47	7,059	.64	11,768	.84	Pwh	1967
Parts*		Mde	3,312	.47	7,059	.64	11,768	.84	Pwh	1977
Electronic components	367		9,260	1.31	21,214	1.91	31,591	2.26		1954
Television tubes*	3671-3	Mdc	910	.13	1,307	.12	1,339	.10	Prod.	Units, factory sales of picture tubes, EIA. 1954
Semiconductors*	3674-9	Mde	8,350	1.19	19,907	1.79	30,252	2.17	Pwh	Units, factory sales of semiconductors, EIA for 1963-66. Production worker hours for 1954-62.1954
Misc.electrical supplies	369		4,931	.70	6,994	.63	12,569	.90		1954
Storage batteries*	3691	Ca	928	.13	1,203	.11	1,704	.12	Prod.	Units; shipments of automotive replacement batteries. Battery Council International. 1954
Misc.electrical equipment*	3692-4,9	Mdc	4,003	.57	5,791	.52	10,865	.78	Pwh	1954
Transportation equipment	37		64,291	9.13	84,158	7.57	136,955	9.80		1947
Motor vehicles and parts	371		37,022	5.25	34,294	3.09	65,036	4.65		1947
Motor vehicles			20,758	2.95	17,529	1.58	39,140	2.80		1947
Autos			12,826	1.82	11,310	1.02	22,358	1.60		Units, Ward's Automotive Reports. 1954 From 1967 to 1972, split into large and small autos based on Ward's Automotive Reports data, current split is based on market segmentation estimates from Dept. of Commerce.

188

Names of groups and series in them	Classification[2] SIC code (1977)	Market	Value Added[3] 1977 Millions of dollars	1977 Proportion	1982 Millions of dollars	1982 Proportion	1987 Millions of dollars	1987 Proportion	Type of series[4]	Series sources, units, and beginning date
Consumer		Ca	8,196	1.16	6,334	.57	12,968	.93	Prod.	1972
Business*		Ebt	4,630	.66	4,976	.45	9,390	.67	Prod.	1972
Trucks and buses			7,286	1.03	5,627	.51	15,665	1.12		1954
Consumer		Ca	4,416	.63	3,072	.28	7,715	.55	Prod.	Pick up trucks, small vans, utility vehicles, and recreational vehicle chassis designed mainly for consumer use. Partly estimated by Federal Reserve from units reported by Ward's Automotive Reports, Recreation Vehicle Industry Assn. 1967
Business		Ebt	2,870	.41	2,555	.23	7,950	.57	Prod.	Trucks and buses other than personal-use vehicles. Ward's Automotive Reports. 1967
Truck trailers	3715	Ebt	645	.09	592	.05	1,117	.08	Prod.	Units, shipments, Census. 1954
Motor vehicle parts	3714		16,264	2.31	16,765	1.51	25,896	1.85		1954
Original equipment*		Mdc	12,588	1.79	11,953	1.08	20,463	1.46	Pwh	Annual levels based on auto & truck output. 1954
Repair*		Ca	3,676	.52	4,812	.43	5,433	.39	Est.	Federal Reserve estimates. 1954
Aerospace and misc. transp. equip.	372-6,9		27,269	3.87	49,864	4.49	71,919	5.15		1954
Aircraft and parts*	372		14,732	2.09	29,402	2.65	42,102	3.01		1954
Aircraft, complete*	3721	Ebt	8,134	1.15	15,641	1.41	16,747	1.20		1954
Commercial aircraft*		Ed	3,539	.50	6,591	.59	6,330	.45	Pwh	1954
Military aircraft*			4,595	.65	9,051	.81	10,417	.75	Pwh	1954
Aerospace eq. and parts,n.e.c*	3724,8	Ebt	6,598	.94	13,760	1.24	25,355	1.81		1954
Comm. aircraft eq., n.e.c.*		Ed	1,952	.28	3,853	.35	7,505	.54	Pwh	1954
Military aircraft eq.,n.e.c.*		Mde	1,914	.27	4,403	.40	8,595	.61	Pwh	1972
Aircraft parts*			2,732	.39	5,504	.50	9,255	.66	Pwh	1972
Ships and boats	373		4,682	.66	7,808	.70	7,658	.55		1954
Ship building and repairing*	3731	Ebt	3,825	.54	6,379	.57	5,227	.37		1954
Commercial ships*		Ed	2,039	.29	3,961	.36	852	.06	Pwh	1954
Military ships,priv.yds*		Ca	1,786	.25	2,418	.22	4,375	.31	Pwh	1954
Boats*	3732	Ebt	857	.12	1,429	.13	2,431	.17	Pwh	1954
Railroad and misc. transp. eq.	374-6,9		7,855	1.11	12,654	1.14	22,159	1.59		1954
Railroad equipment*	374	Ebt	1,883	.27	418	.04	1,284	.09	Prod.	Units, new and rebuilt locomotives and new and rebuilt freight cars. Freight cars only for 1954-73. Assn. of American Railroads. 1954
Motorcycles and bicycles*	375	Ca	370	.05	402	.04	356	.03	Pwh	Production worker hours for 1954-66. 1954
Guided missiles, space vehicles and parts*	376		4,422	.63	9,857	.89	18,152	1.30	Kwh	1972

Names of groups and series in them	Classification SIC code (1977)	Classification Market	Value Added 1977 Millions of dollars	Value Added 1977 Proportion	Value Added 1982 Millions of dollars	Value Added 1982 Proportion	Value Added 1987 Millions of dollars	Value Added 1987 Proportion	Type of series	Series sources, units, and beginning date
Guided mis. & space veh.*	3761	Ed	3,565	.51	7,026	.63	15,000	1.07	Pwh	1972
Missile and space vehicle parts*	3764.9	Mde	857	.12	2,831	.25	3,152	.23	Pwh	1972
Misc. transportation equipment*	379		1,180	.17	1,977	.18	2,367	.17	Pwh	1972
Travel trailers and campers*	3792	Ca	510	.07	442	.04	691	.05	Prod.	Units; Recreation Vehicles Industry Assn. 1972
Tanks*	3795	Ed	437	.06	1,158	.10	993	.07	Pwh	1972
Transp. equip., n.e.c.*	3799	Ca	233	.03	377	.03	683	.05	Pwh	1972
Instruments	38		18,762	2.66	33,672	3.03	45,514	3.26		1947
Scientific & medical instruments	381-4		10,689	1.52	21,454	1.93	30,859	2.21		1954
Scientific & optical goods*	381,3	Ebl	2,185	.31	4,469	.40	7,540	.54	K-Pwh	Production worker hours for 1954-62. 1954
Measuring instruments*	382	Mde	5,242	.74	10,007	.90	11,823	.85	Pwh	Kilowatt-production worker hours, 1963-66; production-worker hours from 1954-62. 1954
Medical instruments*	384	Ebl	3,262	.46	6,978	.63	11,496	.82	K-Pwh	Kilowatt-production-worker hours for 1963-66; production workers hours for 1954-62. 1954
Watches and eyeglasses*	385,7	Ch	1,341	.19	1,358	.12	1,580	.11	Pwh	1972
Photographic equip. & supplies*	386	Ebl	6,732	.96	10,860	.98	13,075	.94	Pwh	1972
Miscellaneous manufactures	39		10,291	1.46	14,059	1.27	17,381	1.24		1947
Misc. consumer goods	391,3,4,6	Ch	5,939	.84	8,046	.72	9,088	.65	Kwh	Production worker hours for 1954-62. 1954
Misc. business supplies	395,9	Ib	4,352	.62	6,013	.54	8,293	.59	Kwh	Kilowatt-production-worker hours for 1963-66; production worker hours for 1954-62. 1954
Gov. owned & operated ordnance*		Ed	7,656	1.09	10,649	.96	16,506	1.18	Pwh	1954; End-of-qtr. number of civilian wage board employees, Depts. of Army and Air Force. 1954
Air Force & Army ord. plts*			4,012	.57	6,867	.62	10,644	.76	Pwh	Production worker hours for last month of quarter, Dept. of Army and Air Force. 1954
Navy ordnance plants*		Ed	911	.13	1,215	.11	1,883	.14	Pwh	Production worker hours for last month of quarter, Dept. of Navy. 1954
Navy shipyards*		Ed	2,733	.39	2,567	.23	3,979	.28	Pwh	Production worker hours for last month of quarter, Dept. of Navy. 1954

Names of groups and series in them[1]	Classification[2] SIC code (1977)	Classification[2] Market	Value Added[3] 1977 Millions of dollars	1977 Proportion	1982 Millions of dollars	1982 Proportion	1987 Millions of dollars	1987 Proportion	Type of series[4]	Series sources, units, and beginning date
UTILITIES.................			41,961	5.96	92,925	8.36	106,592	7.63		Dept. of Energy data. 1919
Electric utilities..............	491,493pt		29,413	4.17	69,569	6.26	83,957	6.01		1947
Generation................			12,418	1.76	28,384	2.55	35,598	2.55		1967
Fossil fuel..............		Me	9,934	1.41	21,033	1.89	20,255	1.45	Prod.	Kilowatt hours, conventional steam and internal combustion. 1967
Hydro and nuclear.......		Me	2,484	.35	7,351	.66	15,343	1.10	Prod.	Kilowatt hours, hydro includes pumped storage.1967
Sales....................			16,995	2.41	41,185	3.71	48,359	3.46		1967
Residential.............		Cs	6,696	.95	15,980	1.44	19,585	1.40	Prod.	Kilowatt sales. 1954
Nonresidential..........		Me	10,299	1.46	25,205	2.27	28,774	2.06	Prod.	Kilowatt sales, classified by industrial users. 1967
Industrial...........		Ib	4,793	.68	12,149	1.09	12,670	.91	Prod.	
Commercial and other.........		Ib	5,506	.78	13,056	1.17	16,104	1.15	Prod.	Combined kilowatt sales to small privately operated commercial and industrial accounts (reported as "commercial" by Federal Power Comm.) and "other" sales. 1954 / 1947
Gas utilities.............	492,493pt		12,548	1.78	23,356	2.10	22,635	1.61		
Gas transmission*........		Me	4,465	.63	9,756	.88	7,737	.55	Prod.	Cubic feet, sales by major pipeline companies of gas for transmission. 1967
Sales*.................			8,084	1.15	13,600	1.22	14,898	1.07		1967
Residential*..........		Cs	3,296	.47	5,100	.46	7,732	.55	Prod.	Cubic feet, sales. 1954
Nonresidential*.......			4,787	.68	8,500	.76	7,166	.51	Prod.	
Industrial*..........		Me	3,251	.46	5,848	.53	3,635	.26	Prod.	Cubic feet, sales. 1954
Commercial and other*..		Ib	1,536	.22	2,652	.24	3,531	.25	Prod.	Cubic feet, sales. 1954

FOOTNOTES:

1. **Group and series:** Series with asterisks are included in published totals but are not shown separately in the monthly report. The following abbreviations are used: n.e.c. = not elsewhere classified; pt = part; misc. = miscellaneous.

2. **Classification:** SIC numbers are from the *Standard Industrial Classification Manual*, 1977 edition. Market classification codes are as follows:

Consumer goods
    Ca - Automotive products
    Ch - Other durable goods
    Cs - Consumer nondurables

Equipment
  Business equipment (Eb)
    Ebi - Information processing
          and related equipment
    Ebn - Industrial equipment
    Ebt - Transit equipment
    Ebo - Other equipment

  Defense and space equipment (Ed)
  *Oil and gas well drilling and
    manufactured homes (Es)*

Intermediate products
    Ib - Business supplies
    Ic - Construction supplies

Materials
  Durable goods materials (Md)
    Mdc - Consumer durable parts
    Mde - Equipment parts
    Mdn - Durable materials n.e.c.
  Energy materials (Me)
  Nondurable goods materials (Mn)
    Mnc - Containers
    Mnn - Nondurable materials n.e.c.
    Mnt - Textile, paper, and chemical

3. **Value added:** The value-added weights are compiled from information contained in the Census of Manufactures and the Census of Mineral Industries and in reports from the Department of Energy, the Department of Defense, the Edison Electric Institute, the American Gas Association, and trade groups. They are used to calculate the combinations of series such as aggregates and groupings. The index now uses 1977 value-added weights for 1977-81; 1982 weights for 1982-86; and 1987 weights for 1987 to the present. The figures may not add to totals because of rounding.

4. **Type of series:** The following codes appear:
   Prod - Physical product, unless otherwise noted. (Most of these series are adjusted for the number of working days per month.) These data are obtained from various government agencies and private trade associations.
   KWH - Kilowatt hours, data collected by the Federal Reserve System.
   PWH - Production-worker-hour data, collected by the Bureau of Labor Statistics unless otherwise noted.
   K-PWH - Kilowatt hours and production-worker hours combined.
   Est - Estimated currently by the Federal Reserve because raw physical product data have become unavailable.

5. Includes steel mill products manufactured for independent forgers (nec), rail transportation, ship building, aircraft, oil and gas drilling mining, agricultural machinery, industrial equipment, electrical equipment, other domestic and commercial equipment, and ordnance.

192

Summary of methodology for calculating capacity utilization:

The Federal Reserve seeks to obtain monthly rates of industrial utilization that are consistent both with current data on production and periodic survey data on utilization. Because there is no direct monthly information on overall industrial utilization rates, various sources are used to calculate monthly capacity indexes that, together with the production indexes, yield the utilization rates. In this scheme of measurement, the short-term movements in utilization typically approximates the difference between the change in the production index and the growth trend of capacity because the estimated monthly capacity indexes change slowly.

Six basic steps are involved in calculating the utilization rates publish by the Federal Reserve.

Step 1. Calculate the preliminary implied end-of-year indexes of industrial capacity by dividing a production index by a utilization rate obtained from a survey for that end-of-year period. These ratios are expressed, like industrial production, as percentages of production in 1987 and give the general level and trend of the capacity estimates.

Step 2. Refine the annual movements of the preliminary capacity indexes to give consideration to alternative indicators of annual capacity changes; these alternatives include capacity data in physical units, estimates of capital stock, and the direct estimates by businesses of their annual percentage change in capacity.

Step 3. Interpolate by month between the final end-of-year capacity indexes to obtain a continuous time series.

Step 4. Apply an adjustment—called annual capacity adjustment—to estimates of capacity that appear to reflect short-term peak capacity rather than a sustainable level of maximum output.

Step 5. Apply value-added weights to the monthly capacity indexes and sum them to appropriate groups.

Step 6. Calculate utilization rates for the individual series and groups by dividing the pertinent production index by the related capacity index. Thus, utilization rates for published groups are not aggregated directly but are derived from aggregate production and capacity indexes.

The table that follows shows the industry structure and series composition of the industrial capacity and utilization estimates. The table includes the value-added weights mentioned in step 5 for 1977, 1982, and 1987, as well as, the annual sources of information that are used in steps 1 and 2 to estimate and refine the capacity indexes.

193

Industry structure and series composition of industrial capacity indexes and utilization rates: classifications, value-added proportions, and description of series (Footnotes follow the table.)

Industry name	SIC Code (1977)	Value-Added Proportions			Series sources, units, and beginning date
		1977	1982	1987	
TOTAL INDUSTRY...........		100.00	100.00	100.00	1967
Manufacturing...........		84.21	74.71	84.44	1948
Durable.................		49.10	42.36	47.27	1967
Nondurable..............		35.11	32.36	37.17	1967
Mining..................		9.83	16.92	7.93	1967
Utilities..............		5.96	8.36	7.63	1967
MINING.................	10	9.83	16.92	7.93	1967
Metal mining..........	10	.50	.29	.32	1967
Iron ores*............	101	.15	.07	.05	Capacity estimates and production, tons, Bureau of Mines. 1967
Copper ore*...........	102	.15	.06	.09	Capacity estimates and production, tons, Bureau of Mines. 1967
Lead and zinc ores*...	103	.05	.02	.01	Capacity estimates and production, tons, Bureau of Mines. 1967
Gold and silver ores*.	104	.02	.06	.12	FR estimate based on peaks in tonnage production. 1972
Ferroalloy ores*......	106	.04	.01	.01	Capacity estimates and production of molybdenum ores, tons, Bur. of Mines. 1967
Misc. metal ores*.....	105,8,9	.09	.07	.03	FR estimate based on trends through peaks in production index. 1972
Coal..................	11,12	1.60	1.68	1.22	1967
Anthracite*...........	11	.02	.02	.01	FR estimate based on trends through peaks in production index. 1967
Bituminous coal*......	12	1.58	1.66	1.21	FR estimate based on trends through peaks in production index. 1967
Oil and gas extraction.	13	7.07	14.39	5.73	1967
Texas crude oil*......	131 pt	1.34	2.36	.76	The FR estimates of crude oil and natural gas capacity are based on trends in
Alaska and California crude oil*.	131 pt	.57	2.12	1.13	regional production and on estimates of proven reserves, and on
Louisiana and other crude oil*.	131 pt	1.54	2.99	1.19	analyses by the Department of Energy, the American Petroleum Institute, the
Natural gas*..........	131 pt	2.16	3.87	1.77	American Gas Association, and others. 1967
Propane*..............	132 pt	.05	.06	.02	FR estimate based on trends through peaks in production index. 1967
Liquified petroleum*..	132 pt	.42	.74	.27	FR estimate based on trends through peaks in production index. 1967
Oil and gas well drilling..	138	.99	2.25	.58	Capacity based on available rigs; physical utilization is ratio of active to available rigs from the Reed Tool Company, Annual Rig Census. 1967
Stone and earth minerals..	14	.66	.56	.67	1967
Stone, sand, and gravel*..	141,2,4	.36	.29	.43	FR estimates based on trends through peaks in production index. 1967
Chemical and fertilizer mat.*....	147	.20	.20	.14	Capacity estimates and output, tons of soda ash, phosphate rock, salt, barite, and frasch sulfur, Bureau of Mines. 1972
Misc. stone and earth minerals*..	145,8,9	.09	.08	.10	FR estimates based on trends through peaks in production index. 1972

Industry name	SIC Code (1977)	Value-Added Proportions 1977	1982	1987	Series sources, units, and beginning date
MANUFACTURING		84.21	74.71	84.44	1948
Primary Processing[1]		31.66	23.61	26.71	1948
Advanced processing[2]		52.56	51.11	57.73	1948
Foods	20	7.96	7.96	8.76	Census and McGraw-Hill/DRI; capital stock. 1948
Tobacco products*	21	.62	.81	1.02	Census survey; capital stock. 1967
Textile mill products	22	2.29	1.67	1.84	American Textiles Manufacturers Institute and McGraw-Hill/DRI surveys. 1948
Fabrics*	221-4	.77	.53	.53	Census survey; capital stock. 1967
Yarn and thread*	228	.32	.21	.27	Census survey; capital stock. 1967
Misc. textiles*	229	1.20	.93	1.04	Census survey; capital stock. 1967
Apparel products	23	2.79	2.35	2.36	Census survey; capital stock. 1967
Lumber and products	24	2.30	1.41	2.00	1967
Logging and lumber*	241,2	1.05	.56	.84	Census survey; capital stock. 1967
Lumber products*	243-5.9	1.25	.84	1.16	Census survey; capital stock. 1967
Furniture and fixtures	25	1.27	1.15	1.45	Census survey; capital stock. 1967
Paper and products	26	3.15	3.00	3.58	McGraw-Hill/DRI survey. 1948
Pulp and paper*	261-3	1.33	1.24	1.64	1967
Wood pulp*	261	.44	.10	.16	Capacity and output, tons, American Paper Institute. 1967
Paper*	262	.44	.81	.98	Capacity and output, tons, American Paper Institute. 1967
Paperboard*	263	.44	.34	.50	Capacity and output, tons, American Paper Institute. 1967
Paper products*	264,5,6	1.81	1.76	1.94	Census survey; capital stock. 1967
Printing and publishing	27	4.54	4.90	6.37	Census survey; capital stock. 1967
Chemicals and products	28	8.05	6.81	8.60	McGraw-Hill/DRI survey. 1948
Basic chemicals*	281	.92	.79	.79	Census survey; capital stock. 1972
Synthetic materials*	282	1.11	.85	1.28	1967
Plastics materials*	2821	.59	.43	.78	Capacity and output, pounds, major thermosetting and thermoplastic resins, Society of the Plastics Industry, Inc. 1967
Synthetic rubber*	2822	.08	.08	.09	Capacity, tons, International Institute of Synthetic Rubber Producers; production, tons, Rubber Manufacturers Association. 1967
Synthetic fibers*	2823,4	.44	.34	.41	Capacity and production, pounds, Fiber Organon. 1967
Industrial organic chemicals*	286	1.83	1.11	1.54	Census survey; capital stock; trade reports on physical capacity. 1972
Chemical products*	283-5,9	3.65	3.60	4.54	Census survey; capital stock. 1967
Agricultural chemicals*	287	.54	.46	.45	1967
Fertilizer materials*	2873-5	.36	.19	.18	Census survey; capital stock. 1967
Agricultural chemicals, n.e.c.*	2879	.18	.27	.28	Census survey; capital stock. 1972

Industry name	SIC Code (1977)	Value-Added Proportions			Series sources, units, and beginning date
		1977	1982	1987	
Petroleum products..........	29	2.40	1.99	1.32	Capacity and gross input to crude distillation units at petroleum refineries, millions of barrels per calendar day, Department of Energy. 1948
Rubber and plastics products......	30	2.80	2.45	3.02	McGraw-Hill/DRI survey. 1948
Tires*..........	301	.62	.42	.40	Census survey; capital stock. 1967
Other rubber products*..........	302-4,6	.51	.42	.44	Census survey; capital stock. 1967
Plastics products, n.e.c.*..........	307	1.67	1.61	2.18	Census survey; capital stock. 1967
Leather and products..........	31	.53	.43	.30	Census survey; capital stock. 1967
Stone, clay, and glass products....	32	2.72	2.12	2.46	McGraw-Hill/DRI. 1948
Glass*..........	321,2,3	.78	.63	.67	Census survey; capital stock. 1967
Cement*..........	324	.24	.16	.16	Kiln capacity and production of cement clinker, tons, Bureau of Mines. 1967
Stone and clay products*..........	325-9	1.70	1.32	1.63	Census survey; capital stock. 1967
Primary metals..........	33	5.33	2.73	3.32	1967
Iron and steel..........	331,2	3.49	1.54	1.95	Capacity and output of raw steel, tons, American Iron and Steel Institute. 1948
Raw steel..........		.51	.12	.11	Capacity and output of raw steel, tons, American Iron and Steel Institute. 1967
Nonferrous metals..........	333-6,9	1.85	1.19	1.38	1948
Primary copper..........	3331	1.13	.04	.03	1967
Copper smelting*..........		.05	.02	.01	Capacity and output, tons, contained copper, Bureau of Mines. 1967
Copper refining*..........		.08	.02	.02	Capacity and output, tons, contained copper, Bureau of Mines. 1967
Primary aluminum..........	3334	.28	.10	.14	Capacity and output, metric tons of ingot, Aluminum Association, Bureau of Mines. 1967
Other nonferrous metals & prods*.	333pt,334-9	1.44	1.05	1.21	Census survey; capital stock. 1967
Fabricated metal products..........	34	6.46	5.30	5.38	Census and McGraw-Hill surveys; capital stock. 1948
Nonelectrical machinery..........	35	9.54	9.20	8.55	McGraw-Hill/DRI survey. 1948
Engine,farm,constr. & allied eq*.	351-3	3.16	2.58	2.01	Census survey; capital stock. 1967
Office and computing machines*....	357	1.41	2.10	2.46	Census survey; capital stock. 1967
Other nonelectrical machinery*....	354-6,8,9	4.97	4.52	4.08	Census survey; capital stock. 1967
Electrical machinery..........	36	7.15	7.61	8.62	McGraw-Hill/DRI survey. 1948
Appliances and television sets*....	363,5	1.19	.81	.75	Census survey; capital stock. 1967
Communications equipment*..........	366	2.01	2.55	3.01	Census survey; capital stock. 1967
Semiconductors*..........	3674-9	1.19	1.79	2.17	Census survey; capital stock. 1967
Other electrical eq. and parts*...	361,2,4,6,9	2.77	2.47	2.69	Census survey; capital stock. 1967

Industry name	SIC Code (1977)	Value-Added Proportions 1977	1982	1987	Series sources, units, and beginning date
Transportation Equipment..........	37	9.13	7.57	9.80	1967
Motor vehicles and parts..........	371	5.25	3.09	4.65	McGraw-Hill/DRI survey prior to 1977. 1948
Autos and light trucks............		2.67	1.39	2.35	1977
Autos*............................		1.82	1.02	1.60	Physical output and capacity based on line speeds and peaks in physical output on for individual plants as reported in Ward's Automotive Reports since 1977. 1977
Light trucks*.....................		.85	.37	.75	Same as above. 1977
Med.&heavy trucks,& trailers,etc*		.28	.19	.46	Same as above (data only for medium and heavy trucks). 1977
Motor vehicle parts*..............	3714	2.31	1.51	1.85	Census survey; capital stock. 1967
Aerospace and misc. trans. eq.....	372-6,9	3.87	4.49	5.15	McGraw-Hill/DRI survey. 1948
Aircraft and parts*...............	372	2.09	2.65	3.01	Census survey; capital stock. 1967
Ships and boats*..................	373	.66	.70	.55	Census survey; capital stock. 1967
Railroad & misc. transp. eq*......	374-6,9	1.11	1.14	1.59	Census survey; capital stock. 1967
Instruments.......................	38	2.66	3.03	3.26	Census and McGraw-Hill/DRI surveys; capital stock. 1948
Miscellaneous manufactures........	39	1.46	1.27	1.24	Census survey; capital stock. 1967
Government-owned/operated ordnance*		1.09	.96	1.18	FR estimates based on trends through peaks in production. 1972
UTILITIES.........................	491,493 pt	5.96	8.36	7.63	1967
Electric utilities................		4.17	6.26	6.01	Physical output and capability, megawatt hours, generating plants, North American Electric Reliability Council, Department of Energy, and Edison Electric Institute. 1967
Gas utilities.....................	492,493 pt	1.78	2.10	1.62	FR estimates based on Dept. of Energy, American Gas Assoc. and industry reports. 1967

Note: The following abbreviations are used: n.e.c. = not elsewhere classified; pt = part; misc. = miscellaneous.
* Data are included in published totals but are not shown in the monthly report.
1. Primary processing industries include textile mill products, lumber and products, industrial chemicals, petroleum products, rubber and plastics products, stone, clay, and glass products, primary metals and fabricated metal products.
2. Advanced processing industries include foods, tobacco products, printing and publishing, chemical products such as drugs and toiletries, leather and products, furniture and fixtures, machinery, transportation equipment, instruments, miscellaneous manufactures, and government-owned-and-operated ordnance facilities.

197

8

The Industrial Pipeline

Most goods-producing enterprises have a standard flow of business. Commercial interaction begins with a sales effort that writes an order. The order is translated into production at a factory. Raw materials go in; electricity, machinery, and labor transform the materials into something quite different; and a final product is wrapped and finished. Then the product is shipped and the customer is billed. Failure to deliver on a timely basis or a downturn in the customer's prospects could result in cancelation of the order. In the latter case, the factory's unsold finished inventory will rise unexpectedly. This process can be seen as a pipeline and is diagramed in Figure 8.1. Since the production process begins with orders and inventory positions are the obverse of production, orders and inventories data are critical to tracking the industrial sector.

The Commerce Department issues two monthly reports covering orders and two covering inventories and sales. The *Advance Durable Goods Orders Report* covers just one segment of the *Manufacturing Industries New and Unfilled Orders Report* (known as M3-1 or, more commonly, *Factory Orders*). But it is released seven days prior (i.e., on the seventeenth working day following the close of the month) which generally puts it between the twenty-second and the twenty-seventh. *Factory Orders* is the more comprehensive report because it covers

FIGURE 8.1 The Industrial Pipeline

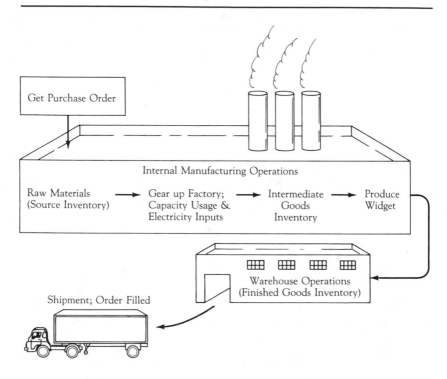

nondurables industries as well as durables and is released one week later. *Manufacturing and Trade Inventories and Sales* are subdivided into wholesale, retail, and manufacturers. An advance report on monthly wholesale trade is also available a week prior to the full report.

Analyzing these data is known as the "art of ex-ing" in large part because officials are often already aware from the financial press that one industry sector is doing well and desire to know whether the good or bad times are spreading to other areas. Thus, analysts look closely at the data "ex" some component, such as autos or defense. As all these reports are compiled in a similar manner from one survey, we will concentrate first on data collection and assembly methods.

DATA COLLECTION

Each month, a sample of about 2,300 firms are asked to file at the divisional accounting level reports with the Commerce Department. These mail reports (see sample in Appendix 8.1) cover the dollar value on a current cost basis of inventories, orders net of cancelations, and shipments (net selling values FOB the plant) by main business line as determined by *Standard Industrial Classification* (SIC) code. The forms are sent out on the twenty-seventh or twenty-eighth of the month and are required to be returned within two weeks. The response rate is high enough that most of the manufacturing giants are included in the advance reports, while the final report generally includes 99% of the sample.

Most manufacturing companies with more than 1,000 employees are included in the survey and selected smaller firms are added to strengthen coverage in individual industries. Separate estimates are made for 79 industry categories. When a company shows an unusually large movement, its data are segregated and computed separately. The sample is linked to a universe using weights determined from an *Annual Survey of Manufacturers* (ASM), and data are reported after seasonal adjustment (using a concurrent process).

The orders and inventories data sometimes experience large revisions, making them notoriously unreliable for financial market participants. Revisions reflect three factors. The difference between the advance and the preliminary reports mainly stems from additional firms' reports being included (delays are common when outside financial accounting or reporting periods end, such as on December 31). But there are also corrections to the sample data: SIC codes may not be detailed enough to describe company operations, or there may be reporting or processing errors. The annual revisions generally stem from benchmarking the monthly reports to the ASM, which covers about 6,000 companies, more than double the monthly sample.

ACCOUNTING PROCEDURES

While dollar data on shipments and orders are solid numbers, standard financial accounting principles allow some leeway in determining the cost of manufacturing inventories. Among the better-known methods are LIFO and FIFO accounting, which stand for *Last In, First Out* and *First In, First Out*, respectively (see Table 8.1). Changes in inventory valuation affect costs and resulting profits. For example, in an inflationary environment most businesses will prefer LIFO accounting because it allows an increasing expense to be recouped faster. This is because higher priced items bought last are assumed to have gone into the production process. In an environment of steady prices, however, average cost or FIFO accounting probably better reflects the reality of how goods flow through factories.

In recognition of the accounting difficulties, the Commerce Department attempted to standardize inventory reporting beginning in 1982. LIFO users are now asked to report the value of inventories prior to the LIFO adjustment, then to report the LIFO reserve and the LIFO value after adjustment for reserve. Data are now compiled on a current cost basis which Commerce Department officials believe approximates replacement cost.

There are two difficulties with obtaining these data by stage of fabrication, however. First, many companies do not keep monthly data at this level of detail, so the survey response rate is lower than for

TABLE 8.1
Inventory Accounting Methods

Item	Cost	Accounting Costs	
1	$120	Assume two items were required from	
2	125	inventory to produce one widget	
3	130	LIFO (items 3 & 4)	$265
4	135	FIFO (items 1 & 2)	$245
Average	127.50	Average Cost (any 2 @ the avg)	$255

overall inventory data. Second, a product considered a finished good in one industry (such as steel mills) may be considered a raw material to another (such as stamping plants). Because the M3-1 contains industries with successive stages of fabrication, the same type of inventories may be included under different categories in the aggregate statistics.

ADVANCE DURABLE GOODS

The advance report on durables does not disaggregate orders to the same extent as does the *Factory Orders Report*. Rather, it contains data in four broad areas and three "supplemental" areas (shown in Table 8.2). The four categories cover orders by end-use—primary metals, two types of machinery, and transportation. The supplemental data eliminate volatile components and help the analyst determine underlying economic activity. A large military order could total billions and will distort the totals depending on the month in which it is reported, so defense and nondefense orders are reported. Nondefense capital goods orders are important because shipments of these items often are of similar magnitude; NDCG shipments are used to construct equipment spending in the GNP accounts.

TABLE 8.2
Durable Goods Orders Components

I.	Categories
	Primary metals
	Machinery excluding electrical
	Electrical machinery
	Transportation
II.	Supplemental series
	Capital goods (defense and nondefense)
	Defense
	Nondefense

Data on durables are scarce. But projections are made using press reports, the inventories component from the NAPM report, auto production data (orders are assumed to parallel production), and Department of Defense data on military expenditures.

FACTORY ORDERS

The term "factory orders" is a misnomer. The *Factory Orders Report* actually covers shipments and orders for manufacturing industries with the data presented SA and NSA in current dollars and as a percent change from the prior month. The major breakdowns are for all industries versus industries with unfilled orders. The latter indicates whether there is a backlog that may keep manufacturing going for a time after demand weakens.

Durables are subdivided into 26 categories covering everything from iron and steel to household appliances and photographic goods. Using the details, the analyst can determine the sources of movements in the *Advance Report*. Nondurables are divided into 24 categories covering three broad areas. These include:

1. Direct consumption items such as food and clothing;
2. Industrial inputs to other products such as paperboard, rubber, and chemicals; and
3. Hard goods that are used to prolong the lives of durable goods such as auto parts and construction materials.

Analysts focus on two items from the *Factory Orders* data, using the SA percent change to gauge their strength. Total new orders will indicate whether industry can keep going, since they lead the production process. *Backlog*, the unfilled orders carried forward from one month to the next and measured as of the end of each month, indicates whether there is any residual demand in the absence of new orders. In many instances, product users double-order during periods of rising demand and cancel only when the outlook turns very dim. Thus, falling backlog for an extended period is indicative of a slowing in factory output. Both new orders and backlog should also be considered ex transportation and ex defense capital goods.

Shipments data (a proxy for industry sales) are subdivided in a manner that parallels the orders numbers. The most important segments are durables and nondurables. Shipments data are used to determine the backlog levels.

WHOLESALE AND RETAIL SALES AND INVENTORIES

Since orders lead the production process and sales determine the ultimate health of an enterprise, the logical intermediary between the two is *inventories*. If a manager guesses incorrectly and overproduces at a time of weakening demand, the result will be unwanted inventory. In an accounting sense, inventories are classified into three categories: raw materials, intermediate goods, and finished products, depending on their stage of processing. But the Commerce Department, instead, uses a classification system that identifies the type of business (wholesalers and retailers) and is subdivided into durables and nondurables. For retailers, the collection process roughly parallels the categories in the *Retail Sales Report* (see Chapter 6), with the important exception that data are also available by region and state. Figure 8.2 shows wholesalers' sales, inventories, and stock/sales ratios from 1983–90.

I/S Ratios

Surging inventories are expected when demand is strong but also occur when orders unexpectedly collapse. Given that inventories are required for production, one is sometimes uncertain about what rising inventory means. One way to determine whether higher inventory is desirable is to consider a ratio of *inventory-to-sales* (generally expressed

FIGURE 8.2 Monthly Sales, Inventories, and Stock/Sales Ratios of Merchant Wholesalers: 1983–90

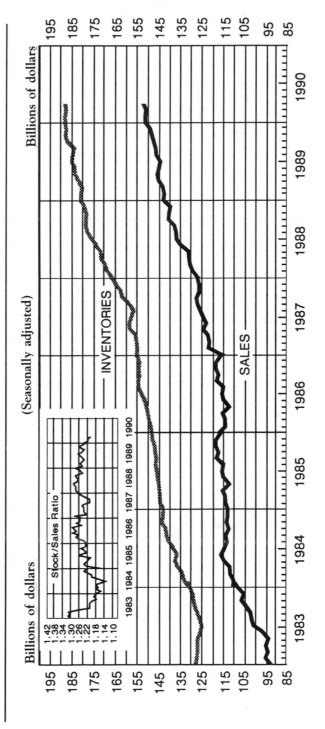

as a number of months). Some businesses have rules of thumb about desired inventory levels. An example is that auto makers should have about a 60-day or two-month supply of cars on hand. Aggregating the *I/S ratio* across industries provides a rough measuring tool.

The I/S ratio is clearly marked in Figure 8.3 for each of the trade reports and is depicted for wholesalers in the inset of Figure 8.2. A ratio under 1.25 is certainly no cause for alarm, since the higher inventories carried by durables producers are often offset by leaner levels in nondurables. However, a ratio approaching 1:3 may signal inventory overhang. One surprising facet of the 1982–90 economic expansion was the failure of I/S ratios to rise significantly as the economy weakened. This is especially surprising since, in each of the prior post-WWII recessions, a significant inventory overhang developed as the economy turned down. But in 1990, the I/S ratio stubbornly remained in a downtrend. One reason may be the massive switch to computer-based ordering that allowed a quick industry response to lower orders.

BUSINESS INVENTORIES

The *Business Inventories Report* is nothing more than a summary of the wholesale and retail trade reports previously discussed plus the same

FIGURE 8.3 Total Business Inventories/Sales Ratios (Based on Seasonally Adjusted Data)

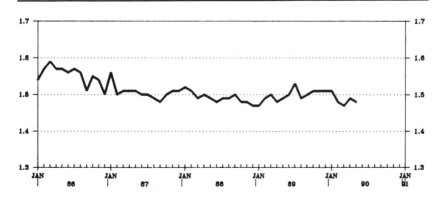

data for the manufacturing sector. At the time of its release, analysts know with certainty all the components, with the exception of retail. Projecting this series involves only compiling wholesale and manufacturing data. Summary inventory and sales data are more closely watched because manufacturers often take the brunt of inventory overhang going into slowdowns. As a result they stop purchasing raw materials and lay off high-paid workers. These actions have significant ripple effects. The new information in this report is the overall I/S ratio (see Figure 8.3), which should not be considered troublesome until it approaches two months.

Note that ratios for durable goods manufacturers tend to be higher than for other industries. These often lead a downturn as consumers postpone buying expensive items when disposable income is down due to high inflation or lost jobs. Note also that I/S ratios are lagging economic indicators because unsold inventory occurs after sales have fallen.

Appendix 8.1

Sample of M-3 Report Form

APPENDIX 8.1 Sample of M-3 Report Form

(For multiunit reporting)

RETURN THIS FORM WITHIN _____ DAYS AFTER RECEIPT ☐   Form Approved O.M.B. No. 41-R0328

REPORT FOR

FORM M-3(MD)
10-2-79

U.S. DEPARTMENT OF COMMERCE
BUREAU OF THE CENSUS

MONTHLY ECONOMIC SURVEY

Please refer to instructions on reverse side

RETURN TO >

NOTICE — This report is authorized by law (title 13, United States Code). By section 9 of the same law, your report to the Census Bureau is confidential. It may be seen only by sworn Census employees and may be used only for statistical purposes. The law also provides that copies retained in your files are immune from legal process. Although you are not required to respond to this statistical survey, your cooperation is needed to make the results comprehensive and accurate.

In correspondence pertaining to this report, please refer to the file number above your name.

Person to contact regarding this report		
CENSUS BUREAU CONTACT	Name	
	Area code	Number
YOUR COMPANY CONTACT – Enter name and telephone number if not shown; correct if wrong.	Name	
	Area code	Number	Extension

(Please correct any error in name and address including ZIP code)

SPECIAL REPORTING INSTRUCTIONS

SECTION I – Changes in Organization or Accounting Practices *(If the answer to any of the following is "YES," please describe in "REMARKS" and indicate the reporting units affected.)*

A. Has there been any change in organization or ownership that affects the completeness of this report or comparability with your previous report?
000
1 ☐ YES   2 ☐ NO

B. Has last-in, first-out (LIFO) been adopted or its use significantly expanded for the figures in this report?
000
1 ☐ YES   2 ☐ NO

C. Have there been any changes in the accounting basis of the figures in this report that affect comparability with previous reports?
000
1 ☐ YES   2 ☐ NO

SECTION II – Report for Individual Reporting Units *(Please report for the individual reporting units listed below. All figures should be reported in THOUSANDS OF DOLLARS)*

Census ID No	Category	Type of reporting unit MFG/DURABLE	Your unit code	Mark the box that describes the CURRENT reporting period	>	☐ Calendar month	☐ 4 weeks ☐ 5 weeks ☐ Other	Ending date _____ Describe in remarks on reverse

Description of this reporting unit

EXAMPLE UNIT:

USUALLY DURABLE MANUFACTURING

Reporting period	SALES	NEW ORDERS	UNFILLED ORDERS	TOTAL INVENTORY	MATERIALS & SUPPLIES	WORK–IN PROCESS	FINISHED GOODS

Census ID No.	Category	Type of reporting unit MFG/NONDURABLE	Your unit code	Mark the box that describes the CURRENT reporting period	>	☐ Calendar month	☐ 4 weeks ☐ 5 weeks ☐ Other	Ending date _____ Describe in remarks on reverse

Description of this reporting unit

EXAMPLE UNIT:

USUALLY NONDURABLE MANUFACTURING

Reporting period	SALES	TOTAL INVENTORY	MATERIALS & SUPPLIES	WORK–IN PROCESS	FINISHED GOODS

Census ID No.	Category	Type of reporting unit	Your unit code	Mark the box that describes the CURRENT reporting period	>	☐ Calendar month	☐ 4 weeks ☐ 5 weeks ☐ Other	Ending date _____ Describe in remarks on reverse

Description of this reporting unit

TOTALS FOR REPORTING UNITS LISTED ABOVE (THESE TOTALS WILL BE USED TO VERIFY COMPUTER PROCESSING OF THIS REPORT)

Reporting period	SALES	NEW ORDERS	UNFILLED ORDERS	TOTAL INVENTORY	MATERIALS & SUPPLIES	WORK–IN PROCESS	FINISHED GOODS

Census ID No.	Category	Type of reporting unit	Your unit code	Mark the box that describes the CURRENT reporting period	>	☐ Calendar month	☐ 4 weeks ☐ 5 weeks ☐ Other	Ending date _____ Describe in remarks on reverse

Description of this reporting unit

Reporting period							

Census ID No.	Category	Type of reporting unit	Your unit code	Mark the box that describes the CURRENT reporting period	>	☐ Calendar month	☐ 4 weeks ☐ 5 weeks ☐ Other	Ending date _____ Describe in remarks on reverse

Description of this reporting unit

Reporting period							

Census ID No	Category	Type of reporting unit	Your unit code	Mark the box that describes the CURRENT reporting period	>	☐ Calendar month	☐ 4 weeks ☐ 5 weeks ☐ Other	Ending date _____ Describe in remarks on reverse

Description of this reporting unit

Reporting period							

Continuation sheets are included if all of your reporting units could not be listed on this page.

*Figures not received when form was prepared.
PLEASE ENTER if not previously submitted.

(For single unit reporting)

RETURN THIS FORM WITHIN _____ **DAYS AFTER RECEIPT** ☐	Form Approved O.M.B. No. 41 R0328

FORM M-3(SD)
(9-26-79)

U.S. DEPARTMENT OF COMMERCE
BUREAU OF THE CENSUS

MANUFACTURER'S SHIPMENTS, INVENTORIES, AND ORDERS

See instructions on reverse side

NOTICE – This report is authorized by law (title 13 United States Code). By section 9 of the same law your report to the Census Bureau is confidential. It may be seen only by sworn Census employees and may be used only for statistical purposes. The law also provides that copies retained in your files are immune from legal process. Although you are not required to respond to this statistical survey, your cooperation is needed to make the results comprehensive and accurate.

RETURN TO ⟩

(Please correct any error in name and address including ZIP code)

Person to contact regarding this report

CENSUS BUREAU CONTACT	Name		
	Area code	Number	
YOUR COMPANY CONTACT *Enter name and telephone number if not shown correct if wrong*	Name		
	Area code	Number	Extension

Description of activities or division(s) to be reported and special instructions.

Mark the box which best describes the current reporting period ⟩

– Calendar month
– Other – Describe in remarks

☐ 4 week   Enter ending date _____
☐ 5 week

Line No.	Description of reporting items *Definition of terms are provided on the back of the form)*	CENSUS USE ONLY	Reporting period – Report all figures in thousands of dollars		
1	SALES	S			
2	NEW ORDERS	N			
3	ORDERS BACKLOG	U			
4	TOTAL INVENTORY	I			
5	MATERIALS AND SUPPLIES INVENTORY	M			
6	WORK-IN-PROCESS INVENTORY	W			
7	FINISHED GOODS INVENTORY	F			
8	HAS LIFO USAGE BEEN ADOPTED OR EXTENDED THIS PERIOD?	H			
	VERIFICATION TOTAL – Sum of lines 1–10 ⟶				

* Figures not received when form was prepared. PLEASE ENTER if not already submitted.

Please complete certification on reverse and return in the enclosed preaddressed envelope.

INSTRUCTIONS FOR COMPLETING THIS FORM

GENERAL INFORMATION

A summary of the instructions for competing this form is provided below. A comprehensive instruction manual is available. Copies of the instruction manual or clarification of instructions or definitions may be obtained by calling the contact on the front of the form or by writing to: **Bureau of the Census, ATTN: Industry Division, Washington, DC 20233.**

- **Purpose of this survey** – This form is designed to collect sales, inventories, and orders data from manufacturing companies for use in the preparation of industry estimates for 79 industry categories encompassing all manufacturing activities. These estimates are widely used as indicators of our Nation's current economic condition and of changes in the business cycle. They also provide important components for estimates of the gross national product (GNP) and related series.

- **Activities to be reported** – A REPORTING UNIT is generally a division, subsidiary, or other operating unit as defined by your company for financial or managerial purposes. Reporting units within the same industry category, as defined in the Instruction Manual, may be combined for reporting purposes. Thus, a reporting unit could also be a complete company if the company operates predominantly in a single industry category. The Census Bureau may request that very large units with diverse activities be subdivided along industry lines for reporting purposes.

  For the purposes of this survey, each reporting unit is to be reported as though a separate entity. Sales (or shipments) should include transfers to other segments of your company, as well as sales to unaffiliated customers. Orders, where applicable, should include orders from other segments of your firm. Finally, the reported figures should be limited to domestic operations (the 50 States and the District of Columbia). Please note that, while the activities of foreign subsidiaries should be excluded, export sales to and orders from foreign subsidiaries should be included.

- **Survey deadlines** – The first report for this survey is based on receipts through approximately the 18th of the month following the reporting period. If possible, please return your report by this time. Otherwise, the figures for your company will be estimated for the early report with actual figures included in the final report only. If a portion of the requested items can be reported early, please call or write so that arrangements for reporting of those data items on a separate form can be made.

- **Use of estimates** – If actual figures are not available, reasonable estimates may be used for reporting. Please indicate in the "Remarks" section below if figures are estimates.

- **Comparability with previous reports** – Please indicate in the "Remarks" section below if there have been any changes in organization or accounting methods that affect comparability with previous reports.

REPORTING DEFINITIONS

A. SALES – Report net sales (or shipments) made during the reporting period. Exclude all taxes that were not included in the cost of goods you purchased. Include sales and transfers to other divisions or subsidiaries of your company.

B. NEW ORDERS – Report net new orders received during the reporting period. Include (1) the sales value of orders received and filled during the reporting period; (2) orders received for future deliveries; and (3) the net sales value of changes to existing contracts. Do not include orders requiring further negotiations, authorization, or funding before the order is final.

C. ORDER BACKLOG – Include orders, as defined above, that have not yet passed through the sales account.

D. TOTAL INVENTORY – Report inventories at current cost or market as of the end of the reporting period. If your inventories are subject to LIFO valuation, report the value prior to the adjustment for the LIFO reserve. The reported figure should include all inventories in the 50 States and the District of Columbia to which you hold title.

The figure for total inventories should be distributed among the following three categories to the extent permitted by your records:

E. MATERIALS AND SUPPLIES INVENTORY

F. WORK-IN-PROCESS INVENTORY

G. FINISHED GOODS INVENTORY

H. AMOUNT OF TOTAL INVENTORY VALUED ON LIFO BASIS – Report the dollar value of inventories included in the total inventory figure that are valued on a last-in, first-out (LIFO) basis. THIS figure should be reported net of the LIFO adjustment or "reserve."

I. LIFO ADJUSTMENT OR "RESERVE" – Report the dollar value of the LIFO adjustment or "reserve" associated with the LIFO INVENTORY.

OPERATIONAL STATUS

☐ Ceased operations
☐ Sold to another company – *Enter name and date in "Remarks"*
☐ Acquired another manufacturing operation – *Enter name and date in "Remarks"*

Remarks

CERTIFICATION

This form is substantially accurate and has been prepared in accordance with the instructions.

Signature of authorized person	Title	Date

M M-3(SD) (3-7-80)

GENERAL INTRODUCTION

The information provided on these forms is used by the Bureau of the Census to prepare monthly estimates for over 79 industry categories in manufacturing. The estimates are widely used by business and government analysts. They also provide major components for estimates of the gross national product (GNP) and related series.

The purpose of this report form is to provide a single report for multi-divisional firms included in the Manufactures' Shipments, Inventories and Orders Survey.

The first release of the manufacturing survey results is the Advance Report for Durable Goods, which is generally released about 22 days after the end of the month covered. Participating companies are entitled to receive a complementary copy of the

publication. If you (or, perhaps, your marketing department) would be interested in receiving this report, please call or write. In addition, any questions you may have about this form or the instructions may be directed to:

Bureau of the Census
ATTN: Industry Division
M-3 Branch
Washington, DC 20233

Telephone: (301) 763-2502

NOTE: A detailed instruction manual is mailed each year with the January reports. If you would like additional copies, please call or write. The instructions provided below are abstracted from the more detailed manual.

INSTRUCTIONS AND DEFINITIONS

1. **Definition of the Reporting Unit** — This form should be used to report the figures for each reporting unit of your firm. A reporting unit is generally a division, subsidiary, or other operating unit as defined by your company for financial or managerial purposes. Reporting units within the same industry category, as defined in the Instruction Manual, may be combined for reporting purposes. However, the Census Bureau may request that certain large operating units be subdivided along industry lines for reporting purposes. In addition, separate defense/nondefense reporting may be requested for the communication equipment, aircraft, shipbuilding, and ordnance categories.

2. **Foreign Subsidiaries** — The figures reported in this survey should be limited to domestic operations (the 50 States and the District of Columbia). While foreign subsidiaries should be excluded, transactions with foreign subsidiaries, as well as with unaffiliated customers, should be included.

3. **Intra-company Transactions** — To the extent permitted by your existing records, transactions between reporting units should be included.

4. **Survey Deadlines** — The first survey results are based on reports received through approximately the 18th of the month following the reporting period. If possible, please return your report by this time. Otherwise, the figures for your company will be estimated for the early report, with actual figures included in the final report only. This is particularly important for the reporting units marked "MFG — DURABLE." If a portion of the requested items can be reported early, please call or write so that arrangements for reporting of those data items on a separate form can be made.

5. **Reporting Instructions for Specific Items**

   a. **PERSON TO BE CONTACTED** — Indicate the name and telephone number of the person in your organization to be contacted about this survey. If preprinted, please check for accuracy and correct if wrong.

   b. **DESCRIPTION OF THE REPORTING UNIT** — This preprinted description is intended to describe the specific reporting unit. Any changes you wish to make in order to clarify the description may be made directly on the form. Your changes will be reflected in the future computer imprinting of the reporting unit description.

   c. **YOUR UNIT CODE** — Space is provided for a six-character code that you may assign to the reporting units. This code is intended for your use. At your request, the "Unit code" will be used to establish the sequence for imprinting the reporting units on the form.

   d. **REPORT PERIOD** — Please indicate the kind of reporting period covered (4 weeks, 5 weeks, calendar month, or other). Reports covering 4 weeks or 5 weeks or other reporting period should also indicate the ending date of the current report period.

6. **EACH OF THE 9 DATA ITEMS COLLECTED IN THIS SURVEY IS DESCRIBED BELOW.**

   a. **SALES** — Report net sales (or shipments) made during the reporting period. Exclude all taxes that were not included in the cost of goods you purchased. Include sales and transfers to other reporting units of your company.

   b. **NEW ORDERS** — Report net new orders received during the reporting period. Include (1) sales value of orders received and filled during the reporting period; (2) orders received for future deliveries; and (3) the net sales value of changes to existing contracts. Do not include orders requiring further negotiations, authorization, or funding before the order is final.

   c. **ORDER BACKLOG** — Include orders, as defined above that have not yet passed through the sales account.

   d. **TOTAL INVENTORY** — Report inventories at current cost or market as of the end of the reporting period. If your inventories are subject to LIFO valuation, report the value prior to the adjustment for the LIFO reserve. The reported figures should include all inventories in the 50 States and the District of Columbia to which you hold title.

   e. **INVENTORY OF MATERIALS AND SUPPLIES** — Include all raw materials and semifabricated purchased material at current cost.

   f. **INVENTORY OF WORK-IN-PROCESS** — Include all inventories undergoing fabrication within plants of the reporting unit at current cost.

   g. **INVENTORY OF FINISHED GOODS** — Include all inventories that are ready for shipment to customer at current cost. Include goods bought for resale requiring no further processing.

   h. **LIFO INVENTORY** — Report the dollar value of inventories included in the total inventory figure that are valued on a last-in, first-out (LIFO) basis. This figure should be reported net of the LIFO adjustment or "reserve."

   i. **LIFO ADJUSTMENT OR RESERVE** — Report the dollar value of the LIFO adjustment or "reserve" associated with the LIFO INVENTORY.

7. **Special Reporting Instructions** — Please refer to the Instruction Manual for additional instructions for reporting:
   - Long-term contracts
   - Reports in the shipbuilding and aircraft industries
   - Reporting of receipts for lease or rental of products which you manufacture.

REMARKS

CERTIFICATION — This report is substantially accurate and has been prepared in accordance with instructions.

Signature of authorized official	Title and organization	Date

FORM M-3(MDI) (4-1-87)

Construction Sector Data

Construction data are used as inputs to the GNP model in investment spending. There are three major construction groupings on which markets trade:

1. Housing starts and permits;
2. New and existing one-family home sales; and
3. Construction spending.

Of these, housing starts are a main focus because residential structures account for about a third of gross private domestic investment. Business structures account for another 20%.

HOUSING STARTS AND PERMITS

As is the case for the industrial sector, since 1959 the Commerce Department has used a sort of input–output analytical structure for housing (see Figure 9.1). Private housing permits are reported by the size of structure. The units are then tracked through start, completion, and eventual sale. The units are subdivided into categories for one-family homes, two units, three and four units, and five or more units

FIGURE 9.1 The Housing Pipeline

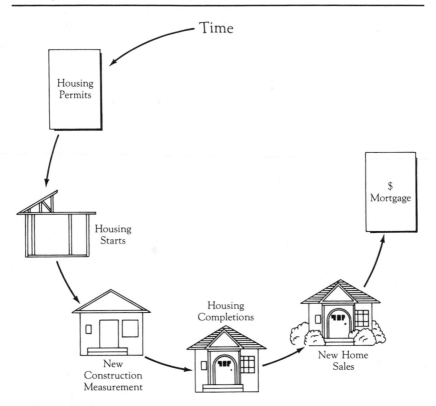

(a catch-all category that mainly covers apartment buildings). Since the tax code allows deductions for home mortgage interest, single-family units are by far the most important, accounting for about 75% of all starts. Starts are also reported by region (Northeast, South, Midwest, and West) and by whether they are inside or outside *metropolitan statistical areas* (MSAs) (see Table 9.1).

Similarly, there are breakdowns for the tables covering privately owned units authorized in permit-issuing places (about 5% of the United States still does not require permits to be filed (mainly rural areas). Separate data are also collected for mobile homes.

These data are compiled from a survey conducted by Census Bureau staff during the first two weeks of each month via face-to-face

TABLE 9.1
New Privately Owned Housing Units Started
(Thousands of units. Detail may not add to total because of rounding)

Period	Total	In structures with— 1 unit	2 units	3 and 4 units	5 units or more	Inside MSA's[1]	Outside MSA's[1]	North-east	Midwest	South	West
ANNUAL DATA											
1980	1,292.2	852.2	48.8	60.7	330.5	913.6	378.7	125.4	218.1	642.7	306.0
1981	1,084.2	705.4	38.2	52.9	287.7	759.8	324.3	117.3	165.2	561.6	240.0
1982	1,062.2	662.6	31.9	48.1	319.6	784.8	277.4	116.7	149.1	591.0	205.4
1983	1,703.0	1,067.6	41.8	71.7	522.0	1,351.1	351.9	167.6	217.9	935.2	382.3
1984	1,749.5	1,084.2	38.6	82.8	544.0	1,414.6	334.9	204.1	243.4	866.0	436.0
1985	1,741.8	1,072.4	37.0	56.4	576.1	1,493.9	247.9	251.7	239.7	782.3	468.2
1986	1,805.4	1,179.4	36.1	47.9	542.0	1,546.3	259.1	293.5	295.8	733.1	483.0
1987	1,620.5	1,146.4	27.8	37.5	408.7	1,372.2	248.2	269.0	297.9	633.9	419.8
1988	1,488.1	1,081.3	23.4	35.4	348.0	1,243.0	245.1	235.3	274.0	574.9	403.9
1989	1,376.1	1,003.3	19.9	35.3	317.6	1,128.1	248.0	178.5	265.8	536.2	395.7
MONTHLY DATA											
Not Seasonally Adjusted											
1989: January	100.1	69.9	1.9	2.8	25.6	84.0	16.1	15.3	11.5	45.4	28.0
February	85.8	59.3	1.3	2.4	22.9	75.8	10.1	8.8	10.5	39.2	27.3
March	117.8	83.5	1.7	2.6	29.9	99.5	18.3	12.2	22.5	49.5	33.6
April	129.4	100.4	2.4	3.5	23.2	104.8	24.6	19.9	25.3	52.0	32.2
May	131.7	101.4	1.6	2.4	26.4	105.1	26.6	17.5	27.7	50.2	36.4
June	143.2	100.3	1.8	3.5	37.7	117.2	25.9	17.9	28.4	52.2	44.6
July	134.7	98.0	2.1	3.3	31.3	109.5	25.2	19.6	29.3	46.0	39.8
August	122.4	91.7	1.5	3.7	25.5	99.8	22.6	14.5	23.5	49.0	35.3
September	109.3	82.4	2.5	1.8	22.6	87.3	22.0	14.4	23.5	40.9	30.6
October	130.1	91.2	1.5	4.3	33.1	102.2	27.9	16.4	28.3	50.1	35.3
November	96.6	71.9	1.2	2.3	21.1	79.6	16.9	14.8	22.1	34.9	24.8
December	75.0	53.4	0.6	2.6	18.3	63.2	11.8	7.2	13.1	26.9	27.7
1990: January	99.2	67.9	1.6	2.4	27.3	84.6	14.6	10.0	14.9	40.1	34.2
February	86.9	65.9	1.1	1.4	18.4	72.4	14.5	9.1	11.4	39.9	26.4
March	108.5	83.2	1.2	1.7	22.4	87.5	21.0	10.0	20.6	46.3	31.6
April	119.0	90.0	2.9	2.3	23.9	93.8	25.2	12.5	28.9	45.5	32.1
May[r]	121.1	92.4	1.2	2.1	25.4	96.8	24.3	12.6	28.4	47.4	32.7
June[r]	116.7	88.3	1.6	2.0	24.7	89.5	27.2	11.4	26.5	50.9	28.0
July[p]	110.8	85.6	1.5	1.3	22.4	88.0	22.8	11.3	24.1	44.1	31.2
Year to date: 1989	842.8	612.8	12.7	20.5	196.9	696.0	146.8	111.2	155.2	334.5	242.0
1990	762.2	573.3	11.1	13.3	164.6	612.6	149.6	76.9	154.8	314.2	216.2
Seasonally Adjusted Annual Rate											
1989: January	1,659	1,188	66		405	(NA)	(NA)	288	304	639	428
February	1,454	1,026	60		368	(NA)	(NA)	219	267	571	397
March	1,405	979	51		375	(NA)	(NA)	163	301	547	394
April	1,341	1,028	62		251	(NA)	(NA)	205	272	529	335
May	1,308	977	43		288	(NA)	(NA)	174	243	515	376
June	1,414	971	55		388	(NA)	(NA)	168	242	553	451
July	1,424	1,029	58		337	(NA)	(NA)	190	276	531	427
August	1,325	987	54		284	(NA)	(NA)	140	236	559	390
September	1,263	969	56		238	(NA)	(NA)	160	247	486	370
October	1,423	1,023	60		340	(NA)	(NA)	174	285	567	397
November	1,347	1,010	47		290	(NA)	(NA)	179	296	498	374
December	1,273	931	53		289	(NA)	(NA)	138	267	440	428
1990: January	1,568	1,099	53		416	(NA)	(NA)	168	373	526	501
February	1,488	1,154	42		292	(NA)	(NA)	224	293	581	390
March	1,307	996	35		276	(NA)	(NA)	139	280	520	368
April	1,216	898	53		265	(NA)	(NA)	124	284	469	339
May[r]	1,206	897	36		273	(NA)	(NA)	127	256	487	336
June[r]	1,179	885	37		257	(NA)	(NA)	114	238	534	293
July[p]	1,148	873	32		243	(NA)	(NA)	108	225	498	317
AVERAGE RELATIVE STANDARD ERRORS[2]											
Annual (percent)	1	1	6	5	2	1	4	2	2	2	1
Monthly (percent)	3	3	14	17	9	3	8	8	6	5	5
Year to date (percent)	1	1	7	5	2	1	4	2	2	2	1

NA Not available. [p]Preliminary. [r]Revised.
[1] Metropolitan statistical areas.
[2] Average Relative Standard Errors (Avg. RSE): Annual—Avg. RSE for the last 2 years; Year to date—Avg. RSE for the current period and the same period last year; Monthly—Avg. RSE for the latest 6-month period (January-June or July-December).

and telephone interviews. Officials choose the counties to be surveyed based on population and the prior volume of private construction activity. Field staff visit local permit offices and sample the applications filed the prior month. They then contact the owner, contractor, or builder and require that forms detailing the value of construction (generally determined from contractors' billings) be filed each month until the project is completed. Seasonal adjustment is done for each category separately and then the results are combined into the overall starts and permits numbers.

Major revisions to starts and permits are rare, with the average error in the rate of change estimated at only plus or minus two percentage points for the year to date. But errors may stem from two sources. First, construction may have begun before a permit had been approved, causing upward revision to prior starts. This is common in the areas where land clearing or pipe laying does not count as construction. Second, there is a substantial misreporting element to this series where builders misclassify their projects. Only after Census Bureau workers have visited the site can this error be rectified. In this case, the composition will change but not the overall starts number.

Housing is one of the most cyclical components of the economy because of its volatility and historically quick response to changes in interest rates. Indeed, building permits are included in the official *Index of Leading Indicators* (see Chapter 14) because they are at the moving edge of the housing industry. Housing is subject to the same influences that dominate *The Employment Report* (see Chapter 4). Income and wealth effects from employment change the market for homes in the short run, while demographics determine whether there is a market. The birth and death rates, immigration, household formations, and the age and health of the population determine the breakdown of the starts and sales patterns.

Table 9.1 shows that overall starts in the one million unit range is indicative of recession (these are the levels posted during the 1981–82 recession). More recently, a healthy housing market has been marked by starts in the one and a half to two million range. The numbers for permits are in a comparable range but generally come in slightly below the starts numbers. This makes intuitive sense in a capitalist economy where some project is always on the drawing board.

NEW HOME SALES

This report is derived from the starts data since units in the original survey are followed through to completion and sale. Its breakdown, therefore, parallels that of the *Housing Starts Report*, with sales subdivided by region. The sales report also gives a median and average price and an I/S ratio expressed in months. The additional data allow the analyst to gauge the underlying strength of housing demand. Rising prices and a low I/S ratio (a rule of thumb is under three months' supply), for instance, will indicate a strong market.

CONSTRUCTION SPENDING

The construction spending report is to housing starts as PCE is to retail sales (see Chapters 5 and 6). That is, construction spending summarizes overall activity using the housing starts numbers as an input for the residential sector (about 45% of the total). But the construction report goes farther, covering nonresidential (about 30%) and public activity (the remaining 25%) as well. The broad categories for the value of new construction put in place are given in Table 9.2.
    New construction is defined to include:

New buildings and structures;
Additions and alterations;
Mechanical and electrical installations;
Site preparation and outside related construction (such as sidewalks, streets, parking lots, utility connections, outdoor lighting, etc.);
Installations of boilers, overhead hoists and cranes, and blast furnaces;

TABLE 9.2
Annual Value of New Construction Put in Place: 1964–89
(Millions of dollars)

Type of construction	Current dollars					Constant (1987) dollars				
	1985ʳ	1986ʳ	1987ʳ	1988ʳ	1989ʳ	1985ʳ	1986ʳ	1987ʳ	1988ʳ	1989ʳ
Total new construction	368,736	398,206	410,208	422,075	432,066	392,754	411,605	410,196	405,212	399,942
Private construction	290,913	313,613	319,639	327,102	333,515	312,493	325,948	319,541	314,367	308,514
Residential buildings	158,474	187,148	194,656	198,101	196,551	172,338	195,377	194,622	190,292	182,045
New housing units	114,662	133,192	139,915	138,947	139,202	124,699	139,052	139,893	133,469	128,944
1 unit	86,123	102,154	114,463	116,649	116,898	93,659	106,621	114,432	112,045	108,279
2 or more units	28,539	31,038	25,452	22,298	22,304	31,040	32,430	25,462	21,424	20,665
Improvements	43,812	53,956	54,741	59,154	57,349	47,639	56,325	54,729	56,823	53,101
Nonresidential buildings	95,317	91,171	91,994	97,102	103,358	102,510	94,794	91,944	93,518	96,033
Industrial	15,769	13,747	13,707	14,930	18,507	16,960	14,293	13,695	14,375	17,188
Office	31,580	28,591	26,430	28,044	28,597	33,967	29,742	26,422	27,012	26,582
Hotels, Motels	7,301	7,451	7,380	6,794	7,617	7,853	7,746	7,381	6,547	7,078
Other commercial	28,048	28,170	29,015	30,059	30,791	30,159	29,283	28,994	28,946	28,601
Religious	2,409	2,702	2,753	2,822	2,972	2,590	2,806	2,751	2,718	2,762
Educational	1,896	2,343	3,438	2,912	3,308	2,039	2,435	3,437	2,806	3,072
Hospital and institutional	5,583	5,422	6,035	7,219	7,537	6,007	5,637	6,031	6,954	7,005
Miscellaneous[1]	2,729	2,745	3,236	4,320	4,028	2,935	2,853	3,233	4,160	3,744
Farm nonresidential	2,197	2,072	2,503	2,270	2,356	2,366	2,154	2,503	2,187	2,190
Public utilities	32,200	30,948	27,858	27,503	28,549	32,528	31,353	27,842	26,338	25,746
Telecommunications	8,397	9,106	9,194	9,801	9,132	8,303	9,195	9,160	9,690	8,198
Other public utilities	23,803	21,842	18,664	17,702	19,417	24,226	22,158	18,683	16,648	17,548
Railroads	4,046	2,891	2,451	2,793	2,716	4,079	2,886	2,454	2,668	2,513
Electric light and power	15,968	15,392	12,656	10,873	11,743	16,369	15,605	12,669	10,186	10,583
Gas	3,517	3,273	3,188	3,659	4,616	3,506	3,372	3,191	3,440	4,144
Petroleum pipelines	272	286	369	377	342	271	294	369	354	307
All other private[2]	2,726	2,275	2,628	2,126	2,702	2,751	2,270	2,630	2,033	2,501
Public construction	77,823	84,593	90,569	94,973	98,551	80,260	85,658	90,655	90,845	91,429
Buildings	27,861	31,115	32,962	36,163	39,202	30,000	32,351	32,955	34,820	36,404
Housing and redevelopment	2,893	3,029	3,262	3,366	3,841	3,146	3,164	3,262	3,233	3,557
Industrial	1,968	1,657	1,457	1,413	1,300	2,118	1,724	1,458	1,361	1,208
Educational	9,329	10,948	11,476	14,267	16,727	10,033	11,368	11,471	13,737	15,534
Hospital	2,497	2,334	2,559	2,693	2,486	2,686	2,429	2,558	2,594	2,310
Other[3]	11,174	13,148	14,208	14,424	14,848	12,016	13,666	14,207	13,896	13,795
Highways and streets	23,741	25,318	26,958	30,141	29,502	23,455	24,909	27,050	28,449	27,368
Military facilities	3,235	3,867	4,324	3,579	3,520	3,341	3,907	4,327	3,417	3,265
Conservation and development	5,144	4,937	5,519	4,728	4,968	5,279	5,005	5,517	4,567	4,589
Sewer systems	6,960	7,654	8,998	8,634	9,229	7,139	7,757	8,994	8,342	8,524
Water supply facilities	2,580	3,183	3,674	3,917	3,923	2,671	3,228	3,669	3,792	3,684
Miscellaneous public[4]	8,302	8,517	8,134	7,810	8,207	8,374	8,500	8,143	7,459	7,593

ʳRevised.
[1]Includes amusement and recreational buildings, bus and airline terminals, animal hospitals and shelters, etc.   [2]Includes privately owned streets and bridges, parking areas, sewer and water facilities, parks and playgrounds, golf courses, airfields, etc.   [3]Includes general administrative buildings, prisons, police and fire stations, courthouses, civic centers, passenger terminals, space facilities, postal facilities, etc.
[4]Includes open amusement and recreational facilities, power generating facilities, transit systems, airfields, open parking facilities, etc.

Fixed, largely site-fabricated equipment not housed in a building; and

Cost and installation of materials inside a building and used to support production, such as concrete platforms and steel girders.

Specifically excluded are:

Maintenance and repairs to existing structures;
Production machinery such as presses, stamping and packaging machines and special purpose equipment;
Drilling of oil and gas wells; and
Land acquisition.

The value of new construction is reported each month in both current dollars and "real" or deflated terms. It includes the cost of materials and labor, the contractor's profit, the cost of architectural and engineering work, associated overhead and office costs, and interest and taxes paid during the construction process.

Private nonresidential buildings, which cover almost a third of the total, fall into eight categories enumerated in Table 9.2. A mail survey is conducted at the end of each month requiring the owners of the buildings to respond with the estimated dollar value of work completed based on contractors' billings. The sample is quite small (the certainty of selection varies by the size of the project, which results in 56 strata having a probability from $1/1$ for the largest projects to $1/150$ for those costing less than $250) and is based on a universe established as of mid-month by the F. W. Dodge Company, which tracks private projects and contracts as they are awarded.

Responses are due by the third week of the subsequent month and are tallied into the total. Under this system, a new project cannot appear until it is at least two-weeks old (e.g., August awards are not in the universe until September 15), so the survey has its own revision process built in. Also, responses are notoriously slow; late responses account for more than half the remaining revisions.

For the remaining construction categories, the sample and data collection procedures vary. Most public utilities are tallied on an annual basis from the data filed with regulatory agencies. The exception is the telephone companies which are polled directly. Federal estimates are based on construction reports filed monthly by 40 different agencies which have building budgets. These are subclassified into nine categories based on the agency responsible for the work. For example, Veterans Administration expenditures are classified as hospital, while Bureau of Reclamation expenditures are classified as conservation and development. State and local expenditures also come from F. W. Dodge data (increased by 5% for nonreporters). Farm nonresidential and "other private" data, which cover private streets, bridges, dams and the like, are largely estimates. The former is based on annual data in the U.S. *Department of Agriculture's Income and Balance Sheet Statistics Report*, while the latter is blown up from the F. W. Dodge Reports.

THE F. W. DODGE INDEX

The F. W. Dodge Company, founded in 1890 in Boston, maintains a network of 1,300 professional reporters and correspondents and 21 full-time researchers in 140 branch offices around the United States. Employees use private and public sources to compile information in a standardized survey format on building and construction projects. In a typical year, Dodge employees make two million personal or telephone interviews on 76,000 sources, including owners; architects; engineers; contractors; federal, state, and local officials; regulatory agencies; and others. Their other data sources include city council minutes, local newspapers, federal procurement data, and attendance at bid openings and meetings of professional associations.

Dodge packages the information in computer programs and in construction reports available to the public for a fee. Since breakdowns are available by region and project cost, the reports are in wide use in the industry as a planning and sales tool. During the third week of each month, F. W. Dodge releases a seasonally adjusted *Index of Contracts and New Construction Value Report* which covers activity in the prior month (see Table 9.3). While its construction is proprietary, the Dodge index differs in two important ways from the Commerce

TABLE 9.3
New Construction

Construction Contracts

Period	Total Value Index (1982 = 100)	Commercial and Industrial Floor Space (millions of square feet)
1980[r]	97	904
1981[r]	100	919
1982[r]	100	690
1983[r]	124	756
1984[r]	136	955
1985[r]	150	1,097
1986[r]	159	1,016
1987[r]	165	1,019
1988[r]	166	973
1989[r]	170	926
		Annual Rates
1989: May[r]	167	909
June[r]	172	916
July[r]	171	915
Aug[r]	169	805
Sept[r]	186	1,008
Oct[r]	180	892
Nov[r]	167	812
Dec[r]	166	805
1990: Jan[r]	160	883
Feb[r]	156	798
Mar[r]	160	828
Apr[r]	148	745
May[p]	156	802
June[p]	153	693

Note: New construction expenditures series revised beginning 1975.
Sources: Department of Commerce (Bureau of the Census) and McGraw-Hill Information Systems Company, F.W. Dodge Division.
r = revised
p = projected

Department's data: it covers only new, not ongoing, construction and it excludes additions and alterations to existing buildings. Thus, it tends to exaggerate movements in construction. Nevertheless, the Dodge Index may be a leading indicator of turns in construction. And since 1986, the Commerce Department has used Dodge data for private nonresidential projects valued at $50,000 or more in the United States except Hawaii.

THE RELATIONSHIP OF CONSTRUCTION SPENDING TO GNP

The construction estimates differ from the gross private domestic fixed investment numbers in the GNP reports because of differences in coverage and estimation procedures. The GNP estimates of structures include several items not in the construction report, namely mobile homes, oil and gas wells, mine shafts, brokers commissions on sales, and purchases by the private sector of used structures from the public sector. The differences in estimation procedures include different seasonals, some definitional discrepancies, and the failure of the GNP accounts to incorporate all the revisions to the value-in-place series. Among the definitional differences are the treatment of dormitories and fraternity and sorority houses (counted as educational structures in the construction reports but as residential structures in GNP). Among the time frame discrepancies, the GNP accounts incorporate land development costs from 1959 forward, but the value-in-place series incorporates them from 1964.

These discrepancies represent only a mild annoyance to the GNP projectionist concerned with the economy's current rate of growth. A good proxy for the nonresidential structures component in GNP is the private nonresidential spending component in the construction spending data. Similarly, the proxy for housing expenditures in the GNP accounts is the new residential units number in this report.

SURVEY OF CAPITAL SPENDING

Initiated in 1947, the Commerce Department's *Survey of Capital Spending* reports five times each year on actual and anticipated *plant and equipment* (P&E) nominal dollar expenditures. Surveys of about 5,000 businesses are taken quarterly, initially in October/November for publication in December to cover the coming year. These are then updated in January/February, April/May, July/August, and October/November. While the actual amounts are reported as the year progresses, the estimated amounts remain subject to variation. This is because firms may not be able to obtain financing or boards of directors may approve different amounts because of a change in business conditions.

Analysts use the latest P&E survey to project the business fixed investment sector of GNP, but recent research indicates the two differ by as much as 2 percentage points. *Nonresidential fixed investment* (NRFI) consists of both producers durable equipment (machinery) and business structures (factories, warehouses, and the like). Differences between the P&E series and NRFI include timing problems (NRFI is based on construction put in place, while P&E expenditures may occur later) and definitional problems (NRFI is a broader series which covers farming, real estate, and professional services as well as industry). Thus, it is not surprising that the correlation loosened during the 1980s as the economy became more service oriented. There has also been a tendency for expenditures to be front-loaded in recent years into the first half of each year. Still, the annual survey is the only available predictor of NRFI.

10

Net Exports

The international sector can be thought of as leakage from the economic system. A country that has closed borders does not trade and its GNP accounts are entirely self-determined. But consider a country that achieves efficiencies by being able to produce something cheaper or faster than its neighbors, reflecting either lower wage rates and higher productivity or readily available natural resources. Then there exists a clear advantage to be gained from trading this product for another which is not so cheap to produce. Foreign trade has been born.

Trade has two sides and each has price and volume aspects. Economists measure the dollar value of *net exports*, which is defined as the difference between *exports* (commodities produced domestically but being shipped outside the country's border) and *imports* (commodities coming in). The *foreign exchange rate* is generally defined as the relative price of two currencies, as reflected in price levels. Put another way, *exchange rates* are the price of one country's money in terms of other countries' money. With perfect asset substitutability (that is, no capital controls) and rational behavior, exchange rates are determined by purchasing power parity. That is, the country with the higher money growth rate and higher inflation will have higher projected returns. These returns are exactly offset by a deterioration in its exchange rate.

Exchange rates affect investment returns and the relative costs of goods to the consumer. So, their movements bring about a chain of decisions about whether to invest at home or abroad and whether to purchase foreign or domestic goods that have the potential to affect the economy. How exchange rates affect the economy has produced a distinct body of theory.

The J Curve

Purchasing power parity gives rise to an expectation for changes in trade imbalances known as the *J curve*. This theory says that when a particular country's currency falls, its exports may not go up in the short run but will rise substantially in the long run. Behavior modification explains the lag. Say U.S. producers react to a lower dollar by lowering the foreign currency prices of their products. This would stimulate overseas sales at the expense of profit margins. Or, domestic prices might be raised to compensate, leaving foreign currency prices constant. In the latter case, export profits would rise helping finance modernization for plant and equipment that would eventually strengthen the United States's competitive position. Hence, exports would rise over the long run but not necessarily in the short run.

The effects of a deteriorating currency on imports are not so clear-cut and depend on consumers' responsiveness to the price changes. Economists call this *elasticity of demand*. In theory, a small country faced with given world prices would reduce its demand for imported goods if its currency fell. But in some cases, the response is more complicated. If the exchange rate is expected to deteriorate further, consumers may instead first step up their purchases of foreign goods. Also, the value of imports may go up immediately after a currency deterioration as goods purchased abroad in previous months and priced in foreign currencies are worth more. Thus, as deliveries are made, recorded imports are initially increased for a given volume of imports. Later, imports would fall if consumers cut back their purchases. This is another example of the J curve effect. In sum, the J curve indicates that the initial response to a deteriorating currency may be an increase in the trade deficit. But over time, the trade gap falls as the currency deteriorates.

History

Until the 1980s, the United States's trade imbalances were relatively small and temporary, averaging within 1% of GNP (see Figure 10.1). But the trade account deteriorated from a position of approximate balance in 1980 to a peak deficit of more than 3% of GNP in 1987. Even though the U.S. trade deficit has improved since 1987, it is still at a historically high level of 1 to 2% of GNP, or around $100 billion. Moreover, the components that comprise trade make up more than 15% of productive capacity. Recent research blames the growth in the trade deficit on *intertemporal shocks* (things that affect the time distribution of supply and demand, thereby encouraging foreign indebtedness). These include:

growth in the federal deficit (which substituted present consumption for future consumption);

a decontrol of capital flows (especially in Japan) which helped reduce U.S. interest rates and prevent adjustment in the dollar; and

cyclical movements in investment (due in part to tax incentives) which reduced the ability to produce consumption goods and, therefore, encouraged international borrowing.

Following the dismantling of the Bretton Woods fixed-exchange rate system in effect from 1944 to 1973, the dollar has moved wildly. Most recently, there was almost a 40% trade-weighted surge in the U.S. unit from 1980 to 1985. After the Plaza Accord of April 1985, central banks began intervening in the exchange markets. The dollar plum-

FIGURE 10.1 Foreign trade.

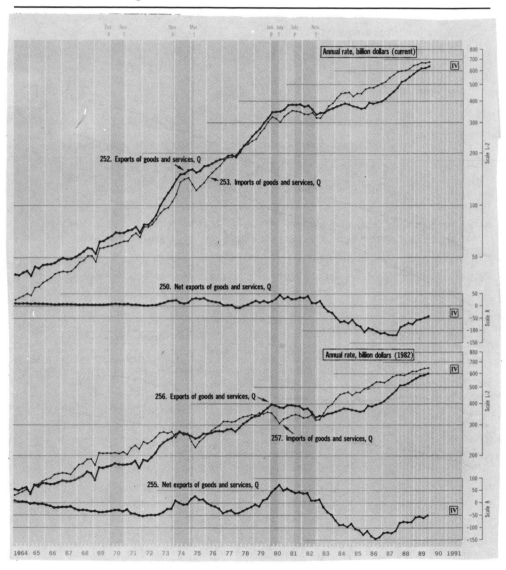

FIGURE 10.1 Foreign trade.

meted by an equal amount, returning to the levels set earlier in the decade. And after improving in late 1989, the dollar renewed its downtrend in 1990. The U.S. trade deficit mirrored these moves, but with a lag, as suggested by the J curve. After peaking at $220 billion in the mid-1980s, the trade gap fell steadily to $109 billion in 1989. Its improvement was impeded but not interrupted in 1990 by the dollar's up-move in 1989.

MERCHANDISE TRADE BALANCE

The primary measure of U.S. trade is the monthly *merchandise trade balance* (the only non-survey, non-judgmental report produced by the Commerce Department). The values for imports and exports in the report are based on actual data obtained from the U.S. Customs Service, a branch of the Treasury Department. In order to properly incorporate these data, the report is released with a lag of about 45 days after the end of the reporting month. It includes seasonally adjusted and NSA data for six end-use categories. They are:

1. food, feeds and beverages;
2. industrial supplies and materials;
3. capital goods;
4. autos;
5. consumer goods; and
6. other merchandise (see Table 10.1).

Separate NSA tables are also included for oil (price and volume), country information (Canada, Western Europe, OPEC, Japan, and Mexico are the main trading partners for the United States), and bilateral trade with all 150 countries of the world.

TABLE 10.1

U.S. Merchandise Exports and Imports (Billions of dollars; monthly data seasonally adjusted)

| Period | Merchandise exports (f.a.s. value)[1] | | | | | | | General merchandise imports (customs value)[3] | | | | | | | | Trade balance | |
| | Total[2] | Principal end-use commodity category | | | | | | Total | Principal end-use commodity category | | | | | | General merchandise imports (c.i.f. value) | Exports (f.a.s) less imports (customs value) | Exports (f.a.s) less imports (c.i.f.) |
		Foods, feeds, and beverages	Industrial supplies and materials	Capital goods except automotive	Automotive vehicles, parts, and engines	Consumer goods (nonfood) except automotive	Other[2]		Foods, feeds, and beverages	Industrial supplies and materials	Capital goods except automotive	Automotive vehicles, parts, and engines	Consumer goods (nonfood) except automotive	Other			
1982	216.4	31.3	61.7	72.7	15.7	14.3	20.7	244.0	17.1	112.0	35.4	33.3	39.7	6.5	254.9	-27.5	-38.4
1983	205.6	30.9	56.7	67.2	16.8	13.4	20.5	258.0	18.2	107.0	40.9	40.8	44.9	6.3	269.9	-52.4	-64.2
1984	224.0	31.5	61.7	72.0	20.6	13.3	24.0	4 330.7	21.0	123.7	59.8	53.5	60.0	7.8	346.4	-106.7	-122.4
1985	5 218.8	24.0	58.5	73.9	22.9	12.6	27.3	4 336.5	21.9	113.9	65.1	66.8	68.3	9.4	352.5	-117.7	-133.6
1986	227.2	22.3	57.3	75.8	21.7	14.2	35.9	365.4	24.4	101.3	71.8	78.2	79.4	10.4	382.3	-138.3	-155.1
1987	254.1	24.3	66.7	86.2	24.6	17.7	34.6	406.2	24.8	111.0	84.5	85.2	88.7	12.1	424.4	-152.1	-170.3
1988	5 322.4	32.3	85.1	109.2	29.3	23.1	43.4	441.0	24.8	118.3	101.4	87.7	95.9	12.8	459.5	-118.5	-137.1
1989	363.8	37.2	99.3	138.8	34.8	36.4	17.2	473.2	25.1	132.3	113.3	86.1	102.9	13.6	493.2	-109.4	-129.4
1989:																	
Apr	30.4	3.2	8.3	11.7	3.1	2.9	1.3	38.7	2.0	11.0	9.0	7.3	8.3	1.1	40.3	-8.3	-9.9
May	30.7	3.2	8.7	11.4	2.9	3.0	1.5	40.9	2.2	11.8	9.8	7.3	8.7	1.1	42.6	-10.3	-11.9
June	31.6	3.4	8.7	11.8	2.9	3.0	1.5	39.5	2.1	11.3	9.7	6.9	8.5	1.1	41.1	-8.0	-9.6
July	29.9	3.0	8.4	11.8	2.5	2.9	1.3	39.0	2.1	11.2	9.3	6.8	8.6	1.0	40.7	-9.1	-10.8
Aug	30.2	3.0	8.5	11.7	2.7	3.0	1.4	40.5	2.1	11.6	9.6	7.2	8.8	1.2	42.3	-10.3	-12.1
Sept	30.1	2.8	8.1	12.3	2.6	2.9	1.4	38.9	1.9	10.5	9.4	7.0	8.8	1.2	40.5	-8.8	-10.4
Oct	31.4	3.0	8.4	12.3	3.1	3.0	1.6	41.6	2.1	11.9	9.9	7.0	9.1	1.4	43.4	-10.2	-12.0
Nov	30.6	3.2	8.3	11.1	3.0	3.4	1.7	40.5	2.1	11.1	10.0	7.2	9.0	1.3	42.3	-9.9	-11.7
Dec	31.3	3.0	7.9	12.3	3.1	3.4	1.6	38.1	2.0	10.4	9.4	6.5	8.4	1.2	39.7	-6.8	-8.4
1990:																	
Jan	31.4	3.1	8.6	12.0	2.5	3.4	1.8	41.6	2.3	12.9	9.8	6.4	8.9	1.3	43.4	-10.2	-12.1
Feb	31.6	3.1	8.0	12.8	2.8	3.4	1.6	38.7	2.3	11.1	9.1	6.7	8.3	1.2	40.4	-7.1	-8.8
Mar	33.3	3.2	8.6	12.8	3.3	3.4	1.8	41.6	2.5	11.5	9.8	7.9	8.7	1.3	43.5	-8.4	-10.2
Apr	32.1	3.0	8.4	12.4	3.0	3.5	1.7	39.4	2.3	10.5	9.8	6.9	8.7	1.3	41.1	-7.3	-9.1
May	32.8	2.9	8.4	12.7	3.5	3.6	1.7	40.5	2.3	11.3	9.5	7.5	8.7	1.3	42.3	-7.7	-9.6

[1] Includes Department of Defense Military Assistance Program grant-aid shipments.

[2] Includes goods other than intransit shipments.

[3] Total arrivals of imported goods other than intransit shipments.

[4] Total includes revisions not reflected in detail.

[5] Total exports are on a revised statistical month basis; end-use categories are on a statistical month basis.

NOTE.—Data shown include trade of the U.S. Virgin Islands.

Data revised beginning 1988. For 1989, adjustments were made for carryover, corrections, distribution of undocumented exports to Canada, and reexports to appropriate end-use and commodity categories. In addition, seasonally adjusted data were revised for 1988 forward.

Source: Department of Commerce, Bureau of the Census.

Imports

Under the 1930 Tariff Act, the U.S. Customs Service is charged with collecting a duty on imports. Since the "chicken wars" of 1964–65, when imported poultry nearly drove domestic farmers out of business, tariffs have been set by commodity class or by country. Most are set either under acts of Congress or by the Commerce and State Departments (which are charged with enforcing the international General Agreement on Tariffs and Trade or GATT*) and are meant to encourage or hinder trade. In a relatively few instances, there are quota requirements. For instance, there is a relatively high 25% tariff on imported trucks which helps to protect domestic market share. The Soviet Union generally pays higher duties than other nations, a result of our historically poor relations. Textiles and apparel imported from Taiwan and other lesser developed countries are still a big quota factor.

About 1.3 million tax documents are filed each month with the Customs Service by brokers identifying the *import value* (based on billings) and the categories of imports. Treasury Department Customs Agents are responsible for testing the contents of shipments and verifying values. Approximately 80% of these documents are catalogued in the *automated broker interface* (ABI) computer system making them easy for Commerce Department staff to interpret. They are encoded into 14,000 categories using a 10-digit system called the *harmonized tariff schedule*. This schedule was developed by the U.S. Trade Representative to determine end-use. The first six digits of the system correspond to international usage under the *Standard International Trade Classification System* developed at the United Nations. The reported imports numbers are "customs valued" only; in the recent past they have been valued for *costs, insurance, and freight* (CIF-valued). Of course, the adjustment will linearly blow up the dollar size of imports.

Not surprisingly, the best predictor of monthly non-oil imports is Treasury customs duties which are reported in the *Monthly Treasury*

Statement (see Chapter 11). The percentage change in customs duties must be seasonally adjusted using the factors in the trade report. For oil imports, the American Petroleum Institute reports the volume and the analyst must guess only at the average price since the spot market's monthly average may differ slightly from the Commerce Department's survey. In large part, import data can be thought of as measuring the strength of domestic demand. That is, a growing economy is consistent with strengthening imports.

Exports

Since there exists no tax reason to obtain data on exports, the Commerce Department developed a form called the *Shipper's Export Declaration* (SED) which is used to determine their value. The SED is filed with the Customs Service at the time of export. It serves the additional purpose of telling agents whether exports fall into categories prohibited by the State or Commerce Departments. After the SED is filed, export data are coded into approximately 9,000 10-digit areas, much like imports. They are valued *free along ship* (FAS) to exclude insurance costs.

The best predictor of monthly exports is factory shipments (a part of the industrial pipeline discussed in Chapter 9). Data from the NAPM report also indicate whether factory exports are higher or lower and should be kept in mind, even though they tend to be less accurate that the factory reports. Again, the appropriate seasonals from the trade report must be applied. Like imports, exports can be thought of as an indicator of demand—but from abroad. Growing economies overseas should expand exports from the United States.

Data Problems

The main error sources in the trade picture stem from two sources: smuggling and carry-over. Commerce Department officials refuse to hazard guesses about the extent of *smuggling*, except to note that drug imports are probably exponentially larger than the official numbers show. Private estimates indicate that the U.S. trade gap may be larger by a factor of $10 billion or more due to drug smuggling.

A far more interesting quirk of the trade data is *carry-over*. Carry-over is defined as the imports or exports that actually occurred in a prior month but were not captured until a later period. These numbers, historically, have been the main source of revisions to trade data. But by the late 1980s, carry-over rates had fallen to under 3% of imports and exports, in large part because the Commerce Department had begun to exchange computer tapes on trade with Canada. For example, although the measurement period for August closes on August 31, data processing will go on for 45 days after. The August trade gap will not be reported until mid-October. During that time, additional data collection may occur because the Customs Bureau may not have forwarded all the SEDs and tax documents to the Census Bureau. In fact, almost 0.6% of goods in the September 1990 trade report were due to carry-over. While this is a small percentage, it resulted in a $1.9 billion swing in the $9.4 billion trade gap, with $1.8 billion due to imports and $0.1 billion resulting from exports.

CURRENT ACCOUNT

The broadest measure of U.S. trade is the *current account* balance. This balance is a current dollar measure that incorporates services and unilateral transfers into the merchandise trade data (see Table 10.2). The bulk of the services and transfers data are estimates with substantial judgmental components (discussed later). During the 1980s, the deterioration in the current account mainly reflected movements in the trade balance and a movement in services from surplus toward deficit. This is because the J curve effects for the current account are not identical to those for the trade balance. Net investment income receipts increase immediately as the dollar falls, reflecting capital gains from asset revaluation. Also, there is a continuing positive effect

TABLE 10.2
U.S. International Transactions

In the first quarter of 1990, the current account deficit fell to $22.9 billion from $26.7 billion in the fourth quarter of 1989.

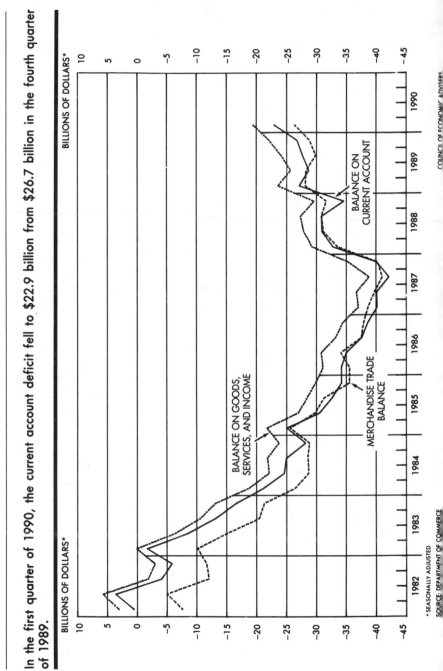

* SEASONALLY ADJUSTED

SOURCE: DEPARTMENT OF COMMERCE

COUNCIL OF ECONOMIC ADVISERS

234

[Millions of dollars; quarterly data seasonally adjusted, except as noted. Credits (+), debits (−)]

Period	Merchandise [1] [2]			Services			Investment income [4]			Balance on goods, services, and income	Remittances, pensions, and other unilateral transfers, net [1]	Balance on current account
	Exports	Imports	Net balance	Net military transactions [3]	Net travel and transportation receipts	Other services, net [4]	Receipts on U.S. assets abroad	Payments on foreign assets in U.S. [3]	Net			
1981............	237,085	−265,063	−27,978	−844	144	12,552	84,975	−53,626	31,349	15,223	−8,331	6,892
1982............	211,198	−247,642	−36,444	112	−992	12,981	85,346	−57,097	28,250	3,907	−9,775	−5,868
1983............	201,820	−268,900	−67,080	−163	−4,227	13,859	81,972	−54,549	27,423	−30,188	−9,956	−40,143
1984............	219,900	−332,422	−112,522	−2,147	−9,153	14,042	92,935	−69,542	23,394	−86,385	−12,621	−99,006
1985............	215,935	−338,083	−122,148	−4,096	−10,788	14,008	82,282	−66,115	16,166	−106,859	−15,473	−122,332
1986............	223,367	−368,425	−145,058	−4,907	−8,939	18,551	80,982	−70,013	10,969	−129,384	−16,009	−145,393
1987............	250,266	−409,766	−159,500	−3,530	−8,298	18,262	90,536	−85,210	5,326	−147,739	−14,575	−162,314
1988............	320,337	−447,323	−126,986	−5,452	−4,060	21,032	110,048	−108,438	1,610	−113,857	−15,005	−128,862
1989............	360,465	−475,329	−114,864	−6,320	659	26,123	127,536	−128,448	−912	−95,314	−14,720	−110,034
1988: I........	76,497	−109,988	−33,491	−1,075	−1,776	4,736	26,980	−24,580	2,400	−29,206	−3,476	−32,682
II.......	79,392	−110,494	−31,102	−1,139	−1,062	5,079	26,739	−26,330	409	−27,815	−3,060	−36,875
III......	80,511	−111,290	−30,779	−1,144	−624	5,391	27,942	−28,083	−141	−27,297	−3,461	−30,758
IV......	83,937	−115,551	−31,614	−2,094	−599	5,829	28,386	−29,445	−1,059	−29,537	−5,008	−34,545
1989: I........	88,267	−116,360	−28,093	−1,763	−57	5,899	30,872	−30,407	465	−23,549	−3,555	−27,104
II.......	91,111	−119,333	−28,222	−1,667	39	6,164	31,932	−33,889	−1,957	−25,643	−3,006	−28,649
III......	89,349	−119,152	−29,803	−1,114	−192	7,031	32,102	−32,085	17	−24,061	−3,530	−27,591
IV......	91,738	−120,484	−28,746	−1,776	870	7,030	32,629	−32,068	561	−22,061	−4,631	−26,692
1990: I [p]......	96,044	−122,415	−26,371	−1,370	1,213	6,468	31,057	−30,449	608	−19,452	−3,489	−22,941

[1] Excludes military.
[2] Adjusted from Census data for differences in timing and coverage.
[3] Quarterly data are not seasonally adjusted.

[4] Fees and royalties from U.S. direct investments abroad or from foreign direct investments in the United States are excluded from investment income and included in other services, net.

See p. 37 for continuation of table.

235

from the translation of income receipts denominated in non-dollar terms. Thus, the J curve for the current account records an immediate improvement, followed by a response in line with that for the trade balance.

CAPITAL ACCOUNT

The *capital account* measures transactions in assets between U.S. residents and non-residents (see Table 10.3). These asset transfers result from foreign trade or from unilateral transfers without a *quid pro quo* (such as a decision to buy a foreign security).

Financial assets encompass claims payable in money (loans, bank deposits, bonds, and equities are all examples) as well as intercompany accounts. The major organizing principle for the capital account is a distinction between U.S. assets abroad (claims) and foreign assets in the United States (liabilities). The functional breakdown distinguishes between U.S. and foreign government claims and those of private individuals.

DATA COLLECTION

The *balance of payments* data are one of the few statistical reports that have legal authority. The collection of information is undertaken under Section 8 of the *Bretton Woods Agreements Act of 1945*, which requires the publication of complete balance of payments information. However, the nature of these data require quarterly or annual mail surveys to be completed by businesses for direct investment, transportation, and services. Data on travel and unilateral transfers are compiled from annual voluntary surveys and so are subject to more uncertainty about timing and revisions. The U.S. Treasury Department supplies data on U.S. reserve assets and on international capital movements from the *Treasury International Capital Survey* (TIC). The latter is administered by the Federal Reserve Bank of New York,

TABLE 10.3

U.S. International Transactions

In the capital accounts, claims on foreigners reported by U.S. banks decreased $45.7 billion in the first quarter of 1990, compared to an increase of $32.7 billion in the fourth quarter of 1989. Liabilities to private foreigners reported by U.S. banks, excluding Treasury securities, decreased $28.1 billion in the first quarter, compared to an increase of $36.7 billion in the fourth quarter.

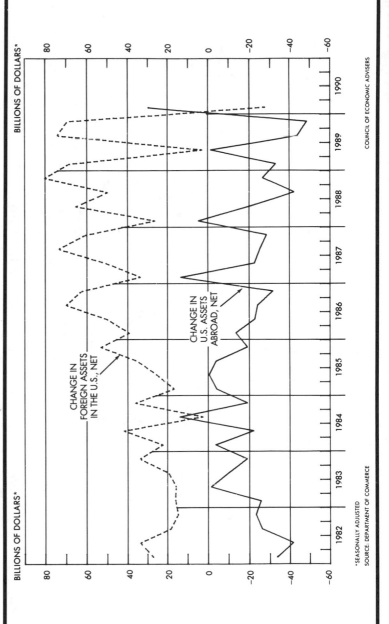

BILLIONS OF DOLLARS*

BILLIONS OF DOLLARS*

CHANGE IN FOREIGN ASSETS IN THE U.S., NET

CHANGE IN U.S. ASSETS ABROAD, NET

*SEASONALLY ADJUSTED
SOURCE: DEPARTMENT OF COMMERCE

COUNCIL OF ECONOMIC ADVISERS

237

TABLE 10.3 (Continued)

[Millions of dollars; quarterly data seasonally adjusted, except as noted]

Period	U.S. assets abroad, net [increase/capital outflow (−)]				Foreign assets in the U.S., net [increase/capital inflow (+)][3]				Allocations of special drawing rights (SDRs)	Statistical discrepancy		U.S. official reserve assets, net[5] (unadjusted, end of period)
	Total	U.S. official reserve assets[3][5]	Other U.S. Government assets	U.S. private assets	Total	Foreign official assets	Other foreign assets			Total (sum of the items with sign reversed)	Of which: Seasonal adjustment discrepancy	
1981	−110,951	−5,175	−5,097	−100,679	83,032	4,960	78,072	1,093	19,934	....	30,074
1982	−124,490	−4,965	−6,131	−113,394	93,746	3,593	90,154	....	36,612	....	33,958
1983	−56,100	−1,196	−5,006	−49,898	84,869	5,845	79,023	....	11,374	....	33,747
1984	−31,070	−3,131	−5,489	−22,451	102,621	3,140	99,481	....	27,456	....	34,934
1985	−27,721	−3,858	−2,821	−21,043	130,012	−1,083	131,096	....	20,041	....	43,186
1986	−92,030	312	−2,022	−90,321	221,599	35,588	186,011	....	15,824	....	48,511
1987	−62,946	9,149	997	−73,091	218,470	45,210	173,260	....	6,790	....	45,798
1988	−84,176	−3,912	2,969	−83,232	221,442	39,515	181,927	....	−8,404	....	47,802
1989	−127,061	−25,293	1,185	−102,953	214,652	8,823	205,829	....	22,443	....	74,609
1988: I	4,569	1,502	−1,594	4,661	26,079	24,840	1,239	....	2,034	2,970	43,186
II	−19,856	39	−847	−19,048	65,270	5,970	59,300	....	−14,539	−2,995	41,028
III	−42,383	−7,380	1,957	−36,960	49,797	−2,015	51,812	....	23,344	−4,630	47,788
IV	−26,508	1,925	3,452	−31,885	80,295	10,720	69,575	....	−19,242	4,656	47,802
1989: I	−32,859	−4,000	962	−29,821	68,402	7,797	60,605	....	−8,439	3,093	49,854
II	−1,381	−12,095	−303	ᶜ11,017	2,794	−4,961	7,755	....	27,236	−1,697	60,502
III	−44,076	−5,996	574	−38,654	74,136	13,003	61,133	....	−2,469	−4,953	68,418
IV	−48,745	−3,202	−47	−45,496	69,320	−7,016	76,336	....	6,117	3,560	74,609
1990: I ᵖ	29,509	−3,177	−486	33,172	−27,489	−8,825	−18,665	....	20,922	3,116	76,303

[5] Consists of gold, special drawing rights (SDRs), foreign currencies, and the U.S. reserve position in the IMF.

NOTE.—All data now shown on pages 36 and 37 are the revised series, as published in Survey of Current Business, June 1990.

Sources: Department of Commerce (Bureau of Economic Analysis) and Department of the Treasury.

238

which polls banks and non-bank financial institutions monthly and quarterly about holdings and portfolio investment. Data on foreign military sales and direct defense expenditures, as well as government grants and pensions, are shared by other government agencies. Services transactions are estimated.

The application of seasonal adjustment to international transactions is limited because many of the data are read quarterly. In the current account, only about half the components are adjusted; in the capital accounts, only two items are adjusted (repayments of U.S. government credits and reinvested earnings flowing out of the United States). The data are reported about 10 weeks after the close of the quarter and include bilateral data for three countries, seven regions, and for international organizations. These data are, therefore, useful for analyzing foreign exchange rate movements.

USING NET EXPORTS IN GNP: IMPORT–EXPORT PRICE INDICES

In large part, incorporating the international sector into the GNP accounts requires deflating the merchandise trade accounts by excluding the military components (which are part of government spending). * Special data series have been developed for this purpose. These are called the *import–export price indices*. They are a measure of a fixed 1985 market basket of goods (a Laspeyres index similar to the producer price index, see Chapter 13) based on a monthly mail survey of dollar-denominated import and export pricing data from U.S. companies. The survey comprises about 4,000 items during eight months of the year, but expands to about 20,000 items quarterly in March, June, September, and December. The survey for the prior month is sent via mail on the first of the month and is due back within two weeks, so that, for example, January data become available in late February.

The import–export price indices have two built-in biases. First, oil imports are measured from a secondary industry source at an average price for the entire month. Thus, they may misstate the actual costs to consumers when there have been sharp swings in demand during the month. Say the demand for oil falls at the end of the winter heating season in late March and the price plunges. The monthly average price will fall, but the bulk of the month's purchases were likely made earlier in the period at the highest levels. Thus, the import price deflator will understate the true costs. For this reason, analysts sometimes harp on the import price index excluding oil.

Second, the index converts prices of goods denominated in foreign currencies at the average exchange rate for the prior month. For instance, the October survey's conversion rates will be the September foreign exchange rates. This assumes a steady dollar (something which is outrageous in the current market environment).

Even with these quirks, the import–export indices are the best deflator of the foreign accounts in the GNP data. Much like the other GNP components, real growth is measured by subtracting the deflators from the nominal percentage change in the trade accounts. However, it should also be noted that the import price deflator is an offset to the overall GNP price deflator. Higher non-oil import prices subtract from domestic inflation, which is what the GNP deflators measure.

NOTE

*During 1991, the Commerce Department began to release seasonally adjusted merchandise trade data which can also be used in the construction of the GNP.

*GATT talks are detailed in Appendix 10.1.

Appendix 10.1

Negotiations for General Agreement on Tariffs and Trade

GATT Talks	Number of Countries	Results
1947	23	General agreement on tariffs and trade founded; 45,000 tariff concessions in 20 areas
1949	13	5,000 tariff concessions
1951	38	8,700 tariff concessions reduce tariffs 25%
1956	26	$2.5 billion in tariff reductions
1960	26	4,400 tariff concessions
1964–67	62	"The Kennedy Round" shifts from products to across-the-board reductions; cuts tariffs by up to 50%
1973–79	99	"The Tokyo Round" establishes preferential treatment for developing nations and reduces tariffs further; unifies customs valuations procedures
1986–present	107	"The Uruguay Round" seeks to broaden agreements into intellectual rights and services

11

The Government Sector

The massive federal apparatus in Washington, D.C. and the April 15 filing deadline for federal taxes immediately come to mind when one speaks of the government sector. But, the 50 individual states and hundreds of local entities also tax and spend, with significant economic effects. Although the federal government has a budget exceeding $1 trillion, these other entities in the aggregate account for more than half of overall net government expenditures.

FEDERAL GOVERNMENT

The federal government is the focus of attention because it is the only body which has the power to create money under the Constitution. While this power currently resides at the Federal Reserve, budget decisions influence the mix of monetary and fiscal restraint that create the environment in which financial markets function. In recent years, historically high interest rates and massive trade flows have been caused in part by the large budget deficits that began in 1980 under the Reagan Administration. The federal budget has also received repeated press attention because there has been little political agreement on the effects of or the need to close high deficits. This has

243

resulted in an elongation of the debate about a normally very cut-and-dried process.

The budget process (see Figure 11.1) begins in early January when the President transmits a budget message to the Congress for the new fiscal year beginning on October 1 (fiscal year 1991, for example, begins on October 1, 1990 and runs through September 30 of the following year). This plan is called the *Budget of the U.S. Government* and is detailed in Figure 11. 2. As indicated in the pie chart, the plan gives the dollar amounts and proportions for spending and taxes by broad category. It also projects the resulting deficit for five years using specified economic assumptions that private analysts dote on modifying.

By February 25 (within two months), the Congressional "appropriations" committees responsible for programmatic decisions should respond to the President's plans. They report the costs of the resulting (modified) programs to the Budget Committees, which were set up in 1974 to provide an overall spending plan. By April 15, a budget resolution giving the overall spending and borrowing plans is reported by the Budget Committees and voted on in both the House and Senate.

By June 15, a "reconciliation" bill is due that meshes both the House and Senate versions of the budget. On June 30, all appropriations actions are expected to have been passed by the House (where they are required under the Constitution to have originated). Thus, the theoretical schedule results in all budget legislation being completed more than two months prior to the start of the spending period. In actuality, anything can, and does, go wrong at any step of the process. This is because Congressional members can modify the plan at any step, adding favorite projects and thus raising the costs.

In recent years, lack of agreement on the overall budget plans has caused massive delays in this process. Theoretically, the government must close its doors if a budget is not in place on October 1. But Congress has taken pains to avoid this action. One ploy has been for the Congress to issue a *continuing budget resolution* that allows spending to continue after the start of a new fiscal year at the levels authorized

FIGURE 11.1

Budget Calendar for 1989

January 3	Congress convenes.
January 9	President Reagan transmits FY 1990 budget.
January 20	Inauguration Day.
February 25	Congressional committees report budget estimates to Budget Committees.
April 15	Action to be completed on congressional budget resolution.
May 15	House consideration of annual appropriations bills may begin.
June 15	Action to be completed on reconciliation.
June 30	Action on appropriations to be completed by House.
July 15	President Bush transmits Mid-Session Review of FY 1990 Budget, including preliminary estimates of the G-R-H baseline.
August 15	Initial snapshot of the G-R-H baseline.
August 25	OMB issues initial G-R-H report to the President and Congress, and President issues initial sequester order.
October 1	Fiscal year begins and initial sequester order becomes effective.
October 15	OMB issues final G-R-H report to the President and Congress, and President issues final sequester order, which becomes effective immediately.

Source: U.S. Budget.

for the prior period. Thus, work on the actual budget for the full fiscal year can be delayed indefinitely.

After a budget is approved, there are two other reasons the results may not come in as planned. These are an increase in spending for means-tested programs (Social Security is an example, where a shift in

FIGURE 11.2

The Federal Government Dollar
Fiscal Year 1991 Estimate

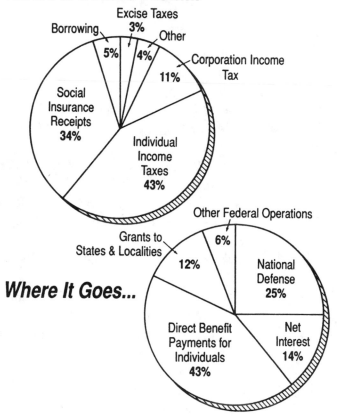

Where It Comes From...

Excise Taxes 3%

Borrowing 5%

Other 4%

Social Insurance Receipts 34%

Corporation Income Tax 11%

Individual Income Taxes 43%

Other Federal Operations 6%

Grants to States & Localities 12%

Where It Goes...

National Defense 25%

Direct Benefit Payments for Individuals 43%

Net Interest 14%

RECEIPTS, OUTLAYS, DEFICIT/SURPLUS UNDER THE PRESIDENT'S PROPOSED POLICY

(In billions of dollars)

	1989	1990	1991	1992	1993	1994	199.
Receipts	990.7	1,073.5	1,170.2	1,246.4	1,327.6	1,408.6	1,48
Outlays	1,142.6	1,197.2	1,233.3	1,271.4	1,321.8	1,398.0	1,47
Surplus or Deficit (+/−)	−152.0	−123.8	−63.1	−25.1	+5.7	+10.7	+

demographics or retirements may cause higher expenses that cannot be controlled), or a weakening in the economy. The last would cut tax receipts and raise involuntary payments (say, unemployment insurance system outlays). So, monitoring the progress of the budget becomes another concern to the economic analyst.

Once set by Congress, the expenditures of the U.S. government are approved by the U.S. Treasury Department and paid through a fiscal agent, the Federal Reserve Banks. They are considered so important that data are released daily via a telephone recording on the operating cash balances and selected expenditure categories. These data are also published in the *Daily Treasury Statement* (see Table 11.1). The data are then corrected, redistributed, and compiled on the twentieth business day of the month as the *Monthly Statement of Receipts and Outlays of the United States Government*, also known as the *Monthly Treasury Statement*. The latter contains information on the deficit (the excess of spending over receipts) on which the financial markets concentrate.

DAILY TREASURY STATEMENT

The DTS contains six tables detailing Treasury operations. Table 11.1, subtable I gives a breakdown of where the available cash balances are held. Under a system established in November 1978, the Treasury can keep cash either in its "checking account" at the Federal Reserve Banks or in special accounts in the commercial banking system. The commercial banks pay interest on their accounts, known as *Treasury Tax & Loan Accounts* (TT&L), at the rate of one-fourth percentage point under the weekly effective Fed funds rate. It is, therefore, advantageous to the government to hold as much as possible in the TT&L depositories. Also, balances held at the Fed drain reserves from the banking system since by definition they are outside of the system. Thus, the breakdown of Treasury cash balances has implications for monetary policy, which may affect one's GNP forecast.

TABLE 11.1

DAILY TREASURY STATEMENT
Cash and debt operations of the United States Treasury
Friday, September 7, 1990
(Detail, rounded in millions, may not add to totals)

TABLE I—Operating Cash Balance

Type of account	Closing balance today	Opening balance		
		Today	This month	This fiscal year
Federal Reserve Account	$ 4,407	$ 5,244	$ 4,453	$13,452
Tax and Loan Note Accounts (Table V)	19,114	18,024	17,869	27,521
Total Operating Balance	23,521	23,267	22,323	40,973

TABLE II—Deposits and Withdrawals of Operating Cash

Deposits	Today	This month to date	Fiscal year to date	Withdrawals	Today	This month to date	Fiscal year to date
Federal Reserve Account:				**Federal Reserve Account:**			
Public Debt Receipts (Table III-B)	$ 733	$ 28,484	$1,428,373	Public Debt Redemptions (Table III-B)	$ 727	$ 19,423	$1,240,403
Customs and Certain Excise Taxes	74	311	18,014	Commodity Credit Corporation (net)	−1	−75	8,225
Deposits by States:				Direct Deposit (EFT) Federal Salaries	76	1,041	41,485
Unemployment	14	46	15,950	Education Grants and Payments	77	298	20,845
Supplemental Security Income	2	61	2,913	Energy Grants and Payments	71	320	15,934
Energy Receipts	25	152	5,721	Federal Employees Insurance Payments	28	146	11,258
Estate and Gift Taxes	33	190	10,587	Federal Highway Administration	87	443	13,159
Farmers Home Loan Repayments	19	89	5,464	Food Stamps	35	112	12,907
Federal Financing Bank (net)	—	21	4,720	HHS Grants (selected)	443	1,462	70,304
Federal Reserve Earnings	—	408	22,041	HUD Payments	38	942	19,505
Foreign Deposits, Military Sales	11	427	7,313	Interest on Public Debt	9	643	151,783
HUD Receipts	39	134	7,622	Labor Department Programs	32	123	7,441
Individual Income and Employment				Medicare	422	1,606	100,502
Taxes, Not Withheld	294	879	150,979	Miscellaneous Food & Nutrition Service	21	114	8,453
Postal Service Receipts	254	1,112	51,807	Natl. Aeronautics & Space Adm. (NASA)	17	209	9,909
Prepayment of Treasury Securities (net)	26	−160	−186	Unemployment Insurance Benefits	70	284	16,313
Taxes Received (Table IV)	1,780	7,414	308,087	Other Withdrawals:			
Tennessee Valley Authority (net)	−2	98	3,783	FSLIC Resolution Fund	247		
Other Deposits:				Rural Electrification Admin.	63		
				Resolution Trust Corp.	593		
Total Other Deposits	—	368	9,578				
				Unclassified	1,916	18,382	582,474
Change in Balance of Uncollected							
Funds (closing balance $90)	+57	+19	+8	Total, Other Withdrawals	2,819	22,689	835,403
Transfers from Depositaries	774	11,581	700,826	Transfers to Depositaries	—	1,899	178,801
Total Federal Reserve Account	4,133	51,633	2,753,601	Total Federal Reserve Account	4,970	51,679	2,762,631
Tax and Loan Note Accounts:				**Tax and Loan Note Accounts:**			
Taxes Received (Table IV)	1,864	10,926	513,619				
Transfers from Federal Reserve Banks	—	1,899	178,801	Transfers to Federal Reserve Banks (Table V)	774	11,581	700,826
Total Tax and Loan Note Accounts (Table V)	1,864	12,825	692,419	Total Withdrawals (net of transfers)	4,970	49,779	2,583,831
Total Deposits (net of transfers)	5,223	50,978	2,566,393	Net Change in Operating Cash Balance	+254	+1,198	−17,452

* less than $500,000

This statement summarizes the United States Treasury's cash and debt operations for the Federal Government. Treasury's operating cash is maintained in account at Federal Reserve banks and branches and in Tax and Loan accounts at commercial banks. Major information sources include the Daily Balance Wires from Federal Reserve banks and branches, reporting from the Bureau of Public Debt, electronic transfers through the Treasury Financial Communications Systems and reconciling wires from the Internal Revenue Service Center. Information is presented on a modified cash basis. Deposits are reflected as received, and withdrawals are reflected as processed.

SOURCE Financial Management Service, Department of the Treasury.

Note The Daily Treasury Statement is now available on the day following the Statement date on the Financial Management Service's *Financial Management Data Base Terminal Access System*. For more information about the system, please call 202-208-1771. Selected information is also available on two separate telephone recordings at 4:00 p.m. Eastern Time on the day following the statement date on 202-208-1690 (shorter version) and on 202-208-1682 (longer version).

TABLE 11.1 (Continued)

Friday, September 7, 1990

TABLE III-A—Public Debt Transactions

(Stated at face value except for savings and retirement plan securities which are stated at current redemption value)

Issues	Today	This month to date	Fiscal year to date	Redemptions	Today	This month to date	Fiscal year to date
Marketable:				Marketable:			
Bills:				Bills	$ —	$ 16,723	$ 912,774
Regular Series	$ 2	$ 18,509	$ 933,356	Notes	3	10	267,867
Cash Management Series	—	—	68,396	Bonds	2	6	1,834
Notes	— *	9,024	353,732	Federal Financing Bank	—	—	5,000
Bonds	—	—	41,108	Nonmarketable:			
Federal Financing Bank	—	—	5,000	Savings and Retirement Plan Series	35	159	7,893
Nonmarketable:				Government Account Series	23,947	84,877	4,218,440
Savings and Retirement Plan Series				Domestic Series	669	782	7,953
Cash Issue Price	40	162	8,111	Foreign Series	—	467	7,847
Interest Increment	—	—	7,218	State and Local Series	19	1,276	27,404
Government Account Series	16,669	100,154	4,325,355	Other	*	*	45
Domestic Series	673	787	26,799				
Foreign Series	—	240	36,848				
State and Local Series	12	299	30,228	Total Redemptions	24,675	104,300	5,457,058
Other	—	—	44				
Total Issues	17,397	129,176	5,836,194	Net Change in Public Debt Outstanding	−7,278	+24,876	+379,136

TABLE III-B—Adjustment of Public Debt Transactions to Cash Basis

Transactions	Today	This month to date	Fiscal year to date
Public Debt Cash Receipts:			
Public Debt Issues (Table III-A)	$ 17,397	$ 129,176	$5,836,194
Premium on New Issues	—	—	294
Discount on New Issues:			
Bills (−)	*	526	60,784
Bonds and Notes (−)	−*	32	17,553
Government Account Transaction (−)	16,664	100,134	4,322,561
Interest Increment on Savings and Retirement Plan Series (−)	—	—	7,218
Total Public Debt Cash Receipts Deposited in Federal Reserve Account	733	28,484	1,428,373
Public Debt Cash Redemptions:			
Public Debt Redemptions (Table III-A)	24,675	104,300	5,457,058
Government Account Transactions (−)	23,947	84,877	4,216,655
Total Public Debt Cash Redemptions	727	19,423	1,240,403

TABLE III-C—Debt Subject to Limit

Classification	Closing balance today	Opening balance Today	This month	This fiscal year
Total Public Debt				
Outstanding	$3,236,567	$3,243,845	$3,211,691	$2,857,431
Less Public Debt Not Subject to Limit:				
Miscellaneous Debt	596	596	596	597
Discount Adjustment[1]	56,590	56,696	57,321	12,360
Federal Financing Bank	15,000	15,000	15,000	15,000
Plus Other Obligations Subject to Limit:				
Guaranteed Debt of Federal Agencies	317	317	316	296
Total Subject to Limit	3,164,698	3,171,870	3,139,090	2,829,770
Statutory Limit	3,195,000	3,195,000	3,195,000	2,870,000

Act of August 9, 1990, temporarily increased the statutory debt limit to $3,195.0 billion through October 2, 1990.
[1]Represents the unamortized discount on Treasury bills and zero-coupon bonds (amortization is calculated daily).

TABLE IV—Federal Tax Deposit

Classification	Today	This month to date	Fiscal year to date
Withheld Income and Employment Taxes	$ 2,861	$ 8,415	$ 680,551
Individual Estimated Income Taxes	—	*	672
Railroad Retirement Taxes	11	86	3,957
Excise Taxes	25	418	34,015
Corporation Income Taxes	48	180	89,411
Federal Unemployment Taxes	3	11	5,731
Change in Balance of Unclassified Taxes (closing balance $19,466)	+697	+9,230	+7,370
Total	3,644	18,340	821,706
These Receipts were deposited in:			
Federal Reserve Account:			
Directly	153	2,018	75,574
Remittance Option Depositaries	1,628	5,395	232,513
Tax and Loan Note Accounts	1,864	10,926	513,619

TABLE V—Tax and Loan Note Accounts by Depositary Category

Type of account	Classification			Total
	A	B	C	
Opening Balance Today	$ 250	$ 576	$ 17,198	$ 18,024
Investments:				
Credits	26	135	1,703	1,864
Transfers to Depositaries	—	—	—	—
Withdrawals:				
Treasury Initiated	—	—	—	—
Depositary Initiated	6	33	735	774
Closing Balance Today	270	678	18,166	19,114

TABLE VI—Income Tax Refunds Issued

Classification	Today	This month to date	Fiscal year to date
Individual	$ 390	$ 397	$ 73,920
Business	9	200	21,327

The DTS also contains information about receipts and expenditures. Table 11.1, subtable II is the most useful because it gives the daily deposits and withdrawals of operating cash flowing through the Fed. Deposits can come from Treasury securities issues, from repayments for government services, or from taxes. The latter are broken down in Table 11.1, subtable IV into income taxes withheld from pay checks, estimated income taxes, retirement and excise taxes, and corporation income taxes.

Income taxes are levied on earnings. They generally increase as income rises and can be either withheld from paychecks or remitted periodically by the individual or corporation. Retirement taxes, such as Social Security, are regressive. They generally represent a fixed percentage of the first x dollars of wages. An excise tax is an internal licensing fee or a tax on a privilege. Some examples are taxes on the production, sale, or consumption of a good such as cigarettes or liquor.

Tax payments have a definite rhythm which is prescribed by law. For example, employers must remit taxes withheld from paychecks to the Treasury each week on a complicated schedule determined by their number of employees and the dollar size of the payroll. These dates may be within three banking days of the end of eight-monthly periods that fall on the third, seventh, eleventh, fifteenth, nineteenth, twenty-second, twenty-fifth, or the last day of the month. Individuals pay estimated taxes on a quarterly schedule on April 15, July 15, October 15, and January 15. One can see the results of these inflows in the cash balances: they rise sharply in the second week of each month and at the quarterly due dates.

Withdrawals of operating cash (the left-hand side of Table 11.1, subtable II) indicate where the Treasury's cash goes, by program. The largest payments are at month-end (military pay and retirement annuities), mid-month when interest is due on debt issues, and on the third of the month (Social Security and supplemental payments). Unfortunately, defense and other security-sensitive payments are lumped into the "unclassified" expenditures, so one must await the MTS to sort them out. Income tax refunds are detailed in Table 11.1, subtable

VI. These become a significant drain on cash in the period from mid-February to mid-May (also when individuals settle their income tax accounts).

Inter-governmental Transfers

Table 11.1, subtable III-A, provides the details of the Treasury's financing operations. These include the marketable bills, notes, and bonds available to the investing public and the issues used to fund the government's trust accounts. The latter deserve further explanation because they are a gimmick used to sell new programs to the public.

One example is the non-marketable "investments" made by the Social Security Trust Funds. Individuals pay social security taxes to the Treasury via deductions from their paychecks. These payments are theoretically "invested" in non-marketable debt that the Treasury issues to the trust funds. But both the trust funds and the Treasury are government agencies, so when the accounts are consolidated the government has simply used the tax money to pay its bills, among which are Social Security benefits. Economists call this process a *transfer* and refer to the Social Security tax as a *transfer payment*.

Issuing non-marketable debt to the Social Security Funds and other like entities has another effect on the *debt subject to limit* (as seen in Table 11.1, subtable III-C). Each year, the Congress sets government budget totals and votes an associated debt limit that should be sufficient to fund the related deficit. By convention, however, issuance of both non-marketable and marketable debt comes under the debt limit. So, overspending in any form (be it for war or the more altruistic payment of Social Security to a deserving worker) causes the debt subject to limit to rise. As indicated in the footnote, the Congress sometimes temporarily raises the debt limit. Most observers agree that the debt limit is arcane in an electronic age which allows close monitoring of Treasury expenditures. Nevertheless, its presence requires Administration officials to return to Congress during the budget year to explain spending overruns.

Market-based Uses of the DTS

First, the movements in cash balances are often correlated with pressures on short-term rates. Other things being equal, a rise in the Treasury's balances held at the Fed should also raise the Federal funds rate because it drains reserves from the banking system. Thus, on days when Treasury securities are issued and individuals make payments to the Treasury's account at the Fed, there is a tendency for overnight rates to spike. The average increase in the Fed funds rate on securities settlements days for the first seven months of 1990, for example, was just under 10 basis points or 0.1% point (a significant amount for highly leveraged securities dealers).

Second, how close the Treasury is to the debt limit has implications for the volume and maturities of securities to be sold. For instance, anticipating no further issuance because the Treasury is at its debt limit has been a reason for bond market rallies. Traders also believe that a small leeway remaining under the debt limit (say, $5 to $15 billion) indicates a risk for a fast auction of short-term Treasury bills. This is because officials sometimes jockey to bolster Congressional action to raise the limit by exhausting the government's current debt limit.

THE MONTHLY TREASURY STATEMENT (MTS)

Converting data from the DTS into the government's monthly budget is, theoretically, very simple. The change in the cash balance plus any market financing gives the deficit. This is demonstrated in Table 11.2 for August 1990. The change in the cash balance was −$2.4 billion (from Table 11.1, subtable I) and the net market financing change was $46.5 billion (from Table 11.1, subtable III-A), indicating the deficit was around $49 billion.

If the conversion process indicates that the DTS can provide insights on the most important information available for the markets,

TABLE 11.2
Converting DTS Numbers to the Monthly Deficit

(1)	Change in cash position	July 31	$24,756 million
		August 31	$22,323
		Change	−$2,433
(2)	Change in debt		
	Issues: Total		$618,466
	Less Non-marketable		430,175
	Net issues		188,291
	Redemptions: Total		575,547
	Less Non-marketable		433,821
	Net issues		141,726
	Net Change:		−46,565
(3)	Sum of the changes		−$48,998

why read the MTS? The MTS was first published in February 1954 as a key to the government's central reporting system. It was established as the statement with which all other government reports must be consistent. It was also designed to integrate all agency-Treasury data on the common basis of cash transactions, so that the actual results can be compared with the budget plan. During the past 35 years, the MTS has evolved dynamically, reflecting the expansion of government operations and the differing budgetary treatments of government financial transactions. But, its purpose as the official publication of fiscal policy results remains unchanged.

Table 11.3 shows that the MTS provides information on both receipts and outlays as well as the resulting deficit for the month and fiscal year (both on and off budget). The terms *on* and *off budget* are accounting anomalies: Congress can choose to exclude a program from the budget but it must be financed in any event. So, the Treasury consolidates all its receipts and expenditures in this statement.

There are three means to finance the budget:

1. changes in the cash balance;
2. borrowing from the public; and
3. other.

The other category includes checks outstanding, accrued interest payable to the public, any increases in deposit fund balances (such as government agency deposits), and *seigniorage* (the difference between the value of money as money and its inherent components of paper and metal). The means indicate the pressures on the financial markets by showing borrowing from the public; the table indicates the proportion of savings that the federal government must absorb. *Borrowing from the public* is defined to include borrowing from the Federal Reserve System, commercial banks and other financial institutions, foreign central banks, and businesses and individuals.

Table 11.4 is a summary of receipts and outlays of the U.S. government. The heart of the statement is just an expansion of the

TABLE 11.3

Summary of Budget and Off Budget Results and Financing of the U.S. Government, July 1990 and Other Periods

[$ millions]

Classification	This Month	Current Fiscal Year to Date	Budget Estimates Full Fiscal Year[1]	Prior Fiscal Year to Date (1989)	Budget Estimates Next Fiscal Year (1991)[1]
Total on-budget and off-budget results:					
Total receipts	72,357	850,102	1,044,228	815,332	1,135,374
On-budget receipts	50,446	614,981	762,768	594,193	823,244
Off-budget receipts	21,911	235,121	281,460	221,140	312,130
Total outlays	98,291	1,039,191	1,264,310	938,991	1,311,700
On-budget outlays	79,844	857,027	1,038,805	767,881	1,076,339
Off-budget outlays	18,447	182,163	225,505	171,109	235,361
Total surplus (+) or deficit (−)	− 25,934	− 189,088	− 220,082	− 123,658	− 176,326
On-budget surplus (+) or deficit (−)	− 29,398	− 242,046	− 276,037	− 173,688	− 253,095
Off-budget surplus (+) or deficit (−)	+ 3,464	+ 52,958	+ 55,955	+ 50,030	+ 76,769
Total on-budget and off-budget financing.	25,934	189,088	220,082	123,658	176,326
Means of financing:					
Borrowing from the public	24,233	220,199	209,628	97,830	174,055
Reduction of operating cash, increase (−)	9,862	16,217	10,973	36,932	. . . .
By other means	− 8,161	− 47,328	− 519	− 11,103	2,271

[1]Based on the Mid-Session Review of the FY 1991 Budget released by the Office of Management and Budget on July 16, 1990.
Note: Details may not add to totals due to rounding.

TABLE 11.4
Summary of Receipts and Outlays of the U.S. Government, July 1990 and Other Periods ($ millions)

Classification	This Month	Current Fiscal Year to Date	Comparable Prior Period	Budget Estimates Full Fiscal Year[1]
Budget Receipts				
Individual income taxes	33,290	383,578	363,732	476,090
Corporation income taxes	2,057	74,555	81,898	98,223
Social insurance taxes and contributions:				
Employment taxes and contributions (off-budget)	21,911	235,121	221,140	281,460
Employment taxes and contributions (on-budget)	5,643	60,370	57,960	72,183
Unemployment insurance	1,701	17,738	18,825	21,778
Other retirement contributions	355	3,762	3,762	4,734
Excise taxes	3,053	29,915	28,993	36,715
Estate and gift taxes	924	9,743	7,361	10,680
Customs duties	1,505	13,807	13,304	16,896
Miscellaneous receipts	1,917	21,513	18,357	25,468
Total Receipts	**72,357**	**850,102**	**815,332**	**1,044,228**
(On-budget)	**50,446**	**614,981**	**594,193**	**762,768**
(Off-budget)	**21,911**	**235,121**	**221,140**	**281,460**
Budget Outlays				
Legislative Branch	164	1,907	1,790	2,317
The Judiciary	228	1,359	1,137	1,684
Executive Office of the President	15	122	105	174
Funds Appropriated to the President	100	8,040	3,448	10,696
Department of Agriculture	3,349	40,346	43,019	47,531
Department of Commerce	405	3,213	2,213	3,933
Department of Defense—Military	22,004	[2]241,428	241,812	290,230
Department of Defense—Civil	2,113	[2]20,685	19,454	24,803
Department of Education	1,207	19,511	17,946	22,929
Department of Energy	915	10,224	9,777	12,319
Department of Health and Human Services, except Social Security	17,345	161,418	141,595	192,369
Department of Health and Human Services, Social Security	19,647	203,061	188,730	244,904
Department of Housing and Urban Development	1,654	16,896	16,645	21,394
Department of the Interior	397	4,673	4,370	6,094
Department of Justice	567	5,655	5,231	6,945
Department of Labor	2,330	21,330	18,753	25,543
Department of State	263	3,263	3,119	3,834
Department of Transportation	2,601	23,439	21,767	28,533
Department of the Treasury:				
Interest on the Public Debt	18,435	228,629	207,253	261,080
Other	-1,424	[2]-8,171	-8,050	-8,691
Department of Veterans Affairs	1,265	24,177	24,155	29,275
Environmental Protection Agency	444	4,175	3,960	5,311
General Services Administration	-371	-460	-754	381
National Aeronautics and Space Administration	1,101	10,341	9,045	12,058
Office of Personnel Management	2,831	26,662	24,344	32,831
Small Business Administration	76	606	65	709
Other independent agencies:				
Resolution Trust Corporation	3,183	[3]35,197	....	57,132
Other	2,051	[4]22,077	18,736	25,765
Undistributed offsetting receipts:				
Interest	-972	-61,303	-51,083	-61,034
Other	-3,634	-29,310	-29,589	-36,742
Total Outlays	**98,291**	**1,039,191**	**938,991**	**1,264,310**
(On-budget)	**79,844**	**857,027**	**767,881**	**1,038,805**
(Off-budget)	**18,447**	**182,163**	**171,109**	**225,505**
Surplus (+) or deficit (−)	**-25,934**	**-189,088**	**-123,658**	**-220,082**
(On-budget)	**-29,398**	**-242,046**	**-173,688**	**-276,037**
(Off-budget)	**+3,464**	**+52,958**	**+50,030**	**+55,955**

[1]Based on the Mid-Session Review of the FY 1991 Budget released by the Office of Management and Budget on July 16, 1990.
[2]Includes a reclassification of clearing accounts for the Department of Defense and the Central Intelligence Agency to a non-budgetary status ($25 million for FY89 and $26 million for FY 1990).
[3]Includes a net adjustment of $64 million ($202 million gross outlays and $266 million applicable receipts) reported in June 1990.
[4]Includes a net adjustment of $31 million ($1,451 million gross outlays and $1,482 million applicable receipts) reported by Federal Deposit Insurance Corporation and $64 million ($202 million gross outlays and $266 million applicable receipts) reported by Resolution Trust Corporation in June 1990.
[5]Includes a net adjustment of $33 million for premiums paid but previously reported as investments by Tennessee Valley Authority (October $51 million, November −$18 million). 1989 respectively.
... No Transactions.

256

totals in Table 11.3. Receipts are presented by major source category, while outlays are broken down by legislative branch, the judiciary, the executive departments, and agencies. In other words, the unclassified expenditures of the DTS are reconciled and the lump-sum business tax collections are broken out into categories. The table gives four time horizons for easy comparison: the current month, the current fiscal year to date, the comparable prior year's fiscal year to date, and the budget estimates for the full current fiscal year. The last column can give the analyst a sense of whether the year's targets are likely to be hit.

It is useful to focus on selected components of Table 11.4 because certain categories are more likely to be swing factors in any fiscal year. Among the receipts, corporation income taxes depend highly on the economic cycle and the tax statutes; they lag downturns and accelerations and adjust quickly to changes in the tax code. Individual income taxes and social insurance taxes are tied to payroll growth. A marked weakening in nonfarm payrolls should be felt in these receipts as soon as layoffs occur.

Among the outlays are Social Security (see Department of Health and Human Services), interest on the public debt (see Department of Treasury), and military spending (see Department of Defense—Military). These are all considered swing factors. The former two are tied to the calendar. A month which has two coupon interest payments on Treasury debt will be reconciled. Say payments are made on the last day of each month but February 28 is a holiday and the payment is made on March 1. The MTS will show the outlays properly so that one each falls into January, February, and March.

Social insurance payments are not subject to the same convention. In the instance where two were made in March, the Social Security outlays number would be bloated, causing the deficit to swell. Analysts should adjust their thinking accordingly, calling for the September surplus to be that much larger.

Defense payments are also predictable, rising at the start of each quarter and then falling back. They also tend to spike up in September, perhaps because there is a last gasp prior to fiscal year-end. For

FY1988 through FY1991 ("FY" stands for "fiscal year"), the independent agency called the *Resolution Trust Corporation* should be another significant item. The RTC outlays cover the thrift bailout and are scheduled to balloon until FY1992, when they should turn negative and start to contribute cash to the Treasury. This will reflect the sale of assets and the recapture of the working capital lent to the thrifts.

The information in Table 11.4 is disaggregated even further into gross receipts, refunds, and net receipts. Each of the major categories are broken into subcomponents in back-up tables. The most important new information in the back-up tables is the percentage of individual income tax receipts stemming from withheld taxes. These should correlate with payrolls for most of the year, making their projection easy. But the withheld percentage sinks to its minimum in April when individuals settle their tax liabilities, making the projection dicey.

Similarly, gross outlays, offsetting receipts, and net receipts for the month and for the current and the prior fiscal year to date are shown in back-up tables. Note that the military expenditures are classified in personnel, operations, procurement, construction, research and development, or family housing. Note also that social security is technically an off-budget item. And, the substantial offsetting receipts for the RTC come from the sale of bank assets taken over from the failed institutions.

STATE AND LOCAL GOVERNMENTS

Barring a process of following the thousands of individual budgets available on differing schedules (due to differing fiscal years) for state and local governments, there exists no comprehensive report detailing these expenditures. Instead, the Commerce Department uses a variety of source data to track municipal outlays. Estimating salaries is easy because the Labor Department and the Social Security Administration obtain firm data on unemployment insurance and employer contributions; these data are shared with the GNP estimators.

Municipal expenditures on structures are covered in the construction surveys. But all other expenditures must be estimated quarterly based on a judgmental trend using data from a quinquennial census and annual surveys.

GNP USES OF THE DATA

Government expenditures are adjusted to a calendar year and delivery timing basis so that federal and municipal spending are consistent. Specifically excluded are financial transactions, transactions in land, interest, subsidies, transfer payments and grants in aid. Included are estimated financial services furnished to the government without payment. Thus, the quarterly NIPA accounts fairly present the value added to the product side of GNP.

Monetary Policy Indicators

The interaction between the government's monetary and fiscal policy is obvious to all financial market participants, in part because it is seen daily in the close working relationships between officials at the Federal Reserve and the U.S. Treasury Department. So, no book on economic indicators would be complete without a section devoted to financial indicators, although they are not required for the construction and understanding of GNP. Presumably, however, there is an optimal mix between monetary and fiscal policy that has implications for GNP and investment decisions. For example, the less stimulative the budget, the more leeway the Fed has to ease interest rates. A well-developed body of monetary theory suggests financial decisions, such as the 1990 credit crunch, could constrain the economy's growth. So, a few of the more important monetary releases are discussed in this chapter.

MONEY'S TRANSMISSION TO THE ECONOMY

A simple form equation (Eq. 1) says that the number of times the money supply changes hands (money times velocity) serves as a cap on the value of the transactions in the economy (the price level times the number of transactions). Thus, economic analysts also concern themselves with the outstanding money supply, how it is created and used, and the behavior of banks.

$$M \times V = P \times T \qquad\qquad \textbf{(Eq. 1)}$$

where M = money supply
       V = velocity
       P = prices
       T = real transactions

The Federal Reserve System reports each Thursday evening on the money supply, bank reserves, and the condition of the central bank. These data are summarized in statistical releases identified by numbers in the letter H series. The Fed creates credit mainly via purchases and sales of securities to dealers called *open market operations*. This new credit is measured as bank reserves and eventually finds its way into an expanding money supply. This is because the United States has a fractional accounting system that requires less than $1 to be held at the central bank in reserves behind each $1 in commercial bank deposits.

THE H.4.1

The analyst's main source for information about Fed operations is the weekly statement on factors affecting reserve balances of depository institutions and condition statement of Federal Reserve Banks, abbreviated as the *H.4.1*. The H.4.1 is the consolidated balance sheet for the 12 district Federal Reserve Banks, showing factors supplying ("above the line") and subtracting ("below the line") reserves from the banking system. The data are reported both for the final Wednesday of the seven-day period and for the week. It also shows the change from the prior week and a year ago (see Table 12.1).

The main supplying factors are the Fed's securities portfolio, float, discount window borrowings, and "other" assets. Although the legal

TABLE 12.1
The H.4.1

FEDERAL RESERVE

These data are scheduled for release each Thursday. The exact time of each release will be announced, when the information is available, on (202) 452-3206.

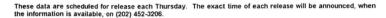

H.4.1

Factors Affecting Reserve Balances of Depository Institutions and Condition Statement of F.R. Banks

December 6, 1990

Millions of dollars

Reserve balances of depository institutions at F.R. Banks, Reserve Bank credit, and related items	Averages of daily figures			Wednesday Dec 5, 1990
	Week ended Dec 5, 1990	Change from week ended		
		Nov 28, 1990	Dec 6, 1989	
Reserve Bank credit[1] [2]	291,872	+ 3,337	+ 25,202	291,084
U.S. government securities				
Bought outright--system account	241,823	+ 3,455	+ 18,820	241,340
Held under repurchase agreements	2,381	- 1,418	+ 2,381	2,006
Federal agency obligations				
Bought outright	6,342	0	- 183	6,342
Held under repurchase agreements	341	+ 109	+ 341	376
Acceptances	0	0	0	0
Loans to depository institutions				
Adjustment credit	15	- 36	- 43	19
Seasonal credit	97	- 36	+ 6	87
Extended credit	25	0	+ 4	24
Float	1,376	+ 1,025	+ 696	1,293
Other F.R. assets	39,472	+ 238	+ 3,180	39,596
Gold stock	11,059	0	- 1	11,058
Special drawing rights certificate account	10,018	0	+ 1,500	10,018
Treasury currency outstanding	20,329	+ 10	+ 770	20,329
Total factors supplying reserve funds	333,278	+ 3,347	+ 27,471	332,489
Currency in circulation*	279,835	- 240	+ 25,998	280,441
Treasury cash holdings*	548	- 7	+ 103	544
Deposits, other than reserve balances, with F.R. Banks				
Treasury	5,651	+ 757	+ 489	5,879
Foreign	245	+ 33	- 81	217
Service-related balances and adjustments[3]	1,885	- 41	- 18	1,885
Other	222	- 16	- 62	214
Other F.R. liabilities and capital	9,488	+ 259	+ 1,024	9,276
Total factors, other than reserve balances, absorbing reserve funds	297,874	+ 745	+ 27,452	298,455
Reserve balances with F.R. Banks[4]	35,404	+ 2,602	+ 19	34,034

On December 5, 1990, marketable U.S. government securities held in custody by the Federal Reserve Banks for foreign official and international accounts were $ 252,573 million, a change of + $ 6,608 million for the week.

1 Net of $ 6,089 million, daily average, matched sale-purchase transactions outstanding during the latest statement week, of which a net of $ 6,089 million was with foreign official and international accounts. Includes securities loaned--fully secured by U.S. government securities.

2 Net of $ 6,553 million matched sale-purchase transactions outstanding at the end of the latest statement week, of which a net of $ 6,553 million was with foreign official and international accounts. Includes $ 228 million securities loaned--fully secured U.S. government securities.

3 Consists of required clearing balances of $ 1,746 million and adjustments of $ 140 million to compensate for float.

4 Excludes required clearing balances and adjustments to compensate for float.

* Estimated (Treasury's figures).

Components may not add to totals due to rounding.

263

scope exists for the Fed to buy almost any type of security, the Fed's portfolio currently consists only of Treasury and Federal Agency securities. These can be purchased permanently or temporarily (the latter is called *under RP* or repurchase agreement with dealers who agree to repurchase the securities at a given price within 14 days). It is conceptually simple to see that the Fed's purchases add reserves to the banking system. When the Fed or any government agency purchases securities, it credits individuals' accounts with money they did not have before. This has an expansionary effect. Temporary purchases have ranged in the $3 to $5 billion area in recent years, though they may be larger around the Christmas holiday season when the Fed is moving to counteract seasonal forces that drain reserves.

Float comes about as a result of the check-clearing process. In order to facilitate trade, the framers of the 1914 Federal Reserve Act indicated the Fed should create an *elastic currency*. So, the Fed immediately credits to banks' accounts any checks that have been presented, regardless of whether the bank on which they are drawn has seen an offsetting debit. So, it is possible that bad weather that produces transportation delays will in turn delay the check clearing process. If so, float rises, adding reserves to the banking system. In recent years, the Fed has moved to reduce float by charging for so-called overdrafts and by posting adjustments as soon as troubles are discovered in the clearing process. As a result, daily spikes in float of more than $1 to $2 billion are rare.

Discount window borrowings are money lent by the Fed to institutions that cannot borrow elsewhere to meet their reserve needs. They fall into three categories, adjustment, seasonal, and extended credit. Adjustment borrowings are temporary and go to healthy institutions experiencing some unexpected difficulty, such as a glitch in the wire transfer system. Seasonal credit goes to small institutions in resort and farm areas that experience extraordinary demands at particular times of year. It peaks during the spring planting season and falls towards zero during the winter. Extended credit goes to troubled banks that are largely locked out of the money market; thus it is apt to remain outstanding for some time. Famous examples are the loans made during banking crises to Franklin National and Continental Illinois.

The Fed's *other assets* is a catch-all category for miscellaneous items. Two items are of particular interest to the financial markets, holdings of foreign currencies and the treatment of accumulated interest on the Federal Reserve System's $250+ billion portfolio. Foreign currencies are revalued at market levels at the end of each month, so a large dollar change in the $2 to $3 billion range can be seen if *foreign exchange* (FX) rates have changed radically. This category also captures any central bank intervention in the FX markets, undertaken at the behest of the U.S. Treasury, which sets dollar policy. Note also that the moves in FX holdings understate the actual intervention levels, since responsibility for FX intervention is allocated equally between the Fed and the *Exchange Stabilization Fund* at the Treasury. Accumulated interest on the securities portfolio is posted daily but, since the Fed is a government agency, must be repatriated to the Treasury weekly.

There are two main factors on the H.4.1 which absorb reserves from the banking system. These are *currency in circulation* (accounting for over 90% of the absorbing factors) and *Treasury balances*. Again, it is conceptually simple to envision why. A rise in currency in circulation causes banks to call in loans or take in more deposits by raising rates, because it must be 100% backed by cash. This has contractionary effects. Similarly, a rise in Treasury deposits means that the government is taking money away from individuals.

Currency in circulation is highly seasonal, rising apace around the summer vacation season and again during the holiday shopping season. It falls during the winter, when people are more productive and replenish their savings. Also, currency in circulation mirrors the overall economy, weakening when the business cycle turns down but more generally growing at a given pace on a year-over-year basis. It also surges before major holidays and ebbs in the days after. Treasury balances, on the other hand, are more predictable. Balances rise during periods of major bond flotations and immediately after tax dates (see Chapter 11) and fall when government payments (such as Social Security benefits and coupon interest) are made.

The difference between the factors supplying and absorbing is the reserve balances with the Fed—over $35 billion in the last line of our example in Table 12.1. This represents the money that commercial banks hold on deposit with the Fed in order to meet legal requirements to hold deposits. The breakdown of these deposits is given in the following two releases.

THE H.3

The *H.3* provides information on aggregate reserves of depository institutions and the monetary base. Reserves accounting is simple if one remembers that total reserves are either required or excess (i.e., in excess of reserve requirements); or borrowed (from the Fed) or non-borrowed. Thus, the right-hand side of the reserves section on the H.3 (see Table 12.2) must sum to the left-hand side.

Analysts look at the NSA data in Table 12.2. These data, however, can be reconciled with the H.4.1. This is because the Fed allows *vault cash* not in use during any two-week accounting period to be counted as an offset to required reserves. So, the NSA required reserves less the vault cash used to satisfy reserve requirements must equal the two-week average for the reserve balances numbers on the H.4.1. Note also that the monetary base is defined as the sum of currency in circulation plus total reserves. While some analysts find it useful to follow the base as a proxy for monetary policy, it is redundant if one has already tracked reserves and the Fed's balance sheet.

A high or accelerating growth rate for reserve balances will portend a pick-up in non-borrowed reserves growth. Acceleration in either of these series will indicate that the banking system has the ability to make larger or more aggressive loans. In turn, this will eventually result in a pick-up in the money supply and either inflation or real economic activity.

TABLE 12.2 The H.3

FEDERAL RESERVE statistical release

H.3 (502)
Table 1

AGGREGATE RESERVES OF DEPOSITORY INSTITUTIONS AND THE MONETARY BASE
Adjusted for changes in reserve requirements[1]
Averages of daily figures, seasonally adjusted unless noted otherwise
Millions of dollars

For Release at 4:30 p.m. Eastern Time

DECEMBER 6, 1990

Date	Reserves of depository institutions					Monetary base	Borrowings of depository institutions from the Federal Reserve, NSA		
	total[2]	nonborrowed[3]	nonborrowed plus extended credit[4]	required	excess NSA[5]		total	seasonal	extended credit[4]
1989—OCT.	59640	59085	59106	58620	1020	282786	555	330	21
NOV.	59646	59297	59318	58601	945	283222	349	134	21
DEC.	60053	59767	59787	59110	922	284946	265	84	20
1990—JAN.	59996	59456	59482	58880	1016	287509	440	47	26
FEB.	60215	58768	59302	59227	989	289714	1448	51	555
MAR.	60297	58173	60123	59436	861	291820	2124	78	1950
APR.	60275	58647	60051	59379	897	293540	1628	122	1403
MAY	59783	58448	59324	58820	962	294401	1335	244	875
JUNE	59732	58850	59196	58958	774	296276	881	311	346
JULY	59322	58565	58845	58460	862	297860	757	389	280
AUG.	59746	58819	58947	58879	868	301121	927	430	127
SEP.	60082	59457	59464	59173	909	304780	624	418	6
OCT.	59609	59199	59217	58763	847	306539	410	335	18
Two weeks ending									
1990—OCT. 3	60359	59843	59852	59237	1122	306435	516	424	9
17	59910	59509	59522	58926	984	305856	401	345	13
31	59148	58751	58776	58498	650	307245	397	307	26
NOV. 14	59753	59471	59496	58746	1007	307308	282	195	25
28p	59979	59786	59811	58941	1038	308185	193	140	25

p--preliminary

pe--preliminary estimate

1. Reserves and monetary base figures incorporate adjustments for discontinuities, or "breaks", associated with regulatory changes in reserve requirements. (For more information, see Table 3.)
2. Seasonally adjusted, break-adjusted total reserves equal seasonally adjusted, break-adjusted required reserves plus unadjusted excess reserves. (Also, see footnote 2 on Table 2 and footnote 2 on Table 3.)
3. Seasonally adjusted, break-adjusted nonborrowed reserves equal seasonally adjusted, break-adjusted total reserves less unadjusted total borrowings of depository institutions from the Federal Reserve.
4. Extended credit consists of borrowing at the discount window under the terms and conditions established for the extended credit program to help depository institutions deal with sustained liquidity pressures. Because there is not the same need to repay such borrowing promptly as there is with traditional short-term adjustment credit, the money market impact of extended credit is similar to that of nonborrowed reserves.
5. Excess reserves NSA equals unadjusted total reserves (Table 2, column 1) less unadjusted required reserves (Table 2, column 3).
6. The seasonally adjusted, break-adjusted monetary base consists of (1) seasonally adjusted, break-adjusted total reserves plus (2) the seasonally adjusted currency component of the money stock plus (3), for all quarterly reporters on the "Report of Transaction Accounts, Other Deposits and Vault Cash" and for all those weekly reporters whose vault cash exceeds their required reserves, the seasonally adjusted, break-adjusted difference between current vault cash and the amount applied to satisfy current reserve requirements. (Also see footnote 3 on Table 2 and footnote 4 on table 3.)

TABLE 12.2 (Continued)

H.3 (502)
Table 2

AGGREGATE RESERVES OF DEPOSITORY INSTITUTIONS AND THE MONETARY BASE

Not adjusted for changes in reserve requirements.
Averages of daily figures, not seasonally adjusted
Millions of dollars

Date	Reserves of depository institutions			Monetary base[3]	Reserve balances with F.R. Banks[4]	Vault cash[5]			Net carryover of reserve balances[8]
	total[2]	nonborrowed	required			total	used to satisfy required reserves[6]	surplus[7]	
1989-OCT.	60397	59842	59378	284328	33123	29910	27275	2636	
NOV.	60989	60640	60044	287189	33941	29549	27048	2502	
DEC.	62810	62544	61888	292554	35436	29812	27374	2439	
1990-JAN.	62931	62491	61914	292131	34090	31301	28841	2461	
FEB.	60623	59175	59654	290025	30929	32489	29693	2795	
MAR.	60658	58535	59797	292377	33407	29581	27251	2330	
APR.	62512	60884	61615	296872	35409	29281	27103	2178	
MAY	60232	58897	59269	297034	32771	29812	27461	2351	
JUNE	61197	60315	60423	300985	33878	29632	27318	2314	
JULY	60943	60185	60081	303387	32946	30457	27996	2460	
AUG.	60728	59801	59860	304995	32448	30843	28280	2563	
SEP.	61452	60828	60544	307211	33303	30622	28149	2473	
OCT.	61052	60642	60206	308848	32127	31516	28925	2591	
Two weeks ending									
1990-OCT. 3	60954	60438	59832	306519	32389	31222	28565	2657	55
17	62004	61603	61021	310456	32833	31673	29171	2502	117
31	60121	59724	59471	307781	33565	31422	28756	2666	228
NOV. 14	62131	61849	61124	312244	33840	30653	28291	2363	69
28p	62048	61855	61009	312994	32924	31633	29124	2510	190

p--preliminary   pe--preliminary estimate

1. Reflects actual required reserves, with no adjustments to eliminate the effects of discontinuities, or "breaks", associated with regulatory changes in reserve requirements.
2. Reserve balances with Federal Reserve Banks plus vault cash used to satisfy reserve requirements.
3. The monetary base, not break-adjusted and not seasonally adjusted, consists of (1) total reserves, plus (2) required clearing balances and adjustments to compensate for float at Federal Reserve Banks, plus (3) the currency component of the money stock plus (4), for all quarterly reporters on the "Report of Transaction Accounts, Other Deposits and Vault Cash" and for those weekly reporters whose vault cash exceeds their required reserves, the difference between current vault cash and the amount applied to satisfy current reserve requirements. After the introduction of CRR, currency and vault cash figures are measured over computation periods ending on Mondays.
4. Excludes required clearing balances and adjustments to compensate for float and includes other off-balance sheet "as-of" adjustments.
5. Dates refer to the maintenance periods in which the vault cash can be used to satisfy reserve requirements. Under contemporaneous reserve requirements, maintenance periods end 30 days after the lagged computation periods in which the balances are held.
6. All vault cash held during the lagged computation period by "bound" institutions (i.e., those whose required reserves exceed their vault cash) plus the amount of vault cash applied during the maintenance period by "nonbound" institutions (i.e., those whose vault cash exceeds their required reserves) to satisfy current reserve requirements.
7. Total vault cash (line 8) less the amount of vault cash applied to satisfy reserve requirements.
8. Consists of carryover only by depository institutions maintaining reserves on the basis of two-week maintenance periods. Reflects excess (+) or deficit (-) reserves eligible to be carried forward into the two-week reserve maintenance period ending on the date shown.

TABLE 12.3

MONEY, CREDIT, AND SECURITY MARKETS

MONEY STOCK, LIQUID ASSETS, AND DEBT MEASURES

M2 rose slightly in June and M3 fell slightly. Both aggregates had declined in May.

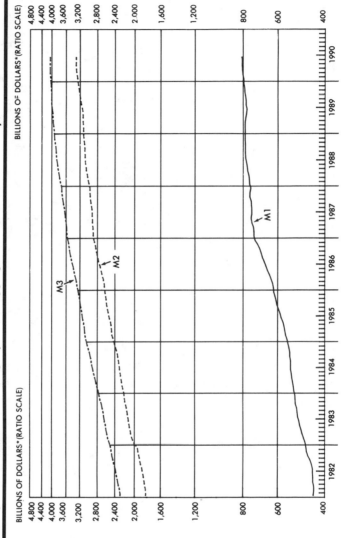

BILLIONS OF DOLLARS* (RATIO SCALE)

BILLIONS OF DOLLARS* (RATIO SCALE)

* AVERAGES OF DAILY FIGURES, SEASONALLY ADJUSTED
SOURCE: BOARD OF GOVERNORS OF THE FEDERAL RESERVE SYSTEM

COUNCIL OF ECONOMIC ADVISERS

TABLE 12.3 (Continued)

[Averages of daily figures, except as noted; billions of dollars, seasonally adjusted]

Period	M1 Sum of currency, demand deposits, travelers' checks, and other checkable deposits (OCDs)	M2 M1 plus overnight RPs and Eurodollars, MMMF balances (general purpose and broker/dealer), MMDAs, and savings and small time deposits	M3 M2 plus large time deposits, term RPs, term Eurodollars, and institution-only MMMF balances	L M3 plus other liquid assets	Debt Debt of domestic nonfinancial sectors (monthly average)[1]	Percent change from year or 6 months earlier[2] M1	M2	M3	Debt
1980: Dec	408.9	1,629.9	1,987.5	2,324.2	3,873.2	6.8	8.9	10.2	9.5
1981: Dec	436.5	1,793.5	2,234.2	2,596.8	4,260.3	6.7	10.0	12.4	10.0
1982: Dec	474.5	1,953.1	2,441.9	2,851.6	4,651.3	8.7	8.9	9.3	9.2
1983: Dec	521.2	2,186.5	2,693.4	3,154.7	5,176.7	9.8	12.0	10.3	11.3
1984: Dec	552.1	2,371.6	2,982.8	3,524.1	5,924.0	5.9	8.5	10.7	14.4
1985: Dec	620.1	2,570.6	3,202.1	3,829.5	6,732.8	12.3	8.4	7.4	13.7
1986: Dec	724.7	2,814.2	3,494.5	4,135.5	7,588.3	16.9	9.5	9.1	12.7
1987: Dec	750.4	2,913.2	3,678.7	4,338.7	8,307.5	3.5	3.5	5.3	9.5
1988: Dec	787.5	3,072.4	3,918.4	4,676.0	9,062.0	4.9	5.5	6.5	9.1
1989: Dec	794.8	3,221.0	r4,042.0	r4,879.2	9,777.6	.9	4.8	r3.2	7.9
1989: June	773.7	3,101.6	3,984.9	r4,784.4	9,414.9	-3.5	1.9	3.4	7.8
July	779.1	3,127.0	4,007.2	r4,810.1	9,465.6	-1.7	3.5	4.1	7.7
Aug	780.4	3,146.7	4,012.2	r4,824.5	9,529.1	-1.6	4.5	3.8	7.6
Sept	782.9	3,163.3	r4,012.3	r4,830.7	9,585.2	-.7	4.9	2.8	7.5
Oct	788.1	3,181.4	r4,016.5	r4,840.2	9,654.8	1.5	6.0	2.6	7.7
Nov	789.4	3,200.6	r4,029.0	r4,856.4	9,732.4	3.4	7.5	3.2	8.0
Dec	794.8	3,221.0	r4,042.0	r4,879.2	9,777.6	5.5	7.7	2.9	7.7
1990: Jan r	794.8	3,229.3	4,044.6	4,880.7	9,825.9	4.0	6.5	1.9	7.6
Feb r	801.4	3,252.4	4,058.6	4,890.2	9,889.9	5.4	6.7	2.3	7.6
Mar r	804.8	3,266.2	4,061.5	4,908.3	9,953.0	5.6	6.5	2.5	7.7
Apr r	807.4	3,271.8	4,065.1	4,917.9	10,005.3	4.9	5.7	2.4	7.3
May r	805.5	3,264.6	4,055.7	4,889.3	10,057.4	4.1	4.0	1.3	6.7
June p	809.6	3,269.9	4,055.0			3.7	3.0	.6	

[1] Consists of outstanding credit market debt of the U.S. Government, State and local governments, and private nonfinancial sectors; data from flow of funds accounts.

[2] Annual changes are from December to December and monthly changes are from 6 months earli-er at a simple annual rate.

NOTE.—See p. 27 for components.

Source: Board of Governors of the Federal Reserve System.

TABLE 12.4

COMPONENTS OF MONEY STOCK AND LIQUID ASSETS

[Averages of daily figures; billions of dollars, seasonally adjusted, except as noted by NSA]

Period	Currency	Demand deposits	Other checkable deposits (OCDs)	Overnight repurchase agreements (RPs), net, plus overnight Eurodollars [NSA]	Money market mutual fund balances[1] — General purpose and broker/dealer	Institution only	Money market deposit accounts (MMDAs)	Savings deposits	Small denomination time deposits[2]	Large denomination time deposits[2]	Term repurchase agreements (RPs) [NSA]	Term Eurodollars (net) [NSA]	Savings bonds	Short-term Treasury securities	Bankers' acceptances	Commercial paper
1980: Dec	115.3	261.4	28.0	28.8	61.6	15.2	0.0	400.1	728.5	260.4	33.5	50.3	72.3	133.5	32.1	98.8
1981: Dec	122.6	231.4	78.2	36.6	150.6	38.0	.0	343.8	823.2	303.0	35.3	67.5	67.8	149.4	40.0	105.3
1982: Dec	132.5	234.1	103.6	39.9	185.2	51.1	43.2	356.7	851.0	327.2	33.4	81.7	68.0	183.6	44.5	113.7
1983: Dec	146.2	238.5	131.6	55.6	138.8	42.8	379.2	305.4	784.1	327.6	49.9	91.5	71.1	211.9	45.0	133.2
1984: Dec	156.0	243.9	146.9	60.6	168.2	62.1	416.8	285.1	886.8	417.4	57.6	82.9	74.2	260.9	45.5	160.8
1985: Dec	167.8	266.8	179.6	73.5	177.2	63.9	513.0	301.2	884.0	437.0	62.4	73.5	79.5	298.3	42.1	207.5
1986: Dec	180.6	302.1	235.5	82.3	208.7	83.8	571.0	370.1	856.2	439.8	80.5	83.8	91.8	280.8	37.2	231.1
1987: Dec	196.7	287.0	259.7	83.2	222.0	89.0	523.8	414.9	917.8	488.8	106.1	91.0	100.6	254.2	44.8	260.4
1988: Dec	211.8	287.0	281.3	83.3	240.9	87.1	500.3	427.8	1,031.0	541.1	121.7	106.0	109.3	272.0	40.6	335.6
1989: Dec	221.9	279.7	285.7	76.8	312.4	102.3	483.7	409.0	1,142.3	558.3	94.9	r81.4	117.5	r330.6	41.2	347.9
1989: June	217.2	276.3	273.0	79.6	268.3	96.3	460.9	403.4	1,114.0	574.9	128.4	93.4	113.6	r295.2	41.2	349.4
July	217.8	279.6	274.5	80.9	277.7	99.0	463.9	403.3	1,122.4	574.7	123.8	91.8	114.3	r297.2	41.9	349.5
Aug	218.6	278.5	276.0	78.3	287.8	101.4	468.2	404.0	1,130.0	570.5	116.9	r89.8	115.0	r300.3	42.6	354.3
Sept	219.3	278.1	278.4	74.8	295.9	101.6	471.9	405.5	1,132.6	565.6	112.9	r85.6	115.7	r311.5	41.0	350.3
Oct	220.0	280.0	280.8	75.3	302.7	101.1	475.3	406.1	1,135.9	562.7	108.3	r90.2	116.2	r317.6	40.0	350.0
Nov	220.4	278.8	282.8	74.9	309.0	101.1	480.8	407.9	1,138.5	561.0	107.2	r79.5	116.8	r318.8	40.5	351.3
Dec	221.9	279.7	285.7	76.8	312.4	102.3	483.7	409.0	1,142.3	558.3	94.9	81.4	117.5	r330.6	41.2	347.9
1990: Jan	224.6	277.3	285.4	80.7	318.1	103.2	485.0	410.2	1,142.5	554.2	91.5	r74.3	117.7	r334.3	40.7	343.3
Feb	226.6	280.2	287.0	81.3	324.5	103.7	489.4	413.6	1,141.2	r549.6	94.9	r68.5	118.2	330.3	38.3	344.7
Mar	228.4	279.3	289.5	80.7	325.0	105.4	494.4	414.6	1,143.8	543.6	93.1	r66.5	119.1	348.0	37.0	342.7
Apr	230.1	277.8	291.8	r78.1	324.8	106.8	498.9	415.8	1,144.1	537.6	92.7	r65.9	119.9	339.7	r35.7	348.0
May r	231.6	274.6	291.6	81.0	319.4	107.3	500.2	415.1	1,145.2	534.6	93.0	68.1	120.7	327.7	35.2	357.5
June p	233.4	274.5	294.0	77.3	321.0	107.3	501.4	415.9	1,143.5	531.7	94.6	64.5				349.9

[1] Data prior to 1983 are not seasonally adjusted.

[2] Small denomination and large denomination deposits are those issued in amounts of less than $100,000 and more than $100,000, respectively.

NOTE.—Travelers checks of nonbank issuers are a component of money stock but are not shown here.

Source: Board of Governors of the Federal Reserve System.

271

THE H.6

The result of the growth in reserves held by the banking system is inevitably growth in money supply, which one should recall is ultimately related to the growth of the economy. Since there is debate among economists about the exact definition of money, the Fed publishes weekly three measures of money supply called M1, M2, and M3. All economists agree that money has some transaction and some savings components, but few know where to draw the line. The higher the numerical designation, the less spendable the money aggregates become. In other words, the higher the numerical designation, the greater the investment components of the money aggregates.

M1 includes travelers checks, currency held outside the banking system, and checking accounts (demand deposits and other checkable deposits). M2 incorporates M1 and other investment components that are easily converted into cash. These components include overnight Eurodollars, overnight and continuing contract repurchase agreements, savings accounts, small denomination time deposits, and balances in general purpose and broker/dealer money market funds. M3 incorporates M2 and large denomination time deposits ($100,000 CDs), term bank liabilities, and balances in taxable and tax-exempt institution-only money market funds (see Tables 12.3 and 12.4).

Taken together, the Federal Reserve releases described here indicate how responsive the central bank is to changes in the economy. Since the economy is both a determinant of monetary policy and results from prior policy changes, the nation's monetary stance is critical to any economic forecast.

13

Price Indices

In the U.S. economy, indices are used to measure the rate of inflation, which is defined as a rise in prices that is "both general and widely diffused."* In turn, the GNP components are deflated so that real or price-adjusted activity can be measured. In this chapter, we will discuss four types of price indices ranging from the most basic to the more complex used in the GNP report. These start with raw inputs and build up to cover the cost of the whole market basket of items that most consumers purchase.

COMMODITY PRICES**

Prices of raw commodities have a strong link to the level of inflation over time because they are inputs to the manufacturing pipeline. Even though the service-oriented economy has loosened commodity prices' historical link to inflation in recent years, these prices became important again in the late 1980s because some Fed officials used them as an early warning signal of inflation. Statistical studies show they lead consumer prices by about nine months and that a permanent 10% rise in commodity prices translates into about a 3 percentage point rise in inflation.

Commodity prices are readily available because some of the components are traded on exchanges. However, this makes them subject to noise. A case in point is the summer 1990 behavior of oil prices which surged but then retreated as the oil availability situation changed almost daily after Iraq's invasion of Kuwait. It is not uncommon for commodities indices to rise or fall by 1% in a given day in reaction to news events. Commodities indices do not incorporate wages, transportation, and distribution costs which modify changes in final prices.

The CRB Index

The *Commodity Research Bureau's Futures Index* (CRB), compiled since 1957, measures prices of nonfinancial contracts traded on public futures exchanges. The CRB contains nearby and deferred (up to but not including one year away) futures prices for 21 separate commodities contracts. The contracts are weighted equally but the index is a geometric average of all 21 prices divided into a base year (currently 1967). The CRB is divided into six groupings listed in Table 13.1. Some commodities, such as oil and metals, are listed in more than one group. So, the sum of the six groups exceeds 100% and the groups are not equally weighted.

Since 13 of the 21 commodities are foodstuffs and the remaining eight are atypical industries, the CRB is not the best indicator of

TABLE 13.1
CRB Component Groups

Imports:	cocoa, coffee, sugar
Precious Metals:	gold, platinum, silver
Industrials:	cotton, copper, crude oil, lumber, platinum, silver
Livestock and Meats:	cattle, hogs, pork bellies
Grains:	corn, oats, soybean meal, wheat
Energy:	crude oil, heating oil, unleaded gasoline

general inflation. It may react to the weather, statistical reports, and news events.

The Journal of Commerce Industrial Price Index (JoC)

Since 1986, the *Journal of Commerce* has tracked in its own index prices of 18 industrial materials and supplies used in the first stage of manufacturing, energy production, or building construction. Geoffrey Moore of Columbia University developed the index, choosing the components because, historically, they have been sensitive to price pressures that show up six to nine months later in the PPI or *consumer price index* (CPI). So, the JoC is more sensitive to actual economic developments than the CRB.

Each commodity in the *JoC Index* is weighted by its importance to overall economic output and how well it predicts inflation. The base year is 1980. The JoC Index is subdivided into three major categories: textiles, metals, and other (see Table 13.2 for components and weights). The JoC Index is smoothed by dividing the daily index by the average of the prior 250 days and converting that ratio to a compounded annual rate. A rule of thumb is that a change over 20%, in the absence of special factors such as strikes or import restrictions, indicates an acceleration in the other price indices in the future.

TABLE 13.2
JoC Index Composition

Textiles:	cotton (5.9%), burlap (5.5%), polyester (2.7%), printcloth (3.3%)
Metals:	scrap steel (6.3%), copper scrap (6.7%), aluminum (6.1%), zinc (5.1%), lead (5.4%), tin (5%)
Miscellaneous:	hides (5.5%), rubber (6.3%), tallow (5.2%), plywood (7.9%), boxes (5%), red oak (6.3%), benzene (4.7%), crude oil (7.1%)

PRODUCER PRICES

The *Producer Price Index* is the oldest series published monthly by the BLS. It began in 1902, with coverage from the years 1890 to 1901, as a response to an 1891 Senate resolution calling for an investigation into the effects of tariff laws on the economy and the price level. Known until 1978 as the *Wholesale Price Index*, the PPI has undergone significant expansion and modification over the years. Weighting was first introduced for the PPI in 1914, and major sample expansions and reclassifications were implemented in 1952 and 1967.

As it stands currently, the PPI measures average changes in selling prices received by domestic producers for their output. Most of the data used in the PPI are obtained by systematic sampling of virtually every industry in the mining and manufacturing sectors. The PPI also contains data from the fishing, agricultural, forestry, services, and utilities industries. Military goods and interplant transfers are included as well. Major PPI categories are detailed in Table 13.3, the summary data release.

Price is defined as the net revenue received by the producer for products shipped during the month. *Excise taxes* (received by the government) are specifically excluded but changes in rebate programs, low-interest financing, and other promotional programs are included. Likewise, changes in transportation fees will be reflected only to the extent they are paid by the producer (this is sometimes called *free on board point of production* (FOB)). A good example of this is the auto rebate programs instituted frequently in the late 1980s. If the auto manufacturer offers buyers a $500 rebate, the manufacturer's net revenue is reduced and the PPI would be lowered. The termination of rebate programs then results in higher PPI numbers in following months.

Surveys for the PPI generally refer to the Tuesday of the week containing the thirteenth of the month, so the pricing date can range from the ninth to the fifteenth. The exceptions to this rule involve commodities. Farm prices are for many other days of the week, refined petroleum prices are an average of the first half of the month, and

TABLE 13.3
Producer Price Indexes and Percent Changes by Stage of Processing

Grouping	Relative importance Dec. 1989 1/	Unadjusted index Apr. 1990 2/	Unadjusted index July 1990 2/	Unadjusted index Aug. 1990 2/	Unadjusted percent change to Aug. 1990 from: Aug. 1989	Unadjusted percent change to Aug. 1990 from: July 1990	Seasonally adjusted percent change from: May to June	Seasonally adjusted percent change from: June to July	Seasonally adjusted percent change from: July to Aug.
Finished goods................................	100.000	117.2	118.0	119.2	5.1	1.0	0.2	-0.1	1.3
Finished consumer goods...................	74.554	115.8	116.9	118.4	5.8	1.3	.1	-.2	1.6
Finished consumer foods..............	25.878	123.2	124.9	125.0	5.3	.1	-.4	0	.8
Crude........................	1.777	118.7	114.2	113.2	.2	-.9	-4.0	3.7	4.0
Processed...................	24.101	123.5	125.6	125.8	5.7	.2	-.2	-.2	.5
Finished consumer goods, excluding foods.....	48.676	112.2	112.9	115.1	6.1	1.9	.4	-.3	2.0
Nondurable goods less foods..............	33.310	107.7	108.5	111.5	7.7	2.8	.2	-.5	2.9
Durable goods........................	15.366	119.3	120.1	120.0	2.6	-.1	.9	.2	.2
Capital equipment........................	25.446	122.2	122.5	122.9	3.3	.3	.4	.3	.3
Manufacturing industries..............	6.690	123.8	124.4	124.7	3.4	.2	.2	.2	.2
Nonmanufacturing industries..............	18.756	121.6	121.8	122.2	3.2	.3	.5	.2	.5
Intermediate materials, supplies, and components.	100.000	112.8	113.0	114.4	2.1	1.2	-.2	0	1.3
Materials and components for manufacturing.....	49.947	118.2	118.4	118.7	.8	.3	.1	0	.4
Materials for food manufacturing........	3.480	117.2	120.9	120.5	6.4	-.3	.2	-.5	.6
Materials for nondurable manufacturing......	15.770	117.0	116.9	116.7	-.6	-.2	0	0	.1
Materials for durable manufacturing..........	11.437	120.8	120.3	121.6	-.4	1.1	-.2	.2	1.3
Components for manufacturing 3/..............	19.260	118.7	118.8	118.9	1.7	.1	.1	.1	.1
Materials and components for construction......	12.645	123.0	122.9	122.9	1.1	0	-.2	.1	.2
Processed fuels and lubricants........	12.250	78.0	78.3	85.7	10.9	9.5	-1.2	-1.0	9.7
Manufacturing industries...........	4.726	79.8	80.1	87.5	9.8	9.2	-.8	-1.3	9.5
Nonmanufacturing industries........	7.524	76.9	77.1	84.6	11.6	9.7	-1.3	-.9	9.8
Containers........................	4.224	127.8	127.4	127.6	1.3	.2	.1	-.2	.2
Supplies........................	20.933	118.9	119.5	119.3	.8	-.2	-.3	.3	0
Manufacturing industries..............	7.589	121.7	121.9	122.1	1.4	.2	.1	.1	.2
Nonmanufacturing industries..............	13.344	117.5	118.2	117.9	.6	-.3	-.3	.2	0
Feeds........................	1.627	101.6	105.2	102.4	-7.8	-2.7	-4.6	2.9	-1.5
Other supplies........................	11.717	119.7	120.0	120.1	1.8	.1	.1	.1	.2
Crude materials for further processing..........	100.000	103.0	101.2	110.2	9.0	8.9	-2.4	.6	9.3
Foodstuffs and feedstuffs..............	41.939	115.1	115.4	113.5	3.2	-1.6	.4	1.0	-.9
Nonfood materials..............	58.061	91.0	88.0	103.2	13.3	17.3	-4.4	.2	17.4
Nonfood materials except fuel 4/..............	42.154	92.7	87.6	111.6	19.6	27.4	-5.8	-1.0	28.1
Manufacturing 4/..............	38.941	87.3	82.1	106.7	20.8	30.0	-6.3	-1.4	30.0
Construction..............	3.214	146.1	147.3	146.8	4.6	-.3	.5	.6	-.3
Crude fuel 3/ 4/..............	15.907	84.7	86.5	80.8	-3.3	-6.6	-.8	4.2	-6.6
Manufacturing industries 3/..............	8.095	82.8	84.8	78.2	-4.4	-7.8	-1.0	5.2	-7.8
Nonmanufacturing industries 3/..............	7.812	86.8	88.4	83.8	-2.2	-5.2	-.7	3.2	-5.2
Special groupings									
Finished goods, excluding foods..................	6/ 74.122	115.2	115.8	117.3	5.0	1.3	.4	-.2	1.5
Intermediate materials less foods and feeds......	7/ 94.893	112.8	112.8	114.4	2.1	1.4	-.2	-.1	1.5
Intermediate foods and feeds..............	7/ 5.107	112.5	116.1	115.0	1.7	-.9	-1.3	.5	-.1
Crude materials less agricultural products 4/ 8/.	9/ 56.211	90.2	87.0	102.7	13.6	18.0	-4.6	.1	18.2
Finished energy goods..:	6/ 9.202	68.0	67.8	74.4	17.0	9.7	-.9	-.5	9.5
Finished goods less energy..............	6/ 90.798	125.0	126.1	126.2	4.0	.1	.3	-.1	.5
Finished consumer goods less energy..............	6/ 65.352	126.1	127.3	127.5	4.3	.1	.3	-.2	.5
Finished goods less foods and energy..............	6/ 64.920	125.6	126.5	126.6	3.4	.1	.6	-.1	.3
Finished consumer goods less foods and energy....	6/ 39.474	127.7	128.8	128.9	3.5	.1	.7	-.2	.2
Consumer nondurable goods less foods and energy..	6/ 24.108	133.8	135.2	135.3	4.2	.1	.6	-.4	.5
Intermediate energy goods......................	7/ 12.354	77.7	78.0	85.3	10.9	9.4	-1.0	-1.2	9.6
Intermediate materials less energy..............	7/ 87.646	120.1	120.3	120.4	.9	.1	0	.1	.2
Intermediate materials less foods and energy.....	7/ 82.539	120.6	120.5	120.8	.7	.2	-.1	.1	.3
Crude energy materials 3/ 4/..................	9/ 40.528	73.1	69.4	87.1	18.5	25.5	-6.2	-.1	25.5
Crude materials less energy..............	9/ 59.472	120.5	120.7	119.9	3.0	-.7	.1	1.0	-.1
Crude nonfood materials less energy 5/..........	9/ 17.533	137.8	137.7	139.9	2.4	1.6		.9	1.8

1/ Comprehensive relative importance figures are computed once each year in December.
2/ Data for Apr. 1990 have been revised to reflect the availability of late reports and corrections by respondents. All data are subject to revision 4 months after original publication.
3/ Not seasonally adjusted.
4/ Includes crude petroleum.
5/ Excludes crude petroleum.
6/ Percent of total finished goods.
7/ Percent of total intermediate materials.
8/ Formerly titled "Crude materials for further processing, excluding crude foodstuffs and feedstuffs, plant and animal fibers, oilseeds, and leaf tobacco."
9/ Percent of total crude materials.

prices of natural gas and some industrial chemicals are for the full prior month.

The PPI is calculated as a modified Laspeyres Index which weights price changes with quantity shipped (the latter using the Commerce Department's gross value of shipments data). Establishments are chosen to participate in the survey based on weighted random sampling from the Unemployment Insurance System covering virtually all employers. After an initial visit by an economist to select items to be priced, the subsequent data-gathering is mainly completed by mail and telephone. The survey is updated every few years in a procedure called resampling which takes account of product changes resulting from new technology and altered industry structure.

Quality Adjustment

The major potential for error in the PPI report stems from quality adjustments which modify products. The BLS treats these adjustments in one of three ways.

1. If the change in the product is very minor, the new price is directly compared to the old price and the PPI changes accordingly.

2. If the product changes are quantifiable, the BLS puts into the PPI only the portion of the price change that reflects added costs. An example is retooling in the auto industry for the model changeover. If the price of a new car rises by $500 but $200 of that amount represents extra product costs and the associated normal profit margins from adding government-mandated safety equipment, then the real price has risen by only $300. The change in the passenger car portion of the PPI index will be $300, not the $500 nominal price rise.

3. If a value for quality adjustment cannot be judged, the BLS will assume that the entire price difference between the old and new items is entirely due to quality adjustment and will apply

an *overlap method*. That is, the BLS will collect prices for both the old and new products over a period of time and choose an *overlap month*. In the overlap month, any difference between the price levels of the two items is factored out. In the following months, the new item alone is included in the PPI. The latter two methods allow much discretion and give rise to measurement error. In particular, the BLS has been criticized for missing economies where new products and technologies cost the producer less than older, inferior products.

Included in the PPI report are:

Price indices for about 500 mining and manufacturing industries, including nearly 8,000 specific products;

Over 3,000 commodity price indices organized by end-use; and

Several major aggregate indices that measure price changes by stage of processing.

The financial markets focus on the latter three measures, known as the PPI for crude materials, the PPI for intermediate goods, and the PPI for finished goods.

Crude

The crude materials PPI measures items which need further processing (such as the raw materials that are used at the first stage of industrial processing). Foodstuffs and feed account for about 41% of this index, fuels for about 15%, and manufacturing materials for about 39%. A spurt in the crude index can be the first indication that profit margins will be squeezed and that price increases are looming. The crude materials PPI differs from commodities indices in that it is available only monthly, but it measures the same pressures, and indeed the commodities indices are used to project it.

Intermediate

The intermediate materials PPI measures materials, supplies, and components that have already had some preparation (for example, they include labor costs and profit margins). About 50% of the items in the index are intermediate inputs to manufacturing, while 13% are used in the construction trades, and another 12% are processed fuels and lubricants.

Finished

The finished goods PPI is the index that makes news headlines. It is the broadest measure of manufacturing inflation and covers all the costs of production (materials, labor, parts, electricity, and so on). Approximately 75% of the finished goods PPI is devoted to finished consumer goods, including foods (26%), gasoline and related products (9%), nondurable goods such as clothing (33%), and durables such as home appliances and autos (15%). The other 25% covers capital equipment purchased by businesses. Sharp rises in the finished goods PPI could portend an increase in consumer prices if profit margins are maintained, so the index is watched closely.

Core

The financial markets focus on the finished goods PPI and one of its components—the PPI excluding food and energy. The latter is known as the *core rate* and covers about 65% of the items in the overall PPI. Figure 13.1 shows the movements in the overall PPI and component series over the course of the last eight years. The chart demonstrates that much of the volatility in the PPI reflected erratic movements in food and energy (items over which Wall Street has decided our policy makers have very little control since they depend on the weather and political acts). Thus, an accelerating or decelerating core PPI has the potential to cause substantial adjustments in the financial markets.

FIGURE 13.1

PRICES

PRODUCER PRICES

In June, the producer price index for all finished goods rose 0.2 percent. Prices of finished consumer foods fell 0.4 percent, while prices of other finished consumer goods rose 0.4 percent. Capital equipment prices rose 0.4 percent.

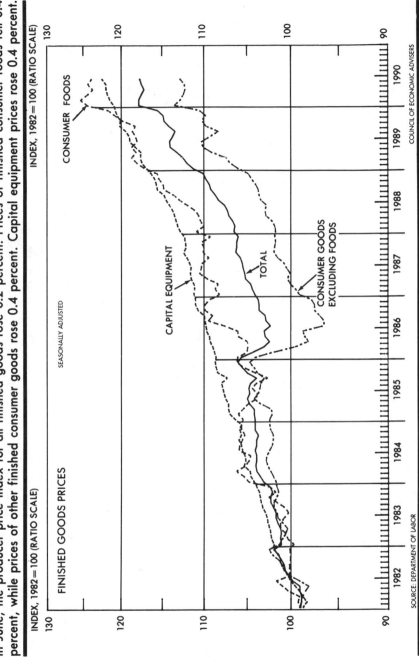

FIGURE 13.1 (Continued)

[1982=100; monthly data seasonally adjusted]

Period	Finished goods								Intermediate materials			Crude materials		
	Total finished goods	Consumer foods	Finished goods excluding consumer foods					Total finished consumer goods	Total	Foods and feeds [1]	Other	Total	Foodstuffs and feedstuffs	Other
			Total	Total	Durable	Nondurable	Capital equipment							
				Consumer goods										
1980	88.0	92.4	86.7	87.1	91.0	85.1	85.8	88.6	90.3	105.5	89.4	95.3	104.6	84.6
1981	96.1	97.8	95.6	96.1	96.4	95.8	94.6	96.6	98.6	104.6	98.2	103.0	103.9	101.8
1982	100.0	100.0	100.0	100.0	100.0	100.0	100.0	100.0	100.0	100.0	100.0	100.0	100.0	100.0
1983	101.6	101.0	101.8	101.2	102.8	100.5	102.8	101.3	100.6	103.6	100.5	101.3	101.8	100.7
1984	103.7	105.4	103.2	102.2	104.5	101.1	105.2	103.3	103.1	105.7	103.0	103.5	104.7	102.2
1985	104.7	104.6	104.6	103.3	106.5	101.7	107.5	103.8	102.7	97.3	103.0	95.8	94.8	96.9
1986	103.2	107.3	101.9	98.5	108.9	93.3	109.7	101.4	99.1	96.2	99.3	87.7	93.2	81.6
1987	105.4	109.5	104.0	100.7	111.5	94.9	111.7	103.6	101.5	99.2	101.7	93.7	96.2	87.9
1988	108.0	112.6	106.5	103.1	113.8	97.3	114.3	106.2	107.1	109.5	106.9	96.0	106.1	85.5
1989	113.6	118.7	111.8	108.9	117.6	103.8	118.8	112.1	112.0	113.8	111.9	103.1	111.2	93.4
1989: June	114.0	117.9	112.7	110.2	117.7	105.6	118.8	112.8	112.3	111.6	112.4	103.3	109.6	94.7
July	113.6	118.1	112.1	109.2	117.4	104.3	118.9	112.1	112.1	113.2	112.0	103.5	108.9	95.5
Aug	113.3	118.5	111.5	108.2	117.8	102.7	119.3	111.6	111.8	112.8	111.8	101.1	109.7	91.3
Sept	114.1	118.1	112.8	109.7	118.7	104.5	120.1	112.5	112.4	112.7	112.2	102.3	109.0	93.6
Oct	114.7	119.7	113.1	110.1	118.6	105.1	120.0	113.3	112.4	112.5	112.4	102.6	109.0	94.1
Nov	114.8	120.7	112.9	109.7	118.7	104.4	120.4	113.3	112.2	113.4	112.1	103.2	111.4	93.5
Dec	115.5	121.6	113.5	110.4	119.2	105.3	120.7	114.1	112.2	113.1	112.1	104.7	113.9	94.4
1990: Jan	117.7	124.4	115.6	113.4	118.6	109.7	120.9	117.0	113.6	113.3	113.6	107.0	114.7	97.5
Feb ʳ	117.7	125.3	115.2	112.7	119.0	108.5	121.4	116.8	112.7	112.3	112.8	107.3	115.4	97.5
Mar	117.4	124.4	115.1	112.3	119.4	107.8	121.7	116.3	112.8	112.8	112.8	106.0	116.3	94.9
Apr	117.1	123.6	115.0	112.1	119.2	107.6	121.9	115.9	112.9	114.2	112.8	102.7	115.4	90.3
May	117.4	124.3	115.1	112.2	119.3	107.7	121.9	116.2	112.8	115.6	112.7	102.6	112.5	91.9
June	117.6	123.8	115.6	112.7	120.4	107.9	122.4	116.3	112.6	114.1	112.5	100.1	112.9	87.9

[1] Intermediate materials for food manufacturing and feeds.

Source: Department of Labor, Bureau of Labor Statistics.

282

CONSUMER PRICES

The *Consumer Price Index* (CPI) is a measure of the average change in prices paid by urban consumers for a fixed-market basket of goods and services. It is calculated monthly from a survey conducted by the BLS for two groups (wage earners and clerical workers and all urban families—CPI-U). The first is a continuation of an index dating from 1919 used in wage negotiations; the second is a broader index representative of the buying habits of over 75% of the population of the United States (the CPI-U).

The CPI was initiated during WW I, when rapid price increases made an index necessary for calculating cost-of-living adjustments in wages. It began as a study of family expenditures in 92 urban centers over the 1917–19 period and expanded to a regular national index covering 32 cities in 1921. The CPI is currently based on a sample of the prices paid for a wide range of goods (food, shelter, clothing, fuels) and services (transportation, medical services) that people use for day-to-day living. Price change is measured by following the same items on a month-to-month basis and comparing the aggregate cost with that of the prior period. The result is a hypothetical expenditure needed to maintain the same standard of living as established in the base period (sometimes called a *cost of living index*).

Weights and Samples

The weight of an item in the CPI is derived from the expenditures in the *Commerce Department's Consumer Expenditure Survey*. Prices are collected by telephone and during in-person interviews in 91 urban areas from about 21,000 retail and service businesses. Rents come from about 40,000 tenants and 20,000 owner-occupied homes. Food, fuels, and a few other items are priced monthly in all 91 areas. Most prices are collected monthly in the five largest urban areas but only bi-monthly in the remaining areas. The survey is taken at varying days during the month for different products or outlets and is published about three weeks following the reference month.

Price changes for the various items within each area are averaged together using weights that represent their importance to the appropriate population group within that area. City averages are computed using local area data. Separate indices are computed for four regions, four size classes, and 27 metropolitan statistical areas. The weights for the overall CPI-U currently are heaviest for food and beverages (17 + %), housing (43%), transportation (17%), and apparel and medical care (each about 6%). See Table 13.4 for index values for some components and Appendix 13.1 for the relative importance of all the components.

Uses

The CPI affects almost the entire population of the United States because of its myriad uses. These uses include:

1. As an economic indicator. The CPI is the inflation indicator used by policy makers to judge their effectiveness because it covers a broad range of items. Private business and labor leaders also use the CPI to make economic decisions such as pricing and wage demands.
2. As a deflator of other series. The CPI and its components are used to adjust other economic indicators for price changes and to translate these indicators into inflation-free or "real" dollars. Retail sales, hourly and weekly earnings, and components of GNP are all deflated using the CPI.
3. As contract adjustments. More than three million workers are covered by contracts that tie wages to the CPI. About 60 million recipients of federal government benefits receive adjustments tied to the CPI. Private firms use the CPI to adjust rents, royalties, and alimony and child support payments.

Figure 13.2 shows the movements in the CPI over time. Major price accelerations are seen in 1973 and again in 1979 (periods of crisis in

TABLE 13.4
The CPI-U

[1982–84=100, except as noted; monthly data seasonally adjusted, except as noted]

Period	All items¹ Not seasonally adjusted (NSA)	All items¹ Seasonally adjusted	Food	Housing Total¹	Shelter Total	Shelter Renters' costs (Dec. 1982=100)	Shelter Homeowners' costs (Dec. 1982=100)	Shelter Maintenance and repairs (NSA)	Fuel and other utilities	Apparel and upkeep	Transportation Total¹	New cars	Motor fuel	Medical care	Energy²	All items less food, shelter, and energy
Rel. imp.³	100.0		16.3	42.0	27.9	7.9	19.8	0.2	7.5	6.1	17.1	4.2	3.2	6.2	7.4	48.4
1980	82.4		86.8	81.1	81.0	....	....	82.4	75.4	90.9	83.1	88.4	97.4	74.9	86.0	80.6
1981	90.9		93.6	90.4	90.5	....	....	90.7	86.4	95.3	93.2	93.7	108.5	82.9	97.7	88.3
1982	96.5		97.4	96.9	96.9	....	....	96.4	94.9	97.8	97.0	97.4	102.8	92.5	99.2	95.1
1983	99.6		99.4	99.5	99.1	103.0	102.5	99.9	100.2	100.2	99.3	99.9	99.4	100.6	99.9	100.0
1984	103.9		103.2	103.6	104.0	108.6	107.3	103.7	104.8	102.1	103.7	102.8	97.9	106.8	100.9	105.0
1985	107.6		105.6	107.7	109.8	115.4	113.1	106.5	106.5	105.0	106.4	106.1	98.7	113.5	101.6	109.0
1986	109.6		109.0	110.9	115.8	121.9	119.4	107.9	104.1	105.9	102.3	110.6	77.1	122.0	88.2	112.7
1987	113.6		113.5	114.2	121.3	128.1	124.8	111.8	103.0	110.6	105.4	114.6	80.2	130.1	88.6	117.0
1988	118.3		118.2	118.5	127.1	133.6	131.1	114.7	104.4	115.4	108.7	116.9	80.9	138.6	89.3	121.9
1989	124.0		125.1	123.0	132.8	138.9	137.3	118.0	107.8	118.6	114.1	119.2	88.5	149.3	94.3	127.3
1989:																
June	124.1	124.1	125.2	122.6	132.3	138.0	136.9	118.3	107.3	118.9	115.7	119.3	94.6	148.7	96.4	127.4
July	124.4	124.5	125.6	123.3	133.2	139.6	137.6	118.4	107.8	118.3	115.3	118.8	92.9	149.6	95.9	127.7
Aug	124.6	124.5	125.9	123.5	133.5	139.1	138.2	118.5	107.8	116.9	114.2	118.5	88.4	150.8	93.8	127.8
Sept	125.0	124.8	126.3	123.7	133.7	138.7	138.7	118.6	108.0	118.6	113.9	118.1	87.1	151.9	93.2	128.3
Oct	125.6	125.4	126.8	124.2	134.4	139.8	139.4	118.6	108.1	119.4	114.5	118.8	88.4	153.0	94.1	128.8
Nov	125.9	125.8	127.4	124.7	135.0	140.5	140.0	119.3	108.7	119.4	114.6	119.8	86.8	154.2	93.8	129.3
Dec	126.1	126.3	128.0	125.2	135.6	141.0	140.6	119.5	109.4	119.0	115.0	120.8	86.3	155.1	94.1	129.7
1990:																
Jan	127.4	127.7	130.5	126.1	136.3	142.3	141.1	120.4	111.6	119.0	117.4	121.6	93.4	156.1	98.9	130.4
Feb	128.0	128.3	131.1	126.3	136.6	143.4	141.0	120.8	110.9	122.9	117.7	121.4	93.6	157.3	98.2	131.5
Mar	128.7	128.9	131.5	126.9	137.6	143.8	142.4	121.2	111.0	124.9	117.6	121.2	92.2	158.5	97.4	132.2
Apr	128.9	129.1	131.2	127.0	137.9	143.9	142.8	121.2	110.5	125.0	117.7	120.9	92.5	159.8	97.0	132.6
May	129.2	129.3	131.2	127.2	138.2	143.9	143.2	122.2	110.5	124.6	117.5	120.7	91.2	161.0	96.3	132.9
June	129.9	130.0	132.2	128.0	139.5	144.5	144.8	121.8	110.3	124.5	118.0	120.5	93.2	162.1	96.9	133.2

¹ Includes items not shown separately.
² Household fuels—gas (piped), electricity, fuel oil, etc.—and motor fuel. Motor oil, coolant, etc. also included through 1982.
³ Relative importance, December 1989.

Note.—Data beginning 1983 incorporate a rental equivalence measure for homeownership costs and therefore are not strictly comparable with figures for earlier periods.
Data beginning 1987 and 1988 calculated on a revised basis.
Source: Department of Labor, Bureau of Labor Statistics.

FIGURE 13.2 The CPI

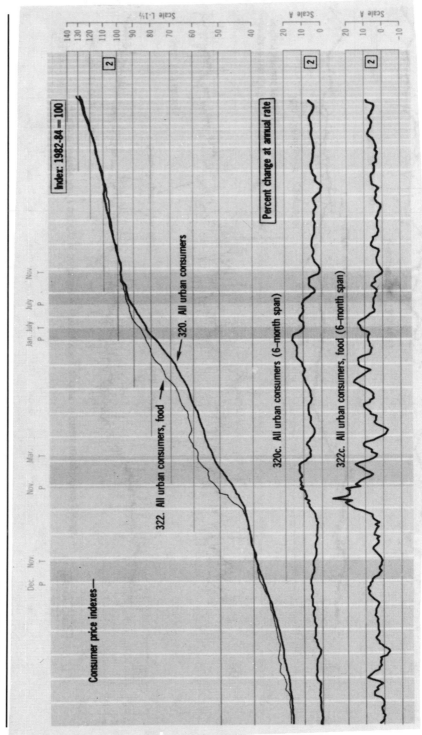

286

the oil markets). See Appendix 13.2 for the index numbers. This is why financial markets focus on the CPI less food and energy, just as they do for the PPI. This is also called the *core rate* for the CPI.

Pitfalls

Historically, there have been two major criticisms of the CPI. These stem from the fixed nature of the market basket of goods measured in the index and from the treatment of housing costs, which in the past soared whenever mortgage interest rates rose. In January 1983, the BLS changed the computation for shelter to an *owners' equivalent rent concept*. The new concept separates out the investment or asset aspects of homeownership from the shelter services of the house by comparing it with rental equivalents. Strictly speaking, the CPI revision means that indices before 1983 are not currently able to be directly comparable to the CPI. It may also mean that inflation was over-measured in prior economic cycles because the CPI assumed that a new home was purchased during periods of credit tightness. In fact, few consumers were actually buying homes during these periods, so rising rates may not have been the constraint that the CPI assumed.

Substitution effects, however, are still not captured by the CPI. Since the index measures a fixed market basket of goods, it fails to capture behavior patterns. (Economists would say the CPI assumes demand is price inelastic.) When prices of beef rise faster than those for chicken, for example, the consumer buys less beef. He substitutes the cheaper good immediately. The index may not capture this change for several months until the next Commerce Department spending survey is conducted. The CPI is also probably not applicable to non-urban residents who have access to farm produce or to any particular subgroup with particular purchasing needs (such as the elderly).

Services and Taxes

The main differences between the CPI and the PPI are that the former covers the services sector and includes taxes paid. Services are both the fastest growing and the most inflationary part of the economy, particularly in the medical field. Note also that the inclusion of taxes paid in the CPI follows the concept of disposable personal income (see Chapter 5). Payment of higher taxes means less spending on discretionary items.

GNP PRICE DEFLATORS

Three deflators are released in the quarterly GNP reports—the *implicit*, *fixed-weight*, and *chain price deflators*. Each has differing uses but all are legitimate inflation measures. The markets focus on the first two, since the chain price index covers only the price movement from one period to the next*** and its change largely duplicates that of the fixed weight deflator.

Implicit deflator

Each component of quarterly GNP, in as fine a detail as possible, is deflated using the indices that make up the CPI (for consumption components) or the PPI (for gross private domestic investment components). The index also incorporates separate deflators for construction costs and export prices. Once deflated, the components are again summed to obtain constant dollar GNP. The overall implicit deflator is found by dividing current dollar GNP by constant dollar GNP. The value of the implicit deflator for any quarter thus depends on the composition of GNP since it is weighted by its components.

In periods when some deflator components are advancing more rapidly than others (particularly the case with nondurable goods, nonresidential construction, and government spending in the 1970s), this is a good inflation measure because it captures any shifts in consumption. Economists call these *substitution effects*. They are easily illustrated by a rise in the price of beef relative to other meats and poultry. Theoretically, consumers will eat more chicken. Thus, their market basket of purchases will shift and the implicit deflator easily captures the price effects. Another practical example is the use of energy. In periods of sharply rising oil prices, consumers will make great adjustments to their lifestyles. They will switch to more fuel efficient cars to reduce gasoline purchases and buy more insulation, storm windows, and space heaters to save on heating fuel. These changes will be captured in the composition of the implicit deflator.

Fixed Weight Deflator

The fixed weight deflator is also an average of the CPI and PPI price indices for the goods and services that make up GNP. In contrast to the implicit deflator, it is weighted by the composition of GNP at some earlier fixed date called the *base period*. It measures the change in the price of a fixed market basket from that date. Thus, it measures only price changes without regard for actual consumption patterns. The fixed weight deflator will overstate inflation when it is rising because it assumes the quality of life remains unchanged, except when consumers step up purchases of high-priced goods in an attempt to outwit still higher prices.

The main differences between the CPI and the GNP deflators are due to weighting differences associated with index definition and the base periods selected. The weighting effect becomes smaller when the base periods are closer together. Historically, differences in weighting patterns have not usually created differences in price measure of more than 0.5% point. But, the effects become bigger the higher the rate of inflation in the economy. The mathematically oriented can study the construction of the indices in Table 13.5.

PRICE THEORY

Rising inflation is said to distort business decisions, hurt savers, and raise interest rates. If the rate of inflation can be divided into trend and cyclical components, the trend has been up. This reflects the three oil shocks to the economy since 1972 and an increased willing-

TABLE 13.5
Laspeyres versus Paasche Indices

	Laspeyres	Paasche
Uses	Market-basket Measure	Shifts with Consumption
Base	Prior Fixed Period	Current Period; It Shifts
Examples	CPI, PPI, Fixed Weight and Chain Deflators	Implicit Deflator

$$\text{Formula } I_{ot} = \frac{\Sigma \, p_t \, q_o}{\Sigma \, p_o \, q_o} = \Sigma \left[\frac{p_t}{p_o} \right] \left[\frac{p_o \, q_o}{\Sigma \, p_o \, q_o} \right]$$

$$I_{ot} = \frac{\Sigma \, p_t \, q_t}{\Sigma \, p_o \, q_t}$$

where o = base period

t = current month

I = index total

p = price

q = quantity

ness on the part of consumers to accept price hikes. The cyclical component rises as the economy operates closer to capacity and ebbs as resource utilization slackens. Theoretically, these forces are known as *cost-push* and *demand-pull inflation*.

Price history is demonstrated in Figure 13.2. Prices, as measured by the CPI, rose relatively modestly for most of the last 40 years with the rate of change averaging just $+4.2\%$. There were four episodes of sharply rising inflation, however. In 1968–69, the expansion of the Vietnam War caused demand-pull inflation, while the episodes in 1973–74, 1979–81 and 1988–90 largely were related to oil prices. In all cases, restrictive monetary policy was used to combat inflation and the rate of price change did not abate until the economy turned down. Thus, inflation numbers are lagging indicators of the economy but may spark policy responses. Note also that, historically, only times of war are associated with double-digit price changes. At those times, wage and price controls were the alternative policy responses to Fed tightening.

Notes

*Moore, Geoffrey H. *The Anatomy of Inflation*, U.S. Department of Labor, Report Number 373, p. 3, 1970.

**My thinking on this section was influenced by the McCarthy, Crisanti & Maffei, Inc. Money Market Critique of July 25, 1989, entitled "Commodity Prices and Inflation," by Astrid Adolfson, with Joseph Plocek and Carl Palash.

***Technically, the chain-weight index is a Laspeyres index that always has its weights taken from the first of any two periods to be compared.

Appendix 13.1

Relative Importance of Components in the Consumer Price Indexes

APPENDIX 13.1

Item and group	U.S. City Average	
	All Urban Consumers (CPI-U)	Urban Wage Earners and Clerical Workers (CPI-W)
All items	100.000	100.000
Food and beverages	17.865	19.768
Food	16.318	18.116
Food at home	10.129	11.454
Cereals and bakery products	1.440	1.638
Cereals and cereal products	.463	.534
Flour and prepared flour mixes	.078	.091
Cereal	.281	.321
Rice, pasta, and cornmeal	.104	.122
Bakery products	.978	1.104
White bread	.238	.293
Fresh other bread, biscuits, rolls, and muffins	.219	.228
Cookies, fresh cakes, and cupcakes	.246	.290
Other bakery products	.274	.292
Meats, poultry, fish, and eggs	3.119	3.654
Meats, poultry, and fish	2.905	3.404
Meats	2.057	2.473
Beef and veal	1.065	1.276
Ground beef other than canned	.381	.474
Chuck roast	.092	.106
Round roast	.055	.063
Round steak	.089	.116
Sirloin steak	.082	.102
Other beef and veal	.366	.415
Pork	.583	.712
Bacon	.094	.112
Chops	.144	.180
Ham	.139	.169
Other pork, including sausage	.206	.251
Other meats	.409	.484
Poultry	.463	.515
Fresh whole chicken	.155	.183
Fresh and frozen chicken parts	.221	.241
Other poultry	.086	.091
Fish and seafood	.385	.416
Canned fish and seafood	.085	.093
Fresh and frozen fish and seafood	.300	.323
Eggs	.214	.250
Dairy products	1.296	1.435
Fresh milk and cream	.651	.760
Fresh whole milk	.380	.472
Other fresh milk and cream	.270	.289
Processed dairy products	.645	.675
Cheese	.370	.382
Ice cream and related products	.163	.177
Other dairy products, including butter	.111	.116

See footnotes at end of table.

293

APPENDIX 13.1 (Continued)

Item and group	U.S. City Average	
	All Urban Consumers (CPI-U)	Urban Wage Earners and Clerical Workers (CPI-W)
Fruits and vegetables	1.813	1.905
Fresh fruits and vegetables	1.150	1.199
Fresh fruits	.612	.630
Apples	.096	.104
Bananas	.069	.074
Oranges, including tangerines	.079	.095
Other fresh fruits	.369	.357
Fresh vegetables	.537	.569
Potatoes	.103	.115
Lettuce	.061	.065
Tomatoes	.081	.095
Other fresh vegetables	.292	.295
Processed fruits and vegetables	.663	.707
Processed fruits	.377	.379
Fruit juices and frozen fruit	.298	.304
Canned and dried fruits	.079	.075
Processed vegetables	.286	.328
Frozen vegetables	.094	.103
Other processed vegetables	.192	.225
Other food at home	2.462	2.822
Sugar and sweets	.348	.391
Sugar and artificial sweeteners	.094	.117
Sweets, including candy	.255	.275
Fats and oils	.267	.306
Nonalcoholic beverages	.797	.926
Carbonated drinks	.422	.519
Coffee	.229	.240
Other noncarbonated drinks	.147	.166
Other prepared food	1.050	1.199
Canned and packaged soup	.086	.095
Frozen prepared food	.191	.210
Snacks	.213	.242
Seasonings, condiments, sauces, and spices	.268	.303
Miscellaneous prepared food, including baby food	.292	.350
Food away from home	6.189	6.661
Lunch	2.187	2.477
Dinner	2.647	2.729
Other meals and snacks	1.034	1.224
Unpriced items	.321	.230
Alcoholic beverages	1.546	1.652
Alcoholic beverages at home	.833	.912
Beer and ale	.432	.540
Distilled spirits	.215	.204
Wine at home	.186	.168
Alcoholic beverages away from home	.713	.740

See footnotes at end of table.

APPENDIX 13.1 (Continued)

Item and group	U.S. City Average	
	All Urban Consumers (CPI-U)	Urban Wage Earners and Clerical Workers (CPI-W)
Housing	42.037	39.509
Shelter	27.908	25.590
Renters' costs	7.871	8.056
Rent, residential	5.955	6.789
Other renters' costs	1.916	1.267
Lodging while out of town	1.675	1.109
Lodging while at school	.206	.129
Tenants' insurance	.035	.028
Homeowners' costs	19.825	17.333
Owners' equivalent rent	19.428	16.998
Household insurance	.398	.336
Maintenance and repairs	.212	.201
Maintenance and repair services	.127	.107
Maintenance and repair commodities	.085	.094
Materials, supplies, and equipment for home repairs	.038	.042
Other maintenance and repair commodities	.046	.052
Fuel and other utilities	7.484	7.691
Fuels	4.214	4.304
Fuel oil and other household fuel commodities	.429	.390
Fuel oil	.307	.264
Other household fuel commodities	.122	.126
Gas (piped) and electricity	3.785	3.914
Electricity	2.587	2.652
Utility (piped) gas	1.198	1.262
Other utilities and public services	3.269	3.387
Telephone services	1.932	1.955
Local charges	1.272	1.292
Interstate toll calls	.364	.361
Intrastate toll calls	.297	.302
Water and sewerage maintenance	.689	.715
Cable television	.468	.539
Refuse collection	.180	.178
Household furnishings and operation	6.645	6.227
Housefurnishings	3.982	3.892
Textile housefurnishings	.394	.372
Furniture and bedding	1.188	1.152
Bedroom furniture	.385	.427
Sofas	.237	.228
Living room chairs and tables	.194	.183
Other furniture	.372	.315
Appliances, including electronic equipment	1.105	1.151
Video and audio products	.597	.650
Televisions	.207	.234
Video products other than televisions	.128	.132
Audio products	.262	.284
Unpriced items	.000	.000
Major household appliances	.348	.381
Refrigerators and home freezers	.103	.113
Laundry equipment	.109	.127
Stoves, ovens, dishwashers, and air conditioners	.135	.141
Information processing equipment	.159	.120
Other housefurnishings	1.296	1.216
Floor and window coverings, infants', laundry, cleaning, and outdoor equipment	.185	.156
Clocks, lamps, and decor items	.260	.210
Tableware, serving pieces, and nonelectric kitchenware	.223	.201
Lawn equipment, power tools, and other hardware	.204	.249
Sewing, floor cleaning, small kitchen, and portable heating appliances	.159	.166
Indoor plants and fresh cut flowers	.173	.152
Unpriced items	.092	.083

See footnotes at end of table.

	U.S. City Average	
Item and group	All Urban Consumers (CPI-U)	Urban Wage Earners and Clerical Workers (CPI-W)
Housekeeping supplies	1.202	1.232
Laundry and cleaning products, including soap	.421	.484
Household paper products and stationery supplies	.389	.383
Other household, lawn, and garden supplies	.392	.364
Housekeeping services	1.461	1.104
Postage	.253	.246
Appliance and furniture repair	.178	.138
Gardening and other household services	.391	.221
Babysitting	.237	.305
Domestic services	.237	.068
Care of invalids, elderly, and convalescents	.051	.037
Unpriced items	.114	.089
Apparel and upkeep	6.131	6.134
Apparel commodities	5.573	5.615
Apparel commodities less footwear	4.750	4.707
Men's and boys'	1.497	1.488
Men's	1.225	1.153
Suits, sport coats, coats, and jackets	.367	.283
Furnishings and special clothing	.288	.274
Shirts	.308	.307
Dungarees, jeans, and trousers	.246	.268
Unpriced items	.016	.021
Boys'	.272	.335
Women's and girls'	2.495	2.438
Women's	2.127	2.014
Coats and jackets	.199	.155
Dresses	.376	.375
Separates and sportswear	1.003	.990
Underwear, nightwear, hosiery, and accessories	.354	.357
Suits	.163	.110
Unpriced items	.031	.028
Girls'	.368	.423
Infants' and toddlers'	.213	.280
Other apparel commodities	.545	.501
Sewing materials, notions, and luggage	.096	.084
Watches and jewelry	.449	.417
Watches	.088	.083
Jewelry	.361	.334
Footwear	.823	.908
Men's	.266	.311
Boys' and girls'	.175	.225
Women's	.382	.372
Apparel services	.557	.519
Laundry and dry cleaning other than coin operated	.297	.228
Other apparel services	.261	.291

See footnotes at end of table.

APPENDIX 13.1 (*Continued*)

Item and group	U.S. City Average	
	All Urban Consumers (CPI-U)	Urban Wage Earners and Clerical Workers (CPI-W)
Transportation	17.102	19.033
Private	15.670	17.939
New vehicles	5.226	5.097
New cars	4.232	3.771
New trucks	.911	1.176
New motorcycles	.083	.149
Used cars	1.237	2.212
Motor fuel	3.152	3.870
Automobile maintenance and repair	1.524	1.589
Body work	.163	.167
Automobile drive train, brake, and miscellaneous mechanical repair	.438	.476
Maintenance and servicing	.505	.482
Power plant repair	.395	.444
Unpriced items	.023	.021
Other private transportation	4.532	5.171
Other private transportation commodities	.720	.907
Motor oil, coolant, and other products	.062	.079
Automobile parts and equipment	.658	.828
Tires	.328	.389
Other parts and equipment	.330	.439
Other private transportation services	3.812	4.264
Automobile insurance	2.274	2.564
Automobile finance charges	.813	1.020
Automobile fees	.725	.681
Automobile registration, licensing, and inspection fees	.339	.369
Other automobile-related fees	.361	.295
Unpriced items	.026	.017
Public transportation	1.432	1.093
Airline fares	.918	.573
Other intercity transportation	.159	.110
Intracity public transportation	.345	.401
Unpriced items	.011	.009
Medical care	6.189	5.260
Medical care commodities	1.179	.968
Prescription drugs [1]	.785	.627
Nonprescription drugs and medical supplies	.394	.341
Internal and respiratory over-the-counter drugs	.256	.257
Nonprescription medical equipment and supplies	.138	.084
Medical care services	5.010	4.292
Professional medical services	3.103	2.633
Physicians' services [2]	1.668	1.420
Dental services [3]	.923	.826
Eye care [4]	.343	.286
Services by other medical professionals [5]	.168	.101
Hospital and related services	1.757	1.544
Hospital rooms [6]	.696	.659
Other inpatient services [7]	.670	.577
Outpatient services [8]	.386	.305
Unpriced items	.005	.003
Health insurance [9]	.151	.115

See footnotes at end of table.

297

Item and group	U.S. City Average	
	All Urban Consumers (CPI-U)	Urban Wage Earners and Clerical Workers (CPI-W)
Entertainment	4.396	4.071
Entertainment commodities	2.079	2.171
Reading materials	.686	.599
Newspapers	.330	.305
Magazines, periodicals, and books	.356	.295
Unpriced items	.000	.000
Sporting goods and equipment	.463	.573
Sport vehicles, including bicycles	.212	.335
Other sporting goods	.251	.238
Toys, hobbies, and other entertainment	.930	.999
Toys, hobbies, and music equipment	.427	.465
Photographic supplies and equipment	.134	.120
Pet supplies and expense	.357	.399
Unpriced items	.011	.015
Entertainment services	2.317	1.900
Club memberships	.384	.212
Fees for participant sports, excluding club memberships	.362	.323
Admissions	.677	.579
Fees for lessons or instructions	.225	.159
Other entertainment services	.648	.614
Unpriced items	.022	.013
Other goods and services	6.281	6.226
Tobacco and smoking products	1.478	1.945
Personal care	1.217	1.168
Toilet goods and personal care appliances	.646	.663
Other toilet goods and small personal care appliances, including hair and dental products	.375	.408
Cosmetics, bath and nail preparations, manicure and eye makeup implements	.271	.255
Personal care services	.571	.505
Beauty parlor services for females	.455	.399
Haircuts and other barber shop services for males	.115	.106
Unpriced items	.000	.000
Personal and educational expenses	3.586	3.113
School books and supplies	.236	.203
School books and supplies for college	.165	.132
Elementary and high school books and supplies	.058	.059
Unpriced items	.012	.012
Personal and educational services	3.350	2.910
Tuition and other school fees	2.159	1.830
College tuition	1.208	.896
Elementary and high school tuition	.392	.313
Day care and nursery school	.337	.409
Tuition for technical, business, and other schools	.134	.136
Unpriced items	.088	.076
Personal expenses	1.192	1.080
Legal service fees	.442	.383
Personal financial services	.315	.260
Funeral expenses	.339	.347
Unpriced items	.095	.090

See footnotes at end of table.

	U.S. City Average	
Item and group	All Urban Consumers (CPI-U)	Urban Wage Earners and Clerical Workers (CPI-W)

Commodity and service group		
All items	100.000	100.000
Commodities	45.088	49.025
Food and beverages	17.865	19.768
Commodities less food and beverages	27.223	29.257
Nondurables less food and beverages	15.967	16.934
Apparel commodities	5.573	5.615
Nondurables less food, beverages, and apparel	10.394	11.319
Durables	11.256	12.323
Services	54.912	50.975
Rent of shelter	27.263	25.025
Rent of residential	5.955	6.789
Household services less rent of shelter	9.075	8.877
Transportation services	6.768	6.947
Medical care services	5.010	4.292
Other services	6.795	5.834
Special indexes		
All items less food	83.682	81.884
All items less shelter	72.092	74.410
All items less homeowners' costs	80.175	82.667
All items less medical care	93.811	94.740
Commodities less food	28.770	30.910
Nondurables less food	17.513	18.586
Nondurables less food and apparel	11.940	12.971
Nondurables	33.832	36.702
Services less rent of shelter	27.649	25.950
Services less medical care	49.902	46.683
Domestically produced farm food	8.878	10.039
Selected beef cuts	.719	.884
Motor fuel, motor oil, coolant, and other products	3.214	3.949
Utilities and public transportation	8.487	8.394
Housekeeping and home maintenance services	1.588	1.211
Energy	7.366	8.174
All items less energy	92.634	91.826
All items less food and energy	76.315	73.710
Commodities less food and energy	25.188	26.649
Energy commodities	3.581	4.260
Services less energy	51.127	47.061

[1] Benefits provided by consumer-paid health insurance constitute 5.9 percent of the relative importance for the U-population and 6.3 percent for the W population.

[2] Benefits provided by consumer-paid health insurance constitute 35.1 percent of the relative importance for the U-population and 30.8 percent for the W population.

[3] Benefits provided by consumer-paid health insurance constitute 8.7 percent of the relative importance for the U-population and 8.7 percent for the W population.

[4] Benefits provided by consumer-paid health insurance constitute 0.7 percent of the relative importance for the U-population and 0.7 percent for the W population.

[5] Benefits provided by consumer-paid health insurance constitute 24.7 percent of the relative importance for the U-population and 29.3 percent for the W population.

[6] Benefits provided by consumer-paid health insurance constitute 61.0 percent of the relative importance for the U-population and 54.4 percent for the W population.

[7] Benefits provided by consumer-paid health insurance constitute 62.6 percent of the relative importance for the U-population and 62.8 percent for the W population.

[8] Benefits provided by consumer-paid health insurance constitute 57.0 percent of the relative importance for the U-population and 53.4 percent for the W population.

[9] Only health insurance premiums paid by the consumer are included in the CPI. The health insurance relative importance includes only that portion of the premium that is retained by the insurance carrier for administrative cost and profit, 9.7 percent of the total premiums for the U population and 10.6 percent for the W population. The portions that are paid as benefits have been assigned to the relevant medical care relative importances.

APPENDIX 13.2 CPI History, 1913–1990

U.S. Department of Labor
Bureau of Labor Statistics
Washington, D.C. 20212

Consumer Price Index

All Urban Consumers - (CPI-U)

U.S. city average

All items

1982-84=100

YEAR	JAN.	FEB.	MAR.	APR.	MAY	JUNE	JULY	AUG.	SEP.	OCT.	NOV.	DEC.	SEMIANNUAL 1ST HALF	SEMIANNUAL 2ND HALF	AVG.	PERCENT CHANGE DEC-DEC	PERCENT CHANGE AVG-AVG
1913	9.8	9.8	9.8	9.8	9.7	9.8	9.9	9.9	10.0	10.0	10.1	10.0			9.9		
1914	10.0	9.9	9.9	9.8	9.9	9.9	10.0	10.2	10.2	10.1	10.2	10.1			10.0	1.0	1.0
1915	10.1	10.0	9.9	10.0	10.1	10.1	10.1	10.1	10.1	10.2	10.3	10.3			10.1	2.0	1.0
1916	10.4	10.4	10.5	10.6	10.7	10.8	10.8	10.9	11.1	11.3	11.5	11.6			10.9	12.6	7.9
1917	11.7	12.0	12.0	12.6	12.8	13.0	12.8	13.0	13.7	13.5	13.5	13.7			12.8	18.1	17.4
1918	14.0	14.1	14.0	14.2	14.5	14.7	15.1	15.4	15.7	16.0	16.3	16.5			15.1	20.4	18.0
1919	16.5	16.2	16.4	16.7	16.9	16.9	17.4	17.7	17.8	18.1	18.5	18.9			17.3	14.5	14.6
1920	19.3	19.5	19.7	20.3	20.6	20.9	20.8	20.3	20.0	19.9	19.8	19.4			20.0	2.6	15.6
1921	19.0	18.4	18.3	18.1	17.7	17.6	17.7	17.7	17.5	17.5	17.4	17.3			17.9	-10.8	-10.5
1922	16.9	16.9	16.7	16.7	16.7	16.7	16.8	16.6	16.6	16.7	16.8	16.9			16.8	-2.3	-6.1
1923	16.8	16.8	16.8	16.9	16.9	17.0	17.2	17.1	17.2	17.3	17.3	17.3			17.1	2.4	1.8
1924	17.3	17.2	17.1	17.0	16.9	17.0	17.1	17.0	17.1	17.2	17.3	17.3			17.1	0.0	0.0
1925	17.3	17.2	17.3	17.2	17.3	17.5	17.7	17.7	17.7	17.7	18.0	17.9			17.5	3.5	2.3
1926	17.9	17.9	17.8	17.9	17.8	17.7	17.5	17.4	17.5	17.6	17.7	17.7			17.7	-1.1	1.1
1927	17.5	17.4	17.3	17.3	17.4	17.6	17.3	17.2	17.3	17.4	17.3	17.3			17.4	-2.3	-1.7
1928	17.3	17.1	17.1	17.1	17.2	17.1	17.1	17.1	17.1	17.3	17.2	17.1			17.1	-1.2	-1.7
1929	17.1	17.1	17.0	16.9	17.0	17.1	17.3	17.3	17.3	17.3	17.3	17.2			17.1	-0.6	-0.0
1930	17.1	17.0	16.9	17.0	16.9	16.8	16.6	16.5	16.6	16.5	16.4	16.1			16.7	-6.4	-2.3
1931	15.9	15.7	15.6	15.5	15.3	15.1	15.1	15.1	15.0	14.9	14.7	14.6			15.2	-9.3	-9.0
1932	14.3	14.1	14.0	13.9	13.7	13.6	13.6	13.5	13.4	13.3	13.2	13.1			13.7	-10.3	-9.9
1933	12.9	12.7	12.6	12.6	12.6	12.7	13.1	13.2	13.2	13.2	13.2	13.2			13.0	0.8	-5.1
1934	13.2	13.3	13.3	13.3	13.3	13.4	13.4	13.4	13.6	13.5	13.5	13.4			13.4	1.5	3.1
1935	13.6	13.7	13.7	13.8	13.8	13.7	13.7	13.7	13.7	13.7	13.8	13.8			13.7	3.0	2.2

YEAR	JAN.	FEB.	MAR.	APR.	MAY	JUNE	JULY	AUG.	SEP.	OCT.	NOV.	DEC.	1ST HALF	2ND HALF	AVG.	DEC-DEC	AVG-AVG
1936	13.8	13.8	13.7	13.7	13.7	13.8	13.9	14.0	14.0	14.0	14.0	14.0			13.9	1.4	1.5
1937	14.1	14.1	14.2	14.3	14.4	14.4	14.5	14.5	14.6	14.6	14.5	14.4			14.4	2.9	3.6
1938	14.2	14.1	14.1	14.2	14.1	14.1	14.1	14.1	14.1	14.0	14.0	14.0			14.1	-2.8	-2.1
1939	14.0	13.9	13.9	13.8	13.8	13.8	13.8	13.8	14.1	14.0	14.0	14.0			13.9	0.0	-1.4
1940	13.9	14.0	14.0	14.0	14.0	14.1	14.0	14.0	14.0	14.0	14.0	14.1			14.0	0.7	0.7
1941	14.1	14.1	14.2	14.3	14.3	14.7	14.7	14.9	15.1	15.3	15.4	15.5			14.7	9.0	5.0
1942	15.7	15.8	16.0	16.1	16.3	16.3	16.4	16.5	16.5	16.7	16.8	16.9			16.3	9.0	10.9
1943	16.4	16.9	17.2	17.5	17.5	17.6	17.7	17.7	17.7	17.7	17.7	17.4			17.3	3.0	6.1
1944	17.4	17.4	17.4	17.8	17.9	17.6	17.7	17.7	17.7	17.7	17.7	17.8			17.6	2.3	1.7
1945	17.8	17.8	17.8	17.8	17.9	18.1	18.1	18.1	18.1	18.1	18.1	18.2			18.0	2.2	2.3
1946	18.2	18.1	18.3	18.4	18.5	18.7	19.8	20.2	20.4	20.8	21.3	21.5			19.5	18.1	8.3
1947	21.5	21.5	21.9	21.9	21.9	22.0	22.4	22.4	23.0	23.0	23.1	23.4			22.3	8.8	14.4
1948	23.5	23.5	23.9	23.9	23.8	24.1	24.2	24.5	24.9	24.7	24.7	24.1			24.1	3.0	8.1
1949	24.0	23.8	23.6	23.9	23.8	23.6	23.7	23.8	24.9	23.6	23.8	23.6			23.8	-2.1	-1.2
1950	23.5	23.5	23.6	23.6	23.7	23.8	24.1	24.3	24.4	24.6	24.7	25.0			24.1	5.9	1.3
1951	25.4	25.7	25.8	25.8	25.9	25.9	25.9	25.9	26.1	26.2	26.3	26.5			26.0	6.0	7.9
1952	26.5	26.5	26.3	26.4	26.7	26.5	26.7	26.7	26.7	26.7	26.9	26.7			26.5	0.8	1.9
1953	26.6	26.6	26.9	26.6	26.9	26.9	26.6	26.9	26.8	26.8	26.9	26.5			26.6	-0.7	0.8
1954	26.7	26.7	26.9	26.8	26.9	26.9	26.8	26.9	26.8	26.8	26.9	26.7			26.9	-0.7	0.7
1955	26.7	26.7	26.7	26.7	26.7	26.7	26.8	26.8	26.9	26.9	26.9	26.8			26.8	-0.4	-0.4
1956	26.8	26.8	26.8	26.9	27.0	27.2	27.4	27.3	27.4	27.5	27.5	27.6			27.2	3.0	1.5
1957	27.6	27.6	27.8	27.9	28.0	28.1	28.3	28.9	28.3	28.3	28.4	28.4			28.1	2.9	3.8
1958	28.0	28.6	28.9	28.8	28.9	28.9	29.0	28.9	28.9	29.0	28.9	28.9			28.8	1.8	2.8
1959	28.0	28.4	28.9	28.9	29.5	29.1	29.2	29.2	29.3	29.4	29.4	29.4			29.1	1.7	0.7
1960	29.3	29.4	29.4	29.5	29.5	29.6	29.6	29.6	29.6	29.8	29.8	29.8			29.6	1.4	1.7
1961	29.8	29.9	29.8	29.8	29.8	29.8	30.0	29.9	30.0	30.0	30.0	30.0			29.9	0.7	1.0
1962	30.0	30.4	30.5	30.5	30.5	30.6	30.7	30.7	30.7	30.8	30.4	30.4			30.2	1.3	1.0
1963	30.9	30.4	30.9	30.5	30.4	30.6	30.6	31.0	30.7	30.6	30.8	30.9			30.6	1.0	1.3
1964	30.9	30.9	30.9	30.9	30.4	30.6	31.1	31.0	31.1	31.1	31.2	31.2			31.0	1.0	1.3
1965	31.2	31.2	31.3	31.4	31.4	31.6	31.6	31.6	31.6	31.7	31.7	31.8			31.5	1.9	1.6
1966	31.8	32.0	32.1	32.3	32.3	32.4	32.5	32.7	32.7	32.9	32.9	32.9			32.4	3.5	2.9
1967	32.1	32.9	33.4	33.4	33.5	33.5	33.9	33.5	33.6	33.7	33.8	34.2			33.9	3.9	2.1
1968	34.1	34.2	34.3	34.4	34.5	34.7	34.9	35.0	35.1	35.3	35.4	35.5			34.8	4.7	4.2
1969	35.6	35.8	36.1	36.3	36.4	36.6	36.8	37.0	37.1	37.3	37.5	37.7			36.7	6.2	5.5

U.S. Department of Labor
Bureau of Labor Statistics
Washington, D.C. 20212

Consumer Price Index

All Urban Consumers - (CPI-U)

U.S. city average

All items

1982-84=100

YEAR	JAN.	FEB.	MAR.	APR.	MAY	JUNE	JULY	AUG.	SEP.	OCT.	NOV.	DEC.	SEMIANNUAL 1ST HALF	2ND HALF	AVG.	PERCENT CHANGE DEC-DEC	AVG-AVG
1970	37.8	38.0	38.2	38.5	38.6	38.8	39.0	39.0	39.2	39.4	39.6	39.8			38.8	5.6	5.7
1971	39.8	39.9	40.0	40.1	40.3	40.6	40.7	40.8	40.8	40.9	40.9	41.1			40.5	3.3	4.4
1972	41.1	41.3	41.4	41.5	41.6	41.7	41.9	42.0	42.1	42.3	42.4	42.5			41.8	3.4	3.2
1973	42.6	42.9	43.3	43.6	43.9	44.2	44.3	45.1	45.2	45.6	45.9	46.2			44.4	8.7	6.2
1974	46.6	47.2	47.8	48.0	48.6	49.0	49.4	50.0	50.6	51.1	51.5	51.9			49.3	12.3	11.0
1975	52.1	52.5	52.7	52.9	53.2	53.6	54.2	54.3	54.6	54.9	55.3	55.5			53.8	6.9	9.1
1976	55.6	55.8	55.9	56.1	56.5	56.8	57.1	57.4	57.6	57.9	58.0	58.2			56.9	4.9	5.8
1977	58.5	59.1	59.5	60.0	60.3	60.7	61.0	61.2	61.4	61.6	61.9	62.1			60.6	6.7	6.5
1978	62.5	62.1	63.4	63.9	64.5	65.2	65.7	66.0	66.5	67.1	67.4	67.7			65.2	9.0	7.6
1979	68.3	69.1	69.8	70.6	71.5	72.3	73.1	73.8	74.6	75.2	75.9	76.7			72.6	13.3	11.3
1980	77.8	78.9	80.1	81.0	81.8	82.7	82.7	83.3	84.0	84.8	85.5	86.3			82.4	12.5	13.5
1981	87.0	87.9	88.5	89.1	89.8	90.6	91.6	92.3	93.2	93.4	93.7	94.0			90.9	8.9	10.3
1982	94.3	94.6	94.5	94.9	95.8	97.0	97.5	97.7	97.9	98.2	98.0	97.6			96.5	3.8	6.2
1983	97.8	97.9	97.9	98.6	99.2	99.5	99.9	100.2	100.7	101.0	101.2	101.3			99.6	3.9	3.2
1984	101.9	102.4	102.6	103.1	103.4	103.7	104.1	104.5	105.0	105.3	105.3	105.3	102.9	104.9	103.9	3.8	4.3
1985	105.5	106.0	106.4	106.9	107.3	107.6	107.8	108.0	108.3	108.7	109.0	109.3	106.6	108.5	107.6	3.8	3.6
1986	109.6	109.3	108.8	108.6	108.9	109.5	109.5	109.7	110.2	110.3	110.4	110.5	109.1	110.1	109.6	1.1	1.9
1987	111.2	111.6	112.1	112.7	113.1	113.5	113.8	114.4	115.0	115.3	115.4	115.4	112.4	114.9	113.6	4.4	3.6
1988	115.7	116.0	116.5	117.1	117.5	118.0	118.5	119.0	119.8	120.2	120.3	120.5	116.6	119.7	118.3	4.4	4.1
1989	121.1	121.6	122.3	123.1	123.8	124.1	124.4	124.6	125.0	125.6	125.9	126.1	122.7	125.3	124.0	4.6	4.8
1990	127.4	128.0															

37.

Bringing It Together

The individual economic indicators that were the focus of the preceding chapters can be used in three ways:

1. to construct a GNP forecast;
2. to anticipate moves in stocks, bonds, and short-term interest rates; and
3. to out-guess our policy makers in Washington, D.C.

All these ends have in common the fact that the economy is cyclical or subject to sometimes radical changes in its rate of growth. Cyclical behavior gives the analyst a framework for interpreting some indicators, in particular the income, inventory, and housing components that have in the past caused massive shifts in the overall GNP growth rate.

THE BUSINESS CYCLE

On average after WW II, the economy has grown for three and three-quarter years before falling into negative territory (see Table 14.1). Human nature gives some insight as to why—anyone or anything can

TABLE 14.1
U.S. Business Cycle History

Dates of		Duration of	
Trough	Peak	Contraction	Expansion
Dec 1854	June 1857	—	30 months
Dec 1858	Oct 1860	18	22
Jun 1861	Apr 1865	8	46
Dec 1867	June 1869	32	18
Dec 1870	Oct 1873	18	34
Mar 1879	Mar 1882	65	36
May 1885	Mar 1887	38	22
Apr 1888	Jun 1890	13	27
May 1891	Jun 1893	10	20
Jun 1894	Dec 1895	17	18
Jun 1897	Jun 1899	18	24
Dec 1900	Sep 1902	18	21
Aug 1904	May 1907	23	33
Jun 1908	Jan 1910	13	19
Jan 1912	Jan 1913	24	12
Dec 1914	Aug 1918	23	44
Mar 1919	Jan 1920	7	10
Jul 1921	May 1923	18	22
Jul 1924	Oct 1926	14	27
Nov 1927	Aug 1929	13	21
Mar 1933	May 1937	43	50
Jun 1938	Feb 1945	13	80
Oct 1945	Nov 1948	8	37
Oct 1949	Jul 1953	11	45
May 1954	Aug 1957	10	39
Apr 1958	Apr 1960	8	24
Feb 1961	Dec 1969	10	106
Nov 1970	Nov 1973	11	36
Mar 1975	Jan 1980	16	58
Jul 1980	Jul 1981	6	12
Nov 1982	Aug 1990*	16	105
Average		17	34

Source: NBER.
*Author's estimate

operate at peak speed only so long before requiring a rest period. In the case of the economy, this rest may not be entirely voluntary, as it may be brought about by financial strains or a collapse in demand. An alternative explanation that found acceptance in the 1970s was *political business cycle* theory (PBC), which held that an incumbent administration, in an effort to increase its chances of re-election, tends to stimulate employment and incomes prior to regularly scheduled election times.

Whichever explanation holds, excesses of any nature cause a pause and reassessment. The latest 1982–90 expansion was extraordinary because it matched the record eight-year expansion of the 1960s (a significantly different era in terms of demographics and political geography). Following an expansion comes the period of retraction known as *recession*. A severe or prolonged recession is called a *depression*.

Economic cycles are dated by the *National Bureau of Economic Research* (NBER), a private research body comprised of distinguished economists. The NBER meets when its members feel the preponderance of statistical evidence on coincident indicators (such as production, incomes, and sales) requires discussion about whether the economy is still expanding. The NBER's standard definition of recession is two or more calendar quarters of decline in real GNP. More recently, observers, particularly Fed Chairman Greenspan, have attempted to broaden the definition of recession to "a significant and broad-based decline in economic activity." The start of recession is labeled the "peak" in our tables and the end the "trough."

The average rate of expansion since WW II in some of the major income-side economic indicators is given in Table 14.2. Appendix 14.1 translates these into product-side components. Consumption is a driving force behind GNP with a growth rate averaging a robust 17% over the course of each expansion. In contrast, surges and stallings in residential construction and business inventories were much more common. With this in mind, the analyst should attempt to find turning points in similar sensitive series.

TABLE 14.2
Post-WW II Recession Detail

Peak	Trough	Duration	Real GNP	Industrial Production	Peak in Unemployment
Nov 1948	Oct 1949	11 months	−1.5%	−10.1%	7.8%
Jul 1953	May 1954	10	−3.2	−9.4	5.9
Aug 1957	Apr 1958	8	−3.0	−13.5	7.3
Apr 1960	Feb 1961	10	−0.9	−8.6	7.0
Dec 1969	Nov 1970	11	−0.8	−7.0	6.1
Nov 1973	Mar 1975	16	−4.5	−14.8	9.0
Jan 1980	Jul 1980	6	−2.4	−5.8	7.8
Jul 1981	Nov 1982	16	−3.5	−9.0	10.8
Average		11	−2.5	−9.8	7.7

Source: U.S. Commerce Department.

HOW TO CONSTRUCT A GNP FORECAST

First, determine the variables important to your decision making. They will probably be dictated by the composition of GNP. Second, study the averaging and distribution methods detailed in Chapter 1. Third, prepare quarterly growth rates for the forecast horizon. Table 14.3 gives one example of a GNP forecast made over a standard four calendar quarter horizon.

Note that the range of variability widens as we move farther into the future. Consumer spending, which accounts for about two-thirds of the total, is critical. *Pocketbook issues* such as tax changes, the price of oil, and job security will affect whether we trend these estimates up or down over the year. Investment spending will usually show a pick-up later in the forecast horizon. Since most surveys of business intentions show little change over the calendar year, failure to start a project late in the year merely delays its implementation. Government is fairly steady and often serves as a counter-balance to slowing private spending.

The data on final sales, unemployment, housing starts, auto sales, and corporate profits associated with our forecast are shown separately. They will determine to a large extent the inventory and net exports components of the forecast. A drop in final sales, for instance, should be associated with rising inventories as manufacturers and distributors pile up unwanted inventory. The CPI and GNP implicit price deflator are also shown separately, as they adjust to the growth implied in the other components, rising with a lag as the economy grows and falling as it contracts.

To a large extent, the components influence even as they are influenced by developments in the financial markets. For instance, rising interest rates will reduce investment because they cut into profits, thus requiring a higher return for a business opportunity to be beneficial. A lower dollar will stimulate exports as their price becomes cheaper to foreign residents. A rising stock market and higher home prices will enhance consumption because individuals feel wealthier.

TABLE 14.3
Economic Forecast for 1991
(annualized percentage changes, unless noted)

	1990:Q4	1991:Q1	Q2	Q3	Q4
Real GNP	-3.0	-3.0	-1.0	2.5	3.2
Personal Consumption	-2.8	-2.0	0.5	2.8	2.5
Autos (MLN units)	6.0	5.6	6.2	6.5	7.0
Government Spending	9.0	5.0	4.5	4.0	4.0
Net Exports*	-45	-40	-37	-40	-57
Change in Inventories*	5	-5	-10	-5	15
CPI	7.0	4.5	3.7	4.0	4.0
Unemployment Rate	5.8	6.2	6.5	6.5	6.3
Associated Market Levels at quarter-end:					
Fed funds	7.0	6.25	5.25	5.375	6.5
30-year Treasury bond	8.125	7.75	7.5	7.75	7.875
FX ($/Yen)	130	120	125	125	130

* = billions of 1982 dollars.

Thus, the composition of real GNP can be as critical to the financial markets as whether the economy is growing. A slowing in final sales and inventory overhang may be greeted as favorably in the bond market as an actual decline in GNP because it portends a further slowing.

THE FED

Inherent in any economic forecast is some reaction on the part of economic policy makers. The body most apt to react to incoming economic data is the Federal Reserve, which controls short-term interest rates. In particular, the appropriate medicine for a slowing economy is an easing of financial market pressures. The Fed accomplishes this by edging down the overnight Federal Funds rate, which is the bedrock cost of credit to securities dealers. Historically, the Fed has tightened credit into recessions and acted to ease too late to prevent an economic downturn. Then, officials have had to ease credit massively.

During the Greenspan era, though, elements of fine-tuning crept in as officials attempted to react more promptly, using small rate changes to either abate inflationary pressures or stall an unwanted cooling of the economy. This is demonstrated in Figure 14.1, which shows the patterns of the Fed's discount rate and Federal Funds rate, as well as the 10-year Treasury and high-grade corporate bond rates over economic cycles. Note, however, that recent research indicates the transmission channels—the cost of capital, wealth effects, and the foreign exchange rate—have not changed. Table 14.4 gives the relative magnitude of the moves in these components four to 20 quarters after the Fed eases (from $15 to $62 billion is added to the economy).

The Beige Book

What's the Fed know that the private analyst does not? Prior to the FOMC meetings, which are held eight times a year, staff from the 12 district Federal Reserve Banks spend time interviewing area business

FIGURE 14.1 Market Interest Rates

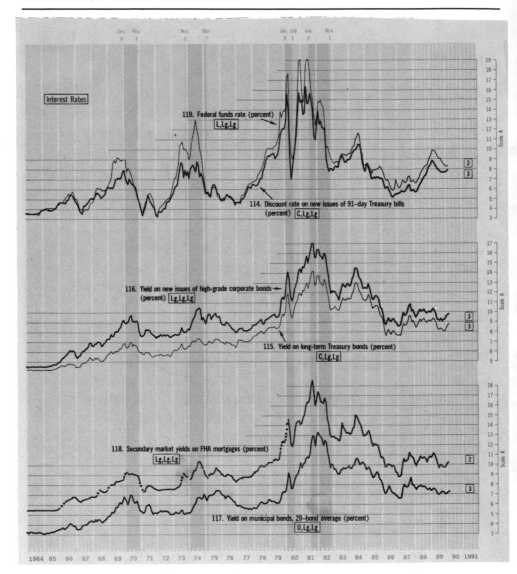

TABLE 14.4
Effects of 1% Point Ease in Fed Funds Rate by Transmission Channel
(billions of 1982 dollars)

Quarters After Reduction	Cost of Investment	Capital Consumption	Wealth Consumption	FX Rate Net Exports
4	7.7	2.8	2.1	2.7
8	12.5	1.3	6.0	7.8
12	19.1	0.6	13.3	10.2
16	27.9	0.5	16.8	6.4
20	34.5	0.2	25.9	2.2

Source: "The Transmission Channels of Monetary Policy," Federal Reserve Bulletin, December 1990.

people and summarizing their findings in a document known as *The Beige Book*. This is officially called a *Summary of Commentary on Current Economic Conditions by Federal Reserve District*, but it gets its nickname from the tan color of its cover when presented to FOMC members. (See the next chapter for a copy.) The Beige Book is released to the public at noon of the Wednesday two weeks prior to the FOMC meeting. It is based on information gathered in the three weeks prior, and the various reports are carefully summarized in an introduction prepared at one of the participating Fed banks.

Note that conditions are deteriorating in the September 1990 Beige Book reproduced in this book. The economy was noted to be uneven, with most districts reporting slowing or declining prospects. Retail sales and construction activity were particularly soft, while manufacturing was stagnant. Staff in seven of the 12 districts noted a slowdown, but the five other areas (notably in the Midwest and West) said the economy was still growing. These anecdotal prospects tipped the balance, so that officials put off an easing.

HOW TO GET A LEG UP: LAGGING, COINCIDENT, AND LEADING INDICATORS

The Commerce Department has classified economic data according to its movement during the business cycle and weighted the data into indices. Leaders tend to precede the turns in the business cycle, coincident indicators show where the economy stands currently, and lagging indicators change only after the cyclical move is well under way. As indicated in Figure 14.2, the leading index turned down two to 20 months prior to recessions in the seven such episodes since 1953. As a rule of thumb, three consecutive declines in the leaders will give a high probability of recession. In 1990, the leaders fell four consecutive times from July to October, predicting a recession. Analysts can project the leaders using proxies for the components (see Table 14.5) and the Commerce Department's weights.

FIGURE 14.2 Composite Indices of Leading, Coincident, and Lagging Indicators

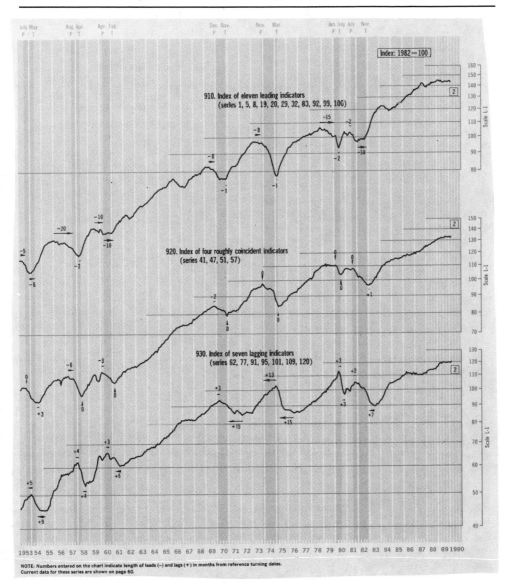

NOTE: Numbers entered on the chart indicate length of leads (–) and lags (+) in months from reference turning dates.
Current data for these series are shown on page 60.

313

TABLE 14.5
Indicators by Economic Cycle Stage

Leaders: average weekly hours worked in manufacturing; average weekly
                initial unemployment claims (inverted); new orders for
                consumer goods and materials; vendor performance
                (inverted); contracts and orders for new plant and
                equipment*; building permits for private housing units;
                change in unfilled orders in durable goods*; change in
                sensitive materials prices; stock prices as measured by
                the S&P 500; M2 money supply*; index of consumer
                expectations.

Coincident: employees on non-agricultural payrolls; personal income less
                transfer payments*; industrial production; manufacturing
                and trade sales*.

Lagging: average duration of unemployment (inverted); ratio of
                manufacturing and trade inventories to sales*; change in
                labor cost per unit of manufacturing output; the average
                prime rate; commercial and industrial loans*; ratio of
                consumer installment credit to personal income; change
                in the CPI for services.

* = in constant 1982 dollars.

FIGURE 14.3 Ratio: Coincident to Lagging Indices

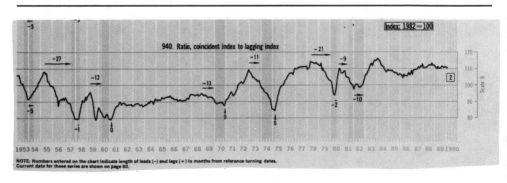

After the Recession

Cyclical upturns can be projected using these data as well. The Commerce Department uses the ratio of coincident to lagging indicators as an indicator of a strengthening economy. This ratio has turned up from two to 27 months prior to the end of recession (see Figure 14.3), signaling an incipient recovery.

LIES, DAMNED LIES, AND STATISTICS

If you have mastered survey techniques, timing and seasonal adjustment, made sure of the scheduled release dates, and put a large dose of logic under your belt, you have more than an average chance of taking in the subtleties of economic indicators. Still, daily bluffs and challenges are common in financial market trading strategies as economic data are discounted into expectations. Pay special attention to your overall GNP forecast, which will take into consideration all the topics discussed in this book. Securities prices will ultimately adjust to the business cycle, so trading and investing can be made profitable with attention to the overview.

Appendix 14.1

Summary National Income and Product Series

APPENDIX 14.1

Summary National Income and Product Series: Annually, 1929-88, and Quarterly, 1960-88

Table 1.—Gross National Product

[Billions of dollars; quarterly data are seasonally adjusted at annual rates]

Year and quarter	GNP	Personal consumption expenditures				Gross private domestic investment				Net exports			Government purchases of goods and services			Final sales	Gross domestic purchases	Percent change from preceding period		
		Total	Durable goods	Nondurable goods	Services	Total	Nonresidential	Residential	CBI	Net	Exports	Imports	Total	Federal	State and local			GNP	Final sales	Gross domestic purchases
1929	103.9	77.3	9.2	37.7	30.4	16.7	11.0	4.0	1.7	1.1	7.1	5.9	8.9	1.5	7.4	102.2	102.8	....	....	....
1930	91.1	69.9	7.2	34.0	28.8	10.6	8.6	2.4	−.4	1.0	5.5	4.5	9.5	1.6	7.9	91.5	90.1	−12.3	−10.5	−12.3
1931	76.4	60.5	5.5	29.0	26.1	5.9	5.3	1.8	−1.1	.5	3.7	3.2	9.5	1.7	7.8	77.5	75.9	−16.2	−15.2	−15.8
1932	58.5	48.6	3.6	22.7	22.2	1.1	2.9	.8	−2.5	.4	2.5	2.1	8.4	1.6	6.7	61.0	58.1	−23.4	−21.4	−23.4
1933	56.0	45.8	3.5	22.3	20.1	1.6	2.5	.6	−1.6	.4	2.4	2.1	8.3	2.2	6.1	57.6	55.7	−4.2	−5.5	−4.2
1934	65.6	51.4	4.2	26.7	20.4	3.5	3.3	.9	−.7	.6	3.0	2.4	10.1	3.2	6.9	66.3	65.0	17.0	15.1	16.7
1935	72.8	55.8	5.1	29.3	21.3	6.6	4.3	1.3	1.1	.1	3.3	3.2	10.2	3.1	7.2	71.7	72.7	11.0	8.2	11.9
1936	83.1	62.0	6.3	32.9	22.8	8.7	5.8	1.7	1.3	.1	3.6	3.5	12.2	5.1	7.1	81.8	83.0	14.1	14.1	14.2
1937	91.3	66.7	6.9	35.2	24.5	12.1	7.5	2.1	2.5	.4	4.7	4.3	12.1	4.8	7.3	88.7	90.8	9.8	8.4	9.5
1938	85.4	64.1	5.7	34.0	24.4	6.7	5.5	2.1	−.9	1.3	4.4	3.1	13.2	5.5	7.7	86.3	84.0	−6.5	−2.7	−7.5
1939	91.3	67.0	6.7	35.1	25.2	9.5	6.1	3.0	.4	1.2	4.6	3.4	13.6	5.2	8.3	90.9	90.1	7.0	5.4	7.3
1940	100.4	71.0	7.8	37.0	26.2	13.4	7.7	3.5	2.2	1.8	5.4	3.7	14.2	6.1	8.1	98.3	98.7	10.0	8.1	9.5
1941	125.5	80.8	9.7	42.9	28.3	18.3	9.7	4.1	4.5	1.5	6.1	4.7	25.0	17.0	8.0	121.0	124.1	25.0	23.2	25.7
1942	159.0	88.6	6.9	50.8	31.0	10.3	6.3	2.2	1.8	.2	5.0	4.8	59.9	52.0	7.8	157.2	158.8	26.6	29.9	28.0
1943	192.7	99.5	6.5	58.6	34.3	6.2	5.4	1.4	−.6	−1.9	4.6	6.5	88.9	81.4	7.5	193.4	194.6	21.2	23.0	22.6
1944	211.4	108.2	6.7	64.3	37.2	7.7	7.4	1.4	−1.0	−1.7	5.5	7.2	97.1	89.4	7.6	212.3	213.0	9.7	9.8	9.5
1945	213.4	119.6	8.0	71.9	39.7	11.3	10.6	1.7	−1.0	−.5	7.4	7.9	83.0	74.8	8.2	214.4	213.9	.9	1.0	.4
1946	212.4	143.9	15.8	82.7	45.4	31.5	17.3	7.8	6.4	7.8	15.2	7.3	29.1	19.2	9.9	206.0	204.5	−.5	−3.9	−4.4
1947	235.2	161.9	20.4	90.9	50.6	35.0	23.5	12.1	−.5	11.9	20.3	8.3	26.4	13.6	12.8	235.7	223.3	10.8	14.4	9.2
1948	261.6	174.9	22.9	96.6	55.5	47.1	26.8	15.6	4.7	7.0	17.5	10.6	32.6	17.3	15.3	256.9	254.7	11.2	9.0	14.0
1949	260.4	178.3	25.0	94.9	58.4	36.5	24.9	14.6	−3.1	6.5	16.4	9.8	39.0	21.1	18.0	263.4	253.8	−.5	2.5	−.3
1950	288.3	192.1	30.8	98.2	63.2	55.1	27.8	20.5	6.8	2.2	14.5	12.3	38.8	19.1	19.8	281.4	286.0	10.7	6.8	12.7
1951	333.4	208.1	29.9	109.2	69.0	60.5	31.8	18.4	10.2	4.5	19.8	15.3	60.4	38.6	21.8	323.2	329.0	15.7	14.8	15.0
1952	351.6	219.1	29.3	114.7	75.1	53.5	31.9	18.6	3.1	3.2	19.2	16.0	75.8	52.7	23.1	348.6	348.4	5.5	7.9	5.9
1953	371.6	232.6	32.7	117.8	82.1	54.9	35.1	19.4	.4	1.3	18.1	16.8	82.8	57.9	24.8	371.1	370.3	5.7	6.5	6.3
1954	372.5	239.8	32.1	119.7	88.0	54.1	34.7	21.1	−1.6	2.6	18.8	16.3	76.0	48.4	27.7	374.1	370.0	.2	.8	−.1
1955	405.9	257.9	38.9	124.7	94.3	69.7	39.0	25.0	5.7	3.0	21.1	18.1	75.3	44.9	30.3	400.2	402.9	9.0	7.0	8.9
1956	428.2	270.6	38.2	130.8	101.6	72.7	44.5	23.5	4.6	5.3	25.2	19.9	79.7	46.4	33.3	423.6	422.9	5.5	5.8	5.0
1957	451.0	285.3	39.7	137.1	108.5	71.1	47.5	22.2	1.4	7.3	28.2	20.9	87.3	50.5	36.9	449.6	443.7	5.3	6.1	4.9
1958	456.8	294.6	37.2	141.7	115.7	63.6	42.4	22.7	−1.5	3.3	24.4	21.1	95.4	54.5	40.8	458.3	453.5	1.3	1.9	2.2
1959	495.8	316.3	42.8	148.5	125.0	80.2	46.3	28.1	5.8	1.5	25.0	23.5	97.9	54.6	43.3	490.0	494.3	8.5	6.9	9.0
1960	515.3	330.7	43.5	153.2	134.0	78.2	48.8	26.3	3.1	5.9	29.9	24.0	100.6	54.4	46.1	512.3	509.4	3.9	4.6	3.1
1961	533.8	341.1	41.9	157.4	141.8	77.1	48.3	26.4	2.4	7.2	31.1	23.9	108.4	58.2	50.2	531.4	526.6	3.6	3.7	3.4
1962	574.6	361.9	47.0	163.8	151.1	87.6	52.5	29.0	6.1	6.9	33.1	26.2	118.2	64.6	53.5	568.5	567.7	7.6	7.0	7.8
1963	606.9	381.7	51.8	169.4	160.6	93.1	55.2	32.1	5.8	8.2	35.7	27.5	123.8	65.7	58.1	601.1	598.7	5.6	5.7	5.5
1964	649.8	409.3	56.8	179.7	172.8	99.6	61.4	32.8	5.4	10.9	40.5	29.6	130.0	66.4	63.5	644.4	638.9	7.1	7.2	6.7
1965	705.1	440.7	63.5	191.9	185.4	116.2	73.1	33.1	9.9	9.7	42.9	33.2	138.6	68.7	69.9	695.2	695.4	8.5	7.9	8.8
1966	772.0	477.3	68.5	208.5	200.3	128.6	83.5	30.9	14.2	7.5	46.6	39.1	158.6	80.4	78.2	757.8	764.5	9.5	9.0	9.9
1967	816.4	503.6	70.6	216.9	216.0	125.7	84.4	31.1	10.3	7.4	49.5	42.1	179.7	92.7	87.0	806.1	809.0	5.8	6.4	5.8
1968	892.7	552.5	81.0	235.0	236.4	137.0	91.4	37.7	7.9	5.5	54.8	49.3	197.7	100.1	97.6	884.8	887.2	9.3	9.8	9.7
1969	963.9	597.9	86.2	252.2	259.4	153.2	102.3	41.2	9.8	5.6	60.4	54.7	207.3	100.0	107.2	954.1	958.3	8.0	7.8	8.0
1970	1,015.5	640.0	85.7	270.3	284.0	148.8	105.2	40.5	3.1	8.5	68.9	60.5	218.2	98.8	119.4	1,012.3	1,007.0	5.4	6.1	5.1
1971	1,102.7	691.6	97.6	283.3	310.7	172.5	109.6	55.1	7.8	6.3	72.4	66.1	232.4	99.8	132.5	1,094.9	1,096.4	8.6	8.2	8.9
1972	1,212.8	757.6	111.2	305.1	341.3	202.0	123.0	68.6	10.5	3.2	81.4	78.2	250.0	105.8	144.2	1,202.3	1,209.6	10.0	9.8	10.3
1973	1,359.3	837.2	124.7	339.6	373.0	238.8	145.9	73.3	19.6	16.8	114.1	97.3	266.5	106.4	160.1	1,339.7	1,342.5	12.1	11.4	11.0
1974	1,472.8	916.5	123.8	380.9	411.9	240.8	160.6	64.8	15.4	16.3	151.5	135.2	299.1	116.2	182.9	1,457.4	1,456.5	8.3	8.8	8.5
1975	1,598.4	1,012.8	135.4	416.2	461.2	219.6	162.9	62.3	−5.6	31.1	161.3	130.3	335.0	129.2	205.9	1,604.1	1,567.4	8.5	10.1	7.6
1976	1,782.8	1,129.3	161.5	452.0	515.9	277.7	180.0	81.7	16.0	18.8	177.7	158.9	356.9	136.3	220.6	1,766.8	1,764.0	11.5	10.1	12.5
1977	1,990.5	1,257.2	184.5	490.4	582.3	344.1	214.2	108.6	21.3	1.9	191.6	189.7	387.3	151.1	236.2	1,969.2	1,988.6	11.7	11.5	12.7
1978	2,249.7	1,403.5	205.6	541.8	656.1	416.8	259.0	129.2	28.6	4.1	227.5	223.4	425.2	161.8	263.4	2,221.0	2,245.6	13.0	12.8	12.9
1979	2,508.2	1,566.8	219.0	613.2	734.6	454.8	302.8	139.1	13.0	18.8	291.2	272.5	467.8	178.0	289.9	2,495.2	2,489.4	11.5	12.3	10.9
1980	2,732.0	1,732.6	219.3	681.4	831.9	437.0	322.8	122.5	−8.3	32.1	351.0	318.9	530.3	208.1	322.2	2,740.3	2,699.8	8.9	9.8	8.5
1981	3,052.6	1,915.1	239.9	740.6	934.7	515.5	369.2	122.3	24.0	33.9	382.8	348.9	588.1	242.2	345.9	3,028.6	3,018.7	11.7	10.5	11.8
1982	3,166.0	2,050.7	252.7	771.0	1,027.0	447.3	366.7	105.1	−24.5	26.3	361.9	335.6	641.7	272.7	369.0	3,190.5	3,139.7	3.7	5.3	4.0
1983	3,405.7	2,234.5	289.1	816.7	1,128.7	502.3	356.9	152.5	−7.1	−6.1	352.5	358.7	675.0	283.5	391.5	3,412.8	3,411.8	7.6	7.0	8.7
1984	3,772.2	2,430.5	335.5	867.3	1,227.6	664.8	416.0	181.1	67.7	−58.9	383.5	442.4	735.9	310.5	425.3	3,704.5	3,831.1	10.8	8.5	12.3
1985	4,014.9	2,629.0	372.2	911.2	1,345.6	643.1	442.9	188.8	11.3	−78.0	370.9	448.9	820.8	355.2	465.6	4,003.6	4,092.8	6.4	8.1	6.8
1986	4,231.6	2,797.4	406.0	942.0	1,449.5	659.4	435.2	217.3	6.9	−97.4	396.5	493.8	872.2	366.5	505.7	4,224.8	4,329.0	5.4	5.5	5.8
1987	4,524.3	3,010.8	421.0	998.1	1,591.7	699.9	444.3	226.4	29.3	−112.6	448.6	561.2	926.1	381.6	544.5	4,495.0	4,636.8	6.9	6.4	7.1
1988	4,880.6	3,235.1	455.2	1,052.3	1,727.6	750.3	487.2	232.4	30.6	−73.7	547.7	621.3	968.9	381.3	587.6	4,850.0	4,954.3	7.9	7.9	6.8
1960: I	516.1	325.5	43.3	150.9	131.3	88.7	49.4	28.4	11.0	4.3	28.7	24.4	97.6	53.0	44.5	505.0	511.8	11.4	7.4	9.6
II	514.5	331.6	44.2	153.8	133.5	78.1	49.6	26.1	2.5	5.1	29.7	24.6	99.6	53.8	45.8	512.0	509.4	−1.2	5.7	−1.9
III	517.7	331.7	43.7	153.5	134.5	77.4	48.4	25.3	3.7	6.5	30.6	24.0	102.1	55.3	46.8	514.0	511.2	2.5	1.6	1.4
IV	513.0	333.8	42.5	154.6	136.7	68.5	48.1	25.3	−4.9	7.7	30.6	22.9	103.0	55.6	47.4	517.9	505.3	−3.6	3.1	−4.5
1961: I	517.4	334.4	40.0	156.0	138.4	69.5	47.1	25.3	−2.9	8.3	31.1	22.8	105.3	56.0	49.2	520.4	509.1	3.5	1.9	3.0
II	527.9	339.1	41.0	156.8	141.2	74.7	48.0	25.5	1.1	7.0	30.0	23.1	107.1	57.7	49.4	526.7	520.9	8.4	4.9	9.6
III	538.5	341.9	42.3	157.3	142.3	81.2	48.3	26.9	6.0	6.6	31.2	24.5	108.7	58.5	50.2	532.5	531.8	8.3	4.5	8.6
IV	551.5	349.1	44.3	159.5	145.3	83.0	49.9	27.8	5.4	6.9	32.0	25.1	112.5	60.4	52.1	546.2	544.7	10.0	10.7	10.1
1962: I	564.4	354.0	45.3	161.5	147.2	87.9	51.0	28.4	8.6	6.3	31.7	25.5	116.2	63.8	52.4	555.9	558.2	9.7	7.3	10.3
II	572.2	359.7	46.6	162.9	150.2	88.0	52.6	29.2	6.1	7.6	33.6	26.1	116.9	63.9	53.0	566.1	564.6	5.6	7.5	4.7
III	579.2	363.7	47.1	164.5	152.1	89.3	53.5	29.2	6.6	7.3	33.6	26.3	118.9	65.0	53.8	572.6	571.9	5.0	4.7	5.3
IV	582.8	370.2	49.1	166.4	154.7	85.4	53.0	29.1	3.3	6.6	33.4	26.8	120.6	65.8	54.8	579.5	576.2	2.5	4.9	3.0
1963: I	592.1	374.0	50.2	167.5	156.4	88.9	52.8	30.2	5.9	6.9	33.3	26.4	122.3	66.0	56.3	586.2	585.2	6.5	4.7	6.4
II	600.3	378.2	51.5	168.2	158.6	92.2	54.3	32.2	5.6	8.5	35.7	27.2	121.4	64.3	57.1	594.7	591.9	5.7	5.9	4.7
III	613.1	385.1	52.2	170.6	162.3	95.7	55.9	32.5	7.3	8.0	36.0	28.1	124.4	65.5	58.8	605.8	605.2	8.8	7.7	9.3
IV	622.1	389.6	53.3	171.1	165.2	95.8	57.7	33.7	4.4	9.5	37.6	28.2	127.2	67.0	60.2	617.7	612.6	6.0	8.1	5.0
1964: I	636.9	398.8	55.4	175.2	168.2	98.2	58.8	34.0	5.5	11.5	39.9	28.4	128.5	67.0	61.4	631.5	625.5	9.9	9.2	8.7
II	645.6	406.4	56.8	178.4	171.2	98.7	60.5	32.8	5.4	10.2	39.5	29.2	130.2	67.0	63.2	640.2	635.3	5.6	5.6	6.4
III	656.0	414.9	58.6	182.0	174.3	100.0	62.5	32.4	5.2	10.9	40.9	29.9	130.1	65.9	64.2	650.8	645.1	6.6	6.8	6.3
IV	660.6	417.1	56.6	183.1	177.4	101.6	63.9	32.1	5.6	10.9	41.8	30.9	131.0	65.7	65.3	655.0	649.7	2.8	2.6	2.9
1965: I	682.7	427.6	62.1	185.6	179.9	114.4	68.6	33.3	12.5	9.0	39.1	30.1	131.8	65.2	66.6	670.2	673.8	14.1	9.6	15.7
II	695.0	434.4	61.9	189.1	183.4	114.0	71.5	33.4	9.1	10.8	44.2	33.4	135.8	67.1	68.7	685.9	684.2	7.4	9.7	6.3
III	710.7	443.4	63.8	192.8	186.9	117.4	74.4	33.0	10.0	9.5	43.3	33.8	140.3	69.0	71.4	700.7	701.2	9.3	8.9	10.3
IV	732.0	457.4	66.1	199.9	191.4	118.8	78.0	32.7	8.0	9.5	45.2	35.7	146.3	73.3	73.0	723.9	722.5	12.5	13.9	12.7
1966: I	754.8	467.7	69.2	204.1	194.5	128.2	81.2	33.2	13.8	8.7	45.6	36.9	150.2	75.1	75.1	741.0	746.1	13.1	9.8	13.7
II	764.6	472.7	66.5	207.6	198.5	129.1	83.4	31.9	13.9	7.6	45.8	38.2	155.2	78.3	76.9	750.7	757.0	5.3	5.3	6.0
III	777.7	481.7	69.1	210.7	202.0	127.6	84.5	30.7	12.4	6.4	46.6	40.2	162.0	83.1	78.9	765.2	771.3	7.0	8.0	7.8
IV	790.9	486.9	69.3	211.4	206.2	129.6	85.0	27.9	16.7	7.3	48.4	41.0	167.1	85.1	82.0	774.2	783.6	7.0	4.8	6.5

APPENDIX 14.1
(Continued)

Table 1.—Gross National Product—Continued

[Billions of dollars; quarterly data are seasonally adjusted at annual rates]

Year and quarter	GNP	Personal consumption expenditures				Gross private domestic investment				Net exports			Government purchases of goods and services			Final sales	Gross domestic purchases	Percent change from preceding period		
		Total	Durable goods	Nondurable goods	Services	Total	Nonresidential	Residential	CBI	Net	Exports	Imports	Total	Federal	State and local			GNP	Final sales	Gross domestic purchases
1967: I	799.7	491.4	67.8	213.7	209.9	125.5	83.5	27.0	15.0	8.0	49.7	41.6	174.8	90.3	84.4	784.7	791.7	4.5	5.5	4.2
II	805.9	500.5	71.2	215.5	213.8	120.6	83.9	30.5	6.2	7.8	48.9	41.2	177.0	91.1	85.9	799.6	798.1	3.1	7.8	3.3
III	822.9	507.5	71.3	217.8	218.4	126.5	84.0	32.2	10.4	7.4	49.1	41.7	181.4	93.9	87.5	812.5	815.5	8.7	6.6	9.0
IV	837.1	514.7	72.2	220.6	221.9	130.1	86.2	34.6	9.4	6.4	50.4	43.9	185.8	95.5	90.2	827.6	830.6	7.1	7.6	7.6
1968: I	862.9	532.4	77.3	227.6	227.5	133.8	90.1	36.1	7.6	5.2	52.1	46.9	191.4	98.0	93.4	855.3	857.6	12.9	14.1	13.7
II	886.7	545.8	79.3	232.6	233.8	137.4	89.2	37.1	11.1	6.1	54.2	48.1	197.4	100.9	96.5	875.6	880.7	11.5	9.8	11.2
III	903.6	561.6	83.6	238.6	239.3	136.8	91.0	37.8	8.0	5.6	56.8	51.1	199.6	100.8	98.8	895.6	898.0	7.8	9.5	8.1
IV	917.4	570.1	83.8	241.2	245.1	139.9	95.2	39.8	4.9	5.0	56.1	51.1	202.4	100.8	101.6	912.5	912.4	6.3	7.8	6.6
1969: I	941.3	581.7	85.8	245.6	250.3	151.3	98.8	41.7	10.8	5.2	52.4	47.2	203.0	99.4	103.7	930.5	936.1	10.8	8.1	10.8
II	955.6	592.7	86.2	250.2	256.3	151.8	100.9	41.8	9.0	5.1	61.8	56.6	206.0	99.6	106.4	946.6	950.5	6.2	7.1	6.3
III	975.4	602.7	86.4	254.2	262.1	158.1	104.5	41.8	11.9	5.3	62.4	57.0	209.2	100.8	108.5	963.5	970.0	8.5	7.3	8.5
IV	983.5	614.3	86.5	258.7	269.0	151.6	104.9	39.3	7.5	6.8	64.9	58.1	210.8	100.4	110.3	976.0	976.7	3.4	5.3	2.8
1970: I	994.2	625.1	85.4	264.7	275.1	146.2	104.5	39.5	2.2	8.1	66.7	58.6	214.7	100.8	113.9	992.0	986.0	4.4	6.7	3.9
II	1,008.9	635.1	86.7	268.2	280.2	148.2	105.6	38.4	4.2	9.8	69.9	60.1	215.7	98.6	117.1	1,004.6	999.0	6.0	5.2	5.4
III	1,027.9	646.8	87.7	271.9	287.2	153.5	106.7	39.6	7.2	8.4	69.4	61.0	219.1	97.3	121.8	1,020.7	1,019.5	7.7	6.6	8.5
IV	1,030.9	653.0	82.9	276.5	293.6	147.3	104.2	44.3	−1.2	7.5	69.6	62.2	223.1	98.3	124.8	1,032.1	1,023.5	1.2	4.5	1.6
1971: I	1,075.2	671.7	93.4	278.3	300.0	166.6	106.4	47.9	12.3	9.4	71.8	62.4	227.5	99.2	128.3	1,062.9	1,065.8	18.3	12.5	17.6
II	1,094.3	685.2	96.2	282.0	307.0	173.4	109.1	54.0	10.3	5.7	72.6	67.0	230.0	98.5	131.5	1,084.0	1,088.6	7.3	8.2	8.8
III	1,113.9	696.8	98.5	284.4	313.9	177.0	110.2	58.0	8.8	6.1	75.3	69.3	234.0	100.4	133.6	1,105.1	1,107.8	7.4	8.0	7.2
IV	1,127.3	712.4	102.2	288.4	321.7	172.9	112.5	60.7	−.3	4.0	69.7	65.7	238.0	101.3	136.7	1,127.6	1,123.3	4.9	8.4	5.7
1972: I	1,166.5	729.3	105.7	293.1	330.5	188.3	117.7	65.8	4.8	2.1	77.8	75.6	246.8	106.8	140.0	1,161.7	1,164.4	14.7	12.7	15.5
II	1,197.2	747.0	108.9	301.5	336.7	199.1	120.5	66.7	11.9	2.2	77.6	75.4	248.9	107.3	141.6	1,185.3	1,195.0	11.0	8.4	10.9
III	1,223.9	764.8	112.3	308.4	344.0	205.7	123.0	68.3	14.4	3.8	81.9	78.1	249.6	104.4	145.2	1,209.5	1,220.0	9.2	8.4	8.6
IV	1,263.5	789.2	118.0	317.4	353.9	214.9	130.7	73.4	10.8	4.5	88.2	83.7	254.8	104.9	149.9	1,252.7	1,259.0	13.6	15.1	13.4
1973: I	1,311.6	813.2	126.3	327.0	359.9	228.0	137.2	75.9	14.8	9.5	100.1	90.6	261.0	106.8	154.2	1,296.8	1,302.1	16.1	14.8	14.4
II	1,342.9	827.9	125.3	333.5	369.1	237.8	144.9	73.5	19.3	13.9	109.4	95.5	263.3	105.6	157.7	1,323.6	1,329.0	9.9	8.5	8.5
III	1,369.4	846.2	125.0	344.0	377.2	237.2	149.4	72.8	15.0	21.1	118.7	97.6	265.0	103.1	161.9	1,354.4	1,348.3	8.1	9.6	5.9
IV	1,413.3	861.6	122.3	353.7	385.7	252.3	152.2	70.9	29.2	22.5	128.3	105.7	276.8	110.0	166.8	1,384.1	1,390.7	13.5	9.1	13.2
1974: I	1,426.2	880.0	120.2	365.6	394.2	238.1	154.4	67.6	16.1	25.0	141.7	116.8	283.1	109.8	173.3	1,410.1	1,401.2	3.7	7.7	3.1
II	1,459.1	907.8	124.3	376.8	406.7	241.3	159.2	66.1	16.0	14.6	151.5	136.9	295.5	114.6	180.9	1,443.2	1,444.6	9.6	9.7	13.0
III	1,489.1	935.3	130.2	388.1	417.0	238.9	163.4	66.2	9.3	10.7	152.9	142.2	304.1	117.8	186.4	1,479.8	1,478.4	8.5	10.5	9.7
IV	1,516.8	943.0	120.3	393.1	429.7	245.1	165.5	59.2	20.4	14.9	159.9	145.1	313.8	122.6	191.2	1,496.5	1,502.0	7.7	4.6	6.5
1975: I	1,524.6	967.4	124.8	400.5	442.1	204.9	160.5	56.9	−12.5	29.3	162.0	132.8	323.1	125.5	197.6	1,537.1	1,495.3	2.1	11.3	−1.8
II	1,563.5	996.6	130.1	411.2	455.3	204.6	160.0	59.8	−15.2	32.7	155.4	122.7	329.7	127.3	202.4	1,578.7	1,530.8	10.6	11.3	9.8
III	1,627.4	1,029.6	140.0	423.2	466.4	229.5	163.4	64.3	1.8	29.4	159.0	129.7	338.9	129.6	209.2	1,625.5	1,598.0	17.4	12.4	18.7
IV	1,678.2	1,057.5	146.5	429.9	481.1	239.3	167.5	68.4	3.4	32.9	168.9	136.0	348.5	134.3	214.2	1,674.8	1,645.3	13.1	12.7	12.4
1976: I	1,730.9	1,091.8	156.4	439.4	495.9	264.6	171.8	75.9	16.8	23.6	170.6	147.0	350.9	132.3	218.6	1,714.1	1,707.3	13.2	9.7	15.9
II	1,761.8	1,111.2	158.9	446.4	505.8	275.8	176.3	79.9	19.6	20.0	175.1	155.1	354.9	134.9	220.0	1,742.2	1,741.9	7.3	6.7	8.4
III	1,794.7	1,139.8	162.4	456.0	521.4	279.6	182.7	79.5	17.4	17.0	180.5	163.4	358.2	137.5	220.8	1,777.2	1,777.6	7.7	8.3	8.5
IV	1,843.7	1,174.6	168.1	466.0	540.6	290.6	189.2	91.3	10.2	14.7	184.8	170.1	363.8	140.7	223.0	1,833.6	1,829.0	11.4	13.3	12.1
1977: I	1,899.1	1,211.8	177.0	477.5	557.4	311.5	200.1	96.3	15.1	4.0	186.3	182.3	371.8	142.7	229.2	1,884.1	1,895.1	12.6	11.5	15.3
II	1,968.9	1,239.2	181.9	485.6	571.7	341.4	209.5	110.2	21.7	4.2	194.0	189.8	384.1	149.9	234.2	1,947.2	1,964.7	15.5	14.1	15.5
III	2,031.6	1,270.2	186.5	491.9	591.7	363.7	218.0	113.0	32.7	5.3	195.9	190.6	392.3	154.3	238.0	1,998.9	2,026.3	13.4	11.1	13.1
IV	2,062.4	1,307.6	192.6	506.8	608.2	359.6	229.0	115.0	15.6	−5.9	190.3	196.2	401.1	157.6	243.4	2,046.8	2,068.3	6.2	9.9	8.6
1978: I	2,111.4	1,332.6	188.9	516.4	627.3	379.7	235.0	118.4	26.3	−6.6	203.8	210.4	405.6	154.9	250.7	2,085.1	2,117.9	9.8	7.7	9.9
II	2,230.3	1,391.1	207.6	534.4	649.0	420.2	257.3	128.5	34.4	1.3	222.1	220.7	417.6	157.1	260.6	2,195.9	2,228.9	24.5	23.0	22.7
III	2,289.5	1,424.6	210.0	548.5	666.1	424.7	266.8	133.4	24.5	6.8	233.2	226.4	433.4	165.4	268.1	2,265.0	2,282.7	11.0	13.2	10.0
IV	2,367.6	1,465.7	215.8	567.9	682.0	442.7	276.9	136.4	29.4	15.0	250.9	236.0	444.2	169.9	274.3	2,338.2	2,352.6	14.4	13.6	12.8
1979: I	2,420.5	1,501.8	215.6	583.4	702.8	446.9	289.0	136.0	21.9	22.7	265.2	242.6	449.2	172.1	277.1	2,398.7	2,397.9	9.2	10.8	7.9
II	2,474.5	1,537.6	214.4	600.9	722.4	463.2	296.3	138.7	28.1	15.2	278.1	262.9	458.6	173.1	285.4	2,446.4	2,459.3	9.2	8.2	10.6
III	2,546.1	1,590.0	223.9	623.6	742.5	461.5	310.1	141.7	9.7	21.8	301.0	279.2	472.8	178.6	294.2	2,536.4	2,524.3	12.1	15.5	11.0
IV	2,591.5	1,637.5	221.9	645.1	770.5	447.8	315.9	139.8	−7.8	15.4	320.6	305.2	490.7	188.0	302.7	2,599.3	2,576.1	7.3	10.3	8.5
1980: I	2,673.0	1,682.2	225.0	662.0	795.1	461.0	326.7	133.9	.4	20.7	346.5	325.8	509.1	197.0	312.2	2,672.5	2,652.3	13.2	11.7	12.4
II	2,672.2	1,688.9	204.9	671.8	812.2	425.0	314.1	110.5	.5	30.1	348.4	318.3	528.2	208.9	319.2	2,671.7	2,642.1	−.1	−.1	−1.5
III	2,734.0	1,749.3	218.7	686.4	844.2	405.4	319.7	115.3	−29.6	46.8	350.1	303.3	532.6	207.2	325.4	2,763.6	2,687.2	9.6	14.5	7.0
IV	2,848.6	1,810.0	228.5	705.2	876.3	456.4	330.5	130.5	−4.6	30.8	358.9	328.1	551.4	219.3	332.1	2,853.3	2,817.8	17.9	13.6	20.9
1981: I	2,978.8	1,862.9	241.1	726.6	895.2	506.9	347.8	131.1	28.0	38.9	380.7	341.9	570.1	229.3	340.8	2,950.8	2,939.9	19.6	14.4	18.5
II	3,017.7	1,896.4	236.0	737.3	923.2	515.3	364.5	128.1	22.7	29.0	383.4	354.4	577.0	233.9	343.2	2,995.0	2,988.7	5.3	6.1	6.8
III	3,099.6	1,940.9	246.9	745.7	948.4	535.9	380.2	120.1	35.7	30.9	382.3	351.4	591.9	245.4	346.5	3,064.0	3,068.8	11.3	9.5	11.2
IV	3,114.4	1,960.2	235.5	752.7	972.0	504.0	384.5	109.8	9.7	36.9	384.8	347.9	613.3	260.2	353.1	3,104.7	3,077.5	1.9	5.4	1.1
1982: I	3,112.6	1,996.3	245.1	758.1	993.1	459.5	382.0	101.7	−24.1	34.7	373.0	338.4	622.1	262.9	359.2	3,136.7	3,077.9	−.2	4.2	.1
II	3,159.5	2,023.8	248.9	762.6	1,012.2	467.8	369.2	103.6	−5.0	42.1	378.9	336.8	625.7	259.3	366.4	3,164.5	3,117.3	6.2	3.6	5.2
III	3,179.4	2,065.6	252.8	776.7	1,036.1	452.2	360.7	100.5	−9.0	14.5	359.9	345.4	647.1	275.3	371.8	3,188.4	3,164.9	2.5	3.1	6.2
IV	3,212.5	2,117.0	263.8	786.6	1,066.5	409.6	354.9	114.7	−59.9	14.1	335.9	321.9	671.8	293.2	378.7	3,272.4	3,198.5	4.2	11.0	4.3
1983: I	3,265.8	2,146.6	266.7	791.0	1,088.9	428.3	340.8	130.2	−42.6	22.7	343.6	320.9	668.1	285.5	382.7	3,308.4	3,243.1	6.8	4.5	5.7
II	3,367.4	2,213.0	284.5	810.9	1,117.6	481.3	344.7	147.8	−11.2	−2.1	344.1	346.2	675.2	287.7	387.5	3,378.6	3,369.5	13.0	8.8	16.5
III	3,443.9	2,262.8	295.2	827.0	1,140.6	519.7	358.1	167.1	−5.5	−19.3	357.7	376.9	680.7	284.9	395.8	3,449.4	3,463.1	9.4	8.6	11.6
IV	3,545.8	2,315.8	310.0	837.9	1,167.9	579.8	383.9	164.9	31.0	−25.8	364.7	390.5	676.1	276.1	400.0	3,514.8	3,571.6	12.4	7.8	13.1
1984: I	3,674.9	2,361.1	322.7	849.9	1,188.6	663.0	392.7	176.2	94.1	−45.7	374.3	420.0	696.5	284.0	412.5	3,580.8	3,720.6	15.4	7.7	17.8
II	3,754.2	2,417.0	335.1	866.9	1,215.1	664.2	413.2	184.3	66.7	−62.8	383.2	446.1	735.8	315.0	420.8	3,687.4	3,817.0	8.9	12.5	10.8
III	3,807.9	2,450.3	337.7	872.8	1,239.7	670.3	423.3	182.1	65.0	−59.3	390.8	450.1	746.6	317.0	429.6	3,742.9	3,867.2	5.8	6.2	5.4
IV	3,851.8	2,493.4	346.7	879.6	1,267.1	661.8	435.0	181.8	45.0	−67.9	385.7	453.6	764.5	326.0	438.5	3,806.8	3,919.7	4.7	7.0	5.5
1985: I	3,925.6	2,554.9	361.4	890.9	1,302.7	639.3	437.7	183.8	17.8	−53.1	376.8	429.9	784.4	336.1	448.3	3,907.7	3,978.7	7.9	11.0	6.2
II	3,979.0	2,599.3	367.1	905.6	1,326.6	652.3	446.1	186.7	19.5	−74.3	372.6	446.9	801.7	339.6	462.1	3,959.5	4,053.3	5.6	5.4	7.7
III	4,047.0	2,661.4	387.2	915.7	1,358.5	626.7	436.6	189.4	.7	−81.2	365.1	446.2	840.2	368.4	471.8	4,046.3	4,128.2	7.0	9.1	7.6
IV	4,107.9	2,700.4	373.2	932.7	1,394.5	654.1	451.3	195.5	7.2	−103.2	369.2	472.4	856.7	376.6	480.1	4,100.7	4,211.2	6.2	5.5	8.3
1986: I	4,181.3	2,734.3	381.8	939.0	1,413.4	683.8	439.3	203.9	40.7	−87.1	395.5	482.7	850.3	358.5	491.8	4,140.6	4,268.4	7.3	3.9	5.5
II	4,194.7	2,761.0	393.6	935.4	1,432.0	657.2	434.5	217.3	5.4	−92.7	390.7	483.4	869.3	368.7	500.6	4,189.3	4,287.5	1.3	4.8	1.8
III	4,253.3	2,826.0	426.4	941.4	1,458.2	647.7	431.2	223.0	−6.4	−100.8	397.3	498.0	880.3	369.9	510.4	4,259.8	4,354.1	5.7	6.9	6.4
IV	4,297.3	2,868.5	422.0	952.1	1,494.4	648.8	435.8	225.1	−12.2	−108.9	402.4	511.3	888.9	368.8	520.1	4,309.4	4,406.2	4.2	4.7	4.9
1987: I	4,388.8	2,914.7	401.2	976.4	1,537.1	673.1	423.9	223.8	25.4	−106.0	416.5	522.5	906.9	375.6	531.4	4,363.4	4,494.8	8.8	5.1	8.3
II	4,475.9	2,989.4	419.2	994.3	1,575.8	684.1	437.5	227.9	18.8	−114.4	437.4	551.8	916.8	378.2	538.6	4,457.1	4,590.3	8.2	8.9	8.8
III	4,566.6	3,055.9	439.3	1,006.0	1,610.6	692.8	457.0	226.2	9.5	−115.3	458.0	573.4	933.2	384.5	548.7	4,557.1	4,681.9	8.4	9.3	8.2
IV	4,665.8	3,083.3	424.5	1,015.4	1,643.3	749.7	458.6	227.7	63.3	−114.6	482.6	597.2	947.5	388.1	559.4	4,602.5	4,780.4	9.0	4.0	8.7
1988: I	4,739.8	3,148.1	446.4	1,022.2	1,679.5	728.8	472.7	226.1	30.0	−82.8	521.6	604.3	945.7	374.1	571.6	4,709.8	4,822.5	6.5	9.7	3.6
II	4,838.5	3,204.9	454.6	1,042.4	1,707.9	748.4	487.1	232.1	29.3	−74.9	532.5	607.5	960.1	377.1	583.0	4,809.2	4,913.4	8.6	8.7	7.8
III	4,926.9	3,263.4	452.5	1,066.2	1,744.7	771.1	493.2	233.2	44.6	−66.2	556.8	623.0	958.6	367.5	591.0	4,882.3	4,993.1	7.5	6.2	6.6
IV	5,017.3	3,324.0	467.4	1,078.4	1,778.2	752.8	495.8	238.4	18.7	−70.8	579.7	650.5	1,011.4	406.4	604.9	4,998.7	5,088.1	7.5	9.9	7.8

NOTE.—GNP=Gross national product; CBI=Change in business inventories.

APPENDIX 14.1
(Continued)

Table 2.—Gross National Product in Constant Dollars

[Billions of 1982 dollars; quarterly data are seasonally adjusted at annual rates]

Year and quarter	GNP	Personal consumption expenditures: Total	Durable goods	Nondurable goods	Services	Gross private domestic investment: Total	Nonresidential	Residential	CBI	Net exports: Net	Exports	Imports	Government purchases of goods and services: Total	Federal	State and local	Final sales	Gross domestic purchases	Percent change from preceding period: GNP	Final sales	Gross domestic purchases
1929	709.6	471.4	40.3	211.4	219.7	139.2	93.0	35.4	10.8	4.7	42.1	37.4	94.2	18.3	75.9	698.7	704.9	.....	.....	.....
1930	642.8	439.7	31.9	203.1	204.8	97.5	76.9	21.5	−.9	2.3	35.6	33.3	103.3	20.6	82.7	643.6	640.5	−9.4	−7.9	−9.1
1931	588.1	422.1	27.5	201.7	193.0	60.2	49.4	17.9	−7.1	−1.0	29.3	30.4	106.8	21.2	85.6	595.2	589.1	−8.5	−7.5	−8.0
1932	509.2	384.9	21.0	187.0	176.9	22.6	29.6	9.4	−16.4	−.5	23.2	23.7	102.2	21.9	80.3	525.6	509.7	−13.4	−11.7	−13.5
1933	498.5	378.7	20.7	181.8	176.2	22.7	25.8	7.7	−10.7	−1.4	22.7	24.2	98.5	27.0	71.5	509.2	499.9	−2.1	−3.1	−1.9
1934	536.7	390.5	23.4	192.4	174.7	35.3	32.4	10.5	−7.6	.1	24.7	24.6	110.7	34.7	76.1	544.3	536.5	7.7	6.9	7.3
1935	580.2	412.1	28.9	201.5	181.7	60.9	40.0	14.7	6.2	−5.9	26.6	32.5	113.0	34.1	79.0	574.0	586.1	8.1	5.5	9.2
1936	662.2	451.8	33.9	224.3	191.4	82.1	54.4	18.7	9.0	−4.2	28.4	32.5	132.5	53.6	78.9	653.1	666.3	14.1	13.8	13.7
1937	695.3	467.9	37.7	232.8	197.4	99.9	65.5	20.2	14.1	−.3	35.7	35.9	127.8	48.9	79.0	681.2	695.6	5.0	4.3	4.4
1938	664.2	457.1	30.4	235.4	191.3	63.1	48.8	20.4	−6.0	6.0	34.1	28.1	137.9	55.0	82.9	670.2	658.2	−4.5	−1.6	−5.4
1939	716.6	480.5	35.7	248.0	196.7	86.0	53.2	28.9	3.9	6.1	36.2	30.1	144.1	53.8	90.3	712.7	710.5	7.9	6.3	7.9
1940	772.9	502.6	40.6	259.4	202.7	111.8	65.0	32.5	14.4	8.2	40.0	31.7	150.2	63.6	86.6	758.5	764.6	7.8	6.4	7.6
1941	909.4	531.1	46.2	275.6	209.3	138.8	76.6	34.4	27.8	3.9	42.0	38.2	235.6	153.0	82.6	881.6	905.5	17.7	16.2	18.4
1942	1,080.3	527.6	31.3	279.1	217.2	76.7	47.4	17.3	12.0	−7.7	29.1	36.9	483.7	407.1	76.7	1,068.3	1,088.0	18.8	21.2	20.1
1943	1,276.2	539.9	28.1	284.7	227.2	50.4	39.4	10.4	.7	−23.0	25.1	48.0	708.9	638.1	70.8	1,275.5	1,299.2	18.1	19.4	19.4
1944	1,380.6	557.1	26.3	297.9	232.9	56.4	52.6	9.0	−5.2	−23.8	27.3	51.1	790.8	722.5	68.3	1,385.7	1,404.3	8.2	8.6	8.1
1945	1,354.8	592.7	28.7	323.5	240.5	76.5	74.2	10.7	−8.4	−18.9	35.2	54.1	704.5	634.0	70.5	1,363.3	1,373.7	−1.9	−1.6	−2.2
1946	1,096.9	655.0	47.8	344.2	262.9	178.1	105.5	44.7	27.9	27.0	69.0	42.0	236.9	159.3	77.6	1,069.0	1,069.9	−19.0	−21.6	−22.1
1947	1,066.7	666.6	56.5	337.4	272.6	177.9	121.7	57.2	−1.0	42.4	82.3	39.9	179.8	91.9	87.9	1,067.7	1,024.3	−2.8	−.1	−4.3
1948	1,108.7	681.8	61.7	338.7	281.4	208.2	127.4	68.6	12.3	19.2	66.2	47.1	199.5	106.1	93.4	1,096.4	1,089.5	3.9	2.7	6.4
1949	1,109.0	695.4	67.8	342.3	285.3	168.8	114.8	63.6	−9.7	18.8	65.0	46.2	226.0	119.5	106.5	1,118.7	1,090.2	0	2.0	.1
1950	1,203.7	733.2	80.7	352.8	299.8	234.9	124.0	86.7	24.2	4.7	59.2	54.6	230.8	116.7	114.2	1,179.5	1,199.0	8.5	5.4	10.0
1951	1,328.2	748.7	74.7	362.9	311.1	235.2	131.7	72.6	30.8	14.6	72.0	57.4	329.7	214.4	115.4	1,297.4	1,313.6	10.3	10.0	9.6
1952	1,380.0	771.4	73.0	376.6	321.9	211.8	130.6	71.2	10.0	6.9	70.1	63.3	389.9	272.7	117.3	1,370.0	1,373.1	3.9	5.6	4.5
1953	1,435.3	802.5	80.2	388.2	334.1	216.6	140.1	73.8	2.8	−2.7	66.9	69.7	419.0	295.9	123.1	1,432.5	1,438.0	4.0	4.6	4.7
1954	1,416.2	822.7	81.5	393.8	347.4	212.6	137.5	79.8	−4.8	2.5	70.0	67.5	378.4	245.0	133.4	1,421.0	1,413.7	−1.3	−.8	−1.7
1955	1,494.9	873.8	96.9	413.2	363.6	259.8	151.0	92.4	16.3	0	76.9	76.9	361.3	217.9	143.4	1,478.6	1,494.9	5.6	4.1	5.7
1956	1,525.6	899.8	92.8	426.9	380.1	257.8	160.4	84.4	12.9	4.3	87.9	83.6	363.7	215.4	148.3	1,512.7	1,521.3	2.1	2.3	1.8
1957	1,551.1	919.7	92.4	434.7	392.6	243.4	161.1	79.3	3.0	7.0	94.9	87.9	381.1	224.1	157.0	1,548.1	1,544.2	1.7	2.3	1.5
1958	1,539.2	932.9	86.9	439.9	406.1	221.4	143.9	81.0	−3.4	−10.3	82.4	92.8	395.3	224.9	170.4	1,542.6	1,549.6	−.8	−.4	.4
1959	1,629.1	979.4	96.9	455.8	426.7	270.3	153.6	100.2	16.5	−18.2	83.7	101.9	397.7	221.5	176.2	1,612.6	1,647.3	5.8	4.5	6.3
1960	1,665.3	1,005.1	98.0	463.3	443.9	260.5	159.4	93.3	7.7	−4.0	98.4	102.4	403.7	220.6	183.1	1,657.5	1,669.3	2.2	2.8	1.3
1961	1,708.7	1,025.2	93.6	470.1	461.4	259.1	158.2	93.6	7.3	−2.7	100.7	103.3	427.1	232.9	194.2	1,701.4	1,711.3	2.6	2.6	2.5
1962	1,799.4	1,069.0	103.0	484.2	481.8	288.6	170.2	102.2	16.2	−7.5	106.9	114.4	449.4	249.3	200.1	1,783.3	1,807.0	5.3	4.8	5.6
1963	1,873.3	1,108.4	111.8	494.3	502.3	307.1	176.6	113.9	16.6	−1.9	114.7	116.6	459.8	247.8	212.0	1,856.7	1,875.3	4.1	4.1	3.8
1964	1,973.3	1,170.6	120.8	517.5	532.3	325.9	194.9	115.3	15.7	5.9	128.8	122.8	470.8	244.2	226.6	1,957.6	1,967.3	5.3	5.4	4.9
1965	2,087.6	1,236.4	134.6	543.2	558.5	367.0	227.6	114.2	25.2	−2.7	132.0	134.7	487.0	244.4	242.5	2,062.4	2,090.3	5.8	5.4	6.3
1966	2,208.3	1,298.9	144.4	569.3	585.3	390.5	250.4	103.2	36.9	−13.7	138.4	152.1	532.6	273.8	258.8	2,171.5	2,222.1	5.8	5.3	6.3
1967	2,271.4	1,337.7	146.2	579.2	612.3	374.4	245.0	100.6	28.8	−16.9	143.6	160.5	576.2	304.4	271.8	2,242.6	2,288.3	2.9	3.3	3.0
1968	2,365.6	1,405.9	161.6	602.4	641.8	391.8	254.5	116.2	21.0	−29.7	155.7	185.3	597.6	309.6	288.0	2,344.6	2,395.3	4.1	4.5	4.7
1969	2,423.3	1,456.7	167.8	617.2	671.7	410.3	269.7	115.4	25.1	−34.9	165.0	199.9	591.2	295.6	295.6	2,398.1	2,458.1	2.4	2.3	2.6
1970	2,416.2	1,492.0	162.5	632.5	697.0	381.5	264.0	109.3	8.2	−30.0	178.3	208.3	572.6	268.3	304.3	2,407.9	2,446.2	−.3	.4	−.5
1971	2,484.8	1,538.8	178.3	640.3	720.2	419.3	258.4	141.3	19.6	−39.8	179.2	218.9	566.5	250.6	315.9	2,465.2	2,524.6	2.8	2.4	3.2
1972	2,608.5	1,621.9	200.4	665.5	756.0	465.4	277.0	166.6	21.8	−49.4	195.2	244.6	570.7	246.0	324.7	2,586.8	2,658.0	5.0	4.9	5.3
1973	2,744.1	1,689.6	220.3	683.2	786.1	520.8	317.3	163.4	40.0	−31.5	242.3	273.8	565.3	230.0	335.3	2,704.1	2,775.7	5.2	4.5	4.4
1974	2,729.3	1,674.0	204.9	666.1	803.1	481.3	317.8	130.2	33.3	.8	269.1	268.4	573.2	226.4	346.8	2,696.0	2,728.5	−.5	−.3	−1.7
1975	2,695.0	1,711.9	205.6	676.5	829.8	383.3	281.2	114.9	−12.8	18.9	259.7	240.8	580.9	226.3	354.6	2,707.8	2,676.1	−1.3	.4	−1.9
1976	2,826.7	1,803.9	232.3	708.8	862.8	453.5	290.6	140.8	22.1	−11.0	274.4	285.4	580.3	224.2	356.0	2,804.6	2,837.7	4.9	3.6	6.0
1977	2,958.6	1,883.8	253.9	731.4	898.5	521.3	324.0	168.1	29.1	−35.5	281.6	317.1	589.1	231.8	357.2	2,929.5	2,994.1	4.7	4.5	5.5
1978	3,115.2	1,961.0	267.4	753.7	939.8	576.9	362.1	178.0	36.8	−26.8	312.6	339.4	604.1	233.7	370.4	3,078.4	3,142.0	5.3	5.1	4.9
1979	3,192.4	2,004.4	266.5	766.6	971.2	575.2	389.4	170.8	15.0	3.6	356.8	353.2	609.1	236.2	373.0	3,177.4	3,188.8	2.5	3.2	1.5
1980	3,187.1	2,000.4	245.9	762.6	991.9	509.3	379.2	137.0	−6.9	57.0	388.9	332.0	620.5	246.9	373.6	3,194.0	3,130.1	−.2	.5	−1.8
1981	3,248.8	2,024.2	250.8	764.4	1,009.0	545.5	395.2	126.5	23.9	49.4	392.7	343.4	629.7	259.6	370.1	3,225.0	3,199.4	1.9	1.0	2.2
1982	3,166.0	2,050.7	252.7	771.0	1,027.0	447.3	366.7	105.1	−24.5	26.3	361.9	335.6	641.7	272.7	369.0	3,190.5	3,139.7	−2.5	−1.1	−1.9
1983	3,279.1	2,146.0	283.1	800.2	1,062.7	504.0	361.2	149.3	−6.4	−19.9	348.1	368.1	649.0	275.1	373.9	3,285.5	3,299.1	3.6	3.0	5.1
1984	3,501.4	2,249.3	323.1	825.9	1,100.3	658.4	425.2	170.9	62.3	−84.0	371.8	455.8	677.7	290.8	387.0	3,439.1	3,585.4	6.8	4.7	8.7
1985	3,618.7	2,354.8	355.1	847.4	1,152.3	637.0	453.5	174.4	9.1	−104.3	367.2	471.4	731.2	326.0	405.2	3,609.6	3,723.0	3.4	5.0	3.8
1986	3,717.9	2,446.4	384.4	878.1	1,183.8	639.6	438.4	195.7	5.6	−129.7	397.1	526.9	761.6	334.1	427.5	3,712.4	3,847.6	2.7	2.8	3.3
1987	3,853.7	2,513.7	389.6	890.4	1,233.7	674.0	455.5	194.8	23.7	−115.7	450.9	566.6	781.8	339.6	442.1	3,830.0	3,969.4	3.7	3.2	3.2
1988	4,024.4	2,598.4	413.6	904.5	1,280.2	715.8	493.8	194.1	27.9	−74.9	530.1	605.0	785.1	328.9	456.2	3,996.5	4,099.3	4.4	4.3	3.3
1960: I	1,671.6	997.1	96.9	460.7	439.6	288.7	161.1	100.9	26.7	−9.4	95.0	104.3	395.2	217.0	178.2	1,644.9	1,681.0	7.0	5.2	5.4
II	1,666.8	1,009.8	99.9	465.9	444.1	261.4	161.4	92.7	7.3	−6.9	98.0	104.9	402.6	220.4	182.2	1,659.5	1,673.8	−1.1	3.6	−1.7
III	1,668.4	1,005.7	98.7	463.1	443.9	258.3	157.7	89.8	10.8	−2.4	99.9	102.3	406.8	221.8	185.0	1,657.6	1,670.8	.4	−.5	−.7
IV	1,654.1	1,007.8	96.4	463.6	447.9	233.6	157.6	89.9	−13.9	2.6	100.5	97.9	410.1	223.2	186.9	1,668.0	1,651.5	−3.4	2.5	−4.5
1961: I	1,671.3	1,009.5	91.2	465.3	453.0	238.3	155.3	90.2	−7.1	3.8	102.1	98.3	419.7	226.9	192.8	1,678.5	1,667.6	4.2	2.5	4.0
II	1,692.1	1,023.5	91.8	470.4	461.3	249.1	157.0	90.5	1.7	−3.0	96.9	99.9	422.4	230.8	191.6	1,690.4	1,695.1	5.1	2.9	6.8
III	1,716.3	1,024.6	93.7	469.2	461.7	270.3	158.0	93.4	17.1	−3.4	100.8	106.2	426.7	233.1	193.5	1,699.2	1,721.7	5.8	2.1	6.4
IV	1,754.9	1,042.9	97.8	475.5	469.7	278.4	162.6	98.4	17.4	−6.0	102.9	109.0	439.6	240.7	198.9	1,737.5	1,761.0	9.3	9.3	9.4
1962: I	1,777.9	1,053.6	99.9	480.2	473.6	287.7	165.5	100.2	22.0	−9.4	102.3	111.7	446.0	248.7	197.3	1,755.9	1,787.3	5.3	4.3	6.1
II	1,796.4	1,063.6	102.0	481.3	480.3	291.2	171.3	103.1	16.7	−5.2	108.9	114.1	446.9	248.1	198.8	1,779.7	1,801.6	4.2	5.5	3.2
III	1,813.1	1,072.8	103.1	485.7	484.0	294.7	173.4	102.9	18.4	−6.5	108.8	115.3	452.1	250.9	201.2	1,794.7	1,819.6	3.8	3.4	4.1
IV	1,810.1	1,085.8	106.8	489.7	489.3	280.7	170.5	102.7	7.5	−9.0	107.5	116.5	452.6	249.4	203.2	1,802.6	1,819.1	−.7	1.8	−.1
1963: I	1,834.6	1,094.1	109.2	492.4	492.6	291.9	168.9	106.1	17.0	−6.6	107.3	113.9	455.2	248.2	207.0	1,817.7	1,841.2	5.5	3.4	4.9
II	1,860.0	1,100.2	111.2	492.2	496.7	306.9	174.3	114.0	18.6	−1.4	114.7	116.1	454.4	245.5	208.9	1,841.4	1,861.5	5.7	5.3	4.5
III	1,892.5	1,115.5	112.9	495.9	506.7	315.6	179.4	116.0	20.2	−2.6	115.8	118.5	464.1	249.5	214.6	1,872.3	1,895.1	7.2	6.9	7.4
IV	1,906.1	1,123.6	113.9	496.5	513.1	314.0	183.9	119.4	10.7	3.0	120.9	117.9	465.5	248.0	217.5	1,895.4	1,903.1	2.9	5.0	1.7
1964: I	1,948.7	1,145.2	118.1	505.1	522.0	324.7	186.5	121.3	16.9	9.7	128.0	118.3	469.2	248.3	220.9	1,931.8	1,939.0	9.2	7.9	7.8
II	1,965.4	1,164.4	120.7	514.6	529.1	323.6	192.3	116.0	15.3	4.8	126.0	121.3	472.7	246.8	225.9	1,950.1	1,960.7	3.5	3.8	4.6
III	1,985.2	1,184.8	124.2	524.4	536.1	324.5	197.9	112.9	13.8	5.6	129.6	124.0	470.3	241.8	228.5	1,971.4	1,979.6	4.1	4.4	3.9
IV	1,993.7	1,188.0	120.3	526.0	541.8	330.8	202.9	111.0	16.9	3.7	131.5	127.8	471.1	239.9	231.2	1,976.8	1,989.9	1.7	1.1	2.1
1965: I	2,036.9	1,208.2	130.7	531.2	546.3	362.1	214.7	115.0	32.3	−3.0	120.1	123.1	469.6	236.3	233.4	2,004.6	2,039.9	9.0	5.7	10.4
II	2,066.4	1,221.7	131.2	536.1	554.4	364.3	224.1	116.4	23.9	−.4	135.8	136.3	480.8	241.3	239.6	2,042.5	2,066.8	5.9	7.8	5.4
III	2,099.3	1,242.3	135.9	544.7	561.7	369.9	231.1	113.3	25.4	−4.3	132.7	137.0	491.5	244.9	246.6	2,073.9	2,103.6	6.5	6.3	7.3
IV	2,147.6	1,273.2	140.8	560.8	571.7	371.8	240.6	111.9	19.2	−3.2	139.3	142.5	505.8	255.2	250.6	2,128.3	2,150.8	9.5	10.9	9.3
1966: I	2,190.1	1,287.6	147.3	563.4	576.9	396.9	247.9	113.3	35.7	−7.9	138.4	146.3	513.5	259.4	254.1	2,154.3	2,198.0	8.2	5.0	9.1
II	2,195.8	1,293.1	140.9	568.6	583.6	390.9	251.2	105.8	33.8	−11.6	136.9	148.5	523.4	267.1	256.2	2,162.0	2,207.4	1.0	1.4	1.7
III	2,218.3	1,305.5	144.8	573.6	587.1	389.1	252.9	102.3	33.9	−18.2	137.8	155.9	541.9	282.9	259.0	2,184.4	2,236.5	4.2	4.2	5.4
IV	2,229.2	1,309.5	144.5	571.5	593.4	385.2	249.7	91.4	44.0	−17.2	140.5	157.8	551.7	285.9	265.8	2,185.1	2,246.4	2.0	.1	1.8
1967: I	2,241.8	1,319.4	142.1	576.3	601.0	368.7	244.5	87.6	36.6	−15.5	144.0	159.5	569.2	300.4	268.8	2,205.2	2,257.3	2.3	3.7	2.0
II	2,255.2	1,336.5	148.4	579.1	609.1	361.7	244.3	99.3	18.1	−16.1	142.3	158.5	573.1	302.8	270.3	2,237.1	2,271.4	2.4	5.9	2.5
III	2,287.7	1,343.3	147.1	578.7	617.5	378.8	243.4	104.3	31.1	−13.5	142.7	156.2	579.1	307.6	271.5	2,256.6	2,301.2	5.9	3.5	5.4
IV	2,300.6	1,351.5	147.2	582.7	621.6	388.4	247.8	111.3	29.3	−22.5	145.2	167.7	583.2	306.6	276.5	2,271.3	2,323.1	2.3	2.6	3.9

APPENDIX 14.1
(*Continued*)

Table 2.—Gross National Product in Constant Dollars—Continued

[Billions of 1982 dollars; quarterly data are seasonally adjusted at annual rates]

Year and quarter	GNP	Personal consumption expenditures				Gross private domestic investment				Net exports			Government purchases of goods and services			Final sales	Gross domestic purchases	Percent change from preceding period		
		Total	Durable goods	Nondurable goods	Services	Total	Nonresidential	Residential	CBI	Net	Exports	Imports	Total	Federal	State and local			GNP	Final sales	Gross domestic purchases
1968: I	2,327.3	1,378.1	155.8	594.2	628.2	387.7	255.7	112.9	19.1	−28.7	149.3	178.0	590.1	309.0	281.1	2,308.1	2,356.0	4.7	6.6	5.8
II	2,366.9	1,396.7	159.1	599.2	638.3	397.2	250.0	115.8	31.4	−27.5	153.1	180.6	600.5	313.4	287.1	2,335.5	2,394.4	7.0	4.8	6.7
III	2,385.3	1,421.5	166.4	608.6	646.5	392.0	252.1	116.8	23.2	−29.2	161.8	191.0	601.0	310.4	290.7	2,362.1	2,414.5	3.1	4.6	3.4
IV	2,383.0	1,427.1	165.3	607.6	654.2	390.2	260.4	119.3	10.5	−33.2	158.5	191.8	599.0	305.7	293.2	2,372.5	2,416.2	−.4	1.8	.3
1969: I	2,416.5	1,442.9	168.8	613.4	660.7	412.0	266.0	119.4	26.6	−31.6	144.9	176.5	593.2	299.0	294.2	2,389.9	2,448.1	5.7	3.0	5.4
II	2,419.8	1,451.7	168.2	616.2	667.3	409.1	267.9	118.3	22.9	−36.9	171.3	208.2	596.0	299.8	296.2	2,397.0	2,456.7	.5	1.2	1.4
III	2,433.2	1,459.9	167.6	617.6	674.7	419.5	273.8	116.5	29.2	−36.6	170.3	206.9	590.4	294.2	296.2	2,403.9	2,469.8	2.2	1.2	2.2
IV	2,423.5	1,472.0	166.7	621.4	683.9	400.5	271.1	107.5	21.9	−34.3	173.3	207.7	585.3	289.5	295.8	2,401.6	2,457.8	−1.6	−.4	−1.9
1970: I	2,408.6	1,481.5	163.5	628.4	689.7	379.9	265.9	108.2	5.8	−31.4	175.8	207.2	578.6	279.8	298.8	2,402.8	2,440.0	−2.4	.2	−2.9
II	2,406.5	1,488.1	165.6	629.6	692.8	376.4	264.3	102.1	10.0	−27.7	181.2	208.9	569.7	268.9	300.8	2,396.5	2,434.1	−.3	−1.0	−1.0
III	2,435.8	1,501.3	166.2	634.3	700.8	390.6	266.9	107.6	16.1	−27.7	178.4	206.1	571.6	264.0	307.7	2,419.7	2,463.5	5.0	3.9	4.9
IV	2,413.8	1,497.2	154.8	637.7	704.6	379.3	259.0	119.2	1.0	−33.3	177.8	211.1	570.6	260.4	310.2	2,412.7	2,447.1	−3.6	−1.2	−2.6
1971: I	2,478.6	1,520.9	170.7	639.4	710.8	415.5	257.7	126.1	31.7	−25.3	178.7	204.0	567.6	255.5	312.1	2,447.0	2,503.9	11.2	5.8	9.6
II	2,478.4	1,533.0	175.1	640.9	717.0	423.1	258.6	139.3	25.2	−41.7	180.2	221.8	564.0	249.1	314.9	2,453.2	2,520.1	0	1.0	2.6
III	2,491.1	1,541.0	180.0	639.0	722.0	425.9	257.6	147.7	20.6	−42.7	187.5	230.2	566.9	251.1	315.8	2,470.5	2,533.8	2.1	2.9	2.2
IV	2,491.0	1,560.1	187.4	641.8	731.0	412.8	259.6	152.2	1.0	−49.3	170.4	219.7	567.4	246.6	320.8	2,489.9	2,540.3	0	3.2	1.0
1972: I	2,545.6	1,581.8	191.7	647.5	742.7	439.5	267.9	163.6	8.1	−52.2	189.5	241.7	576.4	253.6	322.8	2,537.5	2,597.8	9.1	7.9	9.4
II	2,595.1	1,607.9	196.1	661.8	750.0	462.3	272.2	164.5	25.6	−49.2	186.9	236.1	574.1	252.2	321.9	2,569.6	2,644.3	8.0	5.2	7.4
III	2,622.1	1,629.9	201.4	670.4	758.1	473.8	275.9	165.6	32.4	−47.7	196.6	244.3	566.1	241.7	324.4	2,589.7	2,669.8	4.2	3.2	3.9
IV	2,671.3	1,667.8	212.4	682.2	773.2	486.0	292.2	172.8	21.0	−48.6	207.8	256.4	566.1	236.4	329.7	2,650.3	2,719.9	7.7	9.7	7.7
1973: I	2,734.0	1,689.9	225.7	687.8	776.3	515.7	304.5	177.1	34.1	−44.1	227.7	271.8	572.5	240.4	332.2	2,700.0	2,778.1	9.7	7.7	8.8
II	2,741.0	1,687.2	221.8	680.8	784.6	521.7	316.7	165.3	39.6	−36.6	239.2	275.7	568.6	235.8	332.8	2,701.4	2,777.6	1.0	.2	−.1
III	2,738.3	1,694.5	220.0	684.5	790.0	511.4	322.6	158.7	30.1	−23.4	247.8	271.2	555.8	220.0	335.8	2,708.2	2,761.7	−.4	1.0	−2.3
IV	2,762.8	1,686.8	213.8	679.4	793.5	534.2	325.5	152.5	56.3	−22.4	254.1	276.5	564.2	223.9	340.3	2,706.5	2,785.1	3.6	−.3	3.4
1974: I	2,747.4	1,667.5	208.2	664.9	794.4	501.1	324.4	141.4	35.3	11.0	266.8	255.8	567.8	223.9	343.9	2,712.1	2,736.4	−2.2	.8	−6.8
II	2,755.2	1,677.2	209.9	665.4	801.9	496.5	324.7	134.4	37.5	1.4	276.6	275.2	580.2	232.0	348.2	2,717.8	2,753.8	1.1	.8	2.6
III	2,719.3	1,686.7	211.6	670.2	804.9	465.5	316.0	130.6	18.8	−5.5	266.7	272.3	572.6	225.2	347.4	2,700.4	2,724.8	−5.1	−2.5	−4.1
IV	2,695.4	1,664.7	189.7	663.9	811.0	462.2	306.2	114.4	41.5	−3.5	266.7	270.2	572.1	224.4	347.7	2,653.9	2,699.0	−3.5	−6.7	−3.7
1975: I	2,642.7	1,677.1	193.5	666.9	816.7	370.6	285.5	106.9	−21.8	17.4	260.0	242.6	577.5	226.3	351.1	2,664.4	2,625.2	−7.6	1.6	−10.5
II	2,669.6	1,706.0	198.7	677.8	829.6	358.1	277.6	110.8	−30.3	28.2	252.5	224.3	577.2	225.5	351.7	2,699.9	2,641.4	4.1	5.4	2.5
III	2,714.9	1,723.9	211.7	679.8	832.4	394.4	279.6	118.2	−3.4	14.4	256.9	242.5	582.1	225.7	356.5	2,718.3	2,700.5	7.0	2.8	9.3
IV	2,752.7	1,740.4	218.3	681.5	840.5	410.1	282.1	123.6	4.4	15.5	269.3	253.9	586.8	227.8	359.0	2,748.3	2,737.2	5.7	4.5	5.5
1976: I	2,804.4	1,777.5	229.7	696.2	851.7	444.7	284.9	135.4	24.4	−.2	268.5	268.7	582.4	222.1	360.3	2,780.0	2,804.6	7.7	4.7	10.2
II	2,816.9	1,790.4	230.6	705.0	854.8	454.9	286.8	139.1	29.0	−8.7	272.0	280.7	580.3	223.4	357.0	2,787.9	2,825.6	1.8	1.1	3.0
III	2,828.6	1,809.9	232.4	712.1	865.4	452.8	292.8	136.3	23.7	−13.4	277.9	291.3	579.4	225.4	354.0	2,805.0	2,842.1	1.7	2.5	2.4
IV	2,856.8	1,837.8	236.7	721.8	879.4	461.8	297.9	152.4	11.6	−21.8	279.1	300.9	579.0	226.1	352.8	2,845.2	2,878.6	4.0	5.9	5.2
1977: I	2,896.0	1,863.7	246.7	728.8	888.2	492.0	311.5	156.3	24.2	−39.9	277.8	317.7	580.2	223.8	356.3	2,871.8	2,935.9	5.6	3.8	8.2
II	2,942.7	1,869.0	251.8	727.3	889.9	519.0	320.4	172.7	25.9	−32.8	284.8	317.7	587.5	230.8	356.7	2,916.8	2,975.5	6.6	6.4	5.5
III	3,001.8	1,888.0	256.2	728.3	903.5	546.9	327.8	174.4	44.7	−28.1	287.0	315.1	594.9	238.0	357.0	2,957.1	3,029.9	8.3	5.6	7.5
IV	2,994.1	1,914.2	261.1	740.9	912.2	527.2	336.4	169.1	21.7	−41.0	276.9	317.9	593.6	234.8	358.9	2,972.4	3,035.0	−1.0	2.1	.7
1978: I	3,020.5	1,923.0	252.6	745.8	924.6	544.0	339.5	172.9	31.6	−39.0	290.8	329.8	592.5	228.4	364.1	2,988.9	3,059.5	3.6	2.2	3.3
II	3,115.9	1,960.8	272.4	749.1	939.2	584.6	363.6	179.8	41.1	−30.7	307.6	338.3	601.3	230.3	371.0	3,074.8	3,146.6	13.2	12.0	11.9
III	3,142.6	1,970.3	270.9	753.5	945.9	583.3	369.4	180.8	33.1	−22.4	318.5	341.0	611.5	238.3	373.2	3,109.5	3,165.0	3.5	4.6	2.4
IV	3,181.6	1,989.7	273.9	766.3	949.6	595.8	376.0	178.6	41.3	−15.1	333.1	348.2	611.1	237.9	373.2	3,140.3	3,196.7	5.1	4.0	4.1
1979: I	3,181.7	1,997.5	268.9	766.2	962.4	582.2	383.7	174.6	23.9	−4.8	340.4	345.2	606.7	236.4	370.3	3,157.7	3,186.5	0	2.2	−1.3
II	3,178.7	1,994.1	262.9	762.1	969.1	590.1	384.9	172.4	32.8	−12.4	343.6	356.1	606.9	233.9	373.0	3,145.8	3,191.1	−.4	−1.5	.6
III	3,207.4	2,007.9	270.9	766.0	971.0	575.7	394.2	170.6	10.9	12.5	363.5	351.0	611.3	237.3	374.0	3,196.5	3,194.9	3.7	6.6	.5
IV	3,201.3	2,018.0	263.4	772.2	982.4	552.9	394.8	165.7	−7.6	18.7	378.8	360.1	611.7	237.1	374.6	3,208.9	3,182.6	−.8	1.6	−1.5
1980: I	3,233.4	2,015.4	260.6	767.9	986.9	556.7	397.7	154.9	4.1	43.5	398.9	355.4	617.8	243.3	374.5	3,229.3	3,189.9	4.1	2.6	.9
II	3,157.0	1,974.1	231.9	760.9	981.3	499.2	372.9	124.1	2.3	58.6	393.1	334.5	625.1	251.6	373.5	3,154.8	3,098.4	−9.1	−8.9	−11.0
III	3,159.1	1,996.3	242.7	759.9	993.6	467.7	370.4	126.8	−29.5	74.1	383.6	309.6	621.1	248.2	372.9	3,188.6	3,085.1	.3	4.4	−1.7
IV	3,199.2	2,015.6	248.6	761.5	1,005.6	513.5	375.8	142.2	−4.5	52.2	380.6	328.4	617.9	244.4	373.4	3,203.8	3,147.0	5.2	1.9	8.3
1981: I	3,261.1	2,022.9	258.7	763.3	1,000.9	552.3	385.7	139.3	27.3	59.7	394.5	334.8	626.3	252.0	374.2	3,233.8	3,201.4	8.0	3.8	7.1
II	3,250.2	2,022.4	248.4	764.5	1,009.5	551.2	395.3	134.1	21.8	50.2	395.3	345.1	626.4	256.0	370.4	3,228.4	3,200.0	−1.3	−.7	−.2
III	3,264.6	2,031.5	255.5	764.7	1,011.4	560.7	402.7	122.3	35.7	42.1	391.1	349.0	630.2	262.7	367.5	3,228.9	3,222.5	1.8	.1	2.8
IV	3,219.0	2,020.0	240.4	765.2	1,014.3	517.9	397.0	110.4	10.6	45.3	389.8	344.5	635.9	267.5	368.4	3,208.5	3,173.8	−5.5	−2.5	−5.9
1982: I	3,170.4	2,031.2	247.7	764.2	1,019.2	464.2	387.0	101.2	−24.0	40.4	374.1	333.7	634.6	267.0	367.7	3,194.4	3,130.0	−5.9	−1.7	−5.4
II	3,179.9	2,041.0	249.1	768.3	1,023.5	467.5	369.5	103.4	−5.4	41.7	378.5	336.8	629.7	260.5	369.2	3,185.3	3,138.2	1.2	−1.1	1.1
III	3,154.5	2,051.8	251.8	772.8	1,027.2	448.6	358.0	100.1	−9.4	11.7	359.5	347.8	642.5	273.8	368.6	3,164.0	3,142.9	−3.2	−2.6	.6
IV	3,159.3	2,078.7	262.0	778.6	1,038.1	408.8	352.3	115.8	−59.3	11.7	336.0	324.3	660.1	289.5	370.6	3,218.6	3,147.6	.6	7.1	.6
1983: I	3,186.6	2,094.2	263.3	786.3	1,044.6	427.1	341.6	127.8	−42.3	16.1	342.5	326.4	649.2	278.2	371.0	3,228.9	3,170.5	3.5	1.3	2.9
II	3,258.3	2,135.1	280.0	795.7	1,059.4	486.9	348.8	147.4	−9.3	−14.6	341.7	356.3	650.9	278.5	372.4	3,267.6	3,273.0	9.3	4.9	13.6
III	3,306.4	2,163.0	288.5	806.2	1,068.3	524.8	363.9	161.9	−1.0	−35.0	352.8	387.8	653.6	277.6	376.0	3,307.4	3,341.4	6.0	5.0	8.6
IV	3,365.1	2,191.9	300.5	812.7	1,078.6	577.2	390.4	159.9	27.0	−46.2	355.5	401.6	642.2	266.0	376.2	3,338.1	3,411.3	7.3	3.8	8.6
1984: I	3,451.7	2,212.1	312.6	814.5	1,085.0	655.2	401.3	170.5	83.4	−68.6	362.7	431.3	653.0	271.5	381.6	3,368.3	3,520.3	10.7	3.7	13.4
II	3,498.0	2,246.7	322.5	828.2	1,096.1	658.4	422.0	173.1	63.2	−87.3	369.1	456.5	680.2	295.6	384.7	3,434.8	3,585.4	5.5	8.1	7.6
III	3,520.6	2,257.3	324.3	829.6	1,103.5	664.2	433.0	170.3	60.9	−85.5	378.7	464.1	684.5	295.5	388.9	3,459.6	3,606.0	2.6	2.9	2.3
IV	3,535.2	2,281.1	333.1	831.2	1,116.8	655.7	444.4	169.6	41.7	−94.8	376.6	471.4	693.2	300.5	392.7	3,493.5	3,630.0	1.7	4.0	2.7
1985: I	3,577.5	2,319.1	344.8	838.2	1,136.2	634.3	448.2	170.3	15.8	−81.4	371.2	452.6	705.5	309.0	396.4	3,561.7	3,658.9	4.9	8.0	3.2
II	3,599.2	2,337.4	350.3	843.0	1,144.1	647.5	457.8	172.9	16.9	−102.4	367.6	470.0	716.7	313.3	403.4	3,582.3	3,701.6	2.4	2.3	4.8
III	3,635.8	2,375.9	369.1	850.0	1,156.8	618.1	447.1	175.0	−4.0	−107.9	362.6	470.5	749.8	340.9	408.9	3,639.8	3,743.8	4.1	6.6	4.6
IV	3,662.4	2,386.9	356.4	858.3	1,172.2	648.0	460.9	179.4	7.7	−125.3	367.4	492.6	752.7	340.6	412.1	3,654.7	3,787.6	3.0	1.6	4.8
1986: I	3,721.1	2,410.9	363.7	870.1	1,177.1	676.1	448.5	185.7	41.9	−110.0	392.9	502.9	744.1	324.4	419.6	3,679.2	3,831.0	6.6	2.7	4.7
II	3,704.6	2,432.4	374.5	879.8	1,178.0	642.3	438.7	196.5	7.1	−131.2	389.6	520.7	761.2	335.4	425.7	3,697.6	3,835.8	−1.8	2.0	.5
III	3,712.4	2,464.4	401.9	879.1	1,183.4	625.1	430.9	200.1	−5.9	−142.3	399.6	541.9	765.2	334.2	430.9	3,718.3	3,854.7	.8	2.3	2.0
IV	3,733.6	2,477.8	397.5	883.5	1,196.8	615.2	435.7	200.3	−20.8	−135.4	406.5	541.9	776.0	342.4	433.6	3,754.4	3,869.0	2.3	3.9	1.5
1987: I	3,783.0	2,478.3	376.1	887.7	1,214.5	646.3	430.9	197.3	18.1	−118.2	418.7	536.9	776.6	338.1	438.5	3,764.9	3,901.2	5.4	1.1	3.4
II	3,823.5	2,507.7	389.3	889.0	1,229.5	656.7	445.6	197.8	13.3	−115.9	439.5	555.4	774.9	334.7	440.1	3,810.1	3,939.3	4.4	4.9	4.0
III	3,872.8	2,536.5	403.8	891.8	1,240.9	671.7	472.8	192.1	6.8	−118.9	461.3	580.2	783.5	340.7	442.8	3,866.0	3,991.7	5.3	6.0	5.4
IV	3,935.6	2,532.3	389.4	892.9	1,250.0	721.1	472.7	191.9	56.6	−109.8	484.1	593.9	792.1	344.9	447.2	3,879.0	4,045.5	6.6	1.4	5.5
1988: I	3,974.8	2,570.8	408.4	896.6	1,265.9	707.0	483.6	189.1	34.3	−78.2	517.4	595.6	775.1	323.8	451.3	3,940.5	4,052.9	4.0	6.5	.7
II	4,010.7	2,586.8	414.8	899.2	1,272.8	713.5	497.8	194.2	21.5	−72.6	519.7	592.3	783.0	327.9	455.1	3,989.2	4,083.3	3.7	5.0	3.0
III	4,042.7	2,608.1	410.7	910.3	1,287.0	733.6	501.0	195.1	37.5	−74.9	531.9	606.9	775.9	319.8	456.1	4,005.2	4,117.6	3.2	1.6	3.4
IV	4,069.4	2,627.7	420.5	912.0	1,295.2	709.1	492.7	198.1	18.3	−73.8	551.4	625.2	806.4	343.9	462.5	4,051.0	4,143.2	2.7	4.7	2.5

NOTE.—GNP=Gross national product; CBI=Change in business inventories.

APPENDIX 14.1
(*Continued*)

Table 3.—Price Indexes and the Gross National Product Implicit Price Deflator

[Index numbers, 1982=100; quarterly data are seasonally adjusted at annual rates]

Year and quarter	Fixed-weighted price indexes														GNP IPD	Percent change from preceding period			
	GNP	Personal consumption expenditures				Fixed investment			Exports	Imports	Government purchases of goods and services			Final sales		FWPI		GNP IPD	GNP Chain price index
		Total	Durable goods	Nondurable goods	Services	Total	Nonresidential	Residential			Total	Federal	State and local			GNP	PCE		
1959	37.6	35.2	52.3	35.0	31.2	58.0	65.9	30.2	32.8	27.0	25.8	26.9	24.9	37.6	30.4	....	....	2.4	....
1960	38.1	35.7	52.1	35.5	31.9	58.1	66.1	30.3	33.5	27.3	26.4	27.3	25.7	38.1	30.9	1.4	1.5	1.6	1.5
1961	38.4	36.1	51.9	35.8	32.4	58.0	66.0	30.2	34.0	27.0	27.0	27.8	26.4	38.3	31.2	.7	.9	1.0	1.0
1962	38.7	36.4	51.7	36.0	32.9	58.0	66.1	29.9	34.1	26.7	27.8	28.4	27.3	38.7	31.9	.8	.9	2.2	1.2
1963	39.1	36.8	51.6	36.4	33.4	58.0	66.2	29.5	34.4	27.1	28.5	29.3	27.9	39.1	32.4	1.0	1.1	1.6	1.3
1964	39.6	37.2	51.9	36.8	33.9	58.2	66.4	29.6	34.8	27.7	29.3	30.1	28.5	39.5	32.9	1.2	1.2	1.5	1.5
1965	40.1	37.7	51.2	37.5	34.5	58.5	66.7	30.0	35.9	28.1	30.0	30.8	29.3	40.0	33.8	1.4	1.2	2.7	1.8
1966	41.1	38.5	50.6	38.7	35.4	59.3	67.4	30.8	37.1	29.1	31.3	32.0	30.6	41.0	35.0	2.5	2.2	3.6	3.0
1967	42.1	39.5	51.2	39.6	36.5	60.2	68.4	31.6	38.2	29.5	32.7	32.8	32.5	42.0	35.9	2.6	2.5	2.6	2.8
1968	43.7	41.0	52.6	41.2	38.0	61.4	69.5	33.1	39.3	30.1	34.5	34.5	34.4	43.6	37.7	3.7	3.8	5.0	4.3
1969	45.6	42.8	53.8	43.2	39.7	63.2	71.0	36.0	40.9	31.2	36.6	36.4	36.7	45.5	39.8	4.4	4.3	5.6	5.0
1970	47.2	44.7	55.0	45.2	41.9	61.5	68.4	37.4	43.3	33.4	39.6	39.5	39.6	47.2	42.0	3.6	4.6	5.5	5.2
1971	48.8	46.6	56.7	46.6	44.2	60.6	66.6	39.5	45.3	35.6	42.3	42.4	42.2	48.8	44.4	3.5	4.2	5.7	4.8
1972	50.3	48.3	57.1	48.2	46.1	59.8	65.0	41.6	46.5	37.8	45.2	46.0	44.6	50.2	46.5	2.9	3.5	4.7	4.2
1973	53.1	51.0	58.1	52.3	48.3	61.8	66.6	45.1	50.8	42.4	48.8	50.1	47.8	53.0	49.5	5.5	5.7	6.5	5.9
1974	57.2	55.8	61.6	59.0	52.0	64.4	68.5	50.1	59.8	54.5	53.5	54.8	52.6	57.2	54.0	7.8	9.4	9.1	8.9
1975	61.8	60.1	66.7	63.2	56.2	69.0	73.1	54.6	65.4	59.7	58.6	59.4	57.9	61.8	59.3	8.0	7.7	9.8	9.2
1976	65.1	63.5	70.4	65.4	60.4	71.4	75.2	58.4	67.4	61.3	62.2	62.4	62.0	65.1	63.1	5.3	5.6	6.4	5.9
1977	68.4	67.5	73.3	68.5	65.3	72.6	74.9	64.8	70.3	66.1	66.0	65.8	66.2	68.4	67.3	5.1	6.3	6.7	6.1
1978	72.7	72.2	77.3	73.1	70.2	74.5	75.0	72.5	74.5	71.3	70.9	70.6	71.2	72.6	72.2	6.2	7.0	7.3	7.2
1979	78.8	78.6	82.5	80.8	76.0	80.3	80.1	81.2	82.9	80.9	77.3	76.8	77.7	78.8	78.6	8.5	8.8	8.9	8.7
1980	86.1	86.8	89.6	89.6	84.0	86.9	86.1	89.4	90.5	96.3	86.3	86.4	86.2	86.1	85.7	9.3	10.5	9.0	9.0
1981	94.1	94.6	95.8	97.0	92.6	94.5	93.9	96.6	97.7	101.5	94.1	94.9	93.5	94.1	94.0	9.3	9.0	9.7	9.4
1982	100.0	100.0	100.0	100.0	100.0	100.0	100.0	100.0	100.0	100.0	100.0	100.0	100.0	100.0	100.0	6.2	5.6	6.4	6.3
1983	104.1	104.2	102.3	102.1	106.3	100.4	99.9	102.2	101.6	97.7	104.5	104.1	104.8	104.1	103.9	4.1	4.2	3.9	4.1
1984	108.3	108.4	104.1	105.2	111.8	101.5	100.2	106.0	104.3	97.5	109.2	108.0	110.1	108.2	107.7	4.0	4.0	3.7	3.9
1985	111.9	112.2	105.2	107.9	117.2	103.3	101.9	108.3	103.7	95.7	113.2	110.4	115.3	111.8	110.9	3.4	3.5	3.0	3.3
1986	114.9	115.3	106.5	107.8	123.1	105.7	104.2	110.9	103.6	94.0	115.5	110.6	119.2	114.8	113.8	2.7	2.7	2.6	2.5
1987	119.1	120.7	110.3	112.6	129.4	107.8	103.4	115.9	105.6	101.2	119.6	113.3	124.3	118.9	117.4	3.6	4.7	3.2	3.4
1988	124.1	125.9	112.9	117.2	135.5	111.3	109.0	119.5	111.2	106.3	125.1	117.9	130.4	124.0	121.3	4.2	4.3	3.3	3.7
1959: I	37.4	35.0	52.1	34.8	30.9	57.9	65.7	30.2	32.7	26.9	25.5	26.9	24.7	37.4	30.2	....	....	4.1	....
II	37.5	35.1	52.3	34.9	31.0	58.0	65.9	30.2	32.8	27.0	25.6	27.0	24.9	37.5	30.4	1.3	1.1	2.7	1.2
III	37.6	35.3	52.3	35.1	31.3	58.0	66.0	30.2	32.9	27.1	25.7	27.1	25.0	37.5	30.6	1.7	2.1	2.7	1.9
IV	37.8	35.5	52.3	35.3	31.5	58.1	66.1	30.2	33.0	27.1	25.9	27.2	25.1	37.7	30.6	1.4	1.9	0	1.6
1960: I	37.8	35.5	52.2	35.2	31.6	58.1	66.1	30.2	33.4	27.2	26.1	27.2	25.5	37.8	30.9	.9	.4	4.0	1.0
II	38.0	35.7	52.2	35.5	31.8	58.2	66.2	30.3	33.5	27.4	26.1	27.1	25.6	37.9	30.9	1.8	2.3	0	2.0
III	38.1	35.8	52.0	35.6	32.0	58.2	66.2	30.3	33.7	27.4	26.4	27.7	25.8	38.1	31.0	1.5	1.4	1.3	1.8
IV	38.2	36.0	51.8	35.8	32.2	58.1	66.1	30.3	33.6	27.2	26.6	27.7	25.9	38.1	31.0	.6	1.4	0	1.2
1961: I	38.2	36.0	51.8	35.8	32.3	58.1	66.1	30.2	33.6	27.2	26.7	27.7	26.1	38.2	31.0	.5	.8	0	.7
II	38.3	36.0	51.9	35.7	32.4	58.0	66.0	30.3	34.1	27.0	26.8	27.9	26.3	38.2	31.2	.5	−.1	2.6	.6
III	38.4	36.1	52.0	35.8	32.5	58.0	66.0	30.2	34.0	27.0	27.0	27.9	26.5	38.3	31.4	.8	1.2	2.6	1.1
IV	38.4	36.1	51.8	35.7	32.6	58.0	66.0	30.1	34.1	26.8	27.2	28.1	26.7	38.3	31.4	.5	.2	0	.7
1962: I	38.5	36.2	51.8	35.9	32.7	58.0	66.1	30.1	34.2	26.6	27.5	28.3	27.2	38.4	31.7	1.1	1.2	3.9	1.7
II	38.6	36.4	51.7	36.0	32.9	58.1	66.1	30.0	34.1	26.6	27.6	28.4	27.3	38.6	31.8	.9	1.4	1.3	1.3
III	38.7	36.4	51.7	36.0	33.0	58.1	66.1	29.9	34.1	26.6	27.7	28.5	27.4	38.6	31.9	.5	.7	1.3	.8
IV	38.8	36.5	51.5	36.2	33.1	58.0	66.1	29.7	34.2	26.6	28.0	29.0	27.4	38.7	32.2	1.1	1.1	3.8	1.8
1963: I	38.9	36.6	51.5	36.3	33.2	58.1	66.2	29.8	34.2	26.7	28.2	29.1	27.7	38.8	32.3	1.1	1.0	1.2	1.4
II	38.9	36.7	51.5	36.3	33.3	58.0	66.2	29.6	34.3	27.0	28.3	29.2	27.8	38.9	32.3	.9	.9	0	.9
III	39.0	36.9	51.6	36.5	33.5	58.0	66.2	29.3	34.3	27.2	28.4	29.2	27.9	39.0	32.4	1.1	1.6	1.2	1.1
IV	39.2	37.0	51.8	36.6	33.6	58.0	66.2	29.5	34.5	27.5	28.7	29.7	28.2	39.2	32.6	1.7	1.4	2.5	2.4
1964: I	39.3	37.1	52.1	36.8	33.7	58.0	66.3	29.3	34.5	27.6	28.8	29.9	28.3	39.3	32.7	1.3	1.5	1.2	1.3
II	39.4	37.2	51.9	36.8	33.8	58.1	66.3	29.5	34.6	27.7	29.0	30.1	28.4	39.4	32.8	.9	.5	1.2	1.1
III	39.6	37.3	51.8	36.9	34.0	58.3	66.4	29.8	34.9	27.7	29.2	30.2	28.6	39.5	33.0	1.2	1.0	2.5	1.7
IV	39.7	37.3	51.7	36.9	34.1	58.3	66.4	30.0	35.1	27.7	29.3	30.4	28.7	39.6	33.1	1.0	.8	1.2	1.3
1965: I	39.9	37.5	51.8	37.0	34.3	58.4	66.5	30.0	35.8	27.7	29.5	30.6	29.0	39.8	33.5	1.8	1.6	4.9	1.8
II	40.0	37.7	51.5	37.4	34.5	58.4	66.6	29.8	35.9	27.9	29.7	30.7	29.1	39.9	33.6	1.6	1.9	1.2	2.0
III	40.1	37.7	51.0	37.6	34.6	58.6	66.7	30.1	35.9	28.1	29.9	31.0	29.4	40.1	33.9	1.3	.8	3.6	2.2
IV	40.2	37.8	50.5	37.8	34.7	58.7	66.9	30.1	35.9	28.6	30.2	31.4	29.6	40.1	34.1	1.3	.8	2.4	2.2
1966: I	40.5	38.1	50.4	38.3	34.9	58.8	67.0	30.2	36.4	28.6	30.5	31.6	30.0	40.4	34.5	2.6	2.8	4.8	3.3
II	40.9	38.4	50.5	38.6	35.2	59.2	67.3	30.9	36.9	29.1	30.9	31.8	30.5	40.8	34.8	3.8	3.1	3.5	4.2
III	41.2	38.7	50.7	38.8	35.6	59.4	67.6	30.8	37.3	29.2	31.4	32.2	30.9	41.1	35.1	3.1	3.0	3.5	3.3
IV	41.5	39.0	50.9	39.1	35.9	59.7	67.9	31.3	37.8	29.3	31.6	32.3	31.3	41.4	35.5	3.3	3.3	4.6	3.3
1967: I	41.7	39.1	50.8	39.2	36.1	60.0	68.2	31.5	38.1	29.4	32.0	32.3	31.9	41.6	35.7	1.9	1.1	2.3	2.1
II	41.9	39.3	50.9	39.3	36.3	60.1	68.3	31.4	38.1	29.4	32.4	32.6	32.3	41.8	35.7	2.0	1.9	0	2.2
III	42.2	39.6	51.3	39.7	36.6	60.3	68.5	31.6	38.2	29.5	32.7	32.9	32.7	42.2	36.0	3.1	3.6	3.4	3.6
IV	42.6	40.0	51.8	40.1	37.0	60.5	68.7	31.8	38.4	29.6	33.2	33.6	33.1	42.5	36.4	3.8	3.6	4.5	4.3
1968: I	43.0	40.4	52.1	40.5	37.4	60.9	69.0	32.6	38.8	29.8	33.8	33.9	33.7	43.0	37.1	3.9	4.0	7.9	4.9
II	43.5	40.8	52.3	41.0	37.8	61.2	69.3	32.7	39.4	30.1	34.2	34.2	34.2	43.4	37.5	4.3	4.3	4.4	4.5
III	43.8	41.2	52.7	41.4	38.2	61.5	69.6	33.0	39.3	30.2	34.7	34.9	34.6	43.8	37.9	3.5	3.9	4.3	4.1
IV	44.4	41.6	53.1	41.9	38.6	62.1	70.2	33.9	39.6	30.4	35.3	35.3	35.2	44.3	38.5	4.8	4.5	6.5	5.5
1969: I	44.8	42.0	53.3	42.3	39.0	62.7	70.6	35.3	40.2	30.7	35.6	35.5	35.7	44.7	39.0	4.1	3.6	5.3	4.7
II	45.3	42.5	53.7	42.9	39.5	63.1	70.9	35.8	40.4	30.9	36.1	35.8	36.3	45.2	39.5	4.3	4.9	5.2	4.9
III	45.8	43.0	53.9	43.5	39.9	63.4	71.2	36.3	41.0	31.3	37.0	36.9	37.0	45.8	40.1	5.2	4.6	6.2	6.2
IV	46.4	43.5	54.3	44.1	40.5	63.7	71.4	36.8	42.0	32.0	37.5	37.3	37.6	46.3	40.6	4.6	5.2	5.1	5.1
1970: I	46.8	44.0	54.4	44.7	41.0	62.7	70.0	37.0	42.5	32.4	38.5	38.6	38.5	46.7	41.3	3.4	4.7	7.1	6.0
II	47.1	44.5	54.7	45.1	41.6	61.6	68.4	37.9	43.3	32.9	39.2	39.2	39.2	47.0	41.9	2.6	4.1	5.9	5.0
III	47.3	44.9	55.0	45.4	42.1	60.9	67.7	37.2	43.5	34.0	39.9	39.8	39.9	47.2	42.2	1.9	3.9	2.9	3.3
IV	47.8	45.5	55.9	45.8	42.8	60.7	67.4	37.6	43.9	34.5	40.5	40.4	40.5	47.7	42.7	4.1	5.4	4.8	5.2
1971: I	48.3	45.9	56.6	45.9	43.3	60.8	67.1	38.5	44.9	35.3	41.5	41.7	41.3	48.2	43.4	4.3	3.8	6.7	5.9
II	48.7	46.4	56.9	46.4	43.9	60.7	66.9	39.3	45.2	35.3	42.1	42.4	42.0	48.7	44.2	4.0	4.4	7.6	5.2
III	49.0	46.9	56.7	46.8	44.5	60.5	66.5	39.7	45.3	35.8	42.6	42.7	42.5	49.0	44.7	2.5	3.9	4.6	3.7
IV	49.3	47.2	56.4	47.1	45.0	60.4	66.1	40.4	45.7	36.1	43.1	43.4	42.8	49.3	45.3	2.3	2.8	5.5	3.4
1972: I	49.9	47.7	56.8	47.6	45.5	60.3	65.9	40.7	46.2	37.0	44.4	45.4	43.6	49.8	45.8	4.4	4.2	4.5	5.8
II	50.1	48.0	57.1	47.9	45.9	59.7	65.0	41.1	46.4	37.6	44.9	45.8	44.2	50.0	46.1	1.5	2.8	2.6	2.8
III	50.4	48.4	57.3	48.3	46.4	59.5	64.6	41.7	46.4	38.1	45.5	46.2	44.9	50.3	46.7	2.4	3.4	5.3	3.8
IV	50.9	48.9	57.2	48.9	46.8	59.7	64.5	42.8	47.1	38.7	46.2	47.0	45.6	50.8	47.3	3.9	3.7	5.2	4.8
1973: I	51.7	49.5	57.5	50.0	47.2	60.5	65.5	43.2	48.1	39.6	47.3	48.3	46.5	51.6	48.0	6.3	5.5	6.1	5.8
II	52.6	50.5	58.0	51.5	47.9	61.8	66.6	44.7	49.6	41.8	48.3	49.3	47.5	52.5	49.0	7.4	8.2	8.6	7.4
III	53.7	51.5	58.3	53.1	48.6	62.5	67.2	46.1	51.6	43.0	49.4	51.0	48.3	53.6	50.0	8.3	7.8	8.4	8.3
IV	54.4	52.4	58.5	54.5	49.4	62.5	67.0	46.7	53.8	45.5	50.2	51.9	49.0	54.4	51.2	5.9	7.7	10.0	6.8

Table 3.—Price Indexes and the Gross National Product Implicit Price Deflator—Continued

[Index numbers, 1982=100; quarterly data are seasonally adjusted at annual rates]

Year and quarter	GNP	PCE Total	PCE Durable goods	PCE Nondurable goods	PCE Services	Fixed inv. Total	Nonresidential	Residential	Exports	Imports	Gov. Total	Federal	State and local	Final sales	GNP IPD	FWPI GNP	FWPI PCE	GNP IPD	GNP Chain price index
1974: I	55.5	53.8	59.0	56.8	50.3	62.8	67.1	48.0	56.5	49.5	51.5	53.1	50.3	55.5	51.9	8.2	11.2	5.6	8.5
II	56.4	55.2	60.5	58.4	51.4	63.7	67.8	49.4	58.2	53.7	52.5	53.4	51.8	56.4	53.0	6.7	10.1	8.8	8.8
III	57.8	56.4	62.6	59.6	52.5	64.9	68.9	51.0	60.9	56.4	54.2	55.4	53.4	57.7	54.8	9.9	9.4	14.3	12.5
IV	59.3	57.8	64.4	61.1	53.6	66.3	70.4	52.2	63.8	58.3	55.9	57.4	54.8	59.3	56.3	11.2	10.0	11.4	12.3
1975: I	60.4	58.7	65.4	61.8	54.8	68.0	72.1	53.6	65.5	59.6	57.0	58.1	56.1	60.4	57.7	7.8	6.7	10.3	9.3
II	61.1	59.4	66.4	62.3	55.6	68.9	73.1	54.2	65.2	60.3	57.9	58.6	57.4	61.1	58.6	4.6	4.9	6.4	6.0
III	62.3	60.6	67.1	63.8	56.6	69.2	73.4	54.6	65.2	59.5	59.0	59.7	58.6	62.2	59.9	7.7	8.4	9.2	8.3
IV	63.3	61.7	68.1	64.7	57.8	69.8	73.8	55.7	65.7	59.6	60.3	61.1	59.6	63.3	61.0	6.7	6.9	7.6	7.2
1976: I	64.0	62.3	69.1	64.7	58.8	70.7	74.7	56.5	66.4	60.1	61.0	61.6	60.7	64.0	61.7	4.6	4.2	4.7	4.8
II	64.7	62.9	69.9	65.0	59.7	71.4	75.3	57.8	67.0	61.0	61.8	62.0	61.7	64.6	62.5	4.2	4.2	5.3	4.6
III	65.4	63.9	70.7	65.6	60.8	71.7	75.4	58.8	67.5	61.9	62.4	62.2	62.5	65.3	63.4	4.4	6.0	5.9	5.4
IV	66.3	64.8	71.8	66.2	62.1	71.8	75.2	60.3	68.6	62.2	63.4	63.6	63.3	66.3	64.5	5.9	6.2	7.1	6.8
1977: I	67.2	65.9	72.5	67.1	63.5	72.2	75.1	62.0	69.5	64.1	64.6	64.8	64.4	67.2	65.6	5.5	7.0	7.0	6.2
II	68.1	67.0	72.9	68.1	64.7	72.6	75.1	64.1	70.6	65.8	65.6	65.4	65.8	68.1	66.9	5.6	6.8	8.2	6.7
III	68.7	68.0	73.5	69.0	66.0	72.5	74.6	65.0	70.3	67.0	66.2	65.3	66.8	68.7	67.7	3.4	6.2	4.9	4.7
IV	69.7	69.0	74.4	69.7	67.1	73.1	74.6	68.0	70.7	67.6	67.8	67.6	68.0	69.7	68.9	6.0	5.6	7.3	7.5
1978: I	70.7	70.0	75.3	70.6	68.3	73.1	74.4	68.6	72.1	69.0	69.0	69.1	69.0	70.6	69.9	5.4	6.3	5.9	5.8
II	72.0	71.6	76.6	72.7	69.6	73.9	74.7	71.5	73.8	70.9	70.1	69.7	70.3	71.9	71.6	7.7	9.3	10.1	9.1
III	73.2	72.9	78.0	74.0	70.9	74.7	75.0	73.7	74.8	72.0	71.4	70.6	71.9	73.2	72.9	7.0	7.5	7.5	7.8
IV	74.7	74.2	79.2	75.3	72.2	75.9	75.9	76.2	76.9	73.3	73.3	73.0	73.5	74.7	74.4	8.7	7.6	8.5	9.1
1979: I	76.3	75.8	80.5	77.4	73.4	77.6	77.6	77.8	79.5	75.8	74.5	74.1	74.9	76.2	76.1	8.3	8.7	9.5	8.4
II	78.0	77.6	81.9	79.8	74.9	79.6	79.5	80.2	82.3	78.6	76.0	75.2	76.5	78.0	77.8	9.6	10.0	9.2	9.6
III	79.7	79.5	83.0	81.9	76.8	81.3	80.9	82.7	84.0	82.3	77.9	77.0	78.6	79.7	79.4	8.7	9.9	8.5	8.1
IV	81.3	81.4	84.6	83.9	78.7	82.6	82.1	84.2	85.6	86.8	80.8	80.9	80.7	81.3	81.0	8.7	9.9	8.3	8.2
1980: I	83.2	83.7	86.9	86.6	80.8	84.3	83.7	86.3	87.6	92.4	83.0	82.7	83.3	83.2	82.7	9.4	12.1	8.7	9.0
II	85.1	85.8	88.8	88.6	82.9	86.2	85.4	89.1	88.9	95.3	85.4	85.3	85.4	85.1	84.6	9.5	10.1	9.5	9.4
III	86.9	87.8	90.5	90.6	85.1	87.9	87.0	90.9	91.4	98.1	86.8	86.2	87.2	86.9	86.5	9.0	9.9	9.3	9.4
IV	89.3	90.0	92.2	92.8	87.3	89.2	88.5	91.7	94.4	100.0	90.0	91.4	88.9	89.3	89.0	11.3	10.2	12.1	11.3
1981: I	91.5	92.2	93.4	95.4	89.5	91.4	90.7	94.0	96.6	101.9	91.7	92.6	91.0	91.4	91.3	10.0	10.2	10.7	9.8
II	93.1	93.8	95.2	96.5	91.4	93.4	92.8	95.4	97.4	102.5	93.1	93.7	92.7	93.1	92.8	7.5	7.4	6.7	7.5
III	95.1	95.5	96.7	97.6	93.8	95.6	94.8	98.1	98.0	100.2	94.6	95.0	94.3	95.1	94.9	8.8	7.6	9.4	9.0
IV	96.9	97.1	98.0	98.4	95.8	97.7	97.1	99.6	98.7	101.0	96.8	98.1	95.9	96.9	96.7	7.7	6.4	7.8	7.9
1982: I	98.2	98.3	98.9	99.2	97.4	99.2	98.8	100.5	99.7	101.4	98.1	98.7	97.7	98.2	98.2	5.7	5.2	6.4	5.9
II	99.4	99.1	99.9	99.2	98.9	100.0	100.0	100.2	100.1	100.0	99.4	99.6	99.2	99.4	99.4	4.7	3.5	5.0	4.8
III	100.7	100.7	100.5	100.8	100.8	100.6	100.7	100.4	100.1	99.3	100.5	100.0	100.9	100.7	100.8	5.5	6.3	5.8	5.6
IV	101.7	101.8	100.7	101.0	102.7	100.2	100.5	99.1	100.0	99.3	102.0	101.7	102.2	101.7	101.7	4.0	4.8	3.6	4.1
1983: I	102.6	102.6	101.4	100.7	104.3	100.7	100.3	101.9	100.4	98.3	103.0	102.8	103.2	102.6	102.5	3.6	2.8	3.2	3.7
II	103.6	103.7	101.7	102.0	105.5	99.9	99.7	100.4	101.0	97.4	103.9	103.7	104.1	103.5	103.3	3.8	4.6	3.2	3.6
III	104.6	104.8	102.5	102.7	106.9	100.6	99.9	103.2	101.7	97.7	105.0	104.5	105.3	104.6	104.2	4.2	4.1	3.5	4.4
IV	105.7	105.8	103.4	103.3	108.4	100.5	99.6	103.3	103.2	97.6	106.0	105.4	106.4	105.6	105.4	4.0	4.1	4.7	3.9
1984: I	106.8	107.0	103.5	104.6	109.7	100.4	99.5	103.5	103.9	97.7	107.7	106.9	108.2	106.8	106.5	4.5	4.5	4.2	4.5
II	107.8	107.9	104.1	104.9	111.1	101.4	99.9	106.4	104.9	98.1	108.8	107.8	109.6	107.8	107.3	3.8	3.2	3.0	3.8
III	108.7	108.9	104.3	105.4	112.6	101.8	100.4	106.9	104.5	97.4	109.6	108.1	110.7	108.7	108.2	3.4	3.8	3.4	3.4
IV	109.6	109.7	104.5	106.0	113.8	102.3	100.9	107.2	104.0	96.8	110.7	109.0	111.9	109.5	109.2	3.2	3.2	3.0	3.1
1985: I	110.6	110.6	105.0	106.6	115.0	102.6	101.1	107.9	103.8	95.2	112.1	110.4	113.4	110.5	109.7	3.8	3.2	3.7	3.7
II	111.5	111.7	105.1	107.7	116.4	102.9	101.5	107.9	103.9	95.6	112.8	110.9	114.9	111.4	110.6	3.3	4.2	3.3	3.2
III	112.3	112.6	105.1	108.1	117.9	103.5	102.2	108.2	103.5	95.3	113.4	110.0	115.8	112.2	111.3	2.8	3.3	2.6	2.6
IV	113.2	113.8	105.4	109.1	119.5	104.2	102.8	109.0	103.4	96.8	114.4	111.0	117.0	113.1	112.2	3.3	4.3	3.3	3.2
1986: I	113.8	114.3	105.7	108.4	120.8	104.7	103.3	109.7	103.6	95.9	114.9	110.9	117.8	113.7	112.4	2.2	1.6	.7	1.7
II	114.4	114.4	106.0	106.8	122.2	105.5	104.1	110.3	103.5	92.5	115.1	110.5	118.4	114.3	113.2	2.1	.5	2.9	1.7
III	115.3	115.6	106.9	107.7	123.8	105.9	104.4	111.2	103.3	92.9	115.4	110.0	119.4	115.1	114.6	2.9	4.2	5.0	3.1
IV	116.1	116.7	107.5	108.3	125.4	106.4	104.8	112.1	103.5	94.7	116.6	110.7	121.0	116.0	115.1	3.1	3.9	1.8	2.7
1987: I	117.4	118.5	108.7	110.4	127.0	106.9	105.1	113.2	104.2	97.9	118.0	112.1	122.3	117.2	116.0	4.3	6.1	3.2	4.1
II	118.5	120.2	109.8	112.4	128.5	107.3	105.2	114.9	105.1	100.4	119.0	113.0	123.5	118.4	117.1	4.1	5.8	3.8	3.8
III	119.6	121.4	110.9	113.3	130.2	108.1	105.4	117.4	105.8	101.9	120.2	113.6	125.1	119.5	117.9	3.8	4.4	2.8	3.7
IV	120.8	122.8	111.6	114.3	131.9	108.7	106.0	118.2	106.5	103.3	121.3	114.5	126.4	120.6	118.6	3.8	4.5	2.4	3.3
1988: I	121.9	123.6	111.9	114.7	133.2	110.1	107.5	119.2	108.1	104.5	123.1	116.3	128.1	121.8	119.2	3.8	2.6	2.0	3.3
II	123.3	125.1	112.4	116.6	134.7	111.0	108.6	119.3	110.0	106.1	124.4	117.4	129.6	123.2	120.6	4.8	5.1	4.8	4.3
III	124.9	126.6	113.2	118.1	136.2	111.5	109.3	119.3	112.6	106.2	125.9	118.7	131.2	124.8	121.9	5.2	4.6	4.4	4.4
IV	126.2	128.1	114.1	119.4	138.1	112.7	110.5	120.1	113.3	107.3	126.9	119.3	132.6	126.1	123.3	4.3	4.9	4.7	4.1

NOTE.—GNP=Gross national product; PCE=Personal consumption expenditures; IPD=Implicit price deflator; FWPI=Fixed-weighted price index.

Appendix 14.2

The Fed's Beige Book: Summary of Commentary on Current Economic Conditions by Federal Reserve District

SEPTEMBER 1990

TABLE OF CONTENTS

Sixth District—Atlanta
Seventh District—Chicago
Eighth District—St. Louis
Ninth District—Minneapolis
Tenth District—Kansas City
Eleventh District—Dallas
Twelfth District—San Francisco

The Federal Reserve System is comprised of a central body in Washington called the Board of Governors, plus twelve regional Reserve Banks. The framers of the Federal Reserve Act thought in 1914 when the legislation was passed that this unwieldy construction would prevent too much power from being consolidated at the seat of the government, but that it would also serve as a concise information-gathering system for a disparate economy operating over the 3,000 miles of the North American continent. So, from the earliest, the Banks have maintained large economic research and analytical staffs. As a consequence, at FOMC meetings, the Reserve Bank Presidents are expected to contribute information about regional economic trends. This reporting has been formalized in the Beige Book, which summarizes District conditions.

The Beige Book is prepared by each area, but summarized at one Bank (preselected from a rotating schedule) prior to being circulated to Fed staff and voting members before each FOMC meeting. The footnote to the Summary indicates the Beige Book reproduced here was summarized at the Dallas Fed and is based on survey information gathered before September 11, 1990. While economists tend to believe the Beige Book follows recent statistical developments, there is some additional information, however tentative, to be gained from reading the Book in the context of prior conditions. Also, reports in the Beige Book may be prejudiced by its writers, summarizers, or reviewers. In this respect, the disclaimer in the footnote that this does not reflect the views of Fed officials is probably untrue.

The Reserve Bank Presidents are the chief executive officers of their institutions. They are appointed by the Board of Directors of each Bank, with the approval of the Fed Board of Governors, to renewable five year terms. For the most part, the Presidents are career appointees with broad experience in banking matters and economic research. They are usually reappointed, so they range in age from the mid-40s to close to the mandatory retirement 65 and have been in office from two to over 18 years. Even with this degree of professionalism, the Beige Book may be prejudiced by the leanings of the staff or Presidents. So each District in the Beige Book reproduced here has been annotated.

SUMMARY*

Economic activity is expanding more slowly or declining in most Federal Reserve districts, but several districts report continued, modest growth. Weakness is most apparent in the northeastern and mid-Atlantic districts. Although patterns of consumer spending vary widely among districts, rates of increase are generally slowing. The districts' assessments of manufacturing activity range from moderate expansion to absolute declines. On average, however, there seems to be little movement in orders or production. Signs of a construction downturn are widespread, but not universal. While drought persists in some agricultural areas, soil moisture conditions are good or at least improved in most reporting districts. So far, the recent increase in oil prices has not affected domestic oil and gas drilling. Several district reports of credit markets focus on soft loan demand and some district banks offer examples of tighter credit conditions.

*Prepared at the Federal Reserve Bank of Dallas and based on information gathered before September 11, 1990. This document summarizes comments received from businesses and other contacts outside the Federal Reserve and is not a commentary on the views of Federal Reserve officials.

Consumer Spending

Retail sales patterns vary widely among districts, but growth appears to be ebbing. While Minneapolis cites "good" sales increases, Atlanta and Boston note flat to modest expansion. New York and Philadelphia report absolute declines in dollar volumes from a year earlier. Sales of big ticket items are said to be particularly soft, but clothing sales continue to show strength in some districts. Several districts mention the negative impacts of higher oil prices. Despite demand weakness in some districts, most retailers say their inventories are at desired levels.

Auto sales are up in Minneapolis and Cleveland but are weak or slowing in Atlanta, St. Louis, Kansas City, and San Francisco. One district says that credit tightening has caused some potential auto buyers difficulty in finding financing.

Manufacturing

Demand for manufactured products shows little overall change in either direction. Minneapolis and San Francisco characterize their manufacturing sectors' performances as mixed, while growth in Atlanta is moderate except for construction and auto-related products. Orders to Boston, Richmond, and Philadelphia firms are down, and sales have not changed lately in the Dallas District.

Sales patterns differ greatly among industries. Atlanta, Chicago, Cleveland, Dallas, and San Francisco mention strength in demand for primary metals, while Boston and Dallas note weakness in orders for computer, and some construction-related products. Some districts report increased producer uncertainty about future demand.

In some cases, export demand appears to be stronger than domestic sales. Richmond notes exports of manufactures as among the few district manufacturing indicators that are not negative. Minneapolis says that strong foreign demand for producers' equipment has more than compensated for declines in domestic orders. In the Boston district, however, export sales are below a year earlier.

With respect to changing costs of operation, a number of districts cite rising freight costs in the wake of energy price hikes. Several districts, including Philadelphia, Richmond, and Chicago report increasing prices of inputs, but Atlanta reports prices of industrial commodities as steady.

Construction and Real Estate

References to declining construction activity and weakening real estate markets are common. Increases in homebuilding in the Dallas and Minneapolis markets are exceptions, but Minneapolis also notes marked declines in overall construction contract values in the Minneapolis-St. Paul area. While Kansas City mentions recent upturns in housing starts, homebuilding there remains below a year earlier. According to the San Francisco report, construction activity is slowing in many parts of the west. Moreover, Boston, Chicago, St. Louis and New York all refer to weakening residential construction or weak housing sales and Cleveland notes high office and retail vacancy rates. Several reports say that respondents expect continued construction weakness in the near future.

Agriculture

Reports on agricultural production are generally positive, in part, because the soil moisture problems mentioned in the last beige book have ameliorated. In the Richmond District, rainfall in August was mostly above normal and soil moisture levels are now said to be adequate, but the dry weather in June has lowered corn yields. The Dallas District reports that rainfall has improved soil conditions there. Crop conditions are also good in the Chicago, Kansas City, and Minneapolis districts. Inadequate soil moisture continues to impede crop development in portions of the St. Louis district. The St. Louis and Dallas districts discuss the negative effects upon rice prices of the embargo on sales to Iraq. St. Louis also notes that recent increases in freight and insurance costs have discouraged exports to other Middle Eastern countries. Several district reports mention generally falling grain prices.

Energy

Despite marked increases in oil prices in the wake of Iraq's invasion of Kuwait, reporting districts say they have seen few effects on drilling so far. Dallas and Kansas City note recent declines in drilling activity, although the rig count remains above a year earlier in both districts. Moreover, industry observers in both districts say they do not expect the recent price shock to have much of an effect until oil prices remain high for an extended period and natural gas prices rise as well.

Finance and Credit

Most reporting districts say that lending activity is soft. Atlanta, Cleveland, and Philadelphia all mention recent slowdowns in lending, while New York notes signs of weaker demand for business loans. St. Louis cites slow loan growth at the large banks, but Kansas City district bankers report moderate increases in loan demand—including demand for commercial and industrial, consumer, and home mortgage loans. Financial organizations in several districts note tightening credit policies for at least some borrower groups. Banks' and thrifts' concerns over the viability of economic growth is said to have discouraged some lending.

FIRST DISTRICT—BOSTON

The First Fed District spreads over Massachusetts and most of New England. President Richard Syron (b. 1943) was appointed on January 1, 1989 and holds a Ph.D. in economics from Tufts University. His prior work experience includes stints at the U.S. Treasury and as former Fed Chairman Volcker's assistant at the Board. Because of this association, he is generally considered an inflation hawk, though he is not dogmatic and generally votes with the FOMC's majority. The Boston Reserve Bank staff is very professional and highly regarded in the economics field. Their economic commentary in the Beige Book tends to be concise and based on business sectors but does not stem from primary surveys. In September 1990, the commentary indicates that district conditions were poor and slipping further.

Economic activity continues to slow in the First District. Retailers and wholesalers generally report flat or marginally higher sales compared to a year ago, but some are recording substantial declines. Most manufacturers are finding 1990 tougher than expected. A majority of manufacturing contacts face sales below year-ago levels, and several are eating into their order backlogs. Three-fourths have cut employment levels, and half are paring their capital spending plans. Neither retailers nor manufacturers see reason to expect improvement during the next 6 to 12 months, although some retailers believe their promotional activities or cost controls provide a buffer against the poor economic climate.

Retail

For the most part, retailers and wholesalers report flat or marginally higher sales compared to a year ago. Only pharmaceutical sales are said to be rising at a double-digit rate. Some retailers are experiencing declines of up to 20 to 30 percent for building materials and higher-priced clothing. Respondents generally note that consumers are emphasizing essentials, trading down, and shopping around for bargains. Sales in the northern areas are holding up better than in the three southern states and the southern parts of New Hampshire and Maine.

Respondents report little increase in prices, and many durable goods prices are down from a year ago. About half the sample reported that gross margins are stable, and half declining.

In the context of much negative economic news, the majority of respondents expressed satisfaction with successful strategies in advertising and promotions, or in control of inventory and capital costs. No respondent expects an upturn soon. The majority think that demand will be flat for another year, but a significant minority expect further declines before the economy stabilizes.

Manufacturing

According to First District manufacturers, this year is turning out to be "rougher than expected." A majority of these firms report that shipments are flat to down from year-ago levels, with declines ranging from 2 to 10 percent. The respondents with sales increases saw gains of 2 to 6 percent. Companies reporting slowing orders or dwindling backlogs outnumber those seeing improvement.

Products reported to be facing relatively strong demand include "recession proof" consumer necessities, plastics for the auto industry (where current production levels may reflect strike preparations) and equipment with long lead times, such as power-generating and medical systems. Demand is weak for paper goods and for products related to the computer, construction or defense industries. Even the export markets appear less robust. Only one firm reports strong export growth (albeit slower than in 1989); others mentioning exports say they are flat or down versus their 1989 performance. Accordingly, while a majority of contacts describe their inventory levels as satisfactory, a sizable minority find them excessive and are trying to bring them down.

In this environment, all respondents describe materials prices as stable or below 1989 levels so far. They mention declines in prices for metals and computer components in particular. By contrast, in the aftermath of recent oil price increases, plastics prices are expected to rise by year-end. As for selling prices, while discounting prevails in the computer industry, one-half of all respondents have raised prices in 1990, generally by 3 to 5 percent.

Employment and capital spending plans are being cut. Three-fourths of the First District manufacturing respondents have reduced their employment levels—by 2 to 15 percent—during 1990. Over one-fourth expect additional layoffs before year-end. Most contacts had budgeted capital spending for 1990 to be equal to or less than 1989 levels. Half have now pared these spending plans or have made "judicious delays."

A minority of First District manufacturers contacted expect 1991 to be flat with 1990. The rest are less sanguine and, "seeing problems everywhere," are revising their forecasts downward. They cite the bite of decreased defense spending, deferred capital spending, declining consumer confidence, high debt levels, conservative banks, and, most recently, uncertainty about the Middle East and the price of oil.

Residential Real Estate

First District realtors agree that the real estate market is slow this summer. A general uneasiness about the regional economy is the most frequently cited cause. Realtors also feel that recent world events and uncertainty over the national economy have contributed to the slowdown. Prices are falling; sellers are listing their homes at more realistic levels in order to move them, and smaller homes (for first-time buyers) are selling better than larger homes. New construction has slowed considerably since this time last year. Realtors do not expect an upswing in home sales this fall unless the regional economy turns around.

SECOND DISTRICT—NEW YORK

The Second District covers New York, a few counties in Connecticut, and northern New Jersey. E. Gerald Corrigan (b. 1941), the President since 1985, is a permanent voting member of the FOMC, reflecting the pride of place that New York has in the financial system in the U.S. Corrigan holds a Ph.D. in financial economics from Fordham University and is a career Fed staffer who was also once an assistant to

Fed Chairman Volcker. He is also considered an inflation hawk, though his is a safe vote because he almost always supports the Fed Chairman. The huge New York District research staff, whose members enjoy the most prestige in the System, generally follows a GNP model in reporting about economic developments (note the subdivisions—consumer spending and construction). While this summary admits that District conditions are soft, note the upbeat tone and attempt to point out positive developments. This may be a hint that officials in the second District were not convinced that easier Fed policy was necessary to counter a weak economy.

Developments in the Second District economy continued mixed to somewhat soft during recent weeks. On the positive side, unemployment rates remained below the national average and the pace of office leasing was good in much of the region. Retailers reported disappointing sales results, however, and homebuilders reported no improvement in market conditions. Most respondents surveyed at small and medium-size banks described current economic conditions as soft or slow.

Consumer Spending

District retailers reported disappointing sales results since they were last contacted and a worsening of conditions as the period progressed. All our contacts reported year-over-year declines in August as consumers seemed increasingly reluctant to spend. This compares with over-the-year sales gains that were somewhat below plan but, in most cases, positive during July. Big ticket items such as furniture and rugs were especially hard-hit and other types of home furnishing were also weak. Sales of men's and women's apparel showed some improvement, though.

Over-the-year sales results in July ranged widely—from −6 percent to +14 percent—but in August results clustered in a −10 percent to −2 percent range. Despite the below-plan sales volume, however, inventories were reported at comfortable levels and, in some cases, below plan. One retailer did remark that if consumer spending continues weak, a cutback in the targeted level of inventories will probably take place.

Residential Construction and Real Estate

District homebuilders report no improvement in market conditions during recent weeks. In downstate New York and northern New Jersey residential construction activity continues to be very slow and respondents do not anticipate an improvement in the foreseeable future. Housing starts have also declined in some upstate New York areas, but the over-the-year slowdown was from a previously high level of activity and has not been as severe as in other parts of the region. The shortage of credit for acquisition and construction loans continues to be a problem. In addition, some respondents noted that potential buyers are hesitant because of softness in the economy and uncertainly about the impact of the Middle East crisis.

The pace of office leasing remained good in much of the District during recent weeks as tenants continued to avail themselves of generous landlord concessions. Leasing in midtown Manhattan also expanded. However, with the addition of two newly completed buildings in mid-Manhattan, the midtown vacancy rate moved somewhat higher though the downtown rate held steady. Westchester County reports a reduction in the amount of leasing activity as very few large-scale transactions have recently taken place, and the absorption of vacant space in northern New Jersey has also slowed.

Other Business Activity

District unemployment rates remained below the national average in August. New York's rate declined to 5.0 percent from 5.3 percent in July while New Jersey's rate was unchanged at 4.8 percent. Employment conditions vary greatly within the District, however, with increased weakness in the New York metropolitan area coupled with strength in some other areas. A recent BLS study found that during the first five months of this year a loss of several thousand private sector jobs occurred in New York City and northeastern New Jersey—the first drop in local private employment since 1982. On the other hand, some areas in upstate New York and parts of New Jersey have reportedly been experiencing labor shortages.

The percentage of Buffalo purchasing managers reporting an increase in new orders rebounded in August after a sharp drop in July. The percentage with stable or greater production also rose. In the July survey of Rochester managers, however, only 25 percent of respondents anticipated improved conditions over the next three months, down from 47 percent in June. The outlook for capital investment in both areas was described as generally weak.

Financial Developments

Most respondents surveyed at small and medium-size banks in the District described current economic conditions as soft or slow. All of the banks that make business loans reported weaker demand, while demand for consumer and home equity loans has been mixed. Although several bankers stated that real estate loan demand had declined significantly, two bankers noted increased activity in August after a decline in July.

Just under half of the bankers surveyed said that they had begun to tighten credit standards on all types of loans. Over sixty percent of those making business loans had tightened standards on those loans. While none of the surveyed banks have raised interest rates as a means of tightening credit, about half have reduced the maximum lines of credit available to new borrowers and increased collateral requirements. One banker stated that his bank will scrutinize loan applications more carefully because of an anticipated recession. All of the bankers tightening credit gave a less favorable economic outlook as the main reason, and almost three quarters cited a deterioration in the quality of their loan portfolios as well. About half mentioned that they had faced more loan defaults and increasing regulatory pressures. Of the banks which had not tightened credit only one expected to do so in the near future. Most of the others will continue to lend both because they have an adequate supply of funds, and because qualified borrowers are still in the market.

THIRD DISTRICT—PHILADELPHIA

The Third District includes most of Pennsylvania and southern New Jersey. Its President since 1981 has been Edward Boehne (b. 1940), a Ph.D. economist who has spent his career at the Fed. Boehne is a moderate who votes the Chairman's party line, so the Philadelphia staff is unlikely to prejudice its commentary to suit. Economic activity in this district was notably slipping in September 1990, and the Beige Book duly noted the situation. This concern probably reflected the concentration of heavy manufacturing in the area.

Economic activity in the Third District appeared to be slowing across the board in August and early September. Manufacturers reported a continuing decline in business, leading them to trim employment. Retailers generally indicated that sales in August fell from the prior month and year, and they said that the slowdown was continuing in September. Bankers reported a decline in overall lending triggered by a falloff in business and real estate lending; consumer lending continued to increase, but the pace of growth was slackening.

Business contacts expect the downward trend in business to continue. For the most part, they do not have positive views regardless of the outcome of the Middle East crisis. Manufacturers forecast declining activity over the next six months, and they plan to trim capital spending and to make more cuts in employment. Retailers say consumer confidence is ebbing, and they expect consumer spending this fall to drop below the year-ago level, in real terms. Bankers anticipate continued declines in business and real estate lending, and they expect consumer loan growth to slacken further. In general, bankers expect business to decline well into next year.

Manufacturing

According to Third District manufacturers contacted in late August business was generally declining. Half of the firms queried reported a drop in activity, and almost half indicated that business was flat; very few were experiencing improvement. Among the major manufacturing industries in the district, slowing business was reported by producers of lumber, rubber and plastics, primary metals, nonelectrical machinery, and transportation equipment. Business was generally steady for makers of apparel, textiles, electrical machinery, and fabricated metal products. Improvement was common only among chemical companies and producers of stone, clay, and glass products.

For the Third District manufacturing sector as a whole, shipments and orders were declining, prompting area firms to cut working hours and payrolls. In particular, makers of consumer goods reported that cutbacks in orders from retailers were becoming more widespread. Despite the drop in activity, inventories were edging down, overall.

The balance of opinion among Third District manufacturers contacted in late August is that business will continue to ease over the next two quarters. Overall, area firms plan to make further reductions in employment over the fall and winter months, and they plan to trim capital spending.

Despite their assessment that business is slowing, and will continue to do so, manufacturers reported spreading increases in input prices, and they expect further hikes. Most indicated that cost increases, current and anticipated, are for specialized inputs used directly in the production of the goods they make, and not necessarily for petroleum-based materials or for energy.

Retail

Third District retailers contacted in early September generally indicated that sales in August slowed from their early summer rate and that the dollar volume of sales for the month was below that of August of last year. Most also said that sales in the first week of September were below the year-ago period. According to merchants the slowdown has affected all categories of goods, including back-to-school merchandise.

Retailers said they believe consumer confidence is ebbing, and they expect the rest of the fall season to be slow. The consensus of forecasts is that sales through the rest of the year, in current dollars, will only equal the year-earlier period. Store officials did not express concern about current inventory levels, but they were being very cautious in their orders to suppliers, and they said extensive price markdowns are a possibility later in the season if consumer spending declines much further.

Finance

Total loan volume outstanding at major Third District banks has declined since mid-July, and bankers contacted in early September said the downtrend was continuing. Commercial and industrial lending was edging down, according to bank loan officers, partly due to implementation of tighter credit standards but mainly because of a falloff in demand for business credit. Real estate loan volume was declining as payoffs reduced outstandings at area banks while they were booking virtually no new real estate-based loans except home .equity credit lines. Bankers generally reported increases in personal lending, but they said the rate of growth appeared to be slipping. Auto loans were declining at most banks, while credit card lending was described as flat to up slightly by bankers.

Looking ahead, Third District bankers expect total loan volume to continue to fall. Several banks noted that requests for business financing, especially for capital investment, were tapering off. Most of the bankers contacted said they anticipate flat or declining economic activity through the rest of this year and into next, and they expect business lending to shrink over the same time period. They also expect real estate lending to continue to fade, and they anticipate slackening consumer loan demand.

FOURTH DISTRICT—CLEVELAND

The Fourth Fed District comprises Ohio, eastern Kentucky, and parts of Pennsylvania and West Virginia. President W. Lee Hoskins (b. 1941) holds a Ph.D. in economics from U.C.L.A. and has been in office since October 1987. He is another well known inflation hawk with broad background at the Fed and in banking. Note the cautious tone of the summary, which fails to come out and indicate the economy is falling. Instead, the note concentrates on inflation and the "big picture," which were more troubling than District conditions. This may reflect the President's leaning. Note also that manufacturing accounts for a large proportion of District jobs, so significant space is given to the auto, steel, and capital goods industries.

Summary

Fourth District respondents expect that the economic expansion will be sustained at least through the final quarter of 1991, despite short-run effects of the oil-price shock. The worst of the inflation bubble is expected to occur next quarter. The oil-price shock is expected to weaken consumer spending further, but District retailers generally report their August sales turned out to be better than expected. Manufacturers are cautious about short-term prospects for output, but generally acknowledge that effects of the oil-price shock so far have been relatively minimal. Lending activity by banks and thrifts appears to have slowed further in recent weeks.

The National Economy

District respondents generally expect that the expansion will be sustained at least through 1991, despite short-term dampening effects of the oil-price shock. A panel of 21 Fourth District economists expects that growth in real GNP will slow to about 1% between 1989:IVQ and 1990:IVQ, which is about one-half the increase they expected last May. Only a handful expect a two to three quarter contraction in real GNP, of 1% to 3% at annual rates, beginning either in 1990:IIIQ or 1990:IVQ, and extending into 1991:IQ. For 1991, the panel expects slow but steadily rising growth in output from the first quarter through the fourth quarter. The median forecast of real GNP shows growth of 1.9% for the year, somewhat less than they expected last May. There are no recession forecasts for 1991.

Inflation Outlook

The recent jump in crude oil prices is generally expected to have temporary effects on inflation. An inflation bubble is expected between 1990:IIIQ and 1991:IQ, with the worst of inflation expected to be at nearly a 5% annual rate next quarter. Thereafter, inflation is expected to revert to a 4% rate through the balance of the 1991. While most of the panel of 21 forecasters expects a temporary burst in prices at slightly below a 5% rate, several expect that the GNP implicit-price deflator will rise between a 5% and 9.5% rate into early 1991 before moderating.

Consumer Spending

The oil-price shock has weakened the near-term outlook for real consumer spending, according to the Fourth District panel of forecasters. They now believe that real consumer spending between 1990:IIQ and 1990:IVQ will increase by about 1% instead of the 2% they expected last May. Nevertheless, sales reported by retailers and producers of consumer goods in August were generally as good as, or better than, sales in July.

Department store retailers in this District are less optimistic about sales prospects for the fall season. Most report, however, that sales in August rose from July, but that increases were smaller than in the previous month. Retailers generally expect that price promotions will be necessary to sustain sales over the next few months. Retailers in Cleveland report that their back-to-school sales in August were as good as, or better than, sales last year. Auto retailers report August sales were about as expected, and, in some cases, better than in July. Some report a step-up in consumer interest in fuel-efficient cars, and most dealers report buyers are still leaning toward more expensive rather than mid-priced cars.

According to some auto producers, car sales in August were better than they expected in their pre-oil-shock forecasts. Some believe that the timing of the consumer confidence surveys may have biased the survey results, and expect future surveys to show some recovery in consumer confidence.

Manufacturing

District respondents in manufacturing and utilities are typically cautious about short-term prospects for production and profits because of uncertainties over the oil situation. They report no unusual deferments or cancellations of orders or spending in response to the oil-price shock. They emphasize a lessened dependence on oil, a more efficient capital stock that has been installed in anticipation of even higher real prices for oil than at present, and the relatively small price increase in crude oil now compared with episodes in the 1970s.

The steel industry is still operating at close to effective capacity, and producers report a strong third quarter for orders and production. A producer reports that orders for October are being booked at a good pace. There is a tone of less confidence over the short-term outlook because of uncertainty about the effects of the oil situation on the auto and appliance industries. Steel producers point out that their industry is more energy efficient now than even five years ago. Crude-oil costs are a relatively small part of production costs, but the added fuel cost will hurt already squeezed profit margins because additional costs cannot be passed through to steel consumers.

Some capital-goods producers are less optimistic about short-term output and spending plans, because they expect that the uncertainty over the oil situation will temporarily erode business confidence. Some expect that there could be a temporary deferring, or postponing, of short-lead-time equipment from this year into early next year. They also emphasize that capital stock additions in recent years anticipated real oil prices even higher than at present prices.

Auto production next quarter will likely exceed new car sales, barring work stoppages, but dealers' caution about holding inventories and deterioration in consumer confidence are likely to be constraints on auto output plans. Light truck output will be hampered by a 100-day inventory. Heavy-duty truck output is reviving slowly from a trough in late 1989 and early 1990, and output this quarter will likely be the best so far this year.

A major electric power utility in Ohio believes that the effect of the oil-price shock is minimal because their facilities have become marginal users of crude oil. Also, more efficient energy use by the utility's industrial accounts have sharply reduced the effects of oil price increases.

Financial Developments

Some banks and thrifts report a further slowing in lending activity in recent weeks. Mortgage interest rate increases of at least one-half point on fixed-rate mortgages since early August have dulled mortgage lending. Some lenders also state that concerns about rising delinquencies and increasing nonperforming loans that are reported nationally are contributing to more cautious lending policies. While some expect near-term cutbacks in consumer spending, they also believe that consumers will not curtail spending as much as most forecasters expect.

High office and retail vacancy rates in many metropolitan centers, coupled with tightened lending terms, have moved some developers to shift their operations into other kinds of construction. A large shopping mall developer, for example, will increasingly focus on construction of residential communities. Another developer has been moving into apartment construction from office building.

FIFTH DISTRICT—RICHMOND

The Fifth District, covering Maryland, Virginia, North and South Carolina, and most of West Virginia, is led by Robert Black (b. 1927). Black holds a Ph.D. in economics from the University of Virginia and is a career Fed employee who also feels strongly that inflation is a major economic danger. Since this is a well diversified district, with ports, tourism, high technology industries, and light manufacturing, it may weather economic woes well. But the Fifth District economists, who are generally more wordy and include more anecdotal evidence than their Northern counterparts, also note that their area slowed somewhat in late 1990.

Overview

District economic activity slowed somewhat in recent weeks. Retail stores, tourist areas, and manufacturing plants reported that business conditions softened. Higher oil prices raised manufacturers' costs and pushed up prices for finished goods. At financial institutions, the demand for consumer loans fell slightly. In most District areas that are highly sensitive to defense spending, business continued to slow. In some local economies heavily dependent on military personnel, the Mideast deployment crimped consumer demand. On a positive note, exports rose more than imports at District ports, and prospects for District farmers are generally good.

Consumer Spending

Retail activity apparently softened in August while profit margins shrank. Responses to our regular mail survey of retailers indicated that sales, especially of big ticket items, declined from July to August. Retail employment was also down from our previous survey. Two-thirds of our survey respondents reported increases in the prices they paid, while only one-third noted increases in the prices they charged.

District tourism was lackluster in the last month of the summer season. Our telephone survey of hotels, motels, and resorts indicated a slower August and Labor Day weekend than a year ago. Respondents who experienced declines blamed a generally weaker economy. Only one resort manager thought that higher gasoline prices kept tourists away. Most of those surveyed reported that fall bookings were about even with last year's. Respondents remained optimistic about tourist activity in coming months, but they were less so than in our previous survey.

Manufacturing

Our regular mail survey showed that manufacturing activity slowed from a month earlier. All survey indicators except prices and new export orders declined. Almost half of the producers identified poor sales as the most important problem they faced.

Virtually all manufacturers were adversely affected by higher crude oil prices. Raw materials prices and transportation costs rose for all but a few respondents. To adjust to these increased expenses, half said they had raised or would raise their prices, a third said they would try to decrease other nonemployment costs, and one-tenth planned to cut employment.

Manufacturers' assessments of current conditions and their forecasts were more pessimistic in August than in July. A larger majority believed that their local economies and the national economy weakened in the latest month, and only one-fifth now expect business conditions to improve in the next six months.

Ports

District port activity continued to shift toward exports, which rose in August from July and from a year ago. Imports were down from July but were generally unchanged from a year ago. All three major District Ports—Baltimore, Charleston, and Hampton Roads (Norfolk)—expect exports to increase faster than imports in coming months.

The volume of coal exports has apparently not yet been affected by developments in the Middle East. Some of the largest coal shippers, however, expect to export more if crude oil prices remain high.

Financial

A telephone survey of District financial institutions suggested that the demand for consumer loans fell slightly in August from July. More lenders reported decreases than increases in new consumer loans. Respondents indicated that declines in installment credit more than offset increases in revolving credit. Additionally, nearly all lenders reported no change in the rates charged on consumer loans in August.

Agriculture

As of the second week of September, the fall harvest was on schedule and most crop yields were expected to be about average around the District. Corn yields, however, will probably be below average in Virginia and in the Carolinas, due to June's hot, dry weather during the corn crop's crucial pollination period. Rainfall in August was above normal across most of the District, and soil moisture levels were reported to be generally adequate.

Defense Impacts

Business leaders in the Washington and Norfolk areas indicated that the adverse economic effects of defense budget cuts intensified this summer. They said that cutbacks in current and projected defense spending lowered the use of contract personnel and support services such as advertising, printing, and travel; they blamed these effects, in part, for continued declines in real estate values and construction activity.

The Mideast military deployment slowed business in parts of Virginia and the Carolinas. In areas where large numbers of military and support personnel had been stationed and were sent overseas, local business leaders said that retail sales were off sharply; automobiles, appliances, and fast food were particularly hard hit. Contacts in the Washington area noted that the Mideast crisis diverted defense funds away from local contractors that primarily provide long-term, research-oriented services, and toward items of immediate use in the field. The call-up of reserves and the departure of troops, many of whom held second jobs, depleted the supply of workers in some areas where labor markets were already tight. The Mideast deployment, however, evidently gave a boost to some District manufacturers. A textile producer, for example, recently received a large government order for tent fabric.

SIXTH DISTRICT—ATLANTA

The Sixth District covers the states of the Deep South, which are generally less developed and poorer than the norm. Finance, light manufacturing, and tourism are major industries. Robert Forrestal (b. 1931) is an attorney who has spent his career at the Fed, and has held the Presidency of the Atlanta Reserve Bank since December 1983. He is an inflation fighter, but staff take this report more seriously than in other districts. As a result, the data are obtained from more formalized surveys and the report tends better to reflect business sentiment in the area than the prejudices of the Bank's officers.

Overview

Business contacts throughout the Southeast indicate some further deceleration from the slow pace of growth reported in recent months. Uncertainties associated with the Mid East crisis and higher oil prices are reportedly adding to consumer caution. Retailers report that they are generally reducing orders for new inventory in light of anticipated consumer resistance and their expectations that sales growth will remain sluggish through the fourth quarter. Auto dealers confirm that sales remain soft and note particular weakness in the markets for high priced autos and used cars. District bankers indicate that growth in consumer and real estate lending was weak while commercial lending declined this past summer. Southeast manufacturers, however, still report generally moderate growth except for products related to the construction and auto industries. Shortages of skilled workers continue in a number of areas.

Retail

Reports from southeastern retailers indicate flat to modest sales growth during July and August relative to the same period of 1989. Expenditures on both durable and nondurable goods varied considerably around the District but generally durables were weak while apparel sales showed a bit of strength associated with back-to-school clothes purchases and summer clearances. A representative of a large retail chain indicated that furniture and fine jewelry sales were off significantly from 1989 levels in July and early August, for the first time this year. The general sentiment among southeastern retailers is that already weak consumer confidence has been negatively impacted by the Mid East crisis and oil price advances during the last six weeks. As a result, these retailers are reducing the size of their orders to manufacturers expecting that growth in sales will remain sluggish through the fourth quarter.

Auto dealers continue to report that sales were well below levels seen a year ago, especially during the first two weeks of August. Foreign models again sold better than domestic ones. A few dealers indicated consumers are more resistant to the higher priced models and said that sales of new autos priced under $15,000 were comparatively better. Some noted that it was too soon to detect any switch toward more fuel-efficient models.

Financial Services

Bankers in the District generally report that slow growth in real estate and consumer loans over the summer was not sufficient to offset declines in commercial lending. The weakness in commercial lending is said to be related to some deferred capital expansion plans and lean business inventories. A few bank contacts indicated they had further tightened credit standards in the last month. A number of others said they had not tightened standards but were adhering more closely to existing criteria. Most bankers, however, agreed that money is available for good projects and that reports of tighter credit seem exaggerated.

Growth of consumer loans in July and August was reportedly "anemic." Bankers indicate that demand for auto loans continues to weaken, but they continue to indicate a moderate expansion in home equity lending and single family mortgages.

Manufacturing

Manufacturers in the Southeast indicate moderate growth in sales except for construction and auto-related products. Paper mills are reported to be running at capacity levels, partially due to export activities and coal production is picking up. Pipe manufacturers report demand by the domestic oil and gas industry is strong. Chemical and plastic producers also noted a continuation of a recent slowdown from strong growth.

Weak new and existing home sales continue to impact the southeastern textile industry. Carpet producers indicate demand continues to be soft and that downward price pressures are evident at the wholesale level. They do not anticipate any improvement for some time. New layoffs by southeastern tire producers were reported and an auto assembly plant was closed for a week due to poor orders. Apparel producers note continuing weakness, adding that competition from imports is intense.

Wages and Prices

Scattered reports that skilled workers are in short supply continue to come in from around the region, especially from the oil and gas producing areas. But these shortages have not resulted in any new upward wage pressures. A union contact indicates that wages among his constituents rose 3.8 percent during the last 6 months compared to 3.5 percent for the previous 6 months. Prices of industrial commodities were steady, with the exception of sharp increases in the energy sector. Freight costs are reportedly up 1.5 percent since early August due to the recent fuel price increases. Most industries report that the higher energy costs are not yet being passed on to consumers.

SEVENTH DISTRICT—CHICAGO

The Seventh Fed District spans the farm belt and the industrial Midwest through southern Michigan and Wisconsin. President Silas Keehn (b. 1930) is a Harvard M.B.A. who spent many years at Mellon Bank and Pullman prior to being appointed Fed President in 1981. He is a moderate without strong monetary policy views. As a result, District staff tends to give accurate though brief contributions to the Beige reports. In September 1990, the Chicago area noted slow but uneven growth.

Summary

Economic conditions in the Midwest were somewhat uneven in August, but most of the District's economy continued on the slow growth path reported in recent months. Consumer spending in the District generally showed modest growth, except in Michigan. Purchasing manager surveys around the District gave mixed signals, but anecdotal evidence indicated slow expansion in the manufacturing sector. Construction and real estate activity slowed, but remained healthier in the Midwest than in the nation as a whole. While most large banks have not changed lending standards, some District loan officers reported a slight tightening, citing a less favorable economic outlook. District reports indicated no acceleration in the overall inflation rate since the recent rise in the price of oil. Crop conditions continued to be favorable.

Consumer Spending

Consumer spending growth in the District has been modest but stable in recent weeks, although local surveys conducted after the Middle East crisis showed sharp declines in consumer confidence. A spokesman for a department store chain reported "below-plan" national sales growth in recent months, but noted that growth in the Midwest remained intact during the summer. A representative of a discount chain stated that sales of back-to-school items were "very good," but overall sales in the Midwest were weak relative to other regions, in part due to unseasonable cool weather limiting sales of fans and air conditioners. An analyst for a general merchandise chain reported that August sales, after being down in the first week of the month, increased over the year-earlier period. District sales were mixed for this chain, however, with strength in some Midwestern markets partially offset by significant weakness in those areas of Michigan and Indiana linked to the auto industry. Results of several independent surveys in August, however, showed sharp declines in consumer confidence around the District.

Auto sales nationally were little changed in August from recent months, with sources indicating that the Middle East situation has not yet influenced sales. One Midwest dealers' association executive noted that orders for larger cars have not yet been cancelled. A District import car distributor experienced record July sales and reported that August sales were on track to be the best single month in the history of the distributorship. However, a domestic automaker estimated car sales in the remainder of 1990 could drop roughly 500,000 units (saar) below previous estimates, if oil prices stabilize in the neighborhood of $25 per barrel.

Manufacturing

Manufacturing activity in the District generally continued to expand at a slow pace in recent weeks, although some soft spots exist. An auto economist reported production in the summer months to be slightly above normal, due to model changeovers taking place earlier in the year than normal. Downward revisions in production schedules over the remainder of the year will be resisted, in the hope of addressing union concerns about job security. A supplier of truck engines reported that sales softened in late July and early August, however, and truck producers recently lowered their 1990 sales estimates, citing the absence of a previously anticipated increase in demand for trucks produced prior to the introduction of new fuel efficiency standards for 1991 models. A steel economist reported full order books for the third quarter, and stated that fourth quarter bookings were doing "quite well." A major capital goods producer reported little change in July shipment growth from the steady growth experienced in earlier months, and new orders continued their slow upward trend. A producer of electronic and computer components, however, reported lower domestic sales growth than expected, which was attributed primarily to a slowdown in the development of new technology rather than to a fundamental shift in demand.

Purchasing manager surveys in the District showed mixed results for August, continuing an uneven pattern. On a seasonally adjusted basis, the Chicago index showed conditions improving slightly in August, led by production, new orders, and prices. The Milwaukee report was mixed, but indicated new strength in the new orders component. The Detroit index in August showed its sharpest drop since November 1987, with both the automotive and non-automotive sector indexes showing contraction. On balance, however, recent District activity has been relatively stronger than that reported in the national survey.

Construction and Real Estate

District construction and real estate activity slowed somewhat in recent weeks, but continue to fare well relative to the national trend. A supplier of gypsum board reported that Midwest residential and non-residential contract awards (in floor area) posted solid gains year-to-date (through July) in 1990, while awards declined nationally. A cement producer reported that industry shipments in the Great Lakes region grew on a year-over-year basis in the first half of the year, and that the firm's Chicago-area backlog in early August increased significantly from both a month earlier and a year earlier. However, a District service firm involved in the early construction process reported recent new building activity in several major metropolitan areas of the District has "slowed to a trickle."

Area housing sales grew in July, compared to a national decline. The Midwestern market remains one of the "healthiest in the nation," according to a District realtor. However, this contact reported softening overall housing sales in recent weeks, citing a recent rise in mortgage rates, increased uncertainty generated by the Middle Eastern crisis, and a slowdown in company transfers. The Detroit market was

reported to be running below last year's pace in the first half of the
year, and slowed further recently.

Financial Markets

While lending standards at several large District commercial banks
have changed little in recent weeks, their loan officers cited some
tightening in selected sectors. Several loan officers told of tighter
standards for middle market commercial and industrial customers,
while one reported stricter standards for both large and small firms.
Stricter standards were generally attributed to a less favorable economic outlook, but one contact cited stress on the bank's capital position.
Tightening occurred most often in the form of stricter covenants and
collateral requirements. To the extent that tightening has occurred,
standards for construction, land development, and other commercial
real estate loans have been tightened somewhat more than for commercial and industrial loans.

Prices

Despite the recent rise in the price of oil, several District contacts reported downward pressures on the prices of a variety of goods. An
analyst with a major retail chain reported that pre-Christmas type
discounting by competitors is already beginning to occur. Although
housing prices are holding up relatively well in the Midwest, the rate
of increase has slowed substantially in recent months. On the manufacturing side, the price component of the Chicago purchasing manager survey indicated more respondents paying increased prices in
August than in July, although the trend was basically unchanged from
that in June and July. One District manufacturer of heavy moving
equipment reported prices declining in the face of weaker demand.
Crop prices have fallen in recent weeks.

Agriculture

Midwest crop conditions appear favorable. A high proportion of the corn and soybean acreage is rated good-to-excellent in District states. Recent warm temperatures are believed to have added somewhat to the harvest potential and eased concerns about an early frost on this year's late maturing crops. Crop prices, especially for corn, have retreated considerably in recent weeks as export prospects have deteriorated and the forthcoming harvest promises adequate (but still relatively tight) supplies for the year ahead. The declining corn export prospects reflect a large world wheat harvest this year and the likelihood that wheat will displace some corn in livestock feeding rations.

EIGHTH DISTRICT—ST. LOUIS

The Eighth District includes Arkansas, southern Illinois and Indiana, and parts of the Middle South. Since 1985 its Presidency has been filled by Thomas Melzer (b. 1944), a former New York investment banker who holds an M.B.A. from Stanford University. This area contains some large defense contractors but its main industries are agriculture and resource extraction. Note the attention devoted to those sectors. District staff have a distinct monetarist bent, paying careful attention to the interrelationships of money supply growth and the economy, as seen in the banking and credit section. Note that this area was weakening in September 1990.

Summary

District contacts indicate that the economy has weakened slightly in recent weeks, implying that the District's growth rate borders on zero. Higher oil prices and consumer uncertainty stemming from the Persian Gulf crisis are expected to exacerbate the economic slowdown.

The level of District employment has fallen this summer. Retail sales are reported as flat to up moderately and several contacts have an optimistic outlook for the rest of the year. Manufacturing activity has weakened in recent months, as have the construction and real estate industries. Despite moderate deposit growth, loan growth is flat at the District's largest banks. Most District crops are in fair-to-good condition, although some are being stressed by extreme heat and inadequate soil moisture.

Consumer Spending

Reports on recent District retail sales are mixed. Most contacts, however, report sales as flat to up moderately from a year ago. Many retailers report that recent sales met or exceeded their expectations and were obtained without excessive price-cutting. Inventories are generally at desired levels. Several contacts have an optimistic outlook for the rest of the year, but some are concerned about the potential negative effects of higher oil prices. Most retailers expect retail prices to remain stable through the end of the year, although a few think prices will rise this fall, in part because of higher oil prices. It is feared that the deployment of soldiers from a base in Kentucky will result in a sharp decline in business activity in nearby communities. Contacts indicate that sales of new autos are generally weak while sales of used cars are strong.

Manufacturing

District manufacturing activity has weakened since the first quarter. Producers of home appliances, chemicals and electrical equipment expect flat or weakening demand in the next few months, as much of their demand is related to activity in the motor vehicle and construction industries, sectors that have been weak and are not expected to grow soon. One home appliance producer plans to lay off more than a thousand production workers in September, partly because of planned seasonal cutbacks, partly in response to a recent weakening of demand that is expected to persist. A car manufacturer recently announced that it will postpone the closing of a Missouri assembly plant until May 1991, delaying the expected November layoff of approximately 2,000 workers.

The conflict in the Persian Gulf has caused two manufacturers to be more cautious in extending credit to customers in the Middle East; one is holding up shipments of capital goods until previous bills are paid. No substantial price increases in chemical products due to higher oil prices are expected.

Construction and Real Estate

Residential real estate contacts in Little Rock, Memphis and St. Louis report weakness in new and existing home sales. These contacts believe residential real estate conditions will worsen in the next few months and anticipate no increase in construction over the next 12 months. Residential construction unemployment is high relative to historical levels in St. Louis and Little Rock and is expected to increase in the next several months. Contacts in Louisville, however, report that residential real estate conditions are better than they had anticipated.

Banking and Credit

Despite moderate deposit growth, loan growth continues to be very slow at the District's 11 largest banks. Although real estate and consumer lending are up substantially from year-ago levels, overall loan growth remains weak because of a marked decline in commercial and industrial loans at Louisville and Memphis banks. Sluggishness in the residential housing market appears to be more demand-driven than supply-driven, as mortgage financing is plentiful.

Agriculture and Natural Resources

Most District crops are in fair-to-good condition. In some areas, however, a lack of adequate soil moisture and extreme heat are hampering crop development, especially soybeans and pastures. District coal production is running about 7 percent above last year because of strong exports, stockpile rebuilding and increased U.S. electric output. Recent oil price increases are not expected to have a significant effect on the demand for coal or coal prices. Contacts report that exports of rice and Southern pine lumber will be lower than previously expected because of the embargo of exports to Iraq and recent increases in freight and insurance costs for shipments to other Middle Eastern countries. Nonetheless, Southern pine lumber mills report that orders, production and shipments are all up compared to a year ago.

NINTH DISTRICT—MINNEAPOLIS

The Ninth District covers the upper Midwest but also the Dakotas and Montana. Its President, Gary Stern (b. 1944), was sworn into office in March 1985. Also a former Volcker associate and career Federal Reserve employee, Stern, who holds a Ph.D. in economics from Rice University, tends to take a hard anti-inflation line. Farming and natural resource extraction are the main industries in the District, and staff, who take a GNP-oriented overview in Beige Book contributions, duly noted that these areas were stronger than the rest of the country in the Fall of 1990. In part, this also may have reflected the President's views.

Ninth District economic conditions have been moderately good lately. While labor market and manufacturing conditions have been mixed and construction activity has been weak, tourist spending has been strong, and new-car sales and retail sales in general have been fairly good. Resource-related industries have been doing well. In general, wage and price increases have been moderate. The Gulf crisis has not yet affected the district's economy much.

Employment, Wages, and Prices

Labor market conditions have been mixed in the district. After showing signs of improvement during the second quarter of the year, Minnesota's unemployment rates have begun to drift up. The state's overall unemployment rate was 4.6 percent in July, up from 4.2 percent in June and 4.1 percent in July 1989. In the district's other states, unemployment rates in June and July were roughly at the same level as last year. At the same time, firms throughout the district continue to report difficulties in filling entry-level and part-time positions, even at wages well above the minimum wage.

Wage and price increases in the district have remained moderate. Wages have generally increased only at annual rates of 3 to 5 percent. The Gulf crisis has not resulted in a sharp acceleration in the district's inflation rate—though, as is to be expected, gasoline prices have risen sharply. Some prices charged by freight companies have also increased. Prices of agricultural products have recently been declining, though they are still well above the levels of a year ago.

Consumer Spending

District retailers of general merchandise report good sales growth lately. One major retailer reports that, compared to a year earlier, sales in August were up 8 percent and sales in the first eight months of the year were up 6.1 percent. An appliance retailer reports that sales in August were 3 percent higher this year than last. In North Dakota and Montana, retailers report that shoppers from Canada have contributed to strong sales. In North Dakota, sales tax collections have risen sharply from a year ago. Throughout the district, inventories are reported to be at acceptable levels.

Tourism remains the brightest spot in the district's economy. Motorcycle enthusiasts recently held their 50th annual gathering in the Black Hills of South Dakota. This rally reportedly brought an estimated $30 million into the local economy. Also, resort owners in the Upper Peninsula of Michigan, Wisconsin's Arrowhead region, and northern Minnesota report fairly high levels of reservations for the fall colors viewing season. However, district resort owners generally are apprehensive that the recent rise in gasoline prices may crimp tourist activity.

New-car sales have been fairly good recently. One major dealer reports that sales at the end of August were strong. Dealers are cautiously optimistic about prospects for the second half of the year. Inventories of cars and trucks are reportedly at comfortable levels.

The district's housing activity has improved recently, after having shown signs of softening earlier in the year. The number of new housing permits issued in Minnesota, for example, was 6 percent higher this July than last. The number of houses sold in the Minneapolis-St. Paul area during the first eight months of the year was 6.6 percent higher than a year ago.

Construction and Manufacturing

Conditions in the district's construction industry in general have been weak recently, particularly in the Minneapolis-St. Paul metropolitan area. In that area, the dollar value of contracts for future construction in June was 27 percent below the value a year ago. This area's weakness is expected to continue for at least a couple of years.

Conditions in the district's manufacturing industries have been mixed lately. Domestic orders for producer equipment have been lower than last year, but strong foreign demand has more than made up for that. The medical technology industry has grown strongly, but the electronics industry has continued to struggle. Manufacturing firms, in general, express serious concern about the increased probability of a recession.

Resource-Related Industries

The district's resource-related industries appear to be fairly healthy. Excellent rainfall throughout the district has improved the outlook for farmers. The spring wheat harvest in Minnesota is expected to be the best in three years. In that state, the corn harvest is expected to be 5 percent higher than last year, but the soybean harvest is expected to be 10 percent lower, due primarily to fewer acres being planted. Farmers in North Dakota have had the best wheat crop on record. The mining industry is also doing well. However, the lumber and paper products industry, which has been growing strongly for the last two years, reports recent setbacks. Prices of products used in home construction have declined sharply. And according to several firms, finished paper inventories have been rising.

TENTH DISTRICT—KANSAS CITY

The Tenth District includes the states of Colorado, Kansas, Nebraska, Oklahoma, Wyoming, and parts of Missouri and New Mexico that comprise the old West. President Roger Guffey (b. 1929) took office in 1976 and was trained as an attorney (J.D., University of Missouri). Prior to becoming a Fed staffer, he was in private practice; he rarely makes public statements and is considered a moderate. This is a major farming and ranching area that also depends on resource extraction (note the long section devoted to agriculture and the separate energy section). Slow but ongoing growth was noted in the area. Note that Mr. Guffey has announced his retirement for 1992.

Overview

The Tenth District economy is growing slowly. Retail sales have weakened over the last three months, with auto sales slumping as some potential buyers are finding it difficult to obtain financing. But

rural business conditions generally continue to reflect the improvement in the farm economy over the past three years, an improvement
that is expected to continue as bumper crops are harvested this fall.
Retailers are trimming inventories, while manufacturers are trying to
maintain or reduce their stocks. In the energy sector, drilling activity
has slipped in recent months but remains above the level of a year ago.
Housing starts are up from last month despite a slight increase in
mortgage rates.

Retail Sales

Most district retailers have been trimming inventories in light of
weakening sales over the past three months, especially in July. Expectations are mixed for sales over the next three months, while prices are
expected to change little. New auto sales have dropped in most district states over the last month and are expected to drop further during
the rest of the year. Some potential buyers are having financing
problems due to credit tightening. Most dealers are trimming inventory levels to make room for new models.

Manufacturing

Purchasing agents report higher input prices from a year ago but
generally stable prices over the last three months. Some prices have
risen recently due to the Gulf crisis as fuel price increases have pushed
up transportation costs. Agents generally expect more increases in input prices in the next three months. Agents are having little difficulty
in obtaining inputs and most expect few problems for the rest of the
year. Most firms are maintaining or reducing inventories.

Energy

Despite significantly higher oil prices since Iraq invaded Kuwait, ex-
ploration and development activity in the district has declined recently. The district rig count fell from 303 in July to 282 in August. None-

theless, the rig count remains about 9 percent above the year-ago level. Industry observers do not anticipate much improvement in drilling activity unless oil prices remain above $25 a barrel for an extended period and natural gas prices are eventually pulled up by higher oil prices.

Housing Activity and Finance

Housing starts in most areas of the district are up from last month, though still below levels a year ago. Sales of new homes remain mixed. Several builders report increases in lumber costs and a shortage of labor. The outlook for new home sales is mixed but biased toward a slowdown for the remainder of the year.

Most district savings and loan respondents report net outflows of deposits over both the last month and the last year. Mortgage demand is constant to down slightly and is expected to decline over the next three months due to seasonal factors. Mortgage rates have risen slightly at most institutions but are expected to decline slightly in the near future.

Banking

Commercial bankers report that total loan demand rose moderately over the last month. Demand increased for commercial and industrial loans, consumer loans, and home mortgages, while demand for commercial real estate loans and agricultural loans decreased. Loan-to-deposit ratios did not change over the last month but are down slightly from a year ago. Total deposits increased moderately over the last month, with increases in demand deposits, NOW accounts, MMDAs, and small time and savings deposits. Large certificates of deposit, IRAs, and Keough accounts were unchanged. Bankers report no major changes in their prime rates or consumer lending rates, and few expect any changes in the near future. About half of the respondents report that other loan terms—for example, collateral requirements and loan covenants—have recently been tightened or are being reviewed for possible future tightening. Although a few rural bankers report that credit standards have been tightened due to regulatory pressures or concerns about an economic slowdown, most indicate that credit standards for small businesses have not changed.

Agriculture

District crops are generally in excellent condition. Bumper crops of corn, soybeans, and milo are expected in Kansas, where a record wheat crop was harvested earlier this year. The Oklahoma cotton and peanut crops could be the best in years. Development of late-planted crops in eastern Kansas, Missouri, and Nebraska, however, is one to three weeks behind normal, making crops in those areas vulnerable to substantial yield reductions if an early frost occurs.

Higher fuel prices have not yet affected district farming activities, although harvesting costs will be pushed up. Prices of some fertilizers, pesticides, and other petroleum-based products may also rise if petroleum prices remain high. If this happens, farmers will reduce their use of these products next spring.

Business conditions in rural communities across the district generally reflect the rebound in the farm economy over the past three years. Still, the improvement in the district's Main Street businesses has not been uniform. Small businesses continue to struggle in some rural communities, while both established and new businesses thrive in others.

ELEVENTH DISTRICT—DALLAS

The Eleventh District reaches over the states of Texas, northern Louisiana and southern New Mexico, and should be considered the country's oil patch. President Robert Boykin (b. 1926) is an attorney (J.D., University of Texas) but has spent his career at the Fed. As a result, he generally takes a tough stand on limiting national inflation and growth, while promoting the best interests of the District. The District staff noted in the Fall of 1990 that the area economy was still growing, attributing the strength to services and good manufacturing orders. Note that the growth was likely due to the effects of higher oil prices on related industries. As this book went to press, the Eleventh District Presidency was being assumed by Robert McTeer, a career Fed economist who is a protégé of Richmond Fed President Black.

The District economy continues to grow slowly. Orders for manufactured goods have shown little overall change. Retail sales have recently slowed. Auto sales slowed in early August but have since improved. Economic activity has increased in the service sector. The construction sector continues a mild improvement. Higher oil prices are stimulating increased production from existing wells but have not yet motivated new drilling. Recent rains have improved conditions for District farmers and ranchers.

Overall, *manufacturing* production and orders have not changed significantly during the past month, although orders for construction-related products have declined. Manufacturing inventories generally are at desired levels. Most respondents are concerned about the outlook for the U.S. economy now that oil prices have risen. Also, many industries are concerned about higher transportation costs due to the jump in oil prices. One food wholesaler is already planning to curtail costs by reducing deliveries from five to four per week. Recent oil price increases have had only a small effect on the demand for oil field machinery but respondents expect strong gains next year if oil prices remain high. Chemical producers say that product demand remains strong and they are switching feedstocks to reduce the impact of rising oil prices. Orders and production continue strong in the petroleum refining industry and producers are increasing product prices in line with crude costs. Refiners say that they have not experienced any shortages of oil. Steel production continues at high rates due to declines in imports, and producers continue to be optimistic about demand in the near future. Primary metal producers in the District generally say that oil is not a significant energy source in their production process. Respondents in the apparel industry note a mild increase in sales and are cautiously optimistic about the next few months. For electronics producers, orders generally remain weak but several noted that sales to the telecommunications industry are strong. Demand for fabricated metals remains soft. Among stone, clay, and glass producers, a glass producer says sales have decreased significantly and a producer of concrete pipe notes a gradual slowing. Lumber and wood products producers say that demand from home builders has declined but one producer noted an increase in demand from lumber yards.

District *retail* sales have slowed significantly over the last few weeks. Respondents feel that uncertainty about problems in the Middle East has caused consumers to hold back purchases. Weakness is widespread across most product lines but respondents note a particular softness in durable goods. Discount stores continue to experience slightly stronger sales than other retailers.

District *auto* sales increased moderately in July. Sales growth was strong in the Houston area and mild in the Dallas/Ft. Worth area. Sales flattened in the first two weeks of August but picked up slightly during the second half of the month. Respondents note no increase in the relative demand for fuel-efficient vehicles.

Activity in the District *service* sector has increased. Temporary employment agencies say that demand is increasing strongly. A respondent in San Antonio said much of the demand is from firms which are reluctant to hire full time workers because the economy is slow. An accounting firm says that activity has picked up due to demand from the Resolution Trust Corporation. Consulting firms note continued increases in the demand for office automation and management services. An increase in economic activity in Austin and Houston has created a slight increase in demand for legal services.

District *construction* activity continues to grow slowly. Most of the recent growth stems from increased residential construction in Texas. Single and multifamily building permits have increased. District nonresidential and nonbuilding construction remain weak. Nonresidential contract values are up but remain below levels reached last year. Respondents do not expect an upturn in commercial and industrial construction for at least another year. Nonbuilding contract values have fallen and respondents note that expenditures on state highways should continue to decrease in Texas but increase in Louisiana.

Recent gains in the oil price have not stimulated new drilling. The District drilling rig count declined in July and August. Respondents in the *energy* industry say that they are uncertain about what price will be sustained. Production from existing wells should increase, though, as increased revenues are used to upgrade old wells and reopen dormant wells. Most of the work will be done on stripper wells which produce less than ten barrels of oil per day. Some enhanced recovery procedures have also become profitable. Production should increase about 1.1 percent due to the lifting of production ceilings by the Texas Railroad Commission. One respondent noted that about half of the current drilling is for natural gas which has not yet increased in price.

Recent rainfall has improved conditions for District *farmers and ranchers*, although some dryland cotton and corn crops were already destroyed. Ranges and pastures have improved significantly in many areas. August prices received by Texas farmers and ranchers increased 7 percent from last year and 2 percent from July. Rice prices continue to drop and are now 9 percent below a year earlier. Rice prices are expected to remain depressed until mills find alternatives to their Iraqi customers.

TWELFTH DISTRICT—SAN FRANCISCO

The Twelfth Federal Reserve District ranges from Alaska and Hawaii in to California, Arizona, Nevada, Utah, and up to the Pacific Northwest. President Robert Parry (b. 1939) holds a Ph.D. in economics from the University of Pennsylvania and has work experience

at the Fed Board and Security Pacific Bank. Parry, in office since
1986, is another Volcker-era inflation-fighter who favors tight money
and lower growth. His hawkish views are often recorded in dissents at
FOMC meetings. Note that the broad base of business activity in this
diverse district probably prevented staff from reporting that activity
had slowed in the Fall of 1990.

Summary

Economic activity in the West is growing at a modest pace, following
some slowing in recent months. Since the Iraqi invasion of Kuwait,
western business leaders' expectations of future national economic
growth have weakened sharply. Price inflation remains around 5
percent, with the exception of the recent large increase in oil prices.
Retail activity appears to be softening in most parts of the District.
Manufacturing conditions are mixed, with strength in commercial aircraft and aluminum offset by weakness in some other sectors. The
situation in the Middle East has shaken up energy-related industries,
while agricultural conditions remain generally strong. Real estate and
construction activity continue to cool off in the District's coastal
areas, while most inland areas remain strong. Financial institutions
note recent weakening in lending activity.

Business Sentiment

Western business leaders' expectations of future economic activity
have deteriorated significantly since Iraq's invasion of Kuwait. 39 percent now expect a national recession during the next 12 months, compared with only 4 percent six weeks ago, and only 5 percent of respondents now anticipate that growth will be as strong as 2½ percent,
compared with 30 percent last time. Most respondents indicate that
the Iraqi invasion has not yet caused changes in their business plans,
beyond a renewed interest in energy conservation. One firm, how-

ever, has put new Middle East business on hold while a few others are approaching future capital investments with increasing caution.

Wages and Prices

Price inflation remains around 5 percent, with the exception of the recent large increase in oil prices. Gasoline prices are up sharply throughout the District. Jet airplane fuel prices in Seattle are up 62 percent since the end of July.

Most respondents indicate that wages have risen by about 3 to 5 percent from their year-earlier levels. However, the cost of benefits continues to rise at a faster pace, with rising health care costs cited as the major factor.

Retail Trade

Retail activity appears to be softening in most parts of the District. Auto sales have slowed and auto manufacturers continue to fatten rebates to prevent sales from eroding further. Sales of other durable goods, like farm machinery and home furnishings, also are reported to have weakened. Sales of nondurable goods are reported to be softening. A retailer in Southern California indicates that, excluding the effects of promotions, sales fell 5 to 6 percent in August from a year ago. Another West Coast retailer reports that, since July, sales have been up just 3 percent from a year ago, well off the 10 percent growth seen in earlier months. However, reports indicate that sales gains were considerably more robust in California's Central Valley, Alaska, Hawaii, and Utah.

Manufacturing

Manufacturing activity in the District is reported to be mixed overall. Aluminum manufacturers continue to run at about 90 percent of capacity, and one observer suggests that an increase in demand for aluminum products may occur as the Defense Department builds up its inventory of spare parts. Newsprint manufacturers continue to do well, but the packaging and paperboard side of the industry has slowed significantly since last year. Orders for commercial aircraft have been relatively stable for the past three months, and most manufacturers continue to face multi-year backlogs. A paint and coatings manufacturer reports that some of his markets are starting to show signs of slowing, which represents a deterioration from last year when all markets were accelerating.

Agriculture and Resource-Related Industries

Conditions in agriculture remain good overall. Agricultural prices continue strong for most crops except wheat and some feed grains, and livestock markets have held up better than expected. California's almond crop will be the largest ever, but the resulting downward price pressure may put prices below production costs. In the lumber industry, weaker sales are depressing prices and increasing inventories.

Interest in new oil drilling activity has increased in some areas of the District since the Iraqi invasion of Kuwait. One natural gas firm plans to increase capital expenditures by 65 percent this year over last year's level.

Construction and Real Estate

Real estate activity continues to cool in the District's coastal areas, but conditions inland remain strong. Home price appreciation in the Seattle area is slowing and the inventory of unsold homes is growing. Commercial leasing activity in southern California continues at a good pace, but net effective rents have declined 4 to 6 percent from last year as a result of persistently high vacancy rates. Home prices in Bakersfield and Sacramento continue to rise, but reports suggest that price increases may be slowing from their earlier phenomenal paces. Construction activity is slowing in many parts of the West.

Financial Sector

Financial institutions report generally good conditions, despite weakness in lending activity. One southern Californian bank reports declining deposit levels while another indicates that consumer, commercial, and construction loan volumes have weakened in recent weeks. One banker reports that loan activity continues to grow in Oregon and Washington, but at half of last year's pace.

Taken as a whole, the September 1990 Beige Book indicates that seven of 12 Districts show slower growth. This should have been one factor propelling the Presidents whose backgrounds are summarized here to vote in favor of edging down interest rates.

Glossary

Auto sales unit car and truck sales data are reported on a 10-day basis by the manufacturers; the data are seasonally adjusted into an annualized selling pace in the millions by the Commerce Department.

Average hourly earnings the average hourly pay for employees.

All-urban CPI a measure of consumer inflation for city-dwellers.

Agricultural prices measured from mid-month by the Agriculture Department for raw farm produce.

ARIMA AutoRegressive Integrative Moving Average statistical analysis which projects a current trend by adding the average move onto the end of a data series.

BFI Business Fixed Investment refers to money spent on durable fixed items, such as factories, production equipment, delivery vehicles, and the like.

Business inventories items produced and held for future sale; typically economists look at non-farm inventories because the latter are perishable.

BLS The Bureau of Labor Statistics is the agency within the U.S. Labor Department responsible for gathering and disseminating data on wages, prices, and productivity.

371

Big 3 refers to the three largest American auto-producers, Chrysler, General Motors, and Ford.

Business Week Index a private weekly data series covering the output of the nation's mines, factories, and utilities; the primary difference between this and the official Fed measure is that the BW Index follows rail and highway tonnage as a proxy for production.

Base period the time frame chosen to normalize some data series; typically a base period in the recent past will be used as a basis of comparison for future price movements.

Capital markets market for loanable funds; usually refers to a longer-term market, such as for stocks or bonds.

Cash market refers to trading of physical commodities, as opposed to futures exchanges.

C Consumption, which is also known as consumer spending, is the driving force behind the U.S. economy.

Civilian unemployment rate a measure of the utilization of the human resources in the economy; this is defined as the ratio of those outside the armed forces who are unemployed and looking for work, over the labor force.

CPI Consumer Price Index, refers to the change in prices at the level of the average person.

Census Bureau the area within the Commerce Department that is charged with gathering and compiling data on population and business trends.

Commerce Department a branch of the U.S. government set up to serve the needs of business.

CBO The Congressional Budget Office is a branch of the Congress that analyzes and reports independently of the executive branch on budget trends and spending plans.

Capacity utilization a measure of existing factory space in use, it is defined as the ratio of space in use to available facilities.

Capital consumption allowance known as depreciation in accounting terms, CCA measures how much of a good is being used up in the production process.

Demand   the need for a good or service.

Durables   a good with a useful life of more than three years.

Deflator   an inflation measure used to adjust down a data series; the most commonly discussed are the fixed weight and implicit price deflators of the GNP series.

Discouraged workers   individuals who are no longer looking for work because they have been unemployed for a long time.

Deficit   an excess of spending over receipts.

Department store sales   dollar volume of sales reported monthly by the largest chain stores.

Diffusion index   the difference between the items in a survey rising and those falling, expressed as a percentage.

Exports   goods and services produced domestically but sold abroad.

Employment report   the mass of labor market data (unemployment rate, payrolls, wages, and so on) collected in the week containing the twelfth of the month but disseminated on the first Friday of the following month.

ECI   Employment Cost Index is a measure of labor market inflation; it takes into account both wages and benefits.

Farm income   the profits produced by the agriculture sector via the growing of crops.

Farm prices   also called *agricultural prices.*

FRB   The Federal Reserve Board meets in Washington, D.C. and is responsible for setting monetary policy; comprised of seven governors who are nominated by the Administration and confirmed by the Senate; they reflect the business and commercial interests of the country.

Federal Reserve Banks   the 12 regional central banks that along with the FRB comprise the Federal Reserve System; the Banks provide business analysis from the regions and give a broad range of services to member commercial banks.

Fixed   denotes an index with set weights.

Foreign Exchange   claims payable abroad in foreign currencies.

Goods   hard commoditism, as opposed to services.

GNP   Gross National Product measures the overall output of the economy in dollar terms.

G   the government sector, including all levels—local, state, and federal.

General merchandise   the sector of the retail sales report in which department store sales are captured.

Hourly earnings   the wages paid to trades members.

Housing Starts   the number of new homes for which ground has been broken in a given month.

Home sales   the number of completed homes sold during the month.

Investment   the alternative to savings; the amount of money put into hard goods that will have fairly long-term productive uses, such as residences, business investment, and inventories.

Inventories   items held for future sale.

Industrial production   the output of the nation's factories, utilities, and mines.

Imports   items produced abroad but purchased in another country.

IVA   inventory valuation adjustment is the marking of various inventory items, which can be valued in five or more ways, to a standard accounting method.

Implicit price deflator   a GNP deflator that shifts its weights to reflect the current pattern of consumer spending.

Instrument   any type of financial debt paper.

Inflation   the overall change in the price level in an economy.

Interest rate   a return on capital that takes into account risk and time value of money.

JEC   the Joint Economic Committee of the U.S. Congress which is charged with tracking the performance of the economy and overseeing the CBO.

Labor Department   a part of the executive branch of the federal government that produces economic statistics.

Laspeyres index   measures characteristics of a fixed market basket of items.

Margin   the mark-up or profit on a good or service.

Marginal propensities   the change at the margin in behavior, such as to consume.

Net exports   the difference between exports and imports; produces leakage from GNP if a country imports too much.

Net   a residual after adjustments are subtracted from a "gross" or larger number.

Nondurables   goods with an initial useful life of less than three years.

Net operating income   the profit produced by a business entity after subtracting all expenses.

NIPA   the National Income and Product Accounts, which are a system used to track and monitor GNP.

NSA   not seasonally adjusted.

NAPM   the National Association of Purchasing Managers, which polls business members each month for data on whether production, orders, prices and inventories are better or worse.

Output   the finished items that flow out of a factory.

OMB   the Office of Management and Budget is the executive department responsible for producing the federal budget and monitoring spending.

Population   all the people in a country or the universe for a survey.

PPI   the Producer Price Index sometimes is also called wholesale prices and is meant to measure the cost of inputs to the production process.

PI   Personal Income is the sum of money that individuals earn and get from passive activities; they theoretically have this sum available to spend.

PCE   Personal consumption expenditures, the amount of spending that is done each month.

Prices   the overall measure of costs in an economy.

Profits   the difference between aggregate selling prices and all costs, sometimes called corporate profits.

Philadelphia Fed Index   expressed as a diffusion index, this measures the health of the manufacturing sector within the third Federal Reserve District which covers eastern Pennsylvania and southern New Jersey.

Quantity   the volume of any commodity, as opposed to its price.

Retail trade   monthly data on the dollar volume of sales and inventories that are available for the firms that sell to the public.

Savings rate   the residual of income after consumption has been measured.

SA   Seasonally adjusted, indicating a data series has been smoothed for weather, calendar, and holiday fluctuations.

Treasury Department   the department of the federal government responsible for paying bills and borrowing enough cash to fund expenditures.

Time series   data measured over the course of time, such as the calendar year.

Unemployment rate   the ratio of those looking but unable to find jobs to the labor force; reported as two series, for civilians and the overall population (the former will be higher because by definition all members of the armed forces are employed).

Utilization   the ability to put to use an inanimate object, such as a piece of equipment.

Wages and salaries   the money individuals earn via personal employment.

Wholesale trade   data on inventories and sales from one company to another, presumably because the second company will re-sell to the public.

Weekly earnings   a data series that multiplies hours worked times hourly earnings to get a seven-day total.

REFERENCES

Chapter 1

Abken, Peter A. "Innovations in Modeling the Term Structure of Interest Rates," *Economic Review of the Federal Reserve Bank of Atlanta*, July–August 1990.

BEA Methodology Paper No. 1: Introduction to National Economic Accounting, U.S. Commerce Department, 1985.

Carson, Carol S. "GNP: An overview of Source Data and Estimating Methods," Survey of Current Business, July 1987.

Fitzpatrick, Terry J. and Miller, Preston J. "A Simple Way to Estimate Current-Quarter GNP," Federal Reserve Bank of Minneapolis Quarterly Review, Fall 1989.

Heller, Robert. "Implementing Monetary Policy," *Federal Reserve Bulletin*, July 1988.

"Model of the U.S. Economy," *Federal Reserve Bulletin*, February 1987.

"Monetary Policy with a New View of Potential GNP," *Business Review of the Federal Reserve Bank of Philadelphia*, July–August 1990, ISSN 0007-7011.

377

"Stocks, Bonds Plunge, Weak Economy Seen," *The Wall Street Journal*, August 17, 1990, page C-1.

Swardson, Anne. "Statistics can do a Number on the Economy," *The Washington Post*, Washington Business Section, October 29, 1990.

Zadrozny, Peter A. "Estimating a Multivariate ARMA Model with Mixed Frequency Data: An Application to Forecasting U.S. GNP at Monthly Intervals," *Working Paper 90-6*, August 1990, Federal Reserve Bank of Atlanta.

Chapter 2

Bureau of Labor Statistics, *The BLS Seasonal Factor Method*, 1966.

Dagum, Estela Bee. "The X-11 ARIMA Seasonal Adjustment Method," *Statistics Canada Catalogue No. 12-564E*, January 1983.

McIntyre, Robert. "Review of Seasonal Adjustment," *Employment and Earnings*, U.S. Department of Labor, January 1990.

"Seasonal Adjustment Factors, Appendix Table 4," *Federal Reserve Board Release H.6*, December 1989.

U.S. Department of Commerce, Bureau of the Census, "The X-11 Variant of the Census Method II Seasonal Adjustment Program," *Technical Paper No. 15* (1967 Revision).

U.S. Department of Labor, *BLS Handbook of Methods*, Bureau of Labor Statistics, April 1988.

Chapter 3

Bureau of Labor Statistics, *A Guide to Seasonal Adjustment of Labor Force Data*, Bulletin 2114, 1982.

U.S. Commerce Department Computer Bulletin Board, "Economic News Releases for the Months of January to December 1991 Reference Period."

U.S. Department of Commerce, "The Current Population Survey:

Design and Methodology," Bureau of the Census, *Technical Paper No. 40*, 1978.

U.S. Department of Labor, *BLS Handbook of Methods*, Bureau of Labor Statistics, April 1988.

Chapter 4

Berry, John M. "Do Job Surveys do the Job?," *The Washington Post*, April 6, 1990.

"Economic Statistics: Handle With Care," *Business News & Trends*, PNC Financial Corp., Spring 1990.

National Commission on Employment and Unemployment Statistics, "Counting the Labor Force," 1979.

Policy Record of the Federal Open Market Committee, meeting held July 2-3, 1990.

President's Committee to Appraise Employment and Unemployment Statistics, "Measuring Employment and Unemployment," 1962.

U.S. Department of Labor, *Handbook of Labor Statistics*, Bureau of Labor Statistics, August 1989.

U.S. Department of Labor, "How the Government Measures Unemployment," Report 742, Bureau of Labor Statistics, 1987.

Webb, Roy H., and Whelpley, William. "Labor Market Data," *Economic Review of the Federal Reserve Bank of Richmond*, November/December 1989, Volume 75/6.

Chapter 5

Carson, Carol S. "GNP: An Overview of Source Data and Estimating Methods," *July 1987 Survey of Current Business*, U.S. Commerce Department.

"Economic Indicators," U.S. Government Printing Office, July 1990.

"Introduction to National Income Accounting," *BEA Methodology Paper No. 1*, 1985.

"Monthly Estimates of Personal Income, Taxes and Outlays," *November 1979 Survey of Current Business*. U.S. Commerce Department.

"State Personal Income: Estimates for 1929-82 and a Statement of Sources and Methods," 1984 (GPO Stock No. 003-010-00125-9).

Chapter 6

"Advance Monthly Retail Sales, May 1990," *Current Business Reports*, U.S. Department of Commerce.

Avery, Robert B., Elliehausen, Gregory E., and Kennickell, Arthur B. "Changes in Consumer Installment Debt: Evidence from the 1983 and 1986 Surveys of Consumer Finances," *Federal Reserve Bulletin*, October 1987.

Consumer Confidence Survey: October Results, November 1990, The Conference Board.

"Consumer Installment Credit, G.19," *Federal Reserve Statistical Release*, August 7, 1990.

"General Motors 1990 Calendar Year Sales Release Days," General Motors Corporation.

Hershey, Robert D., Jr. "Viewing the Economy With Consumer Eyes," *The New York Times*, Wednesday, April 4, 1990.

Linden, Fabian. "The Consumer as Forecaster," *The Public Perspective*, January/February 1990.

"Methodology for Compiling Consumer Confidence Index," The Conference Board, October 1990.

"Seasonal Factors for Selected Components of Auto Output," Bureau of Economic Analysis, U.S. Department of Commerce, July 1990.

Stertz, Bradley A. "Chrysler, With an Eye on the Japanese, Plans to Discontinue 10-Day Sales Data," *The Wall Street Journal*, Monday, December 3, 1990.

Surveys of Consumers, Survey Research Center, University of Michigan, November 1990.

Chapter 7

Armitage, Kenneth and Tranum, Dixon A. "Industrial Production: 1989 Developments and Historical Revision," *Federal Reserve Bulletin*, April 1990.

Bauer, Paul W. "A Reexamination of the Relationship between Capacity Utilization and Inflation," *Economic Review of the Federal Reserve Bank of Cleveland*, Vol. 26, No. 3, 1990 Quarter III.

"Industrial Production," 1986 edition, Federal Reserve Board.

"Industrial Production and Capacity Utilization," *Federal Reserve Statistical Release G.17 (419)*, July 17, 1990.

Palash, Carl J. "Interpreting the Purchasing Managers Index," *McCarthy, Crisanti & Maffei, Inc. Money Market Critique*, March 27, 1987.

Raddock, Richard D. "Recent Developments in Industrial Capacity and Utilization," *Federal Reserve Bulletin*, June 1990.

Raddock, Richard D. "Revised Federal Reserve Rates of Capacity Utilization," *Federal Reserve Bulletin*, October 1985.

"Source and Descriptive Information: Industrial Production and Capacity Utilization," Federal Reserve Board, August 1990.

"The Index Shows a Strong Recovery," *Business Week*, October 21, 1972.

Chapter 8

"Manufacturers' Shipments, Inventories, and Orders: 1982-1988," *M3-1(88) Current Industrial Reports*, Bureau of the Census, U.S. Department of Commerce, August 1988.

"Manufacturing and Trade Inventories and Sales," U.S. Department of Commerce, May 1990.

"Monthly Retail Trade: Sales and Inventories," *Current Business Reports*, U.S. Department of Commerce, March 1990.

"Monthly Wholesale Trade: Sales and Inventories," *Current Business Reports*, U.S. Department of Commerce, March 1990.

Chapter 9

Anderson, Gerald H. and Erceg, John J. "How Credible are Capital Spending Surveys as Forecasts?," *Economic Commentary*, Federal Reserve Bank of Cleveland, December 1, 1990.

Current Construction Reports: Expenditures for Residential Upkeep and Improvement, First Quarter 1990, U.S. Department of Commerce, Bureau of the Census, November 1990.

"Housing Starts, July 1990," *Current Construction Reports*, C20-907, U.S. Department of Commerce.

"The Dodge Construction Information Network," F.W. Dodge Division of McGraw Hill, 1990.

"Value of New Construction Put in Place, May 1990," *Current Construction Reports*, C30-9005, U.S. Department of Commerce.

Chapter 10

"Balance of Payments of the U.S.: Concepts, Data Sources, and Estimating Procedures," *Methodology Paper of the U.S. Department of Commerce*, August 1990.

"GNP: An Overview of Source Data and Estimating Methods," Methodology Papers: *U.S. National Income and Product Accounts*, U.S. Department of Commerce, September 1987.

Hill, John K. "The Trade Balance and the Real Exchange Rate," *Economic Review of the Federal Reserve Bank of Dallas*, November 1990.

Koenig, Evan F. "Recent Trade and Exchange Rate Movements: Possible Explanations," *Economic Review of the Federal Reserve Bank of Dallas*, September 1989.

Kubarych, Roger M. *Foreign Exchange Markets in the United States*, Federal Reserve Bank of New York, March 1983.

Meade, Ellen E. "Exchange Rates, Adjustment, and the J Curve," *Federal Reserve Bulletin*, October 1988.

Pauls, Dianne B. "U.S. Exchange Rate Policy: Bretton Woods to Present," *Federal Reserve Bulletin*, November 1990.

Plocek, Joseph E. "International Currency Forecasting: Partial Equilibrium Analysis in the Real World," in Harvey A. Poniacek (ed.), *Case Studies in International Corporate Finance*, John Wiley & Sons, New York, 1990.

Sachs, Jeffrey D. "The Current Account and Macroeconomic Adjustment in the 1970s," *Brookings Papers on Economic Activity*, January 1981.

Shafer, Jeffrey R. and Loopesko, Bonnie E. "Floating Exchange Rates After Ten Years," *Brookings Papers on Economic Activity*, January 1983.

Chapter 11

"A Glossary of Terms Used in the Federal Budget Process," U.S. Government Printing Office, March 1981.

BEA Methodology Paper No. 5: Government Transactions, U.S. Commerce Department, 1988.

Budget of the United States Government, Fiscal Year 1991, U.S. Government Printing Office.

General Accounting Systems Staff, "Guide to the Monthly Treasury Statement of Receipts and Outlays of the United States Government," Bureau of Government Financial Operations, Department of the Treasury, May 1983.

Executive Office of the President, *Midsession Review of the Budget, July 16, 1990*, Office of Management and Budget.

Chapter 12

Meulendyke, Ann-Marie. *U.S. Monetary Policy and Financial Markets*, Federal Reserve Bank of New York, December 1989.

Samansky, Arthur W. *Statfacts: Understanding Federal Reserve Statistical Reports*, Federal Reserve Bank of New York, 1981.

Chapter 13

Carlson, Keith M. "Do Price Indices Tell Us About Inflation? A Review of the Issues," *Review of the Federal Reserve Bank of Cleveland*, November/December 1989.

CRB Index Futures: Turning Opportunity into Action, New York Futures Exchange, NYFE Publication No. 3028, 1986.

Moore, Geoffrey H. *Business Cycles, Inflation, and Forecasting, 2nd edition*, Ballinger, 1983.

Producer Price Indices for June 1990, U.S. Department of Labor, Bureau of Labor Statistics.

Producer Price Measurement: Concepts and Methods, Bureau of Labor Statistics, June 1986.

Relative Importance of Components in the Consumer Price Indices, 1989, U.S. Department of Labor, Bureau of Labor Statistics, Bulletin 2359, April 1990.

Survey of Current Business, Bureau of Economic Analysis, U.S. Department of Commerce, May 1985 and July 1987.

"The Consumer Price Index," Chapter 19 of the *BLS Handbook of Methods*, U.S. Department of Labor, Bureau of Labor Statistics, Bulletin 2285, April 1988.

Triplett, Jack E. "Reconciling the CPI and the PCE Deflator," *Monthly Labor Review*, U.S. Department of Labor, September 1981.

Wallace, William H. and Cullison, William E. *Measuring Price Changes: A Study of the Price Indices, 4th edition*, Federal Reserve Bank of Cleveland, June 1981

"Macroeconomic Price Indexes," Webb, Roy H. and Willemse, Rob. *Economic Review of the Federal Reserve Bank of Richmond*, July/August 1989.

Chapter 14

Anderson, Gerald H., Bryan, Michael F., and Pike, Christopher J. "Oil, the Economy, and Monetary Policy," *Economic Commentary of the Federal Reserve Bank of Cleveland*, November 1, 1990.

Business Conditions Digest, March 1990, U.S. Department of Commerce, Bureau of Economic Analysis.

Hoffman, Stuart G. "Assessing the Consequences of the Middle East Turmoil on the U.S. Economy," *Business News & Trends*, Pittsburgh National Bank Publications, Fall 1990.

Huh, Chan Guk. "Political Business Cycles," *Federal Reserve Bank of San Francisco Weekly Letter*, December 14, 1990.

Mauskopf, Eileen. "The Transmission Channels of Monetary Policy: How Have They Changed?", *Federal Reserve Bulletin*, December 1990.

Palash, Carl J. and Radecki, Lawrence J. "Using Monetary and Financial Variables to Predict Cyclical Downturns," *Federal Reserve Bank of New York Quarterly Review*, Vol. 10, No. 2, Summer 1985.

Index

Q-R

S